THE LIUS OF SHANGHAI

THE LIUS
OF SHANGHAI

SHERMAN COCHRAN

ANDREW HSIEH

HARVARD UNIVERSITY PRESS
Cambridge, Massachusetts
London, England
2013

Library of Congress Cataloging-in-Publication Data
Cochran, Sherman, 1940–
The Lius of Shanghai / Sherman Cochran and Andrew Hsieh.
p.   cm.
Includes bibliographical references and index.
ISBN 978-0-674-07259-6 (alk. paper)
1. Family-owned business enterprises—China—History—20th century.
2. Liu family.   I. Xie, Zhengguang.   II. Title.
HD62.25.C63   2013
338.092'251132—dc23   2012039399

For Macu and Ming

Contents

IV ADAPTING TO REVOLUTION, 1946–1956

Preface

On a cold winter day in 1992, I saw letters in the Liu family's correspondence for the first time. I was seated in a solid, wooden, straight-backed chair at the Center for Research on Chinese Business History in the Shanghai Academy of Social Sciences (SASS) when Professor Huang Hanmin, the director of the Center, delivered the letters to my desk. By the standards of American archives and libraries, it was not a comfortable place. According to China's policies at the time, public buildings south of the Yangzi River were not heated in winter, and since Shanghai is located on the Yangzi River, it was one of the northernmost cities wholly lacking in this amenity. But if my personal discomfort initially distracted me, I became completely focused as soon as I opened the first box of the Liu family letters and began to read.

Instantly I felt transported into the world of the Liu family. Four hours later I was startled when Professor Huang pointed out that it was time for lunch. I had sat through the morning without moving a muscle except to turn the pages of the old and fragile onionskin paper on which the letters were written. At that moment I resolved to write a book about the Liu family that would somehow allow readers to share with me what I had experienced on that bitterly cold and utterly exhilarating day.

Why was I immediately drawn into these letters? Admittedly, I had preexisting reasons for taking an interest in the Center's holdings in general and its materials on the Lius in particular. I had been visiting SASS regularly for nearly a decade (since 1983), and in the early 1990s I had teamed up with two of SASS's most distinguished Chinese scholars,

Professors Zhang Zhongli and Ding Richu, in applying successfully for a grant from the Luce Foundation to build the Center that now housed the Liu family letters. Moreover, I had just finished research at the Center on the family's father, Liu Hongsheng, whose career became the subject of a chapter I was writing for a book in Chinese business history. My research on Liu had convinced me that he was a major historical figure—significant for his political relations with Chiang Kai-shek, Mao Zedong, and Zhou Enlai as well as his economic success as a dynamic and wealthy industrialist—but in learning about him I had consulted financial accounts, internal memos, legal contracts, and other business records that had not mesmerized me as his family's letters did.

Some of the Liu family letters captured my attention because they made me feel like a voyeur peering into intimate scenes that were being described by one family member for another and were not intended for readers like me or anyone else outside the family. Other letters caused me to imagine that I was a member of the family who could see into the future, because I had read many of them out of chronological order and learned about later outcomes before I read about earlier decisions that led to them. As I came upon the letters dated earlier, I wanted to warn the writers: "Don't marry him!" "Don't go abroad!" "Don't make that investment!" "Father is right this time—take his word for it!"

Still other letters drew me in because they were intellectually engaging. While some seemed full of emotional outbursts, others contained closely reasoned arguments. Were these written words transparent expressions of inner feelings and thoughts? Or were they crafty maneuvers carried out by skilled and self-posturing negotiators? I found it challenging to try to discern which passages were spontaneous and which were calculated, guarded, or manipulative.

How could I write a book that would do justice to the Liu family letters? This question became more and more challenging as I read more and more letters. On each subsequent research trip, I was greeted with the news that Professor Huang and his successor as head of the Center, Professor Lu Xinglong, had discovered more family letters that had been buried in the vast business records of the Lius' firm.

Before long I began to experiment with possible approaches for framing and presenting the Liu family letters. First, I collected a selection of them in a documentary history, adding editorial comments to each one and photocopying them for distribution to students in my courses. Then I experimented with the form of an epistolary novel, except in this case I selected authentic historical letters written by the Lius rather than making up letters and attributing them to fictional characters in correspondence with each other. After that, I tried extracting bits of data from the letters and using them as a basis for addressing social scientific theories.

My experiments yielded results that have found their way into some of the following chapters, but after reading more of the Lius' letters, I began to have doubts about adopting the form of the epistolary novel or structuring the book exclusively or even primarily around social scientific theories, especially when I consulted my friend Andrew Hsieh about it.

In 1997, after I had been collecting and studying the Liu family letters for five years, I told Andrew about them. By then I had made two research trips to SASS in search of more Liu letters, and I had found some that I could not read because of the idiosyncratic calligraphy used in the Lius' handwriting. Ever since we had been classmates in graduate school during the late 1960s and early 1970s, I had known about Andrew's deep learning and remarkable ability to decipher the most difficult Chinese texts and discern allusions and multiple meanings in them, and I asked him to take a look at some of the Liu letters. As he pored over them, he also became engrossed in them, and we decided to collaborate as we had done on a previous book.

From then on, between 1997 and 2008, sometimes together and sometimes separately, we made research trips to SASS almost every year, ultimately finding about two thousand family letters written by the father, the mother, and their twelve children between the late 1920s and the early 1950s. We agreed that I would organize and write the book and that he would translate letters and other documents to be quoted and cited in it. Since then, as I have drafted chapters, he has commented on them, and along the way he has consistently expressed his preference for a focus on the letters themselves rather than on fictional forms or social scientific theories.

It is easy to see why Andrew believes that readers should have direct access to the Liu family letters. The collection is unlike almost any other in Chinese history because it includes letters from all members of a family during a tumultuous period in Chinese history that spanned the Sino-Japanese War of 1937–1945 and the Communist Revolution of 1949. In the course of their educations, almost all of the Lius learned to write fluently and even elegantly in two languages, Chinese and English. Although the father never studied abroad, he acquired his languages as a student in Shanghai at St. John's Middle School and St. John's University, which were sponsored by the American Episcopal Mission and offered courses in English as well as Chinese. After leaving St. John's, he used English on the job, at first holding a full-time job and later a part-time position with a large Sino-British coal company, Kailuan Mining Administration, where he spoke both languages on a regular basis throughout nearly his whole career in China.

By the time his eldest children reached school age, the father had worked for Kailuan for several years and had come to recognize the advantages of having full command of both Chinese and English. Determined to give his nine sons an early start as language learners, he had them tutored in Chinese and English at home before sending each of them to the same schools he had attended, St. John's Middle School and St. John's University, or other bilingual institutions in Shanghai. In addition, he sent them abroad to colleges and universities where all, except one (the youngest son, who had learning disabilities), spent between four and seven years in the English-speaking countries of England or the United States or studied English as well as Japanese in Japan. He also enrolled his three daughters in Shanghai schools that offered courses in both Chinese and English and then sent them abroad—one to Japan and one to England for less than a year each and one to the United States for four years.

While still in their early teens, the Liu children wrote to their parents and each other in somewhat stilted Chinese as though following models for letter writing (which were then available in Shanghai), but by the time they reached their late teens, their written Chinese became smoother. In learning English, they followed a similar pattern. In their early teens, their written English was initially awkward—far less expressive than their written Chinese—and they did not begin to write letters confidently in English until after they had lived for a while abroad. In their first letters home from England and the United States, they apologized to their father for writing in Chinese rather than following his instructions to use and practice their English. But in every case their English soon improved, and throughout their lives, they corresponded with their parents and each other in both languages. The notes at the end of this book indicate whether each of the Lius' letters quoted or cited here was originally written in Chinese or English.

Only one member of the family, the mother, was not literate enough to write letters in Chinese, English, or any other language, and even she was a prolific correspondent. Unable to write for herself, she dictated her letters to a secretary, Song Guanlin, a blind former English teacher who took the mother's dictation in Shanghai dialect and simultaneously translated and typed it in English-language letters.

If the collection is extraordinary for its inclusion of letters from all members of a big family, it is also extraordinary for its size. It is by no means the only collection of letters that has survived in China, but as far as we know, it is the largest readily available one that reveals interactions within a rich and powerful elite family based in China. Reading these letters is a rare privilege, and Andrew has convinced me of the importance of allowing the letter writers' distinctive voices to be heard, especially in relation to each other.

Fortunately, he and I have been able to find an approach to the Liu family letters that is acceptable to both of us. We have structured each chapter around a debate between two or more members of the family, and we have quoted extensively so that the Lius can be heard making their arguments in their own words. We prefer this form because it takes us inside the family, reveals what its members argued about, and shows who had the power to make its decisions.

Sherman Cochran
Cornell University

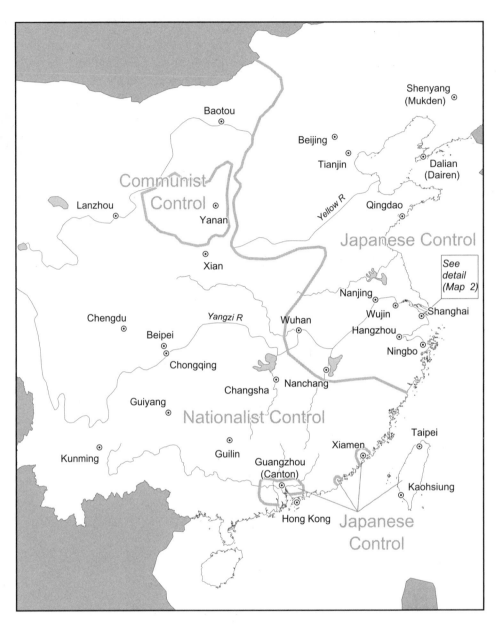

Map 1. Wartime China.

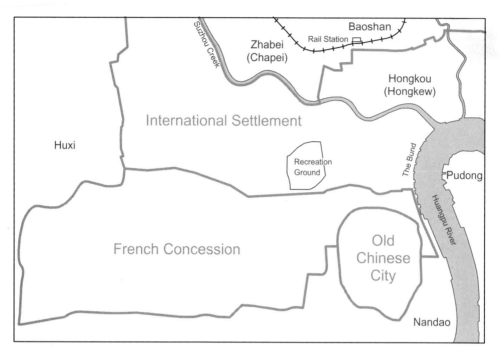

Map 2. The Chinese districts of Shanghai were under Japanese occupation for the duration of the Sino-Japanese War, from 1937 to 1945; the International Settlement was under Japanese occupation from 1941 to 1945; and the French Concession was not under Japanese occupation.

THE LIU FAMILY TREE

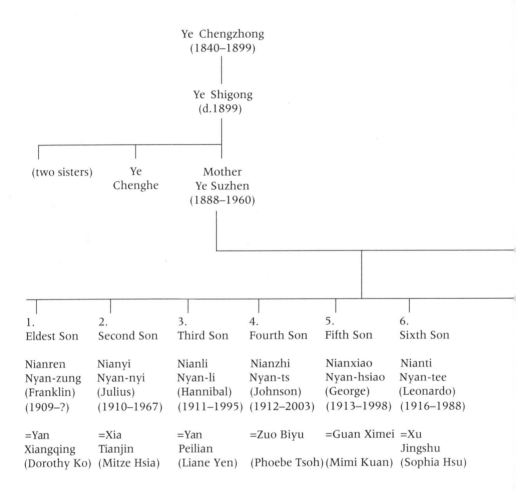

Ye Chengzhong
(1840–1899)

Ye Shigong
(d.1899)

(two sisters)   Ye
Chenghe

Mother
Ye Suzhen
(1888–1960)

1. Eldest Son	2. Second Son	3. Third Son	4. Fourth Son	5. Fifth Son	6. Sixth Son
Nianren Nyan-zung (Franklin) (1909–?)	Nianyi Nyan-nyi (Julius) (1910–1967)	Nianli Nyan-li (Hannibal) (1911–1995)	Nianzhi Nyan-ts (Johnson) (1912–2003)	Nianxiao Nyan-hsiao (George) (1913–1998)	Nianti Nyan-tee (Leonardo) (1916–1988)
=Yan Xiangqing (Dorothy Ko)	=Xia Tianjin (Mitze Hsia)	=Yan Peilian (Liane Yen)	=Zuo Biyu (Phoebe Tsoh)	=Guan Ximei (Mimi Kuan)	=Xu Jingshu (Sophia Hsu)

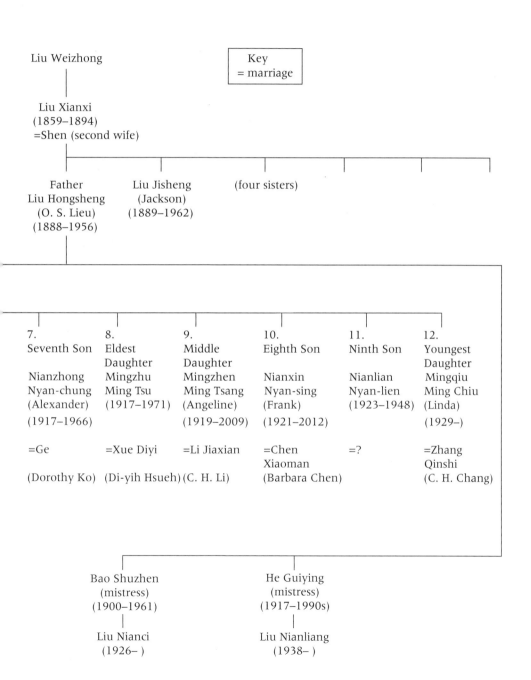

Liu Weizhong

Key
= marriage

Liu Xianxi
(1859–1894)
=Shen (second wife)

Father
Liu Hongsheng
(O. S. Lieu)
(1888–1956)

Liu Jisheng
(Jackson)
(1889–1962)

(four sisters)

7.
Seventh Son

Nianzhong
Nyan-chung
(Alexander)
(1917–1966)

=Ge

(Dorothy Ko)

8.
Eldest
Daughter

Mingzhu
Ming Tsu
(1917–1971)

=Xue Diyi

(Di-yih Hsueh)

9.
Middle
Daughter

Mingzhen
Ming Tsang
(Angeline)
(1919–2009)

=Li Jiaxian

(C. H. Li)

10.
Eighth Son

Nianxin
Nyan-sing
(Frank)
(1921–2012)

=Chen
Xiaoman
(Barbara Chen)

11.
Ninth Son

Nianlian
Nyan-lien
(1923–1948)

=?

12.
Youngest
Daughter

Mingqiu
Ming Chiu
(Linda)
(1929–)

=Zhang
Qinshi
(C. H. Chang)

Bao Shuzhen
(mistress)
(1900–1961)

Liu Nianci
(1926–)

He Guiying
(mistress)
(1917–1990s)

Liu Nianliang
(1938–)

THE LIUS OF SHANGHAI

Introduction

Family Dynamics under Patriarchy

IN THE first half of the twentieth century, the Lius of Shanghai became one of China's preeminent business families, presiding over an industrial empire that produced matches, woolens, cotton textiles, cement, and briquettes. At the same time, the father and mother in the family prepared for the future by giving international educations to almost all of their twelve children—nine boys and three girls—sending them not only to schools in China but also to Cambridge University, Harvard Business School, University of Pennsylvania's Wharton School of Business, Massachusetts Institute of Technology (MIT), Tokyo Institute of Technology, and other leading institutions of higher learning in the West and Japan. Moreover, the father and some of his sons became politically influential, accepting appointments to high official posts and dealing in person with top leaders such as Chiang Kai-shek in the Nationalist government and Mao Zedong and Zhou Enlai in the People's Republic. Even during the two most tumultuous events in twentieth-century Chinese history—the Sino-Japanese War of 1937–1945 and the Communist Revolution of 1949—the Lius retained high positions in China's economic, social, and political life.

In all these ways, the Lius distinguished themselves, and since they were by no means ordinary, they should not be regarded as typical of all families in Chinese history. Yet this family is worth comparing with other Chinese families to see whether it fits the general characterization that has been made of them. In a concise summary of this characterization, the sociologists Martin Whyte and William Parish have observed: "Perhaps the predominant image of urban as well as rural

families in imperial and republican China is that they were 'patriarchal,' a term which conveys the image of a male family head ruling over
a unit that was strictly and hierarchically ordered in terms of generation and sex, with younger members subordinate to older members and
females subordinate to all males."[1]

If Chinese families were generally patriarchal in this sense, were
the Lius patriarchal too? Did their male family head rule? If he did not
retain total authority, how did the power to make decisions come to be
dispersed among younger male and female members of the family? In
this book we have the opportunity to see the internal dynamics of decision making in the Liu family. To take full advantage of this opportunity, we begin by noting how, by comparison, other families in Chinese
history made their decisions.

Father Power

As described by historians and social scientists, Chinese business families like the Lius have been overwhelmingly patriarchal, leaving the
power to make decisions in the family and the family firm almost exclusively in the hands of the father. This point has been forcefully made
in an elegant model constructed by the sociologist Siu-lun Wong. "As a
father," Wong has written, "the head of the family firm has maximum
flexibility in his action. In theory, he can run the business as he sees fit
without consultation with other *jia* [family] members."[2] With full authority in a father's hands, he was in the enviable position of being able
to make quick decisions while remaining completely confident that
other members of the family would accept them and carry them out.

Historians have discovered and documented several examples of
patriarchs dictating decisions in Chinese business families not merely
in theory but in practice. In a case when a lineage formed a corporation,
it was the family hierarchy that directed its members' activities.[3] In other
family firms, whether the patriarch's sons cooperated or competed with
each other, they all deferred to patriarchal authority.[4] If family firms
lasted very long, their durability was attributable not to business institutions or relations between generations but solely to the patriarch.[5]

Even when members of a Chinese business family were separated
from each other, the patriarch retained control and kept the family
intact. During the Sino-Japanese War, according to a study by Parks

Coble, the father-entrepreneurs in Chinese firms took advantage of trusted family members so that they could place them in locations across enemy lines—stationing some sons in parts of China under the Japanese military occupation and some in unoccupied parts—and manage all branches of the family firm by remote control. After the war, these Chinese fathers followed the same survival strategy when they encountered the Communist Revolution of 1949. Such dispersal of a family and a family firm was possible because the father's authority was unquestioned and the business family's deference to his authority remained intact.[6]

Thus, according to studies of Chinese business families, the patriarch appears to have been all-powerful, and his wife and children seem to have been fully compliant. This standard interpretation has been based on sophisticated social scientific modeling and rigorous historical research, but it has not been based on family correspondence or other sources that reveal contentious private exchanges among members of a Chinese business family over a sustained period of time. In reading the personal correspondence of the Liu family, do we find that the father was a patriarch who behaved as other fathers are said to have done in Chinese business families?

The father in the Liu family occupied a position in his family firm comparable to that of the patriarchs cited in previous studies of Chinese business families. Like them, he founded his family firm and held formal authority over it throughout his career. To give his authority institutional protection, he went even farther than many other heads of Chinese family firms by maintaining an accounts office that served as a kind of internal bank within his family firm and kept him involved in all of its major financial arrangements and current transactions.[7]

So if we assess the power of the father on the basis of his formal position in the Lius' business organization, he might be considered to have been an omnipotent patriarch—the man at the top holding unchecked authority. But if we assess the father's power on the basis of his interactions with other members of his family (as we have the opportunity to do in nearly every chapter of this book), his omnipotence is called into question, because these other members of the family also exercised power in the family and the family firm. To explain this broad participation in the family's decision making, we cannot rely solely on the concept of father power. Fortunately, thanks to recent work by specialists in women's history, we have available to us another helpful concept, mother power.

Mother Power

Since the father has generally been portrayed as possessing the power to make virtually all decisions in Chinese business families, it is hardly surprising that mothers have scarcely been mentioned as decision makers.[8] But recently Dorothy Ko, a specialist in Chinese women's history, has challenged what she has called "the myth of an omnipotent patriarchy." In analyzing elite Chinese families (not specifically business families), she has suggested that historians should look not for who has power or who is deprived of it but rather "for changing distributions of power." By shifting the focus from the patriarch to relations among members of the family, Ko has discovered that "even in a society as thoroughly patriarchal as China, kinship systems and family relations may not have been the workings of men alone."[9]

In Chinese history, mothers had opportunities to derive power from at least two sources. First, between the seventeenth and late nineteenth centuries, elite mothers drew power from moral authority that was based on their considerable education, high literacy, and sophisticated writing.[10] Second, in the twentieth century, if not earlier, both elite and nonelite mothers acquired another kind of power that did not require them to be literate. When they married out of their natal families and into their husbands' families, they initially became subordinated to their in-laws in their new homes, but they did not remain powerless for life. Once they became mothers, they formed emotional ties with their sons and constructed subunits in their families that did not include their husbands, whom they sometimes considered to be the enemy. In this way, according to the anthropologist Margery Wolf, Chinese mothers developed "sufficient backing to maintain some independence under their powerful mothers-in-law and even occasionally to bring the men's world to terms."[11]

Did the mother in the Liu family exercise either of these two kinds of mother power? She certainly did not derive power from her high literacy and academic sophistication. Having received little formal education, she was nearly illiterate. But she did express her views on family issues and engage in arguments with her husband and children through the letters she regularly dictated to her secretary.[12] In these letters, even though she made no claim to having literary eloquence or scholarly accomplishments, she resembled the elite mothers of pre-twentieth-century China to the extent that she consistently used written words to lay claim to her moral authority and try to impose it on her husband and children.

The mother in the Liu family also attempted to generate the second kind of mother power by bonding with her sons, forming a subunit within her family, and mobilizing it on her behalf against her husband. By these means she repeatedly sought to buttress her moral authority in the domestic sphere, especially when she had to endure separations from family members. In perhaps her most forceful exercise of her power, she set out to end her husband's long wartime separation from her by resorting to actions that spilled over into the business world, threatening to split not only the family but also the family firm.

Child Power

If we find examples of mother power in the history of the Liu family, do we find examples of child power too? In general, the concept of child power has been conspicuously absent from studies of Chinese family history. It has been commonly assumed that the father formed a relationship with his children, especially his sons, that kept them dependent on him and left them powerless in the family. As Lloyd Eastman has vividly characterized this relationship, "Chinese fathers never conceived of the notion, so widespread in the United States today [in 1988], that they should be pals with their sons. Rather, they tended to be stern, harsh, and remote, convinced that this demeanor was necessary if they were to be effective teachers and role models. For the child, the father thus loomed as an awesome and dour figure, best avoided if at all possible. Thereafter [beginning when sons were six years old], true warmth between a father and his sons was the exception rather than the rule."[13] Only if a father died prematurely did his sons acquire the power to achieve independence.[14]

In general, it has been assumed that such stern, awesome, and cold fathers must have prevented their children from becoming independent and exercising any power at all in Chinese families. But specialists in the history of Chinese childhood have recently begun to question this assumption. Between the seventeenth and nineteenth centuries, according to Ping-chen Hsiung, Chinese families did not regard their children as purely passive and dependent. In her words, "beneath the surface of self-motivation and high morality, children were seen as active agents with their own 'independent' responses."[15] Chinese children achieved independence, according to Jon Saari's analysis of the process in the nineteenth and early twentieth centuries, in two ways. Some reacted to their fathers' denial of their autonomy by becoming "mischievous," and others developed "inner selves" that remained distinct from their outer, public behavior. Thus, they resolved their "autonomy crisis" and took steps toward "an independent, self-reliant youth and adulthood."[16]

In the early twentieth century, young Chinese found new opportunities for achieving independence as a result of their experiences outside the family, according to a recent history of a Chinese family by Joseph Esherick. While in residence at boarding schools and colleges, they became committed to ideas that competed with the ones they had been taught in the family, and during the Sino-Japanese War and Communist Revolution, they left the family behind and set out on their own. In seeking independence, they disengaged from their natal families and pulled them apart.[17]

Did the children in the Liu family experience an autonomy crisis, resolve it by achieving independence, and pull apart their natal family? Because we have relied heavily on their correspondence, we know less about them as small children and more about them as young people over the age of fifteen (when they began writing letters regularly) and as adults. In their late teens and early twenties, they almost all engaged in debates with their father that culminated in the question whether each child should be considered independent within the family. The father and his sons also considered whether the sons should make decisions independently within the family firm and whether sons and daughters should leave the family and lead lives totally separate from it.

In some cases, a child took a stand as an individual confronting his or her father or mother. In other cases, children formed alliances with each other against their parents (providing evidence of a commonly overlooked phenomenon in Chinese family life, the impact of siblings on each other).[18] Whether as individuals or in concert with each other, nearly all of the children in the Liu family expressed their desire for independence (frequently using this word) and argued with their parents about how much power they could exercise in making their own decisions.

The children in the Liu family were nearly all educated outside their home and for that matter outside China, and some of them lived away from their hometown of Shanghai during the Sino-Japanese War and the Communist Revolution. But their quests for independence and their experience away from home did not cause the Liu family to disintegrate during the first half of the twentieth century. Even while the children as well as the father and mother all sought to exercise power, they nearly all remained committed to the family and played active roles in its decision making.

Internal Dynamics

We have discussed father power, mother power, and child power because we believe that they are helpful as concepts for understanding the history of the Liu family. But in pointing out that the Lius did not leave all power in the hands of the patriarch, we do not mean to imply that their family was categorically nonpatriarchal. We realize that patriarchy as an abstract model is bound to differ in some respects as it applies to every concrete example of a family. Our aim is not to dismiss the patriarchal model as an inaccurate description of the details in the Liu family's history but rather to emphasize that even though the father possessed patriarchal power, he was not the sole decision maker in this family. If, as suggested here, the father, mother, and children all had power, then how can we analyze decision making in the family and uncover the internal dynamics that lay beneath it?

We believe that we have a rich basis for addressing this question because of the nature of our sources, especially the Lius' personal correspondence with each other. As mentioned in the preface, we have had access to the Liu family letters in the archives of the Shanghai Academy of Social Sciences, and as far as we know, this collection is unique in Chinese history by virtue of its sheer size (including more than two thousand letters) and wide range of contributors (a father, a mother, and all members of a large family).[19]

These letters allow us to see not merely a father issuing orders unilaterally but also a mother and children exchanging views with a father and each other bilaterally and multilaterally. We believe that the greatest strength of this collection is that it shows how the Lius resolved tensions that arose among them as they argued with each other over family decisions. So we have organized the book around their debates over various topics, focusing on one debate in each chapter.

Needless to say, the Lius did not devote their letters exclusively or even primarily to arguments with each other. On the contrary, they wrote mostly about nonargumentative subjects, and they frequently expressed affection for each other (as is evident in quotations that appear in almost every chapter). But we have focused on their debates to show how freely they expressed themselves as individuals, how intensely they argued with each other, and how subtly they negotiated in devising their strategies and resolving their differences.

In these passionate debates, who won? Did the patriarch triumph over his wife and children or the other way around? If viewed in these stark terms, the outcomes of the debates vary from one chapter to another, with the patriarch or another individual member of the family winning some debates and losing others, or winning some rounds of a fight and losing others within a single debate.

To understand the internal dynamics of the Liu family, we believe it is worth asking different questions: What power did members of the family have in relation to each other? How did father power, mother power, and child power interact as the Lius made their decisions in shifting historical contexts? When the Lius clashed, what centrifugal forces pulled them away from each other and what centripetal forces held them together as a family? The letters the Lius exchanged give us a basis for addressing these questions.

The Lius' Letters in Their Historical Contexts

In this book, we have quoted extensively from the Lius' family letters. We have provided a frame for each chapter—a brief introduction at the beginning and an equally brief conclusion at the end. In the body of each chapter, we have quoted from the Lius' letters, and where it has been necessary to go beyond the letters, we have consulted and cited other sources: interviews with surviving members of the family, memoirs written by members of the family, academic records of family members as students, official documents, newspapers, and other publications.

We have divided the book into four parts to indicate how the Liu family's debates varied in different historical contexts. Parts I and II are set in the late 1920s and 1930s, a period of relative openness when Chinese traveled freely within and outside their country. During this time, the father's business empire was expanding, and he seized opportunities to send his children abroad for their educations. He wanted them to learn how to operate throughout the capitalist world and succeed at perpetuating a multigenerational business dynasty based in China. His children set out from Shanghai on their educational ventures voluntarily and even enthusiastically, and once they settled into their schools and lives abroad, he and they argued about decisions with long-term implications, especially regarding their educations, careers, and choices of marriage partners.

Part III is set in a very different historical context—a period when China became largely cut off from the West and torn apart by the Sino-Japanese War of 1937–1945. The war threw the Lius on the defensive. Quite contrary to their original plan, the father and some of his children involuntarily fled Shanghai following the Japanese military invasion and left behind the mother and the rest of the children. Throughout the war, they discussed short-term strategies for survival more than long-term plans for the future. They continued to debate with each other over family matters such as marital discord, psychiatric breakdown, and business policies, but their debates became inextricably bound up with political issues: whether to cooperate with the Japanese forces that were occupying their hometown, Shanghai; or align with Chiang Kai-shek's Nationalist government and relocate to his wartime capital of Chongqing, nine hundred miles west of Shanghai; or join the Communist movement under the leadership of Mao Zedong at its base in Yan'an, a thousand miles northwest of Shanghai.

Part IV shows that the Lius found themselves in another radically transformed historical context as a result of the Communist Revolution of 1949. In the wake of this event, some of the Lius argued with others in the family about whether they should stay in China, flee China, or return home to China from abroad. In May 1949, when the People's Liberation Army took over Shanghai, the father left behind his wife and most of his children and moved to the British colony of Hong Kong. Over the next six months he debated with them whether he should rejoin them (as they and emissaries sent by Zhou Enlai from Beijing urged him to do) or stay abroad (as his business associates in Hong Kong counseled). After he finally decided to go back to Shanghai, he then urged the last two of his children who were still receiving educations in the West to come back to China once they had completed their degrees. In the early 1950s, his exchanges with one of his sons on this subject turned into a Cold War debate over whether freedom had been lost in China since the Chinese Communist Party had assumed power there.

In all four parts, we have given primacy to the Lius' letters over other sources because these letters convey the intimacy of the family members' exchanges as they dealt with their most pressing disagreements in the historical contexts of their times. In our history of the family, we begin with the initial intimate exchange between the father and mother: their first glimpse of each other on their wedding day.

I

PLANNING A BUSINESS DYNASTY
1907–1932

1

Parents Who Dreamed of a Business Dynasty

ON OCTOBER 30, 1907, Liu Hongsheng and Ye Suzhen were married in their hometown of Shanghai.[1] Their families arranged their marriage "in every respect of the old fashion," Liu later recalled.[2] Following well-established customs, the couple did not see each other until he lifted her veil after the wedding ceremony had been conducted. At that moment, they were both delighted to discover how each other looked. She was an attractive young woman by traditional standards, with delicate skin, fine-boned facial structure, big eyes, and bound feet covered by elegant silk shoes that she had embroidered herself. He was nearly six feet tall and gazed down at his diminutive new bride through intelligent eyes that were set wide apart in a broad and handsome face.

From that moment on, Ye did not doubt that Liu was the one man for her. Nor did she want ever to share him with another woman, even though men who could afford it still took concubines in China at that time. As she later told her children, for her it was love at first sight.[3] Liu's memory of the moment when he lifted Ye's veil was equally positive and nearly as romantic. Writing to one of his sons twenty-five years later, he remembered feeling about himself and his bride that "had either of us been given the free will we could not have chosen better."[4]

Negotiating a Marriage Agreement

For Ye and Liu, both age nineteen, the lifting of the veil was remembered as a spontaneous, romantic, emotionally charged moment, but for their families, the wedding was the outcome of a calculated, protracted, and tense process of negotiation. Both the bride and the groom came from business families, and in arranging the marriage, each family set its own business conditions.

On the Lius' side, their biggest asset was Liu Hongsheng's future promise as a new-style, forward-looking businessman. For a young man, he had already inherited or acquired a very impressive set of business credentials. Born in Shanghai, he had parents whose native place was Ningbo, a prefecture ninety miles southeast of Shanghai that was known for its successful merchants and financiers. The tie to one's native place was different from loyalty to a hometown or a place of birth. All Chinese inherited native places from their fathers (in the same way that they inherited surnames), and in general Chinese preferred to deal with native-place associates rather than other Chinese because they spoke each other's local dialects and expected eventually to retire in their native places, where they would be accountable for their lifelong treatment of their native-place associates. In the case of sojourners from Ningbo, the native-place tie was famously strong. Since the tenth century and especially in the nineteenth century, Ningbo had built up a reputation for producing merchants who migrated widely in China, created powerful networks for managing finance and long-distance trade, and showed fierce loyalty to their native place, making the native-place bond especially significant in this case.[5]

At a relatively young age, Liu Hongsheng felt the need to begin making native-place connections and laying plans for his future in business because his father, Liu Xianxi, had died prematurely at the age of thirty-five in 1894, when Liu Hongsheng was only six years old. During Liu Xianxi's lifetime, he had held a job at China's largest Chinese-owned shipping firm, China Merchants Steam and Navigation Company, and had provided adequately, if not lavishly, for his wife and five children, two boys and four girls. But after Liu Xianxi's death, his family lived very modestly.

Although not from a wealthy family, Liu Hongsheng was able to attend St. John's Middle School and St. John's University on a scholarship. His education in these schools, which were founded and operated by the American Episcopal Mission, was vital for his future in business, because St. John's was the premier institution in Shanghai for producing a business elite.[6] Besides learning English and studying business at St.

John's, Liu made contacts there with classmates who would prove useful to him for the rest of his life. Strapped for funds as a teenager, he left St. John's University before graduation. In 1906, he took advantage of his bilingual command of Chinese and English to land a job as an interpreter for the British-led police in the International Settlement of Shanghai while he continued to look for a position in business.

All of these credentials—Ningbo native-place ties, education at St. John's, command of English—showed that Liu Hongsheng was well prepared to become an internationally connected businessman, but as a prospective marriage partner in a wedding between business families, he was lacking in one important respect: he was not wealthy. No matter how talented, trained, and well connected he might have been, he could not count on his family to provide financial backing for any investments he might wish to make.

Ye Suzhen came from a family that could provide Liu with substantial financial backing, but during the negotiations before the wedding, her relatives were initially reluctant to approve the marriage because of the discrepancy between the two families' wealth and prestige. The members of the Ye family were willing to entertain the idea of this marriage because they recognized that they had much in common with the Lius: both families came from merchant backgrounds, resided in Shanghai, and had Ningbo as their native place. But the members of the Ye family considered themselves superior to the Lius.

The Ye family members saw themselves as part of a distinguished merchant dynasty that had descended from Ye Chengzhong, one of Shanghai's richest Chinese merchants, who had bequeathed to the Ye family on his death in 1899 between eight and ten million ounces of silver (taels; the equivalent of US$12.4–15.5 million at the time).[7] Ye Suzhen's father, Ye Shigong, had helped to sustain the Ye merchant dynasty by founding and managing the Xiecheng Match Mill, one of China's early industrial enterprises. Admittedly, Ye Shigong had not left his children an inheritance as large as the one from Ye Chengzhong, but he had had less time to build up his fortune because his career had been cut short by his untimely death in 1899, the same year Ye Chengzhong died.[8] Even though the fortunes of the Ye family had declined a bit in the aftermath of these two deaths, Ye Suzhen's relatives had doubts about her taking Liu as a husband because they believed she would be marrying down.

Ultimately the members of the Ye family overcame their misgivings about the Lius and approved the marriage because they came to realize that they needed Liu Hongsheng to sustain the Ye business dynasty. Ye Suzhen's mother and father were both deceased by the time she was eleven years old, leaving her and her two younger sisters and brother in the care of their maternal grandmother.[9] The three girls, especially Ye Suzhen, were considered beauties, but they had no experience in business and took pride in their exclusive devotion to domestic matters, as Ningbo women were renowned for doing.[10] None of the three sisters had much formal education; in fact, they were virtually illiterate and spoke only Shanghainese—not Mandarin or even Ningboese and certainly no foreign languages.[11] In addition, they were ill equipped to bear business responsibilities because they were all prone to anxiety and depression from an early age. Similarly, their only brother, Ye Chenghe, who was the youngest child, also suffered from depression and showed no ability or even interest in business. As a young man he was already notorious for squandering money on food, drink, women, and most of all, gambling. His relatives feared that if the family fortune were left in his hands it would soon be gone, bringing the family's merchant dynasty to an end.[12]

After prolonged haggling about what each family's contribution to the marriage should be, the members of the Ye family came to an agreement among themselves and with the Lius that the couple should wed for the sake of sustaining and extending a business dynasty. In this union, the bride was expected to bring to the marriage resources her family had accumulated in its business dynasty of the past, and the groom was meant to use these resources to develop and perpetuate a business dynasty in the future.

Opening Enterprises and Bearing Children

Once they were married, Liu Hongsheng and Ye Suzhen pursued the goal of achieving a business dynasty by establishing enterprises and producing children at a remarkable rate. Each of them predominated in a separate sphere, with her bearing the children and him opening the businesses. But each of them also crossed the line between the domestic household and the business enterprise, with Ye making a timely contribution to the founding of the businesses and Liu playing a decisive role in the education of the children.

Ye Suzhen helped Liu Hongsheng make a start in business by bringing a dowry with her into the Liu household and serving as a conduit for the transfer of other funds from the Ye family to the Lius. Following Chinese custom, she married out of her natal family and into her husband's family, and as soon as she had done so, she became aware of the Lius' demands on her and her family. As she later recalled, the Lius "had to get a lift" from the Ye family to launch her young husband's career in business, and her widowed mother-in-law was the one who put the financial squeeze on her. In Ye's words, since her husband "was not yet in any real position, [my mother-in-law] often 'cracked me like a walnut in order to eat the meat inside,' and that was because my own parents had money."[13] She surely did not enjoy being "cracked" by her mother-in-law, and like many Chinese daughters-in-law, she never did feel fully at ease with her mother-in-law, who did not die until 1931—twenty-four years after Ye married into the Liu family.[14] Under pressure from the Lius, Ye Suzhen channeled considerable resources from the Ye family into her husband's businesses soon after she married Liu, providing a timely infusion of capital when he needed it to launch his first industrial enterprises.

In the 1910s, Liu Hongsheng supplemented the Ye family's capital by drawing on a variety of other sources. In 1909 he took a job at the Kailuan Mining Administration, a Sino-British coal-mining company, and he rapidly rose up the corporate ladder, especially during World War I (1914–1919), when British managers were called back to Europe, opening the way for his advancement as Kailuan's bilingual comprador in China. He also took advantage of contacts in his Ningbo native-place network to distribute Kailuan's coal and mobilize capital from Shanghai's banks (where Ningbo financiers predominated).[15] In the 1920s, he used this capital to establish several major enterprises, including China Coal Briquette Company, Shanghai Portland Cement Works Company Limited, China Match Company, China Wool Manufacturing Company Limited, East China Coal Mining Company, and Chung Hwa Wharf Company. Perhaps the single most personally satisfying investment for him was one of his first, his purchase of the Xiecheng Match Mills in 1920. This company had been founded by his father-in-law, and when he bought it from his in-laws, he took pleasure in demonstrating to them that they had been wrong to doubt his prospects as a businessman before his marriage to Ye Suzhen thirteen years earlier. If the Lius had once swallowed their pride and deferred to the Ye family in the past, they would not do so in the future.[16] By 1930, still in his early forties, Liu had come to preside over all of these businesses, making him one of China's richest and most powerful capitalists.

During the same years, while Liu Hongsheng was extraordinary for opening industrial enterprises one after another, Ye Suzhen was also extraordinary for having children one after another. In one twelve-year stretch of her marriage (1909–1921), she had nearly one child per year. Altogether she gave birth sixteen times, the last one in 1929. She lost four children in their infancy and brought up the other twelve—nine boys and three girls. Of these twelve, the first seven were all boys.[17]

In raising her children, Ye Suzhen depended heavily on wet nurses, nannies, and other servants, especially when she suffered from an unstable psychiatric condition. In 1930, the year after their last child was born, Liu engaged a physician, a woman named Kwei, to examine Ye's "mental and physical soundness," and Dr. Kwei discovered that Ye suffered from a debilitating disorder that she had apparently inherited. Like her sisters and brother, every few years she had, in her doctor's words, "a period of over-activity, excitement and violence followed by a period of depression and a general slowing up of activity." In her married life, the first such attack occurred in 1917. After catching the flu and having a miscarriage, she began alternating between a manic phase and depression over a period of six months.

For relief, Ye took up opium smoking, a habit that was common in China and especially Shanghai. In the 1920s, she had two more episodes—one in 1923 and another in 1928. In each case she followed the same manic-depressive pattern for six months, and she often slept for as many as twenty hours out of twenty-four. During the five or six years between episodes, she functioned normally, according to her doctor, except that "she absolutely does not recall anything that occurred during an attack but a feeling of weakness and generalized pains."[18]

Despite her condition, Ye Suzhen remained on good terms with Liu Hongsheng and her children, even when her emotions swung to extremes. "When patient is violent," Kwei observed in 1930, "she seldom hits her husband but is apt to be violent toward the servants and dependents. She is perfectly devoted to her husband who is also very kind to her." Interviewing Ye and Liu together, Kwei was impressed by the strength of their marital bond. "The relation between the patient and her husband is very cordial and affectionate," she remarked. Similarly, Kwei concluded that Ye's condition did not prevent her from being a good mother. "She is tender to all of them," Kwei commented, referring to Ye's relationship with her children.[19]

Kwei was convinced that Ye understood her condition and could cope with it. "She has good judgment and insight of her disease," she noted, and she urged Ye to "build her condition up" by adjusting her daily routine: eating and sleeping on a regular schedule, taking long walks and hot baths, quitting opium, and adopting contraception. "These suggestions may not avert the attack," Kwei conceded in her prognosis, but they "may moderate the attacks."[20] Perhaps in 1930 Ye Suzhen took her doctor's advice about adopting contraceptives because she had no more children after 1929. By then she and her husband had already taken the first steps toward creating a business dynasty by giving birth to their children and founding a family firm.

Planning Children's Educations Abroad

In the late 1920s, as their eldest children neared college age, Liu Hongsheng proposed that he and his wife should take the next step in their plans for a business dynasty by sending their sons abroad for college educations. He believed that their children needed to study in other countries because China had made a transition from an era of traditional isolation into one of modern international relations. As he wrote to his sons a few years later, "in the past we, as a nation, lived and prospered in peace secluded. But that day now belongs entirely to history. No nation can now fare all by herself. Modern civilization is so aggressive and invading that we have to keep pace with international culture and progress."[21] In his view, the centers of modern civilization abroad were also the centers of worldwide business, and universities in these places would provide his children with educations that they would need to manage the family firm. "The successful solution of our future commercial, political, economic, and [other] problems will depend more or less on our thorough and comprehensive understanding of others," he wrote to his sons.[22]

While contending that it was essential to acquire understanding from foreigners abroad, he emphasized even more strongly that no matter how long his children were away, they should never let other places become as central to their thinking as China was. Whether they ventured overseas to "the Occident" (Europe and the United States) or "the Orient" (Japan), he told them, they should never lose sight of their home base, "keeping our country as the center of all things."[23] In taking this position, he was by no means unique; several other Chinese businessmen in early twentieth-century Shanghai agreed with him and adopted the same policy of sending their children abroad for college educations to prepare them for business careers in China.[24]

When Liu Hongsheng first suggested to Ye Suzhen this idea of sending their children abroad for college, she opposed it, insisting that they should receive their educations in Shanghai. As Liu Hongsheng lamented to his eldest son, "your mother has always been unwilling to let any of your brothers go abroad. She is, as you know, a fond parent who always thinks it best that her children should all the time be as near herself as ever possible. She belongs to the past century in many ways."[25] Besides urging her children to attend school in Shanghai, Ye maintained that they should marry, have children, and live their entire lives together with her and Liu Hongsheng in one house, in accordance with the traditional Chinese ideal of housing multiple generations—as many as five—under one roof.[26]

In 1927, when their eldest son was eighteen, Liu Hongsheng tried to overcome Ye Suzhen's opposition to overseas educations for their children by showing her some of the places where they might send their children to school. For two months Liu and Ye left their children at home in Shanghai and traveled to the West. According to their passport, they visited the United States, Britain, France, Belgium, Germany, Switzerland, and Italy.[27]

After seeing the West with her own eyes, Ye Suzhen still had reservations about the wisdom of sending her children to reside overseas on a long-term basis. But when she and Liu Hongsheng returned to Shanghai, she agreed to go along with her husband's plan, as long as her children would obey three rules that she and Liu laid down. Before going abroad for higher education, each child had to promise (1) to return and live his or her adult life in China; (2) to work for the family business in Shanghai as needed; and (3) to marry a Chinese—not, under any circumstances, a foreigner.[28]

Under these rules, Liu and Ye laid claim to patriarchal authority over their children. By then, they had already given their children lifelong reminders of the need to show deference to themselves as parents by naming each of their sons after one of the Confucian virtues (in the order that Confucius had ranked them): humaneness *(ren)*, righteousness *(yi)*, propriety *(li)*, uprightness *(zhi)*, filiality *(xiao)*, brotherliness *(ti)*, loyalty *(zhong)*, trustworthiness *(xin)*, and honesty *(lian)*. Since the boys shared the middle name Nian, which means "remember," their names exhorted them to remember these virtues. (The eldest son's name, Liu Nianren, meant Remember Humaneness Liu, the second eldest's name, Liu Nianyi, meant Remember Righteousness Liu, and so forth). The three girls' Chinese names all refer to beautiful jewels: pearl *(zhu)*, precious stone *(zhen)*, and round gem *(qiu)*. Their shared middle name, Ming, means "brilliant," highlighting the jewels in their names: Liu Mingzhu (Brilliant Pearl Liu), Liu Mingzhen (Brilliant Precious Stone Liu), and Liu Mingqiu (Brilliant Round Gem Liu).

Liu and Ye were by no means unique in selecting names derived from Confucian virtues for their sons and feminine ideals of beauty for their daughters. In the early twentieth century, Chinese from orthodox scholarly backgrounds conventionally gave similar names to their children. But the adoption of them in this case shows that Chinese from business families as well as scholarly families followed this convention.[29]

In choosing their children's names, Liu and Ye did not invoke Chinese cultural values to the exclusion of Western ones. In fact, they also gave nearly all of their children Western names, which were, in birth order: Franklin, Julius, Hannibal, Johnson, George, Leonardo, Alexander, Angeline, Frank, and Linda. In these Western names, Liu and Ye did not make reference to a set of cultural values as explicitly as they did in their children's Chinese names, but they did seem to show respect or admiration for heroism and inventiveness in classical European history (Julius, Hannibal, Leonardo, Alexander) and early American history (Franklin as in Benjamin Franklin and George as in George Washington). In the remaining sons' and daughters' Western names (Johnson, Frank, Angeline, and Linda), Liu and Ye made no discernible allusion to cultural values.[30]

The selection of these names is worth noting, we believe, because it signifies values that Liu and Ye wished to inculcate in their children. But for the sake of clarity, we have not used either the Chinese or the Western names of the members of the Liu family in the remainder of this book. Instead we generally refer to the parents in the Liu family (Liu Hongsheng and Ye Suzhen) as Father and Mother, and we use the names of the twelve children based on their places in the birth order: Eldest Son for Liu Nianren, Second Son for Liu Nianyi, Third Son for Liu Nianli, Fourth Son for Liu Nianzhi, Fifth Son for Liu Nianxiao, Sixth Son for Liu Nianti, Seventh Son for Liu Nianzhong, Eldest Daughter for Liu Mingzhu, Middle Daughter for Liu Mingzhen, Eighth Son for Liu Nianxin, Ninth Son for Liu Nianlian, and Youngest Daughter for Liu Mingqiu.

We have adopted these ordinal names because when the members of the family addressed each other in Chinese, they also commonly used names based on birth order: Dage (Eldest Son), Erge (Second Son), Sange (Third Son), and so on. We also prefer ordinal names to avoid confusion that arises because of the similarity of the children's names, sharing, as they do, not only a family name, Liu, but also a generational name— Nian in every boy's name (Liu Nianren, Liu Nianyi, Liu Nianli, and so on), and Ming in every girl's name (Liu Mingzhu, Liu Mingzeng, and Liu Mingqiu).[31]

In the late 1920s, after producing and giving names to all of their children, Father and Mother seemed confident that their eldest sons were close enough to adulthood to take the next step in Father's plan for establishing a business dynasty. According to this plan, all of the sons would eventually enroll at Western and Japanese universities and prepare to work in the family firm by majoring in technical subjects— one each in business administration, accounting, law, economics, agriculture, chemical engineering, commerce, and mechanical engineering. Since his daughters were expected to spend their adult lives managing domestic households, not businesses, he planned for all of them to study home economics.[32]

In proposing this plan to his children, Liu assumed that they would carry it out fully. Just as his family and his wife's family had arranged his marriage, he expected to arrange educations and careers as well as marriages for his children. But once he began to send his children overseas for their educations, he discovered that they did not follow his orders as closely as he had anticipated.

2

━━◈◈◈━━

Sons Who Tried for Admission to Cambridge

ON MAY 18, 1929, Second Son (age nineteen), Third Son (age eighteen), and Fourth Son (age seventeen) set sail from Shanghai, and on July 3 they arrived in England on a mission. Under instructions from Father, they were supposed to gain admission to Cambridge University and earn degrees to prepare themselves to serve as accountants and executives in the family firm at Shanghai.[1] At the time, their prospects for admission were not bright, because only twenty-two students of Chinese descent (including those from the rest of the world as well as China) were enrolled at Cambridge.[2] Father recognized that his sons would not be able to accomplish this mission without help in England, but how could he arrange for people to come to their aid there?

In Shanghai, Father, like other members of the urban elite, had built up a powerful personal network based on ties with other Chinese through kinship, native-place, and alumni associations. To reach outside Shanghai and extend his influence all the way to England, he forged a chain of contacts that included Westerners as well as Chinese.[3] The first link in Father's chain between China and England was F. N. Matthews, a named partner in the international accounting firm of Lowe, Bingham and Matthews, who presided over his business' office in Shanghai. Consulting with Matthews in person in Shanghai, Father outlined his plans for his sons, which included a step-by-step strategy for getting them into Cambridge. He wanted them first to have an English host family who would look after their domestic needs; then to be guided by a well-connected mentor; and finally to be put in touch with the elite in English society who in turn would arrange for their admission to

Cambridge. Following Father's instructions, Matthews wrote to his firm's office in London to make the local arrangements. After the boys arrived, they found that as Father had hoped, they had contact with three key institutions—a host family, elite society, and Cambridge University—but they did not receive a warm welcome from any of them, and they had to learn to fend for themselves.

Encountering Racism in a Host Family

On June 10, 1929, Matthews wrote a confidential letter to his colleague Alfred H. Ballard, a senior partner at Lowe, Bingham and Matthews in London, and recruited him to serve as guardian for the boys in England. He probably chose Ballard over other colleagues because he had been born in China and had lived there up to the age of seven. Matthews assured Ballard that "all finance will be done through ourselves," with Matthews sending a lump sum from Father to Ballard, and Ballard opening a special bank account from which to draw funds for all of the boys' expenses: "Everything—housekeeping, tutors' salary and current account, rent, fees, and so on." In managing these funds, Ballard was expected to keep Matthews and Father informed by sending monthly financial reports to Shanghai in duplicate, one copy for each of them.[4]

On July 2, the day before the boys' arrival, Ballard sent his reply, accepting the assignment. "I shall make a special point of seeing, personally," he promised Matthews, "that these lads are brought up in a healthy atmosphere." To strengthen his hand, he requested power of attorney over the boys. "I think it would be desirable to have some legal document investing me with the necessary authority," he proposed before he had even met his new charges, "just in case any matter arose which would necessitate my taking a firm stand regarding it."[5]

Once the boys had met Ballard and had reported that he had made a good first impression, Father granted Ballard's wish. In a formal statement dated October 9, 1929, and sworn in Shanghai, Father legally empowered Ballard "to act as my Attorney and in my stead as Guardian of my three sons" until each of the boys reached the age of twenty-one or returned to China, whichever came first. Father authorized Ballard to act "in loco parentis" and instructed him "to do for and on behalf of my said sons all and every act or thing which I could do if personally present and acting as father and natural guardian of my said sons."[6] With

Ballard as the boys' surrogate father, he, his wife, his children, and his sister-in-law (whose husband had migrated to Canada) became their host family in England, and the Ballards and Lius all moved into one big house that Ballard rented at Leigh on the Sea in Essex, seventy miles southeast of Cambridge.[7]

Eventually the boys became very close to Ballard's sister-in-law, Mrs. J. G. Ballard, who served as their housekeeper and confidante, and from her they learned how deeply hostile and prejudiced she and other members of the Ballard family had initially been toward them. Before she was introduced to them, she at first refused to take the job because she was afraid to work for Chinese. As she confessed several months later to Second Son (who summarized her confession in a letter to Father), "before she came here, she was staying with her mother in Birmingham. When Mr. Ballard told her of the three Chinese boys, she was quite unwilling to come here. Her mother would not let her go and she herself had a horrible idea of what we look like."[8] In imagining that Chinese looked horrible, Mrs. Ballard was typical of Westerners, according to Second Son. "Father," he declared, "all westerners think that Chinese are such as they have seen in the pictures or in the London China Town." Part of the basis for the English image, Third Son wrote to Father, resulted from their failure to stay up to date with China: "They still think that Chinese are very conservative and have no improvement in their customs and life, such as keeping long nails and hanging pigtails." Another part, according to Second Son, was racial. As he wrote to Father, like other Westerners, Mrs. Ballard "thought we were not so white since we belong to the yellow race."[9]

In attributing racism to what the English had seen in the movies, Second Son was probably referring to a series of popular films featuring the sinister Chinese villain Dr. Fu Manchu. Created by an English writer under the pseudonym Sax Rohmer, Fu Manchu was an immediate sensation as soon as he began appearing in movies that were made in England in the mid-1920s. In 1929, the year the Liu boys arrived in England, the first American-made Fu Manchu film was shown to packed houses there. According to Hollywood studio publicity material, Fu Manchu had "menace in every twitch of his finger, a threat in every twitch of his eyebrow, terror in each split-second of his slanted eyes."[10]

Second Son's other explanation for this racism was that the English had jumped to mistaken conclusions based on their impressions of

Cantonese in London's Chinatown. Mrs. Ballard "has seen many Cantonese," Second Son noted, "but they are mostly sun burnt or rather dark. The fineness of our skin [as Shanghainese] surprised her too."[11] Second Son's point about the English failure to distinguish between the Cantonese and Shanghainese reflected the boys' own racial prejudice toward Cantonese. Third Son expressed this attitude in explicitly racist terms. "I should say the Cantonese is the worse race in our country. They are enterprising people but once they settled they never know how to improve their living. They come to Europe and America to spoil our national character and degrade the name of our country."[12]

Even after Mrs. Ballard had started to work in the boys' house and had begun to recognize that they did not conform to the Fu Manchu stereotype, she still had trouble convincing her English family and friends that they were not "horrible" members of "the yellow race." "Once she went back to see her mother," Second Son reported to Father, and on that occasion, "all her family asked her what do we look like and whether we spit or do any awful thing like that. She said several 'O? No.' She told every thing to them concerning us and surprised them greatly."[13] As her confession implies, Mrs. Ballard overcame her preconceptions while working for the boys, and she eventually became very fond of them. On June 25, 1930, after a year in the same household, Second Son reported to Father that "she loves us very much" and that the boys happily reciprocated: "She treats us like her own sons and so well that we treat her almost like mother." She also became aware of the boys' relationships with their family. As Second Son noted, "Mrs. Ballard once said to me, 'The best thing about you is that you maintain a very close relationship with your parents.'"

Yet, even while the boys came to like and trust Mrs. Ballard, they inferred from her revelations about herself and her family that all Westerners shared her racism, and they had experiences with the English elite that reinforced this conclusion.

Breaking into Elite Society

Even before his sons had arrived in England, Father had emphasized the importance of their making connections with members of elite society there. As early as June 6, 1929, he gave instructions to Matthews (who repeated them to Ballard) that his sons "have to learn customs and English manners and will attend theatres, recitals and dine at restaurants and so on." They needed experience in dealing with the English elite because "it is desired that they shall learn to become equal to holding their own anywhere and in any society."[14] After Matthews paid the boys a visit in England a few months later, he pointed out to Father that they would be better able to hold their own in English society if they would rid themselves of their American accents. "Mr. Matthews told me," Father wrote to his sons (in Chinese, inserting the two English words italicized here), "that your boys' spoken English carries *American accents*. Be sure to pay attention to that problem. Since you received your English lessons in Shanghai from Americans, you had little exposure to pure English. You are now students in England, and you need to rid yourselves of your American accent when speaking English."[15] Father wanted his sons to take advantage of language and every other device for making contacts with the English elite.

As the boys' guardian in England, Ballard readily agreed to take personal responsibility for putting them "into contact with the best class of people."[16] Not a university graduate himself, Ballard felt the need to make contacts with members of the English elite who could exercise their influence to arrange for the boys' admission to Cambridge, and he learned from the boys that Father did not have such contacts in England. As Third Son later remarked to Father, "although you may know many great English men in China, you have very few English friends in England."[17] When Ballard discovered that Father had few such friends, he came up with an idea about how the boys could make their own contacts. As early as July 12, 1929, less than two weeks after their arrival in England, he wrote to Matthews, "during this winter, I hope they will be able to attend the Hunt."[18]

Ballard prepared the boys for foxhunting on horseback by giving them lessons with a riding master, Major Evans, a general's son, who, after losing his father's fortune, had ended up earning his living by teaching horseback riding to children in upper-class families.[19] As soon as the boys were comfortable with their mounts, they joined Essex Union Hunt, which was near their home in Leigh on the Sea, and went on fox hunts, in which they were immediately thrown together with members of the English elite. As Fourth Son reported to Father on April 9, 1930, "while fox hunting, we have come into contact with many high-class people, and we have talked about relations between China and England. Although we did not want to show our true feelings, we could tell from their tone that English people pay a lot of attention to our country's people. Many of them have lived in China, so it was interesting to talk with them."[20] While talking with these high-class people, the boys held back their true feelings when they heard the English belittle Chinese, and they were personally offended when the English expressed doubts about whether they, as Chinese, had the strength and stamina needed for the hunt.

On November 27, 1929, four months after the boys arrived in England, Third Son reported to Father that he and his brothers had been regularly riding in fox hunts, and in the most recent one they had felt particularly challenged to prove their mettle as Chinese. "The English people thought we would be fed up by the wet weather and give up hunt," he proudly noted. "They are really surprised to see that we are still as keen as before. They said that a real proper hunt is in a raining day and we agreed with them. They think that the weather in England is most terrible and the Oriental people will not like it. But what we did was [in] contrast to their thought."[21] From this time on, Third Son and his brothers took deep satisfaction in breaking the English stereotype of Oriental people as physically weak and unathletic by demonstrating their prowess in several sports—tennis, soccer, swimming, and polo as well as fox hunting. "We try to show our spirit and skill in doing every kind of sport," Fourth Son proudly reported to Father.[22]

In these other sports, as in the hunt, the boys felt that the English considered them physically weak simply because they were Chinese. When they aggressively attacked their English opponents in a soccer game, Third Son wrote to Father, "at the beginning of the game all the people thought that we were Japanese because they never thought that the Chinese can be so strong and hard. They were shouting 'Japanese' all the time and Mr. Ballard corrected them."[23] The boys found that even Ballard seemed incapable of imagining that they could have grown to be so strong in China. "Mr. Ballard always gives full credit to our physical energy," Fourth Son wrote to Father, "but I do not appreciate the way in which he tells others about us; he means to show them that we have physically developed since we came to England. As matter of fact we have always been very strong. I will not say that I am much stronger than I was because I live in England."[24] The boys were sensitive to Ballard's failure to give proper credit to their Chinese background not only because they regarded it as an ethnic slur but also because they had attended St. John's University, which had been known for its emphasis on sports while they had been there.[25]

For the boys, a year of hearing themselves condescendingly characterized as Chinese weaklings culminated in their hunt club's refusal to let them to ride in horse races. In December 1930 their requests were initially turned down on the grounds that no Chinese would have the physical strength to keep up with the English in this sporting event. Speaking of the club's refusal to let them race, Third Son posed for Father this rhetorical question: "Why can not we, the Chinese boys, do a thing that is safe for the English boys to do?" Third Son recalled that the boys had had difficulty persuading the English secretary of their club to let them hunt, and now they were having the same difficulty persuading him to let them race. "At first, being Chinese boys, we were not considered strong enough to hunt," he told Father. "Now we want to show the English people that we are not only strong enough to hunt but also strong enough to race."[26] Only after Ballard pressed the case and insisted that the boys were strong enough was he finally able to arrange for them to ride in their club's horse races, and they went on to post several victories.

Ultimately satisfied in this case, the Liu boys became frustrated and angry in other situations when they did not overcome racial prejudice or find a satisfying means of dealing with it. On January 6, 1930, after living in England for six months, Fourth Son vented his rage. "Father," he wrote (in Chinese; English word italicized here), "I often hear English people make fun of Chinese, and I can't stand it. I get angry, and I *hate* even to look at any English people." Bottling up his anger and carrying it around with him, Fourth Son speculated that his hatred of the English for telling ethnic jokes about Chinese might explain why he had become withdrawn since arriving in England. He regarded his shyness as a major shortcoming that had recently become so noticeable that his guardian and brothers had begun to criticize him for it. As he admitted to Father,

I run away when I see a stranger. Maybe it's because I didn't come into contact with many people when I was in Shanghai. Mr. Ballard has urged me not to be shy more than a hundred times with no results. One day, Second Brother scolded me, saying "A man of the world must see and come in contact with the world, if you keep on shying you will never be a great man" [this quotation in English]. I was shaken by these words. I have begun to force myself, and maybe I'll achieve success within half a month.

Fourth Son also wrote to Father that when Ballard asked him "Why do you sometimes keep silence and remain in meditation mood?" Fourth Son replied: "This is habitual, and I always do when I think of anything miserable" (both statements in English).[27] At the time the thing that was making him miserable, he explained in his letter to Father, was hearing the jokes the English told at the expense of the Chinese.

Just as the boys considered racism a barrier between themselves and the English elite, they also believed that it restricted their efforts to gain entrance into Cambridge University. "We are Chinese," Fourth Son wrote to Father in January 1930, after six months of fruitless efforts to register for Cambridge's entrance examinations, "and how can we expect help from the government and businesses of a foreign country?" The boys acknowledged to Father that Ballard as their guardian had tried to make contacts with members of the English elite who might help them get into Cambridge. In fact, Second Son regarded Ballard as the exception to the rule that English people were racists, and he cited Ballard's attempts to sign the boys up for Cambridge entrance examinations as evidence of his altruism and egalitarianism. "Mr. Ballard always wants to help people. He treats everybody else the same as he treats us. He has been running around everywhere asking for people's help to solve our entrance exam problem."[28]

Despite Ballard's efforts on their behalf during their first months in England, the boys' prospects for taking the exams looked bleak—unless they could find and make use of influential contacts. "According to Mr. Ballard," Fourth Son glumly reported to Father in January 1930, six months after their arrival, "you must register to take the entrance examinations three or four years in advance. Or if you have influence you might try using it."[29] Fourth Son implied that the boys needed influential patrons who were English. But when Father came to realize that Ballard had not recruited any English patrons who were willing to exert their influence on behalf of his sons, he put the boys in touch with potentially influential Chinese.

Seeking Chinese Help

On the morning of January 3, 1930, on Father's instructions, the three Liu boys paid a visit to China's highest ranking diplomatic official in England, Minister Shi Zhaoji (Alfred Sao-ke Sze), at his residence on the upper floor of the Chinese legation in London.[30] They were accompanied by Ballard, his sister-in-law, and Charlie Matthews (the son of Father's contact in Shanghai, F. N. Matthews), who remained with them only for the formal introductions to Minister Shi. As soon as the Ballards and Matthews were gone, the boys began to form their first contacts with influential Chinese in England, and they found that they positively enjoyed the experience.

Since the boys had not met Shi or his family before and had not spoken Mandarin during their six months in England, they were initially a bit tentative. As Fourth Son described the scene to Father, "After Mr. and Mrs. Ballard left, we all began to speak in Chinese. At first it seemed rather awkward and unfamiliar because we have not had daily practice, and we have lived in a foreign land for a long time. Mr. Shi was extremely friendly, and he asked us about our lives in England and the question of our further studies."[31]

Soon the boys began to relax, especially after they discovered that Shi, who was born near Shanghai and educated there, spoke their own dialect, Shanghainese.[32] In fact, they were delighted when Shi switched from Mandarin to their beloved Shanghainese. While they had not spoken Mandarin in England, they had spoken Shanghainese to each other every day of their lives in England as well as China. As Second Son jokingly, if proudly, told Father, "we brothers still don't fart foreign farts. We speak our own native tongue all of the time." So it was hardly surprising that, as Second Son went on to say, "I feel warm toward Mr. Shi because he speaks Shanghainese, and we speak very freely."[33]

If at ease with Minister Shi, the boys were also taken with his Cantonese wife. To their surprise, she also spoke Shanghainese. "Mrs. Shi has a Cantonese accent," Fourth Son noted, "but all of us understood every word that she said."[34] Second Son also liked Mrs. Shi's youthful and fashionable appearance. Though an older woman, "Mrs. Shi dresses like a thirty- or forty-year-old woman, half new-style, half old-style."[35]

The boys' good first impressions of Minister Shi and his wife were greatly enhanced by their lunch together. At noon the Shis took the boys from the minister's residence in the legation to a place called Shanghai Restaurant in London and were treated to a mouthwatering meal. "This was our first Chinese meal since leaving Shanghai," Fourth Son wrote to Father. "When we saw steamed meat and eggs, stir-fried shredded meat, fish braised in soy sauce, and wonton noodles, we began to swoon."[36] They also enjoyed the rest of the day—first a trip to the zoo with Shi's secretary and then back for four o'clock tea with Shi and his wife at the minister's residence. Picked up by Ballard at five o'clock, the boys returned to their own residence with the feeling that they had formed a bond with Minister Shi and his wife.

As events later transpired, it turned out that the boys had initiated a relationship with Shi that would eventually deepen and become important to other members of Liu family as well as themselves. But at the time they did not receive much help from him with their own immediate problem of finding a way to register for the entrance examinations at Cambridge. At their meeting, they broached this subject, and Shi agreed to look into the problem, but he did not promise to solve it. As Fourth Son summarized Shi's comments to Father on January 6, 1930, three days after they had met with him, when they spoke about the matter of taking entrance examinations for Cambridge University, "he indicated that it would be rather difficult, but he is trying to arrange to have a discussion with the head of the school. We'll hear from him within the next two weeks."[37] Trying not to sound disappointed, Fourth Son observed philosophically to Father that "major difficulties always arise when studying abroad."[38] After two weeks had passed, the boys continued to stay in touch with Shi, but they recognized that they were not making any progress by following Father's strategy of arranging their admission to Cambridge through the English and the Chinese elite in England. In frustration, they began to formulate their own strategy.

Turning to a Tutor

In late January 1930, after receiving no promise of help with their admission to Cambridge from Minister Shi, the boys decided to take advantage of one of their own contacts, their tutor, Reverend A. H. Gardner, whom Ballard had hired to prepare them for the entrance examinations in mathematics and who had worked with them daily for six months since their arrival in July 1929. An Oxford graduate, Gardner approached the college he had attended and secured a place for one of the Lius to take a kind of preliminary entrance examination there. As Third Son wrote to Father, "this is not a University Examination, it is entirely under Mr. Gardner's personal influence in the college." By passing this college examination, one of the Lius would not automatically gain admission into the university, but he would at least "have the opportunity to try to get in the University."[39]

The boys were elated by the news—the first sign that they would not all be kept waiting for two years or more before taking an entrance examination. "I was extremely happy to hear this," Second Son wrote to Father. As the eldest of the three boys, he was the first in line to become an examination candidate, and his brothers exhorted him to work hard and make the most of it. When Fourth Son wrote home about it, he noted that Second Son "had encountered countless difficulties before he received this good news allowing him to take the exam. He needs to give it his all."[40] In his own letter home, Second Son vowed to do just that. "From now on," he promised Father in late January 1930,

> I'll dedicate my life to studying Latin and other subjects. Good old Third and Fourth [Sons] will continue their studies and wait for other vacancies. The examination date is only eight weeks from now. The next several days will be most crucial. I don't care whether I pass this exam or not, but I'll surely benefit from these two months of devoting myself to my studies. Dear Father, isn't this excellent news?

Referring to himself in the third person, Second Son remarked: "Good old Second Son has had good luck. Let's hope he gets good grades."[41] He realized full well that his brothers pinned their hopes and dreams on him, and he promised to do his best.

After throwing himself into his studies for a week, Second Son heard in more detail about the Oxford examination from Gardner, and his previously rising hopes began to fall. On February 6, 1930, "I received news which rather upsets me," he wrote to Father.

> I was told by Mr. Gardner that I have to take two modern languages besides Chinese in order to fulfill the Oxford entrance requirements. As the examination will come at the end of March, I have no chance to take up another language besides Latin. Mr. Gardner has tried his best efforts to help me, & has written a letter to Oxford concerning this matter. An exact answer has not come yet.[42]

Second Son continued to work hard—eight to ten hours every day, including Saturdays and Sundays—but he became far less optimistic
about his chances for passing. His brothers' enthusiasm also waned for
his prospects and their own. As Third Son wrote to Father on February
27, 1930, a month after the boys had first learned of the possible opening
at Oxford, in spite of Second Son's "hard work, the chance of his examination is still doubtful. The university authority required two other
languages besides Chinese and English, even if they will admit Julius
[Second Son] to take the exam. This suggestion will delay our entrance
to either of the universities one more year."[43] Fourth Son also felt frustrated. "Sometimes I do curse the trouble to enter any English University," he wrote to Father on March 10, 1930, "because I think we are
simply wasting time to wait for their replies."[44]

   During the next few weeks, the boys became confused and dispir-
ited. As Third Son summarized their emotional state in a letter to Father on April 8, 1930:

> We are now like pendulums, swinging around and not knowing which
> direction to go. Mr. Ballard has made many vain attempts to seek help
> from his friends who have influence in the different colleges of the uni-
> versities. Cambridge is full until the next two years so we are hopeless
> to have the examination. As to Oxford, everything is very doubtful
> because they never give us a definite answer. We are required to take
> French besides Latin if we want to take the bachelor degree of art in
> which case we have to spend another two years or at least one and a
> half years to study the language.[45]

Since none of the boys knew any languages besides Chinese and English,
they once again resigned themselves to a long wait before they would
be able to take entrance examinations at Oxford or Cambridge.

   The only apparent alternative to these years of language study was
to major in chemistry or physics, which only required them to take
entrance examinations in English and Latin, two languages that they
were already studying with their tutors in England. But if they majored
in the sciences, they would deviate from Father's plans for their education. "Your plan," Third Son reconfirmed with Father, "is that we are
going to take Charter Account after our university work and one of us
must take Secretary; but what have happened are entirely [in] contrast to
your idea." The boys were determined, above all, to follow Father's plan
for training them as accountants and executives and to avoid being

pushed into academic fields that were different from the ones that he had in mind for them. Third Son ended his report to Father on this subject with a desperate plea in English capital letters: "WE WANT TO SEEK YOUR ADVICE."[46]

Second Son, as the eldest of the three boys, laid out the alternatives and made proposals for Father. In his own case, he had already made the decision to take the Oxford entrance examinations beginning in June and to major in chemistry. "Yesterday after I had a discussion with Mr. Harvey and Mr. Gardner [the boys' two tutors]," he wrote to Father in early April 1930,

> I decided to study Chemistry because they said Chemistry is extremely good at Oxford. If I take an ordinary B.A. degree, then I must study French. They said that if I study French, it won't be easy, and I won't learn much. Chemistry is a subject that I like, and you also want us as your sons to study chemistry. Now I am prepared to study this subject. Once I have mastered it, it will be extremely useful.

Second Son was less decisive in specifying his two brothers' plans than he was his own, but he offered an opinion of what they should do too.

> No decision has been reached about Li's and Zhi's [Third and Fourth Sons'] studies. Wait two years? Or do otherwise? Although they are young, they are fired up. They want to climb up fast. What they lack is French. They are not afraid of the other subjects. If they don't study French, then they will have to follow my lead and study chemistry. I think studying French for two years and still not becoming good at it would slow down careers and cost thousands of times as much money in a foreign land.

On the expensiveness of their educations, Second Son differed with his guardian and other English advisors. "Mr. Ballard and others don't care because it's not their money," he wrote to Father, as if Father needed to be reminded whose money it was. "Their job is to make sure that our studies and our daily lives run smoothly, nothing more."[47]

Although expressing his own opinions about how all three boys should try to get into Oxford, Second Son left the ultimate decision to Father. "Didn't you once tell me," he wrote in early April, " 'don't be afraid to talk with me about anything at all and then leave the final decisions to me.' "[48] But before Second Son's seemingly final letter about Oxford could reach Father and elicit a reply, the boys abruptly turned their attention away from Oxford because they began to find vacancies at Cambridge.

Winning Over Tutors at Cambridge

In late April 1930, after ten frustrating months in England, including four months of mixed results in their investigations at Oxford, the boys were finally given opportunities to take entrance examinations at Cambridge. By this time, Father had recruited his most influential contacts to lobby on behalf of his sons' admissions. His Shanghai business associate F. N. Matthews reported to Father: "We are working every possible channel to secure nominations for the boys, but it is a matter of extraordinary difficulty, owing to the very great number of applications for admission to all the better known Colleges." Matthews alone had "five different people working in our interests and I have little doubt that the matter can be arranged shortly."[49] But as it turned out, the boys' original hopes for taking exams at Cambridge were fulfilled not because of Matthews's efforts to exercise influence through high-level English business people or Father's contacts with Chinese diplomats but rather because of interventions by two of the boys' own personal contacts: their guardian, Alfred Ballard, and their riding master, Major Evans.

On the morning of April 28, 1930, Ballard and Evans took Second Son and Third Son in tow, traveled the seventy miles from Leigh to Cambridge, and led them from one college of the university to the next. Evans had in hand a letter of introduction to a tutor in Trinity College from a Cambridge student who was a friend of his. In all likelihood, Evans knew this student because he had been teaching horseback riding to children in upper-class families for years. "This student is very rich and knows all tutors well," Second Son explained to Father in his report on this crucial day. After Evans handed over the letter of introduction from the rich student to the tutor at Trinity, the tutor immediately promised the boys two seats for the entrance examinations in his college, but then he was informed that he had exceeded a quota. "Only one Oriental," Second Son wrote to Father, "is allowed in each college."[50] Apparently embarrassed about withdrawing one of the two seats, the Trinity tutor compensated for this loss by introducing the group to a tutor at St. John's College, who promised them one seat in his college.

Evans, Ballard, and the Liu boys were delighted to have landed these two places with relative ease, but they had a much harder time finding a third one. "In order to get another seat," Second Son reported, "we walked from college to college and finally we got another one in Jesus College. Father, it is a terrible job to find vacancies, we were rejected seven times and came out with great disappointment."[51] After these seven rejections, they finally confirmed a third examination seat, giving all three boys the chance to take entrance examinations at Cambridge—Second Son in St. John's College, Third Son in Jesus College, and Fourth Son in Trinity College.

The boys were elated with these results, and they were especially pleased to have achieved success by following their own strategy. During their first ten months in England, they had tried Father's indirect approach by relying on members of the English and Chinese elite to act on their behalf, and they had made little progress toward gaining admission at Cambridge. Not until they took a more direct approach by visiting Cambridge in person with their own guardian and riding master did they succeed at registering for entrance examinations in the colleges.

In explaining their breakthrough to Father, the boys gave the credit to Ballard for their successes in winning over the Cambridge tutors. But even in praising Ballard, they made clear that the tutors took their applications seriously because the boys themselves had marched purposefully from college to college at Cambridge and demonstrated in person that they were up to English standards, especially in sports. Second Son realized that Father would never have imagined that the boys' accomplishments in sports would be crucial to their admission to Cambridge, so he carefully explained how Ballard had praised these accomplishments in recommending them for admission. "We are good in riding and quite good in games, and this Mr. Ballard knew already. He got the vacancies by telling the tutors that we are very fond of sports and that we ride and hunt. I know you will hardly believe it, but it is true."[52]

Second Son could hardly believe it himself, and to drive home the point, he cited Third Son's admission to Jesus College as his prime example. This college was known for its athletes, and Third Son received the examination seat from it almost exclusively because of his prowess in sports. If Father thought Second Son was exaggerating, his doubts were surely allayed when he received a copy of the letter Ballard wrote recommending Third Son to the master of Jesus College. In it, Ballard devoted more space to sports than to academic achievements; Third Son, he wrote, is

> a first class horseman, riding well to hounds and is well mounted: only ten days ago his horse won the Adjacent Hunts Race at the Essex & Suffolk Point to Point Meeting. He is also a tennis player of the a high order and I understand plays football, baseball, basketball, etc. well; his education in sport is being continued concurrently with his studies, and I anticipate that he will be of outstanding merit in many forms of sport, including rowing and polo by the time he enters your College.[53]

Second Son was impressed by Ballard's success at recognizing what the Cambridge tutors and masters wanted to hear and characterizing the boys accordingly. "Mr. Ballard is a very eloquent and clever man and it was entirely through his effort that we got the vacancies."[54]

After the boys' experiences with English racism, Second Son marveled that Ballard as a Westerner had gone so far beyond the call of duty—literally walking the extra mile at Cambridge—on behalf of his brothers and himself as Chinese. "Mr. Ballard is very good to us, and so earnest toward us that I can't possibly believe that any European will do so much for us. I will never forget him." Like Second Son, his brothers were thrilled with the opportunity to register for Cambridge entrance examinations and deeply grateful to Ballard for making it possible. Fourth Son reported that they were all "much indebted [to him for making] several attempts to get our names down the exam lists. He told the masters that he would guarantee the perfection of our conduct and work."[55]

Once the Cambridge examinations were lined up, Second Son abandoned his plans for taking entrance examinations at Oxford. Before doing so he consulted Gardner, his mathematics tutor, who had contacted Oxford on his behalf in the first place, and he received Gardner's assurance that Cambridge was a better choice. Second Son was relieved that he no longer had to deal with the Oxford man "who takes charge of oriental students," especially because Gardner had now revealed to him that "most of these men are very unkind and wicked, they are not like men in Cambridge who will do their best for you, though some of them are bad enough. Mr. Gardner advised me to take the Cambridge examination which is miles safer."[56] Glad to be free of Oxford and committed to Cambridge, Second Son concluded his report in May 1930: "Father, now everything is settled."

Everything had been settled, that is, about registering for the entrance examinations. Finding seats had been difficult—far more difficult than the boys had anticipated—and their success at securing places was a great relief to Father as well as themselves. "I am extremely happy," Father wrote from Shanghai in reply to Second Son's news that the tutors had been won over at Cambridge.[57] "It's especially comforting to hear that things are all set for you to take the Cambridge entrance examinations," he added in a note to Third Son on the same day.[58] But nothing was set about the outcome of the examinations, and all the boys' arduous efforts to register would be for nothing unless they passed.

Taking the Entrance Examinations

In mid-June 1930, nearly a year after their arrival in England, all three boys took their first entrance examinations at Cambridge. On June 16 they slept overnight in the Cambridge colleges—Second Son at St. John's, Third Son at Jesus, and Fourth Son at Trinity—and each paid an examination fee of 7 pounds. On June 17, Second Son took examinations on two works of literature, Sir Walter Scott's *Kenilworth* in the morning and Shakespeare's *Twelfth Night* in the afternoon, and on June 19, all three boys took their examinations in mathematics. Before and after the examinations, they anxiously expressed their fear of failure.

In the final weeks of preparation, with the examinations fast approaching, the boys had redoubled their efforts at studying and begun holding mock examinations. "Dear Father," Fourth Son wrote home, "we confess that we have done our duty most willingly and earnestly; for about three weeks we tested each other, questioned each other, until all the mathematics text books were thoroughly mastered." While trying to set high academic standards for each other, they were worried about Cambridge examiners setting still higher ones for them. "We are feeling very nervous," Fourth Son wrote to Father, "for we do not usually see everything as acutely as the examiners. Besides, they give very strict marks to the papers."[59] Third Son expressed this same concern. "We have heard that the examiners are very strict and are quite ready to give low marks," he wrote to Father.[60]

As the time for the examinations grew near, the boys became increasingly troubled about the danger of failing and its implications for their future. On May 25, a month before the examinations, Third Son had shown restraint in expressing this fear to Father, keeping calm and using understated language. "It would be best if we all passed," he observed as a matter of fact. "Otherwise there will be all kinds of problems."[61] A week later, on June 1, as the examinations loomed larger, he became more anxious and resorted to hyperbolic language. Again writing to Father, he declared, "If we get in, it will be the best thing that could possibly happen in the world, and we'll thank heaven and earth. If we don't get in, I'll be angry as hell [literally "angry to death"] because it will cause a lot of trouble and waste a lot of time and energy."[62] His emotionally charged language suggests how tense he was.

In case they were not admitted to Cambridge, the three brothers considered possible alternatives. "We have already discussed this question," Third Son reported to Father, "and we have prepared a request asking you to send us to America." Up to that point, they had not mailed Father the request, and they would not do so without giving it more thought, Third Son assured Father. "If any unfortunate thing happens, we'll discuss it in our conference of brothers. Please rest assured that we won't disappoint you. It won't be long until the exams, and we'll write you as soon as the exams are over."[63]

The boys had no chance to submit their proposal for going to the United States, because Father rejected the idea out of hand as soon as he heard that they were contemplating the possibility. "My only hope is that you can enroll either in Cambridge or Oxford," he replied to his three sons on July 8, 1930. "If you failed your exams and ended up going to the United States instead, you would not be doing what I want. Nor will I ever have this hope for you in the future. So you can get rid of that kind of thinking." His sons had to succeed in England and not even consider any alternative. No matter how difficult the Cambridge entrance exams might be, they could and must earn passing grades, he told them. Writing in Chinese but drawing on Western history for inspiration, he noted: "It is said that in Napoleon's dictionary, the word 'impossible' does not exist. I hope you all will keep that in mind."[64]

When the time for the examination finally arrived, the boys responded to Father's challenge and felt their competitive urges rising to the surface. "I had a peculiar feeling when I stepped in the Examination Hall," Fourth Son wrote to Father on the day after his examinations. "There were hundreds sitting with a hungry and earnest look," causing him to ask himself whether "I could beat them."[65] By the end of the examinations, they were emotionally drained. *"You looked horrible,"* Fourth Son told Third Son in English after seeing him in the examination hall. Quoting these words to Father (in a letter otherwise written in Chinese), Third Son added: "Since I couldn't see my own face, I'll have to take Fourth Brother's word for it that I looked horrible. And I myself know that I couldn't have looked very good during the exam."[66]

After completing the examinations, the boys returned from Cambridge to their home in Leigh, where they appealed to their mathematics tutor, Gardner, for reassurance. As Third Son reported to Father, we "gave him a detailed report on the exam that we took. We also told him the answers that we gave and compared them with Mr. Gardner's answers to the same questions." To their relief, Gardner thought that their answers had been satisfactory. Third Son summarized the conversation in Chinese, but he quoted Gardner's exact words in English for Father's benefit. "In Mr. Gardner's estimation, we should have passed the exam. He said, *'I am pretty sure you can pass. I'll be very much surprised if you don't.'* " Although their fears were allayed to some extent by Gardner's approval of their answers, they still wished that they had done better. "On reflection," Third Son wrote, "we realize that we were too nervous, and as a result, maybe our brains were not functioning as well as usual. Otherwise we could have earned even better grades."[67]

Less than two weeks later, when the results of the examinations were announced, Gardner's prediction came true: all three boys had passed the mathematics examination. Second Son, the only one who had taken examinations in English as well as mathematics, received his test results while he was in the middle of writing a letter home about the examinations. "Father, wait a minute," he said, dramatically interrupting himself at his writing desk. "I heard a telephone calling, it is about my examination I hope." Then, returning to his desk, he joyfully reported the good news. "O, father, I have just heard that I have passed my English and mathematics," he wrote. "I have not slept well since I came back from Cambridge, for I was afraid that I might not have passed in English, now my worry has gone, I can have a sound sleep tonight."[68]

This thrilling climax was the emotional peak for the boys of their first year. After a brief vacation, they continued to study long hours in preparation for more examinations in July and October 1930, but they were much more confident about these examinations than they had been about the first ones. Their only concern was about the language examination, and this concern was greatly eased by Cambridge's approval of their petition to substitute classical Chinese for Latin and waive all other language requirements except English.

Though greatly relieved to be spared the Latin examination, Third Son still expressed doubts to Father about whether he could pass the classical Chinese examination, which was based on the Four Books, the embodiment of Confucian teachings. "I am much disgraced to acknowledge that I am entirely foreign to the Chinese Four Books. I am not a pessimist so I will try very hard. Even if I fail I shall not be too disappointed as long as I know that I have worked at it."[69]

If Third Son expected Father to console him, he was disappointed. In reply, Father chastised him and his brothers for not taking the classical Chinese examination more seriously and preparing more fully. "How much do you really know about the Chinese Four Books?" he demanded of them. "Your command of the Chinese classical language is quite poor, and your knowledge of vernacular Chinese will not do you any good on the examination." Lecturing them, he pointed out: "The [Confucian] Four Books include the Analects, Mencius, the Great Learning, and the Doctrine of the Golden Mean. When Li [Third Son] wrote me last time, he thought that the Four Books constituted a single work. From this I can tell that you boys don't know much about it."[70]

Father cautioned his boys not to jump to the conclusion that the classical Chinese exam would be easy simply because they were taking it from Westerners. "Don't think for a minute that foreigners do not know Chinese, and therefore, that you, with a little luck, can pass the examination. Mr. Giles [a noted British linguist and philologist], for example, has an outstanding command of Chinese, and don't you ever look down on him." If they underestimated their examiners, they ran the risk of humiliating themselves, Father warned. "You boys are Chinese, and if you fail the exam in your own language, you'll lose face in front of the foreigners. I hope you will not think that Chinese will be easy and that you will pay special attention to it."[71]

Contrary to Father's fears, the boys all passed the classical Chinese exam, and when their grades were posted, they became proud of themselves for having taken Chinese in place of Latin or French, which other Chinese students tended to take. With self-satisfaction, Second Son told his uncle in Shanghai:

> Most of the Chinese in England took Latin or French instead of Chinese, for they said to me that Latin & French are much easier than Chinese. I feel very sad indeed to hear that Chinese are afraid to learn their own national language. When I met a tutor in Cambridge, he advised me not to take Chinese because it is difficult. I said to him that I prefer Chinese to any other language & had an interesting talk with him concerning it.[72]

By the time Second Son wrote these words, he knew the results of the Chinese examination, and he added: "I am glad I passed the Chinese, or he would call me a liar."

On October 16, 1930, the three Liu boys received news that they had passed all of their examinations, and Ballard immediately sent a telegram to Father in Shanghai reporting these favorable results. Second Son followed up by letter, proudly conveying to Father how relieved and excited the boys were about their success and how pleased they were that their English friends had given them hearty congratulations.[73] But it was Father's approval the boys wanted to hear, and they did not have to wait long for it. On October 16, the same day that Father received Ballard's telegram, he fired back one of his own printed in capital letters:

> CONGRATULATIONS TO YOU AND YOUR BROTHERS FOR YOUR SUCCESSFUL PASS IN CAMBRIDGE ENTRANCE EXAMINATION FATHER.[74]

Father elaborated by letter, and he expressed pride and even astonishment that the boys could have achieved success in England on their own and with so little assistance. "You boys have been in England for only a little over a year, and on your very first try you have got yourselves into such a famous university that everyone respects and admires. You should really be proud of yourselves."[75]

Father praised his sons for achieving success without the benefit of help from high-ranking patrons in English society. "As the ancient saying goes," he reminded them, " 'After climbing up to the Dragon's Gate, a person's social status soars by leaps and bounds.' Now that you have enrolled yourselves in Cambridge, you have indeed climbed up to the Dragon's Gate. So, it goes without saying that your social status has soared. I hope you will continue to work hard and will rise ever higher."[76] Father found his sons very receptive to this advice because they had already become emotionally attached to their new university, and they could hardly wait to prove themselves there.

Falling in Love with Cambridge

If the boys had any doubts about wanting to attend Cambridge before taking the examinations, they had none from then on. They were deeply impressed by the experience of staying overnight in their colleges and strolling around the campus and town, and even before they received the results of their examinations, they began to fall in love with the place. "Cambridge is a beautiful town with luxuriant woods everywhere," Fourth Son wrote to Father on June 20, 1930, the day after his first entrance examination. Describing his college, Trinity, he remarked that "the college buildings are old but very grand-looking; the lovely lawns have been carefully kept for hundreds of years. Rolling and watering are the chief causes that make them turn out nicely."[77]

Second Son was also smitten. On June 25, the day he heard the good news that he had passed his first examinations, he described for Father, St. John's College, where he had stayed while taking the examinations, in glowing terms.

> Around the college where I lived there is a beautiful stream across which many stone bridges had been built. The most fascinating sight is the green meadows, they are the best I have seen in my life. The students are always proud of them. Another interesting thing is the buildings. They are five or six hundred years old and look very nice outside. But inside the buildings it is all dark and the windows are so old-fashioned that they have iron railing instead of glasses.

Even though he knew that he had to take more entrance examinations, Second Son had already walked through the rooms in St. John's and assessed the possibilities for his future home. He laid out the options for Father: "Each student has his own bedroom, a study, and a tiny room for boiling water and storing food. The rooms have differences in their decorating and furniture. The more money a student pays to the college the better room he can have. Some of the rooms look very good while some look like cottage rooms."[78]

Even while Second Son anticipated a place for himself at St. John's, he also imagined how he would fit into student culture at Cambridge. While in residence for his first examinations, he was fascinated by what he saw of Cambridge students. "It is very interesting," he wrote to Father,

> to watch the huge crowd of students walking very slowly in the streets. Some prefer cars and others bicycles. They have pipes in their mouths and look very smart. To my eyes, most of them have rich parents, for they have luxurious cars which cost about 30000 dollars. They do not seem to work very hard, and whenever they come out, they have their best girls with them. At colleges they laugh together and talk loud. They have luncheons in their own rooms and dinners in the hall. Tennis is one of their favourite games, so some good courts are necessary. I walked around the buildings and had a look at the courts, they are all marvelous.[79]

Whether or not Second Son fully identified with these wealthy, fashionable, self-assured students who laughed and talked together and did not seem to work very hard, he had no doubts about wanting to become their classmate.

To show his parents how beautiful Cambridge was, Second Son sent them pictures of it on July 5, 1930, the day after his second round of entrance examinations. In case his parents did not appreciate Cambridge for its unsurpassed beauty, he compared it favorably with St. John's University in Shanghai. This comparison hit close to home because of Father's own experience as a student at St. John's in Shanghai, his current position as chairman of its board of directors, and his decision to send the three boys to school there before they had left for England.[80] Even if Father and the entire Liu family regarded St. John's as the best and most beautiful university in China, it could not begin to compare with Cambridge in Second Son's estimation. "From the pictures," he triumphantly proclaimed to his parents, "you can tell that going to school in this place is a million times better than attending St. John's in Shanghai."[81]

Like his brothers, Third Son lavished praise on Cambridge. He acknowledged that he and his brothers would not have had this educational opportunity without Father's support, and he assured Father that it was fully worth his while. "After sending us abroad, you got worried about us," Third Son told Father, revealing that he had heard this news from Father's business associate Wu Qingtai (T. T. Woo), who had recently visited England. Wu had told the boys about Father's mixed feelings at the time of their departure from Shanghai. On the one hand, for practical reasons, Father had felt compelled to let his sons go, but on the other, for emotional reasons, he could not bear to let them go. Finding this news touching, Third Son wanted Father to know that he and his brothers appreciated both the personal and the financial sacrifices Father had made to send the boys to Cambridge, and he thanked Father for making them all very happy. "Since you have spent so much money and strength to educate us in England, there is no doubt about our happiness."[82]

Fulfilling Father's Plan

In October 1930 the Liu boys were no doubt happy about achieving Father's goal by passing their entrance examinations at Cambridge, but they were also happy about their success at devising their own strategy for achieving this goal. After arriving in England in July 1929, they had initially followed Father's plan for making contacts with members of the English and Chinese elite and depending on them to arrange for the boys' admission to Cambridge. But in April 1930, after using this strategy to no avail for ten frustrating months, the boys had taken their own initiative in paying a visit to Cambridge, where they, their guardian, and their riding master negotiated face-to-face with tutors for seats in the entrance examinations. By this bold maneuver, they succeeded in registering for the entrance examinations and went on to pass them.

The boys considered their entrance into Cambridge merely the first step in fulfilling Father's plan according to which they were supposed to prepare themselves to serve as accountants and executives in the family firm, and in October 1930, once they had passed the examinations, they took another step toward fulfilling this plan. They had free time during the academic year 1930–31 because they had completed their entrance examinations too late to matriculate at Cambridge in the fall of 1930 and had to wait until the fall of 1931 to start classes. To avoid wasting the year, their guardian Ballard proposed that they serve as apprentices—Second Son and Fourth Son in accounting and Third

Son in law—at Lowe, Bingham and Matthews, the accounting firm where he worked in London. The boys eagerly embraced this proposal. "Father what do you think of this idea?" Second Son asked expectantly, and he gave Father his own answer: "Personally I think it is a splendid idea."[83]

With Father's blessing, the idea was adopted, and it worked out to the full satisfaction of two of the boys. Second Son became an "article" doing his apprenticeship as an accountant with Ballard, and Fourth Son did the same with Ballard's fellow chartered accountant, a man named Coates.[84] In 1930–31, each boy completed a full year of the three-year apprenticeship that was required of accountants for certification in England. Third Son did not make such a fast start in his legal apprenticeship because he had to wait a few months before he was placed in a law firm with a solicitor, a Mr. Moulton. Although Third Son was not at the same company as his brothers, all three boys worked in London, taking up temporary residence on its outskirts, and commuted together by car every day. In the fall of 1931 they began classes at Cambridge, and in the summer of 1932, after completing their first year of college, all three boys landed apprenticeships at Lowe, Bingham and Matthews. Second Son and Fourth Son, who were economics majors at Cambridge, continued their apprenticeships in accounting, and Third Son, who majored in law, continued his apprenticeship in law.[85]

Thus, between their arrival in England in the summer of 1929 and their matriculation at Cambridge in the fall of 1931, the boys made great progress toward the goals Father had set for them, but they had done so by taking their own initiatives. They relied on Father's contacts to the extent that they accepted Ballard as their legally appointed guardian, and they initially followed Father's strategy of gaining admission to Cambridge by cultivating contacts with the English elite and the Chinese minister to England. But when Father's strategy failed to bring results, they abandoned it. In its place, they adopted a direct approach, meeting with Cambridge tutors face-to-face. As a result, they gained admission to Cambridge not through Father's preexisting network so much as through their own network of contacts, which included English people whom Father had never met.

While devising their own strategy, they never wavered in their determination to fulfill Father's plan for them as future accountants and executives in the family firm. Not until January 1932, two and a half years after they had arrived in England, did they have a serious disagreement with Father about any aspect of his plan for them. By then they were well ensconced as students at Cambridge, but after their encounters with English racism, they did not think of themselves as English, so they were shocked when Father suddenly proposed that they should become British citizens.

3

Sons Who Did Not Want to Become
British Citizens

IN 1932 Father urged his three sons in England to become British citizens because he hoped to use their British citizenship to prevent a Japanese military takeover of his Chinese-owned businesses. As a councilor on the Shanghai Municipal Council, he was one of the Chinese leaders who tried to avoid a Sino-Japanese military conflict in the city by meeting the Japanese military's demands in January 1932.[1] These demands, as issued by the Japanese naval commander at Shanghai, Rear Admiral Shiozawa Koichi, required the Shanghai Municipal Council to agree to take three actions: first, suppress the anti-Japanese movement and boycott activity that had grown steadily at Shanghai since Japan had seized Manchuria (northeast China) in September 1931; second, compensate Japanese victims of fights that had broken out between Japanese monks and Chinese workers in front of a Japanese-owned factory in Zhabei, a district of Shanghai outside the foreign concessions, on January 18, 1932; and third, issue an apology for this factory incident and for a Chinese publication that had allegedly insulted the emperor of Japan, Hirohito. In announcing these demands, Shiozawa issued an ultimatum. If they were not accepted by the end of the day on January 28, 1932, then the Japanese forces would occupy the Chinese sectors of Shanghai, leaving untouched the foreign concessions in the city that had been administered by Western powers since the nineteenth century.

On orders from Chiang Kai-shek, head of the Nationalist government of China, Father and other members of the Shanghai Municipal Council agreed to all of Shiozawa's demands. Late in the afternoon on January 28, their message reached the Japanese consul general in

Shanghai, but even this capitulation did not satisfy Shiozawa. Complaining that the Chinese had merely announced and not carried out their plans to satisfy Japanese demands, Shiozawa launched a full-scale attack on Shanghai. He committed three divisions and sent airplanes to bomb the Zhabei district of the city, just north of the British-dominated International Settlement. But to his surprise, the Chinese Nineteenth Route Army, which had been stationed in Shanghai, fought back tenaciously and held its ground in Zhabei. Intense fighting between Japanese and Chinese troops continued for thirty-three days, January 29 to March 1, 1932. It was during this sequence of events, which became known as the Shanghai Incident, that Father proposed to his sons in England that they should become British citizens.[2]

Proposing British Citizenship

On February 14, 1932, after the first two and a half weeks of unabated fighting, Father sent his proposal to his three sons in England explaining why they should become British citizens. Since the Japanese seemed to be on the verge of occupying Shanghai, Father was afraid that they would soon confiscate the Chinese-owned businesses in all parts of the city, including the International Settlement, where his businesses were concentrated. But he predicted that the Japanese would spare Western-owned businesses for fear that such confiscations would provoke the United States and European countries to declare war against Japan. With this scenario in mind, he proposed to his sons that they should become British citizens so that they, as co-owners of the family business, could give it a British legal status that would prevent the Japanese from confiscating it.

When Father made this proposal, he did not anticipate any opposition from his sons. He assumed that they would unquestioningly accept it as part of a strategy for protecting the family business, but he did not simply order them to carry it out. Instead he framed it as one of the Chinese efforts that needed to be considered in dealing with the Japanese. "Undoubtedly," he wrote to the boys, trying to imagine their state of mind, "you must have been reading the papers very minutely concerning the happenings here in Shanghai ever since January 29." Up to January 28, he emphasized, he and others in the Shanghai Municipal Council had maintained peace by accommodating the Japanese at every turn. "The demands made by the Japanese on us at that time were very humiliating indeed. Still we desired to preserve peace to the very extreme point. Hence we yielded to those drastic demands and our assent was accepted by the Japanese Consul General as satisfactory. But Japan has wicked intentions." Father was appalled by this hypocritical contrast, as he saw it, between the mendacious pronouncements of the Japanese in public and their malicious intentions in reality, and he admitted that Chinese policy had been inadequate to deal with it.

> To the Japanese faith is but the breath of a syllable. So in spite of the fact that that our assent had been accepted as satisfactory the Japanese nevertheless opened fire on our men. It is plainer than day that the Japanese have no other intention than make trouble. Hitherto we had adopted the policy of non-resistance. But this policy was suicidal. We had simply been cutting off our own limb with a view to save the body.[3]

Even though Father freely admitted that he and other Chinese had failed in their attempts to deal with Japan through diplomacy, he was heartened by the response of the government and army to the Shanghai Incident. "The morale of our government and army was said to be rotten beyond mending," he pointed out, referring to negative international press coverage in newspapers at the time.

> But, my dear boys, we have now proven to the world that our national spirit lives and it will exist forever. Had we gone on with the policy of non-resistance there was every probability that our country might soon sink to a land of slaves. But we have been forced to resort to armed resistance. We have realized that we cannot and should not expect others to save us out of righteousness or justice's sakes. Salvation of China must come from within our very own selves. This armed resistance may mean tremendous cost and sacrifice, but for a nation this is the better policy.

Because of its national spirit, the Chinese armed resistance gave Father hope despite Japan's superior military technology. "We know they have better weapons of war and their men are better trained for fighting. The Japanese dropped bombs from planes to set fire to houses of the civilians. Also the Japanese have been using heavy guns to bombard Chapei [Zhabei] and the Wusung [Wusong] Forts."[4]

With these advantages, the Japanese expected to have no difficulty capturing Zhabei, the district of Shanghai that had been the original target of the Japanese invasion since January 29. "The Japanese thought they could easily take Chapei [Zhabei] in three hours," Father wrote on February 14, but "have not gained an inch though their troops are coming all the time."

In explaining the high morale and impressive effectiveness of soldiers in the Chinese Nineteenth Route Army and other Chinese defenders of Shanghai, Father emphasized above all to his sons that Chinese in the resistance were driven by their belief in their country. "I want to reassure you here," he concluded in his report on the past two and a half weeks of fighting in Shanghai, "that our national or patriotic spirit is backing our men up to win. Our cause is right and right will inevitably defeat might."

In the very next sentence after this unqualified endorsement of "our national or patriotic spirit," Father introduced his proposal for his boys' adoption of British citizenship. "Now my dear boys," he began, "I want to communicate to you here my particular piece of mind. It may sound outlandish to you at the outset. However, I am imparting it to you after a considerable period of profound deliberation." Trying his best not to sound unpatriotic, he made the following proposal:

> I want you three to put your heads together and devote your deep thought to what I have to say to you in the very next moment. I am of the mind that you make expeditious inquiries as to whether you have lived long enough now to entitle you to the privilege of becoming British subjects. In the event that you are now possessed of this qualification then I expressly desire that you take immediate steps to naturalize yourselves as Britishers. I am earnestly looking forward to your response in regard to this subject.[5]

His phrasing here was not dictatorial. He used the words "I want you three to put your heads together," "I am of the mind," "I expressly desire," and "I am earnestly looking forward to your response," as he invited his sons to give their own opinions. But he implied that he expected to hear opinions that were fully in line with his own. If so, then he clearly underestimated his sons' willingness to take issue with him.

Reacting Nationalistically

Before receiving Father's proposal, the boys in England reacted strongly to the news of the Shanghai Incident. On January 28, 1932, the day the fighting first broke out, they received a telegram from Father, assuring them that all members of the family in Shanghai were accounted for and safe at home, and they read about the fighting every day in English newspapers as well as in mail from home.[6] But they did not receive Father's proposal for them to become British citizens for two weeks, the usual period required for letters to go from Shanghai to Cambridge at this time, and during the weeks of fighting before then, they sent him passionately patriotic letters that criticized not only the Japanese but also the British and other non-Chinese.

On February 10, 1932, Second Son wrote to Father that he identified completely with the Chinese defenders of Shanghai: "Let us encourage those that are fighting in Chapei [Zhabei] and let us not forget to set up a memorial for those who died for their country." He reported that other Chinese students at Cambridge supported the Chinese resistance as passionately as he did. "Most of the students from China are simply furious. One of them told me yesterday that he will go back to China in the summer and will personally go to Chapei [Zhabei] to give honor to the brave soldiers who died."[7] The Lius felt solidarity with not only their Cambridge classmates but also other young Chinese men who expressed their patriotism in anti-Japanese demonstrations in China, Southeast Asia, Europe, and elsewhere at the time.

While angry with the Japanese, Second Son was critical of the English too. "Papers here are showing a little bit of sympathy but some are still justifying Japanese actions in Manchuria and Chapei [Zhabei]," he reported to Father. Even the English with experience in China disappointed him. "Most English people who came back from China don't seem to like Chinese," he bitterly observed. He had no faith in England or other Western countries or the League of Nations as allies for China against Japan. "I know this trouble is going to last for years, as other world powers are not doing anything to stop the Japanese madness. We should no longer listen to the Powers, we have to do what we think is justifiable and right."[8] To stop the Japanese, Chinese had to rely on themselves, Second Son contended, and he had no doubt that Father was leading the way. "How busy you must have been these days being on the Municipal Council," he imagined. "Father, I know you so well, you must have been doing great service for the country in the Crisis."

Third Son was as critical of Britain and other Western powers as he was of Japan. In fact, he went so far as to place all the blame on the

British for preventing the League of Nations from intervening in the Shanghai Incident on China's behalf. "It is entirely due to the British influence that the League of Nations did not take any strong measure against Japanese actions in Shanghai," he claimed.[9]

Besides criticizing Britain for sympathizing with Japan, Third Son found fault with Britain's overall approach in its relations with China. As a student of law, he particularly objected to Britain's and other powers' abuses of legal privileges in establishing concession areas for themselves within China's cities. He considered it outrageous that these areas were governed under the principle of extraterritoriality—the right of a criminal to be judged by his or her own nation's laws on Chinese soil. He traced the origins of these foreign privileges to military victories by Britain and other foreign powers over China in the nineteenth century, and he found absolutely no moral basis for the powers' retention of these privileges in his own time. "It is all very well for Great Britain, Japan, France and all other big powers to say that they have great commercial interests in China which they must protect, but they do not see that to have settlements in a country which is a nation, having full justification for its existence, is fundamentally wrong."[10]

The powers, led by Great Britain, operated by a double standard that was not only wrong but hypocritical, Third Son argued. "Suppose we ask one of the powers what will they think and how will they feel, if her capital and other big and important cities also have concessions to foreigners. They simply will not bear such thoughts. What will Great Britain say if we have a Chinese settlement and extraterritorial rights in London?"[11] After living in England for two and a half years, Third Son knew very well how outrageous this question would seem to the English. He regarded a British settlement and extraterritorial rights in Shanghai as equally outrageous, and he concluded that the Chinese simply had to "clear all the foreigners out."

While retaining no more faith in the English than in the Japanese and wanting all the foreigners out of China, Third Son reaffirmed his faith in Father's judgment on this and all other important issues. "My dear father, I know your worry at this time of trouble is great," he wrote on February 22. Speaking for his two brothers as well as himself, he added: "We share with you in all your worries and anxieties and earnestly hope that you shall escape all the great injuries of war." Besides offering sympathy, he reassured Father, as usual, that he depended for advice on Father as on no one else. "I find that you are the only one man in this world to whom I can speak really frankly with an open heart." This singular relationship to Father made him singularly receptive to Father's instructions. "There is something in life which only a father can teach to his son, and which a son can only learn from his father."[12] In these pledges of devotion to Father, Third Son came very close to saying that he would uncritically accept whatever Father would wish to teach him. But within a couple of weeks, when he and his brothers received Father's letter instructing them to become British citizens, they found that they could not bring themselves to accept these instructions uncritically.

Opposing British Citizenship

After receiving Father's proposal on March 9, all three boys replied almost immediately. They pointed out to Father that they were in no position to act on it until they had learned more about the British procedures for naturalization, and they postponed their final decisions on whether to become British citizens until March 14, five days later, which was the earliest that Second Son could arrange for an appointment to investigate the possibilities at the British Foreign Office in London. But they did not wait until then to give their opinions of Father's proposal. On the day after it arrived, they discussed it among themselves, and then each of them wrote a separate reply.

All three opposed the idea of becoming British citizens because of their antipathy for the British. Third Son, writing to Father on March 11, made the point most bluntly. "I hate the Britishers almost as much as the Japanese. This is why we want to avoid the naturalization." He explained to Father how his and his brothers' nationalistic sentiments had grown since arriving in England and especially during the Shanghai Incident.

> You can see why we do not want to be Britishers if we can help it, especially after staying abroad for a few years our love for our mother country has increased. The Britishers are very pro-Japanese which they still regard as Britain's ally. Most of the daily papers in this country write articles which only give the Japanese point of view. Very often what they say make us feel very unhappy and almost angry.[13]

Fourth Son, writing on March 13, agreed with Third Son's assessment of coverage in the British press as very pro-Japanese, and he cited examples of this bias. "It is enough to break our hearts," he wrote to Father on March 13, "to read comments in English newspapers of such sort as 'Keep out of war!' 'Let Chinese and Japanese fight it out themselves.' 'Japanese should have their right to live!'" He went on to find fault with nearly all strata of English society, particularly the English elite, for favoring Japan at China's expense. "To us," he wrote to Father, speaking for his two brothers as well as himself, "the way in which the English people especially the upper class talk about their vast interests in the Far East and their close alliance with Japan on whom alone these interests are supposed to depend, seems so grossly ridiculous and meaningless."[14]

In his scathing critique of all segments of English society, Fourth Son noted only one exception. "The only bright spot in this gloomy picture is that we have the intellectual class who as a result of their careful and impartial investigation of the causes and effects of the present crisis in the Far East are vigorously attempting to give China justice and to right the wrongs she has been suffering under Japanese hands, to fight the cause for us."[15] But this small bright spot was by no means enough to redeem England in Fourth Son's eyes. It remained, in his estimation, a "cowardly and selfish country."

Second Son, like his brothers, blamed the British for sympathizing with the Japanese, and he lumped the two peoples together. "After all," he wrote to Father on March 13, "British people and the Japs are of the same stock. They in that dark year have threatened to destroy our lives and property. Such vivid impressions of their cruelty are still in my mind. Moreover, the British people are the only party which has been unwilling to help us since the beginning of the Present Crisis. You should read some of their criticism." This current British sympathy for Japan was not the only thing that concerned Second Son. He was worried above all about the long-term consequences for the boys. If we become British, he asked Father, "what will happen to us in the future? Once we are Britishers we are no longer Chinese. This is the chief problem which worries me at present. How can we give up our Chinese citizenship which we love and value so much!"[16]

Not until later did Second Son discover that he had been wrong to assume that adopting British citizenship would have required him and his brothers to give up their Chinese citizenship because British law did not have this requirement, leaving open the option of Anglo-Chinese dual citizenship, which other Chinese held at the time. But he and his brothers were right to conclude that the British—especially British officials and other elites—sympathized more with Japan than with China during the Shanghai Incident and its aftermath.[17]

The boys thus unanimously and passionately opposed Father's proposal, but they did not align themselves against him so definitively that there would be no chance for reconciliation between him and them. To give him the opportunity to withdraw the proposal gracefully, they gently suggested to him that he might have been misled into making it because of wartime conditions that temporarily confused him. As the boys knew from reading the newspapers, the fighting had been intense in Shanghai when Father had written the proposal on February 14, and it had ceased since March 1, nearly two weeks before they wrote their replies to him. So, Third Son hypothesized in writing to Father on March 11,

> it may be that on Feb. 14, when you were writing your letter, the state of affairs in Shanghai was at its very worst and you must have been really anxious about the safety of your factories. At that time, the development of events in and around Shanghai was a cause of great anxiety especially to those like you who have big business interests in that area; nobody knew what was going to happen the next day, very likely one or all of your factories might be destroyed by the Japanese bombs and burnt to ashes.

Since the Japanese bombs had stopped falling, surely Father's attitude had changed, Third Son surmised. "Now the anxiety is over," he imagined, "as fighting has ceased in that area, and the present development of disputes between China and Japan is not likely to lead to another outbreak of hostility in Shanghai. Perhaps now your anxiety may have passed too and you may not think that our naturalization is necessary. Do you think we can do without it now? I am sure the state of your mind must have changed since February 14."[18] Second Son and Fourth Son both made the same point and joined Third Son in urging Father to reconsider his proposal now that the fighting had stopped.

In case Father adamantly defended his proposal, the boys did not wholly exclude the possibility that they would comply with it. However strongly they expressed their opposition to it, they ultimately agreed to hear Father out. Third Son closed his letter by acknowledging: "All this is only my personal opinion with which you may not agree. I also want to make it clear that in saying we should avoid the naturalization if possible, I do not mean that we shall refuse such a suggestion in any case." He was willing to consider naturalization "if you think it is absolutely necessary to our interests."[19]

Similarly, Second Son did not remain completely unbending. He continued to oppose the proposal but left no doubt that he would carry it out if Father insisted. Naturalization "will be very complicated and is a delicate problem. I sincerely wish you to think it over again. My opinion in brief is that such step is unadvisable and will give us danger instead of safety and security. Father, I will do anything for you, don't hesitate to unfold your thought to me."[20]

Only one member of the family took a rigid position and set a defiant tone in reacting against Father's proposal. Eldest Son, who was then a student in the United States, urged his brothers to reject it flatly. After attending St. John's University in Shanghai, Eldest Son had transferred to Baldwin-Wallace College in Berea, Ohio, in the fall of 1931, and he was spending the academic year 1931–32 there when he heard from his brothers in England about Father's proposal for their naturalization. As he and all members of the family knew, he was not legally eligible for American citizenship because all Chinese immigrants were forbidden to become naturalized in the United States at the time. But he was familiar with naturalization procedures in the United States and England because he had studied law at St. John's University in Shanghai for two years, and he held strong opinions on the subject.

Eldest Son opposed naturalization for his brothers or any other Chinese on the grounds that they would never be regarded as genuine citizens because of racism in England and, for that matter, in America. "The white people have deep-seated racial ideas, and they will definitely not abandon such racial ideas just because you have been naturalized. Over here, the Americans treat yellow people in a similar way. Outwardly they act very politely toward the Chinese and the Japanese, but their racial ideas are deep-seated and come to the surface from time to time." Moreover, even if willing to tolerate racial prejudice, his brothers would not achieve Father's goals because they would come under restrictions as British citizens. Writing in Chinese and inserting English words (italicized here and in quotations below), Eldest Son informed Third

Son: "According to *English Civil Law,* once naturalized, both your life and your property will be subject to restrictions imposed by the British government."[21]

These restrictions, Eldest Son contended, would prevent his brothers from using their citizenship to protect the family's businesses in China because the boys would not be allowed to become British citizens in the first place if they tried to do so with this intention. "Law pays a great deal of attention to the question of *intention.* If you become a British citizen simply because you wish to protect your property (and that's your intention), you will still not gain protection from British law, even in an emergency."[22]

If the boys could mask their intentions and secure British citizenship at this time, they would still not be able to recover damages from Father's losses in the Shanghai Incident, Eldest Son maintained, because under the law they would not receive any compensation retroactively. "Legally speaking, the *time element* is extremely important. If Japan destroyed your property prior to your naturalization, since you were then still a citizen of China, the Japanese would treat you just as a Chinese citizen, and would not pay you any compensation." He went on to say: "If naturalization had occurred prior to the Shanghai War, you would have been able to ask for compensation because you were already a British citizen before your property was lost. Even if Japan had declined to pay, Japan would have been forced to pay under pressure from Britain, a nation not involved." Only if the boys had been naturalized before the event in question would Britain have been able to do so. For all of these reasons, Eldest Son urged his brothers not to become British citizens. "All of you should consider carefully the question of naturalization, because this has a lot to do with law and country."[23]

Eldest Son dismissed Father's proposal out of hand as nothing more than an overreaction to momentary wartime conditions. "When Father wrote to ask all of you to become naturalized, maybe he did so because the situation in Shanghai was in an extreme emergency, and for the sake of protecting his property. In case his property was destroyed, he could ask the Japanese government for compensation. Now that the fighting in Shanghai has quieted down, I think that he'll regret what he's said."[24] Although the boys in England had made similar points about Father's reactions to wartime conditions, only Eldest Son went so far as to say that Father would regret making the proposal.

In closing, Eldest Son instructed his brothers in England to forward his letter to Father. By the time they received it, they had discovered a fact neither Eldest Son nor they had known when they had sent their objections to Father. On March 15, 1932, after they had mailed their letters to him with their objections, Second Son paid a visit to the British Foreign Office in London and discussed their eligibility for British citizenship with officials there. He learned that British naturalization law included a five-year residency requirement; the boys would not be eligible to apply for two and a half years—not until mid-1934.

Second Son immediately sent a telegram conveying this information to Father. Knowing that the telegram had been sent to Father two weeks earlier, Third Son forwarded Eldest Son's letter to Father on March 31 with the following note appended to it: "The enclosed letter arrived this morning. Eldest Brother asked me to forward it to you after reading it, so I am enclosing it here. We agree with what Eldest Brother has said. We had not known that we had to have five years of residence before becoming British citizens. Father, after you've read Eldest Brother's letter, what is your reaction?"[25] It was surely difficult for Third Son and his brothers to predict how Father would answer this question. When Father received first the strong objections to his proposal from the boys in England and then the even stronger one from Eldest Son, what would his reaction be?[26]

Reconciling Patriarchy and Nationalism

After hearing about the five-year residency requirement for British citizenship, Father acknowledged that the boys in England were not yet eligible for it, but he did not drop his proposal. Instead, in response to his sons' telegram and letters, he struck a balance between two seemingly conflicting positions. On the one hand, he praised his sons for thinking independently, behaving like adults, and daring to criticize his proposal, and on the other, he retained his ultimate authority in the family firm and reaffirmed his commitment to his proposal.

In March and April, Father replied successively to each wave of his sons' messages: first their telegram, which reached him on March 17, and then their letters, which arrived in April. In response to their telegram, which said simply "British subject impossible unless 5 years residence," he sent a straightforward reply, showing no awareness of his sons' reservations about his proposal.[27] But when the boys' letters began arriving in April, he saw the pressing need to address the differences between their views and his.

In early April, Father wrote each of the three boys in England separate letters in which he praised them for taking strong stands and making forthright criticisms of his proposal. He said that he admired their "outspoken" and "hearty" letters, which showed their "manliness," and he applauded them for thinking independently and expressing themselves freely.[28] Moreover, Father conceded the boys' point that he had formulated his proposal in the heat of battle under extraordinary wartime conditions. Since then, he admitted, circumstances had changed. "As now the immediate danger seems to be over and as five years' residence is the invariable prerequisite, we may as well drop the subject entirely out of our mind[s]. I hope that there may never again arise another similar occasion for contemplating that expedient measure [of your becoming British citizens]."[29] Yet, despite all these concessions, he did not drop the subject of naturalization.

While admitting that wartime conditions during the Shanghai Incident were extraordinary, he foresaw the possibility of equally threatening conditions in the immediate future. "Up to the present moment," he wrote to Third Son on April 6, "the cloud in the political horizon has not yet dispersed. The storm might burst any minute. The scene would be somewhere else. But, if that undesirable case should ever be, the awful effect would be felt and faced all the same."[30] Under these persistent storm clouds of war, "I am not particularly sorry at having made you the proposal [for you and your brothers to become British citizens]," he told Second Son.

After thus planting the idea of his sons' future naturalization, he expected it to germinate during the waiting period that was imposed by the five-year British residency requirement. During these two long years, he told the boys that they should think through all their possible uses of British citizenship, because as British citizens, he emphasized again and again, they could protect the family business from a Japanese takeover of Chinese-owned property.

In June, after the Shanghai Incident had ended, he still did not bring discussion of naturalization to an unconditional end. Instead, he reaffirmed his belief that Japan would continue to pose a threat to China and that he and his sons should therefore keep his proposal for their

British citizenship in the future under consideration. With or without the Chinese government's help, he was determined to take whatever steps he could as a businessman to protect his property. With the threat of war once more looming, he told Second Son that June: "My anxieties over our vast enterprises are again aroused. I have not arrived where I now am overnight. And you know perfectly well that all these last long years have been years of arduous labor and great painstaking for me. Inferring from what Japan has been doing there is no telling of what she is to do next. We businessmen can only prepare and do things that businessmen do. We have to pursue a course that is expedient and rational."[31]

In proposing to pursue such a course, Father did not go so far as to say that he would ever coerce his sons into becoming British citizens, but he did insist that they should continue to discuss the subject. "We will thoroughly consider its pros and cons," he told them. "We will give ourselves the chance to argue out the various antagonistic points concerning the subject." All of them would be free to express their views on this subject, he said, as long as they did not question his patriotism. "It is not that we are not patriotic or less patriotic that we do this [contemplate naturalization]," he told them. "And I know, my dear boys, that you understand me perfectly with regard to this matter."[32] If the boys did understand Father perfectly, then he left them no room to debate whether his proposal was patriotic.

Did Father square the circle by reconciling the boys' independence with his patriarchal authority? In the short run, the question was moot, insofar as the boys could not become British citizens without first meeting the five-year residency requirement. In the long run, the boys implicitly settled the question in their favor by never becoming British citizens—not even after they had fulfilled the five-year residency requirement. But at the time, perhaps the most significant consequence for the family was not in their actions (or nonactions) but in the shift of tone in their exchanges of ideas. For the first time, the boys in England, now aged twenty, twenty-one, and twenty-two, seriously took issue with Father on policies concerning the family firm, Chinese politics, and international affairs. They aligned with each other and against him by questioning his insistence on expediency and by committing themselves to nationalism.

Yet they were not carried away by heady nationalism to the point where they rebelled against parental authority. Like other Chinese students in China and abroad at the time, they achieved some independence as a result of their attendance in boarding schools and college outside their home, and they participated in patriotic demonstrations more publicly than their father had ever done. But within their family, even though they questioned Father's basis for formulating his proposal for their British citizenship and they implored him to reconsider it, they did not flatly reject it or categorically refuse to carry it out.

As the boys negotiated with Father, he negotiated with them. Rather than sternly imposing his patriarchal authority and attempting to pound his sons into submission, he conceded some of their points and praised them for expressing their opinions independently like grown men. Only after presenting them with his own counterarguments did he seek to reassert his authority and convince them to continue to discuss the subject in the future, undoubtedly still holding out hope that they would eventually come around to his position.

Patriarchy and Succession

In conducting these negotiations with his sons, Father was preparing them to join him before long as managers of the family firm and eventual heirs to the family's business dynasty. In the midst of his debates with them about naturalization and the Shanghai Incident, he revealed to them that he was already setting dates for the process of succession from his leadership to theirs. "And here I may as well open my heart fully to you," he wrote to Eldest Son on April 29. "My happy dream or plan is that I wish to retire when I come to fifty-two. By that time I expect you and your brothers in England will be efficiently equipped and qualified to take over all the responsibilities from off my shoulders. I want all my boys to prove themselves worthy and deserving successors of mine."[33] On this schedule, Father projected that he would retire in 1940, only eight years away, and he was already letting his sons know that by then he expected them to be finished with their studies and ready to take over the family business. He delivered the same message to all three, and they replied that they were eager to rise to the challenge and fulfill their family obligations.[34]

Father's broaching of the subject of succession with his sons seemed to imply that he was already beginning to share his authority with them as early as 1932, while they were still in their early twenties. But how much latitude was he willing to grant them when they disagreed with him? During the Shanghai Incident, he assured the three in England that he welcomed their free expression of their opposition to his proposal. As he put it, their opinions gave him "so much joy and comfort." But in their debate over this topic, he became uncomfortable when Eldest Son, writing from the United States, began to make direct criticisms of him. "Your eldest brother has written me an exceedingly outspoken letter," Father confided to Third Son on April 6. "He knows some of my weak spots and he has pointed out the same to me."[35] In this "outspoken letter," Eldest Son had confronted Father more directly than his younger brothers had. But even his views seemed to meet with Father's approval as long as they were confined to the exchange of ideas and did not result in any decisions or actions that deviated from Father's overall plan for his sons' educations and their preparations for service in the family firm.

When Eldest Son and his brothers and sisters took positions or actions that were contrary to the plan Father and Mother had for them, how would the differences among family members be resolved? Before 1932, the members of the family were not forced to face this question, but between 1932 and 1937 they had to deal with it, because some of the children began to behave in ways contrary to their parents' plan.

II

BEHAVING CONTRARY TO THE PLAN
1932–1937

4

A Son Who Wanted to Drop Out of Harvard

FATHER and Mother freely admitted to all of their children that they had a unique emotional attachment to their firstborn son, and they had high hopes that he would be worthy of their special treatment.[1] In this favoritism, they were by no means unique among Chinese parents. In fact, following the principle of seniority, it was common for Chinese families to invest heavily in their firstborn sons, decisively favoring them over younger sons in the funding of education, provision of medical care, and acquisition of brides. Only in distributing their wealth at the time of their death did parents generally treat their sons equally, bequeathing to each of them the same amount (with none for daughters).[2]

But by the time Eldest Son became a teenager, Father began to have doubts about his potential as a leader in the family and the family firm. In 1929 Father showed his loss of confidence in Eldest Son when he decided which of his sons would be the first to study overseas. As noted, he sent Second Son (age nineteen), Third Son (age eighteen), and Fourth Son (age seventeen) to England, conspicuously holding back Eldest Son (age twenty). Not until the fall of 1931 did Father allow Eldest Son to go abroad, and even then it was to Baldwin-Wallace College, a small school in Berea, Ohio, which had none of the fame and prestige of the three younger brothers' illustrious institution, Cambridge University. Only after Eldest Son's departure for the United States did Father begin to revive his hopes that his firstborn might assume a role as a leader in the family after all.

Admission to Harvard

In September 1931, within three weeks after Eldest Son's departure from Shanghai, Father began to raise his estimation of his son. "You," he wrote to Eldest Son, "used to be shy and refrained yourself from mixing with society and the world at large. And now you are gallant enough to brave the Occident all by yourself. It is a very splendid thing, my dear boy, that you can blaze a trail alone, and I have every hope and reason to believe that that trail will lead you to glory and success."[3] Father's optimism was borne out for Eldest Son at Baldwin-Wallace. In June 1932, he was allowed to graduate with a BA in business administration at the end of just one year because he had maintained an average of B or higher.[4] Delighted with this outcome, Father sent wholehearted congratulations. "Since going to the States you have been demonstrating remarkable power in unfolding and asserting yourself," Father told him at the end of the 1931–32 academic year. "Being eldest," he wrote, "you are still the first among your brothers to have a degree."[5]

Eldest Son was pleased with Father's congratulations to him as a worthy eldest child, and he was thrilled to report that he had prospects for even greater academic achievements. Barely able to contain his excitement, he announced to his parents that he had been admitted to both Harvard Business School and the University of Pennsylvania's Wharton School of Finance and Commerce for the fall of 1932. "I would love to attend Harvard," he said without reservation, but he noted that Penn had one advantage: the prospect of completing his MBA there in one year, whereas Harvard required two.[6]

Eldest Son needn't have worried about Father's willingness to cover the expenses of his two years at Harvard Business School. As soon as Father heard that Eldest Son had been admitted, he envisioned the possibility that Eldest Son would graduate from America's leading university just as Second, Third, and Fourth Sons were expected to graduate from England's leading university. "I strongly advise that you go to Harvard," he replied unequivocally.

> This is the very best school in America. It corresponds with Cambridge and Oxford in England. You may cast aside all your thoughts in regard to the "higher expenses" at Harvard. I want all my children to get the very best and highest advantage ever possible in education. Of course, it is very much harder to study at Harvard than at the University of

Pennsylvania. But you have given positive demonstrations of your ability and you are just revealing and evolving yourself intellectually. And so, my dear son, just go ahead and complete your post graduate course at Harvard.[7]

Forceful as this advice was, Father qualified it to the extent that he allowed Eldest Son to make the decision. "Of course, I leave it entirely to your own liking and decision whether to choose Pennsylvania University or Harvard. But if you want me to decide the matter, then my advice is: Go to Harvard."[8]

At this moment, in the summer of 1932, when Eldest Son accepted admission at Harvard Business School, Father's plans for Eldest Son and Eldest Son's plans for himself seemed to coincide perfectly, opening the way for Father to introduce his plan for Eldest Son's future.

Father's Plan

"Now," Father wrote to Eldest Son on October 19, once he had confirmed that Eldest Son had settled into his first semester at Harvard Business School, "I have something from my heart to say to you." Relieved that his son's academic career was properly launched, he chose this moment to unveil his plan for Eldest Son's special place as his first-born son and future business associate. "I have oftentimes been thinking and mapping out plans for you boys," he confided to Eldest Son. "Perhaps it is relevant for me to unburden my heart to you in regard to the map I have roughly drawn for you. You are my eldest boy—very close to my heart—and I have great hopes in you as well as in all your other brothers. I realise that after your graduation from Harvard you will be of real and great help to me."[9]

Father's great hopes would be fulfilled, he revealed, if Eldest Son would specialize in one particular commodity: coal. "In view of our vast interests in coal, it is my heart's desire to make you a coal merchant as I am, and in that particular line I hope you will be more successful than I am."[10] Coal, as Father described it, had been the key to his own enduring success in business. In 1909, at age twenty-one, he had landed his first position in the business world with the Sino-British Kailuan Mining Administration. As a comprador there he had accumulated the capital he had used to open industrial enterprises, including his first match factory, Hongsheng Match Mill (in 1920), a cement plant (in

1923), and a woolen mill and a briquette factory (in 1926). Throughout the 1910s and 1920s, Liu's profits from handling Kailuan's coal had provided by far his largest source of income. In 1917 and 1918 he had earned 1.3 million yuan in this way. As of 1926, even after he had opened several industrial enterprises, his profits from coal sales, at 1.5 million yuan, had dwarfed the profits from the most profitable of his other enterprises, his cement plant (660,000 yuan) and his match mill (140,000 yuan).[11]

In explaining his plans to Eldest Son, Father emphasized the significance of coal for surviving the Great Depression in the immediate present. "I am sure you must have more or less noted," he wrote to Eldest Son in Cambridge, Massachusetts, in October 1932, that the "business depression is hitting the United States." In China, conditions were "far worse," and yet, while many Chinese businesses were suffering, "we have ample reasons to congratulate ourselves. We are decidedly among the few fortunate ones here."[12] In an era of economic depression, Father was surviving and even flourishing, he explained to Eldest Son, partly because he had good luck but mainly because he handled coal. His luck was not "a matter of mere chance," he observed. The key to success "is my coal business." While his other businesses waxed and waned, his coal business never wavered. He considered it his "solid firm rock," which would serve as the basis for the future success of Eldest Son as well as himself. On coal, he told his son, "we now stand and will yet rise."[13]

After introducing this plan to Eldest Son on October 19, Father spelled it out in subsequent letters. "In my previous letter," he wrote on November 3, "I told you roughly what my plan is with regard to your future. Perhaps you will not think it redundant if I go over the map here again briefly." The map, as Father specified the details of the plan, was to guide Eldest Son well beyond the confines of Harvard Business School and into coal mines and factories throughout the United States. As Father instructed him: "I want you to observe and study very minutely and carefully" the coal industry in all of the American cities where it was concentrated. "I want you to make great use of your vacations by visiting especially Duluth, Milwaukee, and Pittsburgh."[14] Moreover, Father expected Eldest Son to track coal through each of its successive stages: extraction, transportation, processing, marketing, and sales. In this way, he assured Eldest Son, "you actually see and learn the various steps that take this particular mineral product from the mine to the consumer."

Father told Eldest Son to conduct his investigation of coal mining in the United States in such a way as not merely to understand its place in America's present but also to discern its relevance to China's future. "I can assure you here that coal is to be a large business in our country. Hence it is altogether necessary that you ought to familiarise yourself there with coal business." As Father envisioned the future, Eldest Son would bring back from the United States both academic training from Harvard and a practical understanding of the American coal industry— a combination that was bound to succeed for him in China. "You should learn all you can about [the] coal industry [so that] you can and will make great success out of the business when you come home after finishing your advanced courses in Harvard University. This is my great expectation and hope in you."[15]

Having laid out his two-year plan for 1932–1934, Father did not stop there. He also had in mind two more years of training for Eldest Son in China from mid-1934 to mid-1936. After graduating from Harvard and returning home, Eldest Son would spend half a year studying coal mining on site in north China. Then he was to spend another six months there concentrating on the region's transportation. Only then, after a full year there, would Eldest Son return to Shanghai and complete another yearlong apprenticeship in Father's headquarters. At the end of these four years—two in the United States and two in China—Father explained to Eldest Son, "you are then fully informed and qualified to come into my office to take in all that I do. You see I want you to know everything pertaining to our trade."[16]

Reflecting on the overall requirements of this four-year plan, Father admitted that it was demanding. But he believed that Eldest Son and all his sons would benefit from enduring hardships as apprentices working from the bottom up. "If I put you into a big position immediately after your return from the States," he told Eldest Son, "then all people may say that you are in an easy job. Other fathers may do that sort of thing with their sons. But you know that I am not that sort of father, and I know you are not that sort of son."[17] Father was the sort of father who challenged his sons rather than spoiling them, and he expected Eldest Son to be the sort of son who rose to challenges both at Harvard and in China.

As Eldest Son's first semester drew to a close at Harvard Business School, Father monitored his academic work but gave higher priority to his mastery of the coal industry, repeatedly reminding him that he should not lose sight of the practical experience to be gained by following Father's plan. On November 30, Father agreed that Eldest Son would be well advised to take courses at Harvard on "Accounting, Finance, Industrial Management, Marketing or Salesmanship, and Transportation." But he distinguished sharply between the knowledge his son would acquire in these courses and the more valuable applied knowledge he would gain under Father's plan for him. "You see, my dear boy," Father wrote, "knowledge is one thing, and the ability to apply or use that knowledge in the right way is quite another thing. This is why I mapped out a rough plan for you in one of my previous letters. I consider that plan quite an essential and important one. It is hard experience that will teach one the art and science of using what knowledge he has." Father left no doubt about whether academic knowledge or applied knowledge was the right way to assure success. "Tactful observation and right discernment will be of real importance and use," he assured Eldest Son. "I don't want your knowledge to smell bookish."[18]

All of this advice from Father, including his elaborate four-year plan, was delivered forcefully and enthusiastically but not without concern for Eldest Son's reactions to it. The very first time Father introduced his plan, on October 19, he ended his letter by inviting Eldest Son to comment on it and suggest revisions. "The foregoing," Father wrote, "is then my rough map for you. What do you think of that? You are at perfect liberty to give me your own opinion regarding the matter. One man's thought is far from complete, and we can always put our heads together for modification and improvement. So I expect that you will write me freely touching the subject whenever you can afford the leisure time."[19] In subsequent elaborations of his plan, Father repeatedly asked what Eldest Son thought of it.

In reply, Eldest Son expressed his agreement with Father's emphasis on the importance of practical experience and the superiority of applied over academic knowledge. Even though Father had characterized an apprenticeship in China as particularly arduous, Eldest Son embraced the proposal without qualification. "You mentioned in your letter that I'll need to acquire practical experience through an apprenticeship after I return to China," he wrote to Father on November 14. "I fully agree."[20]

Eldest Son pointed out that Father's proposed apprenticeships were similar to the internships and other kinds of employment held by his fellow American students at Harvard. "Many students here hold jobs while studying," he noted, and "I deeply respect them for their hard-working spirit." He also cited examples of American captains of industry who had worked their way to the top. "Didn't many of the American entrepreneurs and scientists," he rhetorically asked Father, "work *from the bottom up* [italicized words in English]?" If these Americans could make the climb from the bottom to the top, then, Eldest Son contended, "any one of us brothers can do the same with no problem."[21] Similarly, Eldest Son heartily approved of Father's proposal that he should spend his vacations from Harvard investigating the American coal industry. On November 28, he urged Father to begin making the arrangements. Writing to Father and Mother, he noted: "Father has suggested that I use my vacation time to visit the various mines, and that is precisely what I have in mind. I think it'd be best if I could obtain some sort of letter of introduction from your acquaintances, so that I can be an intern for a while in one of the mines."[22]

Father was delighted with Eldest Son's eagerness to follow his plan, and he began using his American contacts to arrange for Eldest Son's trips to the coal mines the following summer. Working through Julean Arnold, the commercial attaché at the American consulate in Shanghai, he recruited Hugh Butler, director of the Boston office of the U.S. Bureau of Foreign and Domestic Commerce, to advise Eldest Son on his itinerary and make arrangements for his trips to the coal mines.[23]

On the eve of Eldest Son's second semester at Harvard, Father was fully satisfied that Eldest Son had accepted his plan. "I am very happy," he wrote to Eldest Son on January 20, 1933, "that you are in agreement with the plan I mapped out for you in regard to your future career. So, the farther one gets down to the bottom of a trade the higher he will climb in the ascent."[24] As he expressed his complete satisfaction with Eldest Son's acceptance of his plan, Father had no inkling that within the next two weeks his plan would begin to unravel. Even less could he anticipate that during the spring semester he and Eldest Son would engage in an intense and angry war of words over what plan should be followed.

Eldest Son's Revision of Father's Plan

On January 29, only a few days after finishing his fall semester final examinations at Harvard Business School, Eldest Son dropped a bombshell. Knowing full well that Harvard had a two-year residency requirement for the MBA, he announced to Father that he wanted to return to Shanghai at the end of his first year and postpone his second year for two or three years. He recognized that this proposal would take Father by surprise, but he believed, at least initially, that Father would not question it because it was based on the rationale that academic learning was less important than practical experience.

In Eldest Son's plan for himself, he assumed that he would do enough academic work in his first year at Harvard Business School to prepare himself for his apprenticeship in China. "By this summer," he suggested to Father in January 1933, "I should be able to complete my first year's course work here. I am confident that by then I will have accumulated enough basic knowledge about the business world."[25] In distinguishing academic knowledge at Harvard from practical experience in the business world, Eldest Son seized on and utilized the key distinction in Father's plan. But he took Father's argument a step farther by suggesting that he needed practical experience in China before he could make the most of his academic studies at Harvard.

In support of his proposal, Eldest Son cited examples of his classmates who had not gone to Harvard Business School until they had reached the midpoint in their business careers. "Among my classmates here," he wrote,

> there are a number of them who are over forty years of age. When I first arrived, I thought to myself, "They have already reached such an age, why have they still come here?" But now, I've learned to respect their strategy. Because they have worked for many years either in business corporations or banks before coming here, they are much better in classroom discussion than those of us who are recent college graduates. They know very well which courses will be especially useful to them as well as the kinds of knowledge which will be relevant to their own enterprises. If I can work in China for a few years, I will at least develop for myself this power of selection.[26]

As a Chinese, Eldest Son claimed, he needed experience on the job before finishing at Harvard even more than his American classmates did.

American students could rest assured that every course at Harvard Business School had some relevance to the American business world, but Eldest Son felt that he could not assume that every Harvard course had relevance to China.

If Eldest Son continued at Harvard without experience in China, he doubted that he would learn much that he could apply in China. "I'll eventually be working in my own country anyway, and I certainly will get only a shallow understanding of China if I rely entirely on what I learn from the professors and from the books I read. There are major differences between the business world in America and in China, and we cannot simply transplant to China all knowledge from America." He needed to work in China, Eldest Son maintained, to become aware of these major differences between the American and Chinese business worlds, because only then would he be able to make good decisions about what to study at Harvard. "Once I find out the real situations in China, I won't have to keep guessing what to learn. I can then concentrate on the areas that are especially relevant to China's situation and further develop my own interest in these areas."[27]

Eldest Son yearned to come home for the sake of Father and the family business, as well as his own education. His assistance was urgently needed, he noted, because Father had accepted an official appointment as head of a government-owned shipping company on top of all his responsibilities in the family business. "I realize," Eldest Son wrote to Father, "that you must have been extra busy since assuming responsibilities at the China Merchants Steam Navigation Company. Sometimes I wish that I now had the ability to lend you a hand. At other times, I fear that I will never be able to do so, and that wanting to help you may turn out to be nothing more than my own wishful thinking."[28]

If the time was right for Eldest Son to help Father, Eldest Son pointed out, then it was also right to give Eldest Son a chance to prepare the way for his younger brothers. By going home and working in the family business during 1933–1936, he could assist Father until the return of the three sons in England. "After I work for a few years in China," he reminded Father, his three brothers "should be coming home from England to help you, and I can leave for a year at that time."[29] Although he did not say so explicitly, it is very likely that he also wanted to come home sooner than his three younger brothers so that he would be able to solidify his position at the top of the hierarchy of sons before the others joined the family firm.

In making all these arguments, Eldest Son made no mention of wanting to leave Harvard for academic reasons, and in closing he remarked: "The course work here is not too difficult. It just takes lots of time. It is not unusual to spend about ten hours a day to complete all the assignments."[30]

On January 29, when Eldest Son made this proposal, he expressed confidence that Father would find it acceptable. He assured Father that he would follow Father's plan for the summer of 1933 by paying visits to coal mines and factories throughout the United States, and he offered to cover still more ground by then returning to China via Europe and surveying the coal mines and factories of England, France, and Germany. In this part and throughout his proposal, he reaffirmed Father's idea that practical experience and applied knowledge should take precedence over academic pursuits and pure knowledge, and he presented the postponement of his second year at Harvard as though it was nothing more than a tentative suggestion. "What I've said above are only my own thoughts," he remarked. "If you have better suggestions, I will be more than willing to follow them."[31]

Father's Doubts

In reply, Father expressed mixed feelings. He agreed to go along with Eldest Son's proposal for leaving Harvard and returning to Shanghai in the summer of 1933. "My heart comes out to you," he told Eldest Son on February 27, "fully touching the points that you have brought forth in your last letter."[32] But Father questioned Eldest Son's ability to assess the past and present and envision the future. On the future, Father noted, "if, after working for two or three years in your own country, there are some changes in your circumstances, and you no longer wish to go study abroad, you will then fail to realize your idealism of today."[33]

Regarding Eldest Son's evaluation of his current circumstances at Harvard, Father doubted that Eldest Son fully appreciated where he stood in relation to his classmates at Harvard Business School. He did not doubt that Eldest Son had classmates who were older and more experienced in business than he was. What struck Father was Eldest Son's reference to working ten hours every day on his studies. Although

Eldest Son mentioned this fact casually and in passing, Father drew far-reaching inferences from it. "You told me in your last letter," Father reminded Eldest Son, "that the Harvard Graduate School of Business Administration is more or less for elderly people who have already acquired experience and practical training in the commercial world. In this case it will not be of much advantage as well as of real benefit for you to continue and push through your second year in that department."[34]

Father's characterization of Harvard's older students and their advantages roughly summarized Eldest Son's viewpoint, but it provided the reasoning for going a step farther than Eldest Son had gone. If the older students set the standard, then Eldest Son was not up to their standard, Father inferred. "The subjects you are taking may not be difficult for you," Father acknowledged, but "some ten hours for preparation on the outside each day is evident proof that you are not quite at par with the standard." Eldest Son fell short of the Harvard standard, Father maintained, because of his inefficiency. Not blaming Eldest Son for this deficiency, Father noted that efficiency was an acquired trait rather than an innate one. An older student's greater efficiency, he said, "does not mean that he is more able or clever than you. But it does mean that he is wiser than you. Ability or cleverness may be something inborn. But wisdom is certainly something that has a close relation with persistent acquirement. It is wisdom that begets efficiency." For Eldest Son to become more efficient and wiser, all he had to do was gain experience. "We all know," Father reminded Eldest Son, "the adage that 'practice makes perfect.' This is almost synonymous with experience. It is constant contact or practice and experience which give one precision and speed at the same instant."[35]

With this comment about the need for experience, Father offered his rationale for Eldest Son interrupting his education at Harvard. Concern about comparative lack of efficiency and need for wisdom had certainly not appeared in Eldest Son's proposal, but Father ended by granting Eldest Son's request to come home in the summer of 1933.[36]

At the same time, Father expressed his disappointment that Eldest Son would deviate from Father's own plan. It was true, as Eldest Son had pointed out, that Father was busy with his additional duties as the newly appointed official head of the China Merchants Steam Navigation Company, and Father had acknowledged to Eldest Son "you will be of great help to us." But it was not the right time for Eldest Son's apprenticeship in the coalfields of north China, because of political chaos and military conflicts occurring there. "I think we will have to modify our map for the future," Father regretfully remarked, and he offered his son a high-level administrative position in the family firm at Shanghai.[37] He contrasted this appointment with one Eldest Son had held in the family's cement plant at Shanghai as a teenager before he had left for the United States. On that occasion, Father said, he had placed Eldest Son in a low-level position, but now he knew better. "That was more or less my mistake of not putting you in a responsible position. So I think we will have to be a little wiser this time, don't you?"

Father's question implied that he had come to see clearly what Eldest Son wanted and fully expected Eldest Son to respond positively to his job offer and his acceptance of Eldest Son's proposal for returning home. Father's closing words reinforced the impression that he anticipated an amicable reply. "My dear boy," he wrote, "I do not want you to study too hard. Put your health before everything else. Just tell me your every wish, for, besides being father I am always your best friend."[38]

Eldest Son's Anger

Perhaps as Father put this letter in the mail, he did think of himself as Eldest Son's best friend, but after Eldest Son read it, his mood was anything but friendly. In March, he wrote a stream of angry letters pouring out his frustration with Father's reaction to his proposal for postponing the completion of his MBA at Harvard. Even though Father had granted his request, Eldest Son was deeply disturbed by Father's interpretation of his motives for making the proposal. He insisted that he wanted to come home simply because he wanted to help Father and gain experience on the job, and he resented Father's insinuations that he had other hidden motives. "Regarding this point, I recall that I explained it quite clearly in my last letter," he wrote to Father on March 17. He had gone to great lengths to do so because he was afraid that Father might misunderstand. "At that time, I had already anticipated that if I did not explain to you fully, you might think that my desire to come home was motivated by something else. In your response, just as I had expected, even though you agree that my reasons are quite good, you still ask me to take into consideration several questions that you have raised."[39] Now he confronted each of these questions that Father had raised and flatly rejected the answers he thought Father had implied.

Eldest Son dismissed out of hand Father's suggestion that if he came home in the summer of 1933, then he might be prevented from returning to Harvard by unforeseen circumstances. "I don't quite understand the meaning of the word 'circumstances,'" he fired back, quoting the word from Father's letter. "If what you meant was that I would not be able to leave because of my strong commitment to the enterprises, didn't I already discuss this with you in my last letter? I said, 'Once my second, third, and fourth brothers come home to help you, I can return here to complete the last year of course work.'"[40]

Eldest Son suspected that Father had used the word "circumstances" to refer to another issue that, in Eldest Son's view, was completely extraneous. "If by 'circumstances' you refer to the problem of my 'falling in love' or 'having a family,' then I have even more confidence in dealing with such an issue. I am now someone who has experience in love, and will never be as crazy about it as before. Regarding having a family of my own, my principle is this: 'So long as I don't have a bowl of rice for myself, I won't be able to support a wife.'"[41] Eldest Son thus saw no validity in any speculation that he would be prevented from returning to Harvard by an attachment to a woman or any other such circumstances.

If bothered by Father's speculation about future circumstances, Eldest Son was more troubled by Father's suggestion that his real reason for wanting to come home was that he was inferior to his classmates at Harvard. "Please don't be suspicious of this and that," he told Father. He was not at all proposing to come home "because of my health or my inability to continue with my studies here."[42] Eldest Son's fears of Father's suspicions deepened as he received and read more letters. "From your letters," he replied to Father on March 30, "I sense that you suspect that I want to come home to work because I have encountered difficulties at *Harvard Business School*. This makes me think that you have absolutely no *confidence* in me" (words in English italicized). Eldest Son could not understand Father's loss of confidence in his ability despite his assurances to Father that his work was not difficult. "In my last few letters," he wrote, "didn't I tell you repeatedly that the school work keeps me busy but is not difficult. Why is it that right up to now you still have not the least bit of trust in me. If there is no trust between father and son, there will be misunderstandings. I hope that you will get rid of this idea right away."[43]

Fearing that Father had ceased to trust him, Eldest Son launched into a broad defense of his overall academic record in the United States and even his own moral character. "To tell the truth," he pointed out to Father, "if I had wanted to be a good-for-nothing son from a rich family, I wouldn't have bothered to come all the way across the ocean to the United States to study. Every single bit of my life in Shanghai was more comfortable than it is here. If I had wanted to be 'lazy and averse to work,' I would not have selected Harvard and Pennsylvania as places to study."[44]

On the basis of this record, Eldest Son claimed that he had earned his independence from Father. "At my age," this twenty-four-year-old proclaimed, "it's my own business whether I am doing my best in my studies here. I am spending your money, but I am the one doing the studying. I can't be dependent on you forever as though you were Mt. Tai. In the future, I'll have to make my own living and then I'll be somebody."[45]

If he was independent of Father as a student, he would be equally independent as a businessman. Posing perhaps his ultimate threat to the family firm, he claimed that he would take a job outside it. "After my return," he warned Father, "I don't necessarily have to work for you. If you want to hire me, I'll become a member of the staff in your company, but I don't expect you to treat me differently. If I have ability, you can hire me. If you don't feel like it, you can always find someone better. A father has the responsibility to raise his children but you are not responsible for becoming a Mt. Tai that I can lean on forever."[46] Taking this aggressive stance, Eldest Son seemed to be on the verge of declaring independence from his immovable father—Mt. Tai—once and for all.

Father's Retreat

Eldest Son's torrent of intemperate letters upset and alarmed Father. After reading the first one dated February 27, which had taken nearly a month to reach him, he immediately replied on March 23, and he did not disguise the fact that he had been hurt by it. "There is no need for me to tell how disheartened I was to read that letter of yours," he wrote, and he could only explain Eldest Son's use of emotionally piercing words by imagining that "you were somewhat hot and rash when you hastily wrote your last letter to me." Though Father found the letters shocking, after reflecting on them, he took a share of blame for triggering Eldest Son's outbursts. "I was afraid," Father wrote back to Eldest Son, "that my letters had disheartened you more. Otherwise I could scarcely account for the justification of your having to write that letter in that dejected and complaining mood."[47]

At the same time, Father did not take all the blame. While reconsidering what he himself had written, he also found fault with some of Eldest Son's erroneous readings. "I am afraid," he told Eldest Son, "that those letters of mine had not been intelligibly written so as to have given you an unpleasant impression. It might be that you were much spent by labor or exercise and that when you read those letters you were not in the swing physically, and, consequently, you had only noted the letter and not discerned the spirit of those letters in question."[48]

Father was so troubled by Eldest Son's insensitivity to the spirit of his letters that he urged his son to reread them. "And, if you still have those letters of mine with you and care to read them over again you will perceive that the spirit of my writing is quite out of harmony with the impression you seemed to have got." To avoid misunderstanding, Father emphasized that both he and Eldest Son needed to be more thoughtful. "I don't want to make you feel hot or bad in any way and I trust you do not at all mean to make me sad if you just stop a moment to think before you write," he wrote at the end of his reply to the first of Eldest Son's angry letters.[49] While Father hoped that he and his son might reduce the tensions between them by writing to each other more clearly and reading each other's letters more carefully, he also became convinced that they would not reconcile unless he yielded to Eldest Son and granted his requests.

On the specific contentious points Eldest Son had raised, Father gave in. He left the decision about when Eldest Son would return to Shanghai entirely up to him. He replied to Eldest Son's preference for a high-level executive position over a low-level apprenticeship in Shanghai by assuring him that he would be appointed at a high level, not a low one. He withdrew all questions that had, in Eldest Son's estimation, implied that he thought Eldest Son was academically inferior to his classmates at Harvard Business School.[50]

More broadly, Father criticized himself for his loose usage of language and inadequate consideration of future possibilities. For example, he accepted Eldest Son's criticism of his use of the word "circumstances" in his speculation about what might keep him from returning to Harvard after spending a few years in Shanghai. Conceding that "circumstances" was a vague term, Father now claimed that even if it was interpreted as a euphemism for "marriage," being married would not necessarily prevent Eldest Son from going back to Harvard. "Various shades of meaning could be given to this word 'circumstance,'" Father observed. "If marriage was to be dragged in, as you made mention of in your letter, that might turn out to be one of the impossibilities. But that impossibility is not impossible to be made possible. If your wife didn't want you to go abroad again, you might possibly persuade her to go along with you."[51] According to this somewhat tortured logic, anything was possible.

After backing down on all of these points, or at least modifying his position to accommodate Eldest Son on all of them, Father also applauded him for aspiring to achieve the personal goal of independence. "What you said in your letter about your desire to become independent is perfectly legitimate. Any educated youth should have this kind of aspiration." Despite Eldest Son's misreading of Father's letters and unwarranted criticisms of Father's interpretations, Father still admired Eldest Son for seeking independence. "Even though your tone is a little out of line because it results from misunderstandings that I have outlined here, I am still not angry because you have reached the right conclusions." Independence was legitimate, Father agreed, as long as Eldest Son banished from his mind all suspicions that he had about Father. "From now on," he told Eldest Son, "you should never be suspicious of me."[52]

On June 16, at the end of Eldest Son's academic year, Father looked back on their six months of verbal warfare and called a truce. "I am awfully sorry that there had been some rough deviations in the recent course of our correspondence," he wrote to Eldest Son, using a geographical metaphor that seems apt, in light of the miles that physically separated the two men.

> The terribly long distance between us might have generously contributed to that undesirable cause. Nevertheless, no misunderstanding, however complicated or serious, ought to be too difficult or beyond possibility to get untwisted and removed. A deviation in most cases is not

an inevitable detour. As we had, by some mischance, just struck into it, let us not take a single step farther. Rather, let us make a clean round-about face and beat a hasty retreat out of it. It is of paramount importance and necessity that we get back into the straight and natural course.

Once they stopped fighting, they could come to an understanding. Shifting from a travel metaphor to a horticultural one, Father observed: "Any misunderstanding, as we know it, is like a weed. It may seem, at its first appearance, exceedingly insignificant and uneventful indeed. If we ever let it to itself it will almost in no time grow and multiply to choke a whole garden of flowers. It is of vital concern that we uproot the weedling and do the uprooting right away."[53] Yet, however eager Father might have been to root out the misunderstanding, Eldest Son was still cultivating his part of the Liu family garden differently than Father supposed.

Eldest Son's Transfer

For all of Father's concessions and modifications of his original plan, he still held out hope that Eldest Son would carry out two parts of it: the inspection of American coal mines in the summer of 1933 and the completion of a Harvard MBA some day—if not in 1933–34, then two or three years later. On both counts, his hopes went unfulfilled.

In the summer of 1933, Eldest Son decided to visit his three brothers in England rather than conduct inspections of coal mines in the United States. After taking his final examinations in early June, he sailed off to England, and on June 21, he explained to Father why he had made this decision.

> I had originally planned to go visit factories and mines right after finishing my exams, but as I was really tired at the time, and all of my friends suggested that I come here [to England] to rest, I decided to come here for several weeks. Besides, it would have been a little lonely for me to visit the mines all by myself. I've heard that Fifth Brother is planning to come to study in America, and if so, he and I can go visit places together. He can learn about this country, and I can have him keep me company.[54]

Tired and lonely, he preferred, as he noted, to play tennis with his younger brothers in England rather than slog through mines in the United States.

Later in the summer, after he had returned to the United States, he received a letter in which Father exhorted him to complete his inspections of coal mines and submit his reports. Father had written the letter July 24:

> By the time when you receive this letter, you must be on your way to inspect factories and coal mines. As you can learn much more from inspection trips than from text books, I, therefore, hope that in your inspection of factories and coal mines, you would not merely, to quote an old Chinese saying, "look at the flowers on a galloping horse," but should study carefully their respective lay-outs, organizations and managements, so that the time and money thus spent will not be in vain. I am anxiously awaiting your findings and observations, which you have promised to report to me from time to time.[55]

If Father was anxiously waiting to receive Eldest Son's reports in the summer of 1933, he had no relief from this anxiety. Despite repeated promises, Eldest Son did not visit any mines. "This past summer," he wrote to Father on October 16; "I could not visit the coal mines as I had planned because I went to England and to Chicago for the World's Fair." The best he could offer was another promise: "Before coming home next year, I must spend a couple of months in the coal mines and have a good look at them. There was simply not enough time this past summer."[56]

Even more disappointing, Eldest Son abruptly terminated Father's plan for him to receive a Harvard MBA. As late as July 11, he had temporarily reversed his earlier decision to leave Harvard and had promised Father that he would finish this degree in 1933–34. "I will study in Harvard another year," he wrote. "I will not return home until I have completed my studies there."[57] But within a few weeks he had changed his mind again.

On August 6, Eldest Son unceremoniously announced that he would not continue any longer at Harvard Business School. After his wide-ranging arguments with Father over a period of several months, he now flatly stated that he would leave Harvard simply because he did not have enough leisure time there. "I had originally planned to continue my studies at [Harvard] Business School," he wrote to Father on August 6. "But the work there kept me so busy that I didn't even have time for my exercises." He admitted that he was not leaving Harvard because it had disappointed him academically. "I have been very satisfied with all my courses at Harvard Business School, but I don't want to sacrifice my health or recreation." He noted that on his trip to England earlier in the summer he had discovered that Second, Third, and Fourth Sons "have plenty of time in the afternoon at Cambridge to do sports." By contrast, "at Harvard, I have only half a day of free time each Sunday."[58]

That month, Eldest Son considered whether to transfer to the Department of Economics in Harvard Graduate School or the Wharton School of Business at the University of Pennsylvania. On August 25, he announced his choice to Father and revealed additional reasons for leaving Harvard Business School. He was attracted to the Wharton School by its specialized courses on insurance, income taxation, and transportation—all subjects Father had urged him to study, as Eldest Son reminded him. As for Harvard Business School, he was loath to return there because he would be required to repeat a statistics course he had failed during the previous semester.

In stating his own preferences, Eldest Son allowed for the possibility of returning to Harvard Business School if Father absolutely insisted on it. "Of course," he wrote, "if you believe that there is no other way but for me to obtain a degree from Harvard Business School, then I will definitely do it, as long as you allow me to stay in America for another two years." This, he made clear, was not what he wanted to do. "After thinking things through carefully, I have decided to transfer to Wharton School."[59]

A few weeks later, although he had apparently not received Father's approval for his transfer to Wharton, he confirmed his decision: "I will definitely attend Wharton School this year," he wrote to Father on September 16. In support of this decision he noted that one of China's leading bankers, Chen Guangfu (K. P. Chen), was a graduate of the Wharton School. After receiving his Wharton degree in 1910, Chen had returned to China, opened the Shanghai Commercial and Savings Bank in 1915, and built it up into one of the biggest Western-style banks in China.[60]

"After I complete my course work at Wharton School next year," Eldest Son told Father, confidently assuming that he would receive his degree just nine months later in the spring of 1934, "I would like to be an intern in Mr. Chen's bank." He also had plans for doing an internship at an American-owned bank—New York's Chase National or the Guarantee Trust Company—and he asked Father to arrange these internships through Chen, who was Father's good friend.[61] No longer considering a return to Harvard Business School, Eldest Son was already laying plans for a banking career that he would pursue after graduating from Wharton.

Faced with this fait accompli, Father accepted it. "In regard to your transfer to the Wharton School of Philadelphia," he wrote on September 22, after Eldest Son had already matriculated there, "I wish to leave that matter entirely to your discretion." Only four months earlier, on May 16, after conceding numerous other points to Eldest Son, Father had clung to one last hope. "My heart's desire," he had written to his son, "is that you complete your Harvard education whether there be a break or no break."[62] But now he gave up on this possibility and took the position that the Wharton School was equally good. "I am fully aware," he told Eldest Son, "that the courses offered by the Wharton School are just as strong as those offered by Harvard Business School. Personally I am not insistent upon your getting a degree from Harvard Business School."[63]

Father did not reverse his earlier claim that a Harvard degree carried more prestige than one from the University of Pennsylvania, but he assured Eldest Son that he gave less priority to prestige than to academic content. "To me," Father declared, "the academic honor is a thing of less importance in comparing with the real knowledge you can obtain from your education. It is my fervent wish that you should get the full benefit of your education and become a useful man to your country after your return to China."[64] No longer expecting Eldest Son to receive a Harvard degree, Father now urged him to concentrate on wrapping up his MBA at the University of Pennsylvania and returning home in the spring of 1934.

As it turned out, Eldest Son did not achieve even this scaled-down goal. At the beginning of spring semester, he began to realize that he would not finish his thesis in time for graduation from the Wharton School, so he proposed to go home and complete it there. "If only I can find all of the materials that I need," he wrote to Father and Mother on February 28, "perhaps I can complete the writing in Shanghai. I have given much thought to this plan."[65] In a series of replies, Father repeatedly rejected this proposal. "In regard to your returning," he told Eldest Son, "it is my belief that you should by all means finish your thesis before you come back home. It does not strike me as a wise step that you should write your thesis at home, as I said in my last letter to you. My only hope is that you can speed up your work and return to China right after you have handed in your thesis."[66]

Despite Father's pleading and contrary to his explicit instructions, Eldest Son did not do so. Not until the spring of 1935, after another semester had passed, did he return to Shanghai. On the way home in 1935, he paid his long-awaited visit to American coal fields. On a one-day stop in West Virginia, he observed operations at the ground level but did not enter the mines. "It was too bad I caught cold again," he wrote to Father on January 24. "So the superintendent of the mine advised me better not to get into the mine on account of the difference in temperature." On another one-day visit, this time to three mines in Pennsylvania near Pittsburgh, he did venture into the pits and saw the coal being extracted. "It was quite an experience," he proudly reported to Father. "When I got out from the mine, I was as dark & black as a negro."[67]

Belatedly, briefly, and on a reduced scale, Eldest Son at least made this token effort to follow Father's original plan for his visits to coal mines in the days before he left the United States. On January 25, 1935, he departed from New York on the S.S. *Europe* and traveled home via Europe and the Suez Canal.[68] In April, he arrived in Shanghai without an MBA. The Wharton School finally conferred this degree on him in February 1936, four and a half years after he first entered business school at Harvard.[69]

Father and His Eldest Sons

Father found Eldest Son's record in the United States disappointing by comparison with the records of Second, Third, and Fourth Sons in England. Although never openly making this comparison to Eldest Son, he strongly implied it in a letter to Eldest Son about his three brothers' successful completion of their degrees at Cambridge University and their graduation on June 19, 1934.[70]

At the time, Eldest Son was sensitive about having dropped out of Harvard a year earlier and failed to finish his MBA at the Wharton School on schedule a month earlier. Showing no concern for this sensitivity, Father announced with great fanfare in a letter of July 6: "I am pleased to inform you that your three brothers in England have taken their degrees with honour[s]. Mother and I have taken great pride in their scholastic achievement, and have deeply appreciated the honour they will bring back to Lieu's [Liu's] family. From this notable example, your younger brothers will inevitably draw an inspiration which will help them in carrying on their studies with success."[71]

In lavishing this high praise on Second, Third, and Fourth Sons, Father held them up as models setting a standard that Eldest Son had failed to reach. Second, Third, and Fourth Sons had earned their positions as family leaders by achieving academic success and carrying out Father's plan for their education at Cambridge University. By contrast, at the time of Eldest Son's return to Shanghai in 1935, he had not carried out Father's plan. Instead, he had left Harvard in favor of Wharton, failed to complete an MBA, and done no more than a perfunctory investigation of coal mining in the United States.

Eldest Son had not merely done poorly at the tasks in Father's plan. He had confronted Father about how or even whether he should carry out these tasks, adamantly refusing to follow Father's orders and aggressively taking actions without Father's permission. In fact, Eldest Son became the first child in the family to take a stand as an individual against Father not only in expressing opinions about the family firm's business policies (as Second, Third, and Fourth Sons had also done) but also in making decisions concerning his education, professional training, and career plans.

Yet, despite Eldest Son's poor record and defiant attitude, when he returned to Shanghai in 1935, Father offered him a job in the Liu family's accounts office, Liu Hong Ji, and Eldest Son immediately accepted it. Subsequently, Eldest Son remained with the family firm, and he eventually became one of its top managers during the war.

In response to Eldest Son's failures and defiance, why was Father so accommodating? Why did he continue to provide support and try to reach a truce even after Eldest Son had rejected his advice and taken actions directly contrary to his plan? Father's permissive attitude toward Eldest Son is particularly striking by contrast with the commonly held view of the Chinese patriarch as a stern, forbidding, rigid parent dictating all family decisions and giving his offspring no room to maneuver.

One possible explanation is that Father was singularly indulgent in this case because he was dealing with his eldest son and, like many Chinese fathers, was prepared to make the highest possible investment in his eldest son with the expectation that this son would be his successor as leader of the family and the family firm. If so, then would Father be equally accommodating with his younger sons? With Second, Third, and Fourth Sons, the question did not arise in school because they closely followed Father's instructions in choosing their university, selecting their majors, and planning their careers. But with the next child in the birth order, Fifth Son, the question did arise and become critical, because he differed with Father over health issues in which he ran the risk of losing his life.

5

A Son Who Was Sick

IN THE late 1920s and early 1930s, Father assured his sons that he would send all of them abroad for their educations, but he considered making an exception in the case of Fifth Son for medical reasons. From birth, Fifth Son had been a sickly child. Chronically underweight and short of appetite, he was eventually informed by his doctors that his stomach was out of place.[1] His gravest illness was tuberculosis, which nearly killed him during his boyhood in Shanghai.[2] In his healthy phases, he tried to keep up with his athletic older brothers by playing tennis and riding horseback,[3] but by the time he was a teenager, if not earlier, he began to fear that his history of illness would cause Father to deny him opportunities that were given to his brothers.

For Fifth Son, Father had in mind an education in the United States and a career in agriculture, but when the time came for Fifth Son to leave, Father did not let him go. After sending Second, Third, and Fourth Sons as a trio to England in 1929, Father could have sent Fifth Son to join with Eldest Son as a pair in the United States in 1931, but he did not do so. His concern for Fifth Son's health became even more apparent in 1931 and 1932, when he sent Sixth and Seventh Sons as a pair to Japan for further studies while still keeping Fifth Son in China.

Would Fifth Son's physical limitations hold him back, deprive him of an education overseas, and keep him dependent on his family at home? Fifth Son dreaded this prospect as he watched his older and younger brothers set sail one after another for England, the United States, and Japan. More and more desperate to follow their example, he pleaded with Father to let him go abroad too.

Medical Care in China

In 1931–1932, after sending six other sons overseas for their educations, Father kept Fifth Son in China and gave him the best available medical care available there for tuberculosis. For the period January–August 1931, Father withdrew Fifth Son from school and arranged care for him at home, except for his daily trips to the General Red Cross Hospital for injections to combat tuberculosis.[4] In August, after Fifth Son continued to deteriorate, Father sent him to Beijing—first to Peking Union Medical College and then to Sanitarium Hospital, where he was placed under the care of a tuberculosis specialist, Dr. Lu Yongchun.[5] Deeply concerned, Father made the eight-hundred-mile trip north from Shanghai to Beijing and recorded what he saw on his visit in a letter to Eldest Son. "I found him on his back in the sanitarium," Father wrote on October 2, 1931. "Of course, he can get onto his feet and move about all right. Still the doctors have to keep him in bed. Rest is what he needs most. I have and will always see to it that he gets the best comfort and nourishment in the hospital. He is, on the whole, improving. My heart is not quite at rest, though, because he has lost some sixteen pounds since he went to the hospital. Now he weighs 115."[6] Fifth Son's loss of weight so troubled Father that he resolved to send the boy to Switzerland for treatment if he did not soon regain it.

Fortunately, little by little, Fifth Son began to gain weight, but he remained in Beijing and continued to receive care there for several months in 1931 and early 1932. Even after he returned to Shanghai in the spring of 1932, he was not well enough to resume his studies. "Your fifth brother," Father wrote to Eldest Son on March 17, "is improving rather slowly." His condition convinced Father that he was not ready to go back to school in China, much less abroad. "I want him to get completely recovered," he told Eldest Son, "before I will let him attempt any study."[7] At that point, Father had not given up on his plan for Fifth Son, but he continued to postpone taking the next step in it. As he wrote to Eldest Son on March 17: "we must wait for his complete recovery. It may, therefore, be a little while yet before he can come over to the States to study agriculture."

By the summer of 1932, Fifth Son realized that his studies in the United States would be postponed at least beyond the academic year 1932–33 and perhaps indefinitely. In desperation, he resorted to deceiving his parents into thinking that he had fully recovered when in fact he had suffered a relapse. He later confessed to them: "Let me tell you the truth. When I was in China, I had a relapse. It's a thing of the past, and I don't want to say any more about it because there would be too much to tell."[8] Apparently, he was so eager to travel abroad and receive a foreign education that he was willing to risk his health or even his life to get the chance to go. When this ruse did not to allay his parents' fears, Fifth Son adopted a different strategy. He recruited Eldest Son to lobby with Father on his behalf.

Allying with Eldest Son

In the summer of 1932, as Fifth Son remained ill and saw his chances for going abroad slipping away, he wrote letters to Eldest Son seeking help. His aim was to follow the same educational path Eldest Son had taken from Shanghai to the United States, and he urged his brother to convince Father to let him do so. As he pointed out, Eldest Son was the only one of the Liu boys in the United States, and none of the others abroad was alone; Second, Third, and Fourth Sons were all at Cambridge, and Sixth and Seventh Sons were together in Tokyo. By this logic, it was time for Eldest Son to have at least one of his brothers join him in the United States, and Fifth Son presented himself as the ideal candidate. Besides, Father himself had already announced his plan to send Fifth Son to the United States. The only question in Fifth Son's mind was when he would be allowed to go.

At Fifth Son's urging, Eldest Son tried to pave the way for his younger brother's matriculation at Baldwin-Wallace College for the academic year 1932–33. Eldest Son had impressed the dean and the faculty during his year there, 1931–32, and when he left in the summer of 1932, he alerted the dean to the possibility that his younger brother would take his place at Baldwin-Wallace. The dean was very receptive to this idea and readily endorsed it in a letter to Father. Along with Eldest Son's grades for the spring of 1932, the dean enclosed a letter saying: "Please find herewith a copy of your son's grades for the second semester of the present school year. We were very happy to have him with us and he proved himself an honest and faithful student and a gentleman in every respect. We should be glad indeed to have your other son, Nyan-hsiao [Fifth Son], register with us in September, knowing that we could render him a similar service as we did Nyan-Tsung [Eldest Son]." As if these words were not enough to make a parent proud, the dean closed by congratulating Father "on the splendid sons that you have."[9]

Father was tempted by the dean's invitation, but he declined it because Fifth Son was still under treatment for tuberculosis. During June and July 1932, Fifth Son once again made the trip from Shanghai to Beijing to receive China's best medical care.[10] By the end of the summer, he was finally ready to resume full-time study for the first time in a year and a half, and although he had begun his first year at St. John's University before he had fallen ill, he now started his freshman year from the beginning once again. "So," Father reported to Eldest Son on August 21, Fifth Son "is going back to St. John's to study. We want to be perfectly assured that he is wholly recovered, and then we shall go into the consideration of his going far from home. We know he is all right now, but we have to be absolutely sure of that. Otherwise, his going far away from home would be a source of constant anxiety with us."[11] Sparing himself and Mother this anxiety, Father was relieved to have Fifth Son in Shanghai, but he took seriously Eldest Son's pleading on Fifth Son's behalf.

In the spring of 1933, as the prospects for the academic year 1933–34 began to loom on the horizon, Eldest Son sharpened his criticisms of St. John's and intensified his campaign for Fifth Son's study abroad. "Today," Eldest Son wrote to Father on March 19, "I received a letter from Fifth Brother. Although he didn't say it openly, I could tell that he feels his life in Shanghai is getting him nowhere. Didn't he say once that he wanted to study agriculture? Why is he still attending St. John's? There are not many good programs at St. John's."[12]

Eldest Son reported that Fifth Son found St. John's unsatisfying socially as well as academically. Fifth Son had made no close friends there since his best friend, Zhang Xingchun, had left to study in the United States. This lack of prospects for lasting friendships would have posed less of a problem if Fifth Son's brothers had stayed in Shanghai along with him, but with them abroad, he was bound to feel lonely, Eldest Son observed. "Now all of his older brothers are abroad, and Sixth and Seventh Brothers—who are close to him in age—are studying in Japan. It's easy to imagine his loneliness even if he doesn't come out and say it. I remember feeling the same way in Shanghai two years ago." Eldest Son had overcome this loneliness and his other problems at St.

John's by transferring to a college in the United States, and he recommended that Fifth Son be permitted to do the same. "To raise his morale and prepare him for the future, I suggest that you have a good talk with him and allow him to study abroad." In agriculture, Cornell University would be the best school in the United States for Fifth Son because it "has a good major in Agricultural Economics. The courses teach farmers not only how to increase their crops but also how to sell their harvests profitably."[13]

Besides hailing the advantages of an American education, Eldest Son claimed that the American environment would be good for Fifth Son's health. Once again he cited his own past as a model for Fifth Son's future. "As for his health," he wrote to Father, "don't worry about it. When I first arrived here, my health wasn't very good. But now that I have started working and keeping a regular schedule, I'm enjoying a healthy life."[14] Eldest Son's self-evaluation seemed fully borne out by his stellar record at Baldwin-Wallace during 1931–32 and his success at gaining admission to Harvard Business School for the fall of 1932, and Father took Eldest Son's advice to heart.

In the spring of 1933, Father allowed Fifth Son to apply to Baldwin-Wallace, and he told Eldest Son that he did so because he hoped that Fifth Son would follow Eldest Son's example by attaining good grades and good health there.[15] With these expectations that Eldest Son would lead the way, Father entrusted Fifth Son to him. As Father had hoped, Fifth Son was accepted for admission in the fall of 1933 and proceeded to follow Eldest Son's lead. Father did not foresee that Fifth Son would begin to pursue goals that differed from the ones in Father's plan.

Plunging into College Life

In August 1933, when Fifth Son was finally allowed to set sail from Shanghai and go abroad for his college education, he was keenly aware that Mother and Father were still full of anxiety about his health. After a tearful farewell at the time of his departure, he tried to reassure them in letters written en route to his distant new home. On board his ship crossing the Pacific, he wrote to Mother: "First, my spirits are high. Second, my appetite is good. . . . Mother, you really, really shouldn't worry."[16] After completing the next leg of the journey, his train trip from San Francisco to Chicago, he reported to Father: "my weight is up to 130 pounds. I feel as good as I ever have. Father, don't worry about a thing."[17]

On arrival in Chicago, Fifth Son had an exhilarating reunion with his eldest brother and Zhang Xingchun, his old friend and classmate from Shanghai. On September 9, he wrote to Father that as his train pulled into the station, "Eldest Brother and Xingchun came to meet me as expected. We had been apart for two years, and now that we were able to have a reunion, we talked and talked and were indescribably happy."[18]

Immediately Eldest Son took charge, and Fifth Son gratefully placed himself in his older brother's hands. "On my arrival," he wrote Father, "Eldest Brother told me to move in with him at International House so that Eldest Brother could take care of everything for me." Eldest Son also took charge of planning Fifth Son's academic program. He and Zhang initially convinced Fifth Son to abandon the plan for attending Baldwin-Wallace in favor of enrolling at the University of Pennsylvania, where Eldest Son had just transferred and Zhang was also a student. They informed him that the University of Pennsylvania had a good program in transportation, which they urged him to choose as his major. He was completely unfamiliar with this program but readily accepted the other boys' advice. He wrote to Father on September 9: "Since I have no opinion of my own, I have decided to follow their suggestion and would like to change my major to transportation." They convinced him that the University of Pennsylvania "has the best department of transportation, so if I am successful at gaining admission there, I might be held back one year. But I think it's worth it because I plan to use the summer to catch up so that I can rejoin my original class."[19]

After becoming swept up in his brother's and friend's enthusiasm for this proposal, Fifth Son discovered two days later that they had changed their minds. In a letter to Father, Eldest Son explained that they switched from one plan to the other because the administrative changes were too difficult to make at such a late date. "I wanted to send him [Fifth Son] to Wharton School as soon as I learned that he wanted to study transportation, as Wharton offers an excellent program in transportation. But everything at Baldwin-Wallace College had been arranged. Besides, I can introduce him to many students and faculty members at Baldwin-Wallace, so I think his life will not be unhappy there." Taking full command, Eldest Son informed Father: "If Fifth Son gets good grades at Baldwin-Wallace this year, I'll help him transfer to Wharton School to major in transportation."[20] Eldest Son also took it upon himself to select the subjects in which Fifth Son would need to get good grades so that he could later transfer to the University of Pennsylvania.

While Eldest Son exhorted Fifth Son to use Baldwin-Wallace as a stepping stone for transferring as soon as possible, Father cautioned him against moving too fast. Father agreed with the idea that Fifth Son should ultimately attend a prestigious school like Harvard or the University of Pennsylvania, but he was afraid that Fifth Son would put his health in jeopardy if he entered their competitive and rigorous academic programs too soon. Father preferred to have Fifth Son spend at least a year, or more, at Baldwin-Wallace with its less demanding courses, and even there he wanted Fifth Son to take a light load. After Fifth Son confirmed that he would attend Baldwin-Wallace rather than the University of Pennsylvania in the fall of 1933 and mailed a copy of his class schedule home, Father expressed concern that Fifth Son might overtax himself by enrolling in too many courses. "In looking at those many subjects which you have to take for this semester, I cannot help fearing that they may prove too heavy on you. While your ambition is laudable, the strain may be too severe on your health. Knowledge, no matter how useful it is, is yet not as important as health; and you should not develop the one and overlook the other entirely."[21]

This privileging of health over knowledge should govern all of Fifth Son's decisions in his academic work, Father insisted. He urged his son to give less of his attention to his academic work and more to his physical conditioning. "I hope that you will not bury yourself among the books," he wrote, "and that you will give yourself as much mental and physical relaxation as possible, so that a sound mind can have a sound body. I would suggest that for the benefit of your health, you can devote some of your time to some gentle physical exercise. I have been told that physical exercise is a required course for every freshman to take in the States and wonder if you [can] take that course this year."[22] In the United States, as in China, Fifth Son should give priority to his health over all else, Father repeatedly reminded him.

Fifth Son was pleased to receive this letter, the first one from Father since he had arrived in the United States. But he was disappointed to find that his parents were still preoccupied with his health. After plunging energetically into college life, he was convinced that his medical history was a thing of the past, and he replied to Father that neither he nor Mother would ever again need to worry about his health. "It seems to me that Mother and you," he wrote to Father on November 14, "are still much worried concerning my health and thinking that I am still as weak as while I was in China, if not weaker. Now, Father, I wish to explain to you that your present conception of my health is by no means right, because I am exceptionally well since I entered into the school. My weight is increased up to 140 lbs. with clothes on. I well remember that my former weight was only 126 lbs. before I came to the United States. That means I have gained more than 10 lbs. in the past three months and I still believe that my body can be increased more for time to come."[23]

As Fifth Son gained weight, he also gained confidence, and he began to conceive of his quest for good health as part of a larger campaign to convince Americans that the Chinese people had become strong. "In fact, I am much more aggressive than I was before," he wrote to Father. He participated with his classmates in all the meetings and games at Baldwin-Wallace and showed that he was healthy and strong because "that is the way to make them understand that Chinese are no longer a sick and timid people."[24]

While giving this characterization of himself as forceful and robust, Fifth Son recognized that his parents were accustomed to hearing him exaggerate the extent of his good health, so he asked one of his classmates, Lawrence Stone, to vouch for him. In a letter to Father, Stone identified himself by noting that Fifth Son "rooms across the hall from me and we have come to know each other quite well." As the two boys had discussed their families and backgrounds with each other, Fifth Son "told me that he was a very sick boy a few years ago and said that you were worried and would like to know how he is now. Might I tell you that he is in the best of health and is quite strong." In closing, Stone tempered his earnest tone with a touch of humor: "I sincerely hope that this letter will help you understand that George [Fifth Son] is getting along very well in college life at Baldwin-Wallace and is feeling fine. (You should see him eat!)."[25]

Fifth Son's strategy of recruiting a classmate to testify on his behalf impressed Father, though it did not completely eliminate his doubts about his son's health. "I have received your letter of Nov. 14th handing me a letter from your friend, Lawrence Stone," Father replied to Fifth Son on December 19. "It is very considerate of you to alleviate my anxiety over your health by asking your friend to vouch for the great improvement you have made in your health. Nothing pleases me more than to learn that you have gained more than ten pounds in the past three months." Pleased but still not fully reassured, Father asked for more evidence. "I only hope," he went on, "that with the proper care of your health, you can still gain more weight in time to come. I would be glad if you can send me some snap-shots of yourself, so that I can prove by my own eyes that George [Fifth Son] is no longer a weak boy as I used to think."[26]

Father expressed his anxiety about Fifth Son to Lawrence Stone too. In a separate note, he thanked Stone for sending a helpful report, but he made clear that he continued to be concerned. "It is true that George's health has been a source of my constant worry. Being still at his teens, and studious and frugal by nature, he, I fear, may apply himself too diligently to his studies without giving proper regard to his poor health. It is very kind of you to inform me that he is in the best of health and quite strong. This great improvement in his health, I believe, must be due to the wholesome college life, which he has now the privilege to enjoy."[27]

In light of these reports on Fifth Son's health, Father was now willing to allow him to continue his studies in the United States, as long as he remained at Baldwin-Wallace. Father made his position on this point clear to Fifth Son. "It is true that there are many advantages to be said in favor of a Chinese student to enter into a small college for the first one or two years. Besides the opportunity of getting a good insight into the American life and of practicing your English Language, you have better living conditions to live in. To a young man of your health, fresh air and quiet life are essential. Therefore I think that it is very wise for you to stay at Berea [where Baldwin-Wallace was located] for one year."[28] Father's plan seemed to be acceptable to Fifth Son. As late as Christmas Day, 1933, after one semester at Baldwin-Wallace, he wrote to Father that he would remain there. But during the next few weeks, he changed his plans.

From Father's Plan to Eldest Son's Plan

Ever since his arrival in the United States, Fifth Son had received conflicting advice. From Father he had heard that the fragility of his health was the paramount consideration, so he should proceed cautiously, take a light load of courses, and remain at Baldwin-Wallace for at least one year. From Eldest Son he had received assurance that his health would take care of itself, so he should throw himself into his work, take a heavy load, and transfer from Baldwin-Wallace to a big and prestigious university as soon as possible.

Fifth Son strongly preferred the latter plan. After impatiently waiting in China while his brothers forged ahead with Father's plan for their study abroad, he was now eager to seize the opportunity to catch up. Since his first days in the United States, he had been open to Eldest Son's suggestion that he should enter the University of Pennsylvania rather than Baldwin-Wallace. When his admission to Penn could not be arranged in time for him to begin in the fall semester of 1933, Fifth Son had gone to Baldwin-Wallace and performed adequately in the classroom without any apparent ill effects on his health. So over winter break, while visiting Eldest Son in Philadelphia, he decided to transfer immediately and attend Penn in the spring semester of 1934. Just as Eldest Son had transferred to Penn without Father's permission and contrary to Father's plan in the fall of 1933, Fifth Son now did the same in the spring of 1934.

Fifth Son delivered the news to Father as a fait accompli. "Perhaps, you will be surprised to know," Fifth Son wrote to Father on February 5, "that I am no longer studying in Baldwin-Wallace. I left for the University of Pennsylvania as soon as I finished my work in the first semester." He emphasized to Father that "most important of all, I can assure you that I am in good health. I also try to make myself robust and strong and continue to take the best care of my health." He acknowledged that living in the big city of Philadelphia would not be as good for his lungs as breathing the clean air of bucolic Berea had been. But he hastened to add that his new roommate was Eldest Son, who had already agreed to move with him out of the city to a healthier location. He and Eldest Son were living "harmoniously and splendidly" in their Philadelphia apartment, he wrote to Father in early February, "but for the sake of my health, we are planning to move to the country."[29]

Eldest Son reinforced Fifth Son's point by assuring his parents that Fifth Son's health was nothing to worry about. During the fall, Eldest Son had proposed more than once to arrange for Fifth Son's transfer to Penn and had brushed aside Father's instructions that he should counsel Fifth Son to remain at Baldwin-Wallace, postpone his transfer to Penn, and slow down the overall pace of his education for the sake of his health.[30] Now, clearly pleased with Fifth Son's move to Philadelphia and transfer to Penn, Eldest Son wrote to Father and Mother that Fifth Son's "health is much better than it was in Shanghai. He has gained ten pounds. As soon as we have a chance we'll take photographs for you."[31]

Father had not expected the news of Fifth Son's transfer, and he was disturbed by it. "I would say that I am surprised at finding from your letter of Feb. 5th that you have transferred from Baldwin Wallace to Pennsylvania," he replied to Fifth Son on March 10. The transfer "has come sooner than I anticipated, because I have thought that you would stay at B. W. one semester longer yet." Upset at not having been consulted and reluctant to accept this unforeseen move, Father continued to make his case for keeping Fifth Son at Baldwin-Wallace. "It is always my belief," he reminded Fifth Son, "that a small college offers many advantages which you cannot get from a big university. This is especially true with Chinese students who have to pursue undergraduate courses. In a small college which, as a rule, is situated in a small town, not only [are] the living condition[s] wholesome and healthy, but you have more chances to mix up with the American students and to learn their life and language."[32]

While remaining committed to this belief that Baldwin-Wallace was preferable to Penn at this time, Father did not attempt to undo Fifth Son's transfer. He accepted it with one proviso: that Fifth Son should make good on his promise to move his residence out of Philadelphia and into the surrounding countryside. Since Fifth Son had already transferred, Father told him: "It will be out of place to dwell much upon this subject. For the benefit of your health, I strongly urge you to find your lodgings in the country as stated in your letter, as the hurly-burly of big city life will do [good neither] to your health nor to your studies."[33]

As it turned out, Fifth Son did not accommodate even this request from Father. "As to our lodging," he replied to Father on April 10— more than halfway through the spring semester—"we still have not found a better place to move so far as our convenience is concerned.

Most likely, we will not move to any place till the next term." He saw
no need to follow Father's advice about where he should live any more
than about where he should attend college, now that he had put his illnesses behind him. "Fortunately," he assured Father, the move to Philadelphia and Penn "does not trouble me, because I still have confidence
in myself concerning my present health."[34]

From Patriarch to Friend

Fifth Son's rapidly rising confidence in his health and, more broadly, in
himself did not escape Father's notice. On reflection, Father did not
belabor his criticisms of his son for deviating from the original plan.
Instead he noted that it was one of many examples of Fifth Son's quest
for personal independence. Another example, Father observed, was
Fifth Son's tenacious opposition to Father's idea of appointing a guardian for him. Father had in mind for this position Shi Zhaoji, the Chinese diplomat who had assisted Second, Third, and Fourth Sons in England while serving as China's minister there (1929–1932) and was now
serving as China's minister to the United States. But Fifth Son repeatedly insisted that he needed no guardian at all.[35]

Reflecting on the significance of Fifth Son's growing independence,
Father suggested that it required them to adjust their father-son relationship. "By now," he wrote to his son on August 1, 1934,

> you have already been in the United States about one year. Being far
> away from China, you, even with the assistance of a worthy guardian,
> have to, sometimes, do things according to your own judgment. In
> other words, you have to look after your affairs all by yourself. I, of
> course, wish to keep [in] as close personal touch with you as possible,
> but the long distance between us has made this very difficult, if not
> impossible. In order to keep up good understanding between us, I wish
> you [to feel that you] can always speak out your mind without reserve
> and exchange opinions with me frankly and openly.[36]

This frank and open relationship between Father and Fifth Son had
become a model for Father's relationships with all his sons, he said. "As
a matter of fact, the relation between a father and a son should be on
the basis of good friends. It is far from being my wish that I should use
the paternal authority to force my wishes and advices on my sons and
ask them to follow my dictates blindly without reasons. As a ruler of

our house, I wish to be, to use a political parlance, a democratic leader, instead of being an autocrat or a dictator."[37]

In renouncing his autocratic role as a patriarch and offering to be a democratic leader of the family, Father assured Fifth Son that he did not want to dictate decisions to his son unilaterally from thousands of miles away. Even if he wanted to do so, he could not prevent his son from changing his attitude toward authority under the influence of American culture. "Being a generation older than you coupled with my unfamiliarity with the conditions prevailing in America," Father acknowledged, "I am fully aware that my outlook may be considered as conservative and not being compatible with the trend of modern thoughts. In case you find faults with any of my suggestions, do not hesitate to say so. Do not obey just for the sake of obedience. Treat me as a friend, and tell me everything you will do [as you would tell it] to your friend."[38]

As a father seeking to make friends with his sons by letter, Father had found a model for himself in the Earl of Chesterfield (1694–1773), the English statesman and author who had published his correspondence with his son. "In Lord Chesterfield's letters to his son," Father told Fifth Son, "he always referred to himself as his son's best friend," and Father expressed the hope that Fifth Son would "also consider me as your best friend."[39] In deprecating himself as a conservative member of an older generation, and offering to be Fifth Son's best friend, Father seemed to imply his approval of Fifth Son's decision to transfer to the University of Pennsylvania even though it was made against Father's wishes.

Father's willingness to accommodate Fifth Son in the summer of 1934 bore a striking resemblance to his willingness to accommodate Eldest Son in the summer of 1933. Yet Fifth Son's disagreement with Father over transferring from Baldwin-Wallace was fundamentally different from Eldest Son's disagreement with him over transferring from Harvard Business School. Fifth Son did not confront Father so directly or argue with him so aggressively. His strategy was to keep his plans to himself, align himself with an older brother, and then present a fait accompli—a technique Father urged him to abandon when he pleaded with him to "tell me everything you will do." Moreover, compared to Eldest Son's disagreement with Father, Fifth Son's disagreement was less about his academic work and career plans than about his health. As long as Fifth Son was healthy, he pursued his ambitions and threw himself into his work confidently and wholeheartedly without concern for Father's cautionary advice, but when his health deteriorated, he faced the dilemma of whether to hide his illness and carry on or heed his father's warnings and slow down.

Admissions of Failure

If Fifth Son's confidence rose during his first year in the United States, it began to fall at the beginning of his second year. In September 1934, as classes resumed at Penn, he admitted to his parents that his health had not been fully restored and that his living conditions in Philadelphia had slowed his recovery. As always, he tried to put the best possible face on his medical condition, but he no longer claimed that he was physically sound, and in his letters he began to set a darker tone.

On September 15 he wrote to Father: "My health, as I have already told you, is always improving," but now he admitted that the improvement "is somehow very slow and gradual." He also conceded that Philadelphia was not the healthiest place to live in the United States. "Some gentle exercises such as playing tennis seem to be quite necessary for me," he wrote, but "in this city I can hardly find good [places to play]. The weather is becoming disgusting now. It is suffocating and wet and that is the first experience that I have ever known, since I came to this country. Besides this, I always find myself too much confined with city atmosphere. All these are unfavorable to my present health and that was why I at first had a strong desire to study one year in Cornell."[40]

Yet he did not transfer from the urban campus at Penn to the rural setting at Cornell or even move to the outskirts of Philadelphia, because he gave priority to his studies over his health. "Due to my ambition to study Transportation and Insurance," he told Father on September 15, he had decided to abandon plans for study at Cornell and "continue my study here. This is surely a little risk of my health, however, I think I might have a greater future by doing this than otherwise." He risked his health because he believed that by an act of will he could overcome his physical limitations. To fulfill his dreams of academic success, he told Father he would "try every means of what I can do with this body."[41]

On September 20, he wrote an equally sober assessment to Mother. He confessed to her that neither his health nor his academic work had progressed as he had claimed in earlier letters. "The illnesses I have been carrying around for the past several years have improved but not been completely cured," he admitted. "Therefore my life during the past year has been a mess." His academic record, he reported, deserved an equally low evaluation. "During the past year, I have not achieved any of the goals in my original plan. In my studies I have barely scratched the surface, nothing more."[42]

Weighed down by his own physical and academic failures, he seemed further burdened by his awareness of how far he had fallen short of his older brothers' standards. As he recounted their achievements to his mother, the contrast with his own failures was inescapable. "Recently I've heard that Third and Fourth Brothers have returned to the Fatherland. They've been away from home for many years and have crossed many oceans. Now they have returned to our homeland. How can this not bring happiness to the mother who always has her sons on her mind. I hear that they graduated from Cambridge with honors, and this will bring more fame to the already illustrious history of the Liu family." How could Fifth Son close the gap between himself and these two older brothers, Fourth Son (who was only one year older than he was) and Third Son (two years older)? "I don't know what the future year will bring," he wrote to his mother in September, as he threw himself into the fall semester at the University of Pennsylvania. "I have no choice but to work extremely hard."[43]

Father rejected this notion that Fifth Son had no choice and urged him to take his destiny into his own hands by moving away from Philadelphia to a healthier place. He reminded Fifth Son that "one of the principal reasons for you to cross the Pacific and study in the U.S. is to seek good health." If Fifth Son had not found it in Philadelphia, then he should look for it elsewhere. "If personal experience has convinced you that the climatic conditions in Pennsylvania are not as ideal and adaptable to you as those of Ohio or New York, there is, at best, but little force in the argument for you to continue your sojourn in Philadelphia. In your case, as also in everybody else's case, the seeking and attaining of good health should not be considered secondary to the acquisition of knowledge."[44]

With health as the top priority, Father urged Fifth Son to transfer immediately. "The atmosphere and life in the University of Pennsylvania cannot be anything but beautiful and desirable," he acknowledged.

"Nevertheless, since you have found the climatic conditions in Cornell University better and more salutary, I strongly advise that you take actual measures for a transfer."[45] But Fifth Son did not transfer. He continued to live in Philadelphia and work hard at Penn. Sad to say, at the end of the fall semester in 1934, he relapsed into the worst recurrence of tuberculosis that had ever struck him down.

The Relapse

This case of tuberculosis was not discovered until it had reached an advanced stage, because he did not have a physical examination until the end of 1934, a full year after he had arrived at Penn. If he had matriculated at Penn at the beginning of the fall semester, he would have been required to have a physical, but in transferring from Baldwin-Wallace in the middle of the academic year, he had no such requirement. During the summer of 1934, he should have had a physical, but he postponed it until November, probably because he dreaded hearing the results. Only then, when he could no longer put it off, did he see a school physician because he needed a "Dr. Examination Certificate" to continue his studies.[46]

The diagnosis and prognosis of Fifth Son's condition were dire. "The x-ray showed," he wrote to his parents on December 15, "that my tuberculosis had advanced to the second stage." Characteristically, he tried to find a silver lining in the cloud that cast its dark shadow on his health. "The doctor said there is a lot of hope for my recovery," he reported. "It is 90 percent certain. This is a happy thing among all of the unfortunate things." Because of this happy thing, "I myself have great faith in my future recovery even though my illness is more serious than what I've had in the past." For all his boundless optimism, even Fifth Son did not question the University of Pennsylvania doctor's orders that he should withdraw from school. "Under the circumstances, it was absolutely impossible for me to continue my studies. The doctor persuaded me to go to Colorado Springs for a rest." The Cragmor Sanatorium in Colorado Springs was one of the most prominent hospitals for treating tuberculosis in the United States.[47]

Confronted with this diagnosis and recommendation, Fifth Son put the doctor in touch with his guardian, Shi Zhaoji, China's minister to the United States, at the Chinese legation in Washington, D.C. During his first year in the United States, Fifth Son had refused to accept a guardian and had only gone along with Minister Shi's appointment as his guardian in September 1934 after he had begun to admit that he was not fully healthy.[48] But now he fully embraced Shi as his guardian and readily complied with all of Shi's instructions that he should drop out of school, take the train from Philadelphia to Washington, and travel by train with one of Shi's secretaries, W. S. Lao, the two thousand miles from there to Colorado. Within the brief span of two weeks, once Shi took charge in early December, Fifth Son found his life suddenly transformed from that of a student at the University of Pennsylvania to that of a patient at the Cragmor Sanatorium.

Fear of Parental Abandonment

By the time he arrived there, Fifth Son had finally become convinced that he had been wrong and Father had been right about his health all along. No longer defending his own self-evaluation, as he had done during his past eighteen months in the United States, he begged his parents to look after him and give him one more chance. "Since I came to America," he wrote to them, "all of Father's letters to me have conveyed his worries about me and have repeatedly urged me to take care of myself. Father has done all that can be done. Out of respect for Father's good intentions and persuasive instructions, how can I not try to find a way to follow Father's instructions?"[49]

Now Fifth Son placed the blame for his predicament squarely on himself. "Regrettably," he confessed to his parents, "I became foolish and allowed my ambition to run out of control. As a result, I failed to recognize my own limitations, and I allowed my weak body to deteriorate. Whenever I reflect on this, I have incredible regrets and hate myself. I have let my young and precious body come to this point." Full of self-doubt, he now feared that his parents would have doubts about him too or, worse yet, would give up on him. Having flagellated himself for his past foolishness, he went on to say: "What I am asking now is for you to give me another chance! Once I recover, I will definitely never upset or disappoint you again." Without this chance, he could see no hope. "My only hope now is that you are willing to forgive me. The mistakes of my past will be redeemed! So I will never again fail to measure up to your expectations!"[50] In these desperate pleas, he was declaring that he had lost his vision of a future for himself and that he would never have a future without his parents' support.

Fifth Son needed not only his parents' moral support but also their financial backing to cover his expensive medical care. He discovered that Cragmor Sanatorium was more expensive than the hospitals in China, but he thought it was worth the money. Hoping his parents would agree, he wrote them from Cragmor on his first day there, December 15: "If you want me to return to our country for treatment, I'll of course follow your instructions and come home. I myself would like to get treatment in this hospital because it is much better than the hospitals in China; not only is the equipment superior but the doctors are also far more competent. But this is only one way of looking at it because there's no question that it will cost a lot less for treatment in China than in the United States." He left to his parents the decision as to whether they could afford to pay his bills at Cragmor, but he clearly conveyed to them his preference for staying there. "Since I've been admitted to the hospital," he reported after only one day there, "my body has suddenly become comfortable and relaxed. My mental state is much more stable. Sometimes I even feel carefree. Although by myself, I do not feel lonely. I myself realize that if I were not living like this, I would have no way out."[51]

Fifth Son knew from the beginning that he would have a long stay at Cragmor, or wherever he was to be treated, but he was not sure how long. "It is not possible," he told his parents, "to determine how long it will take to cure my illness. Perhaps at most one year? If not, at least half a year. It will all depend on how much progress I can make."[52] He promised to keep his parents informed about his progress, and he assured them that they would also hear about his condition from his attending physician, Dr. Alexius Forster, and from Minister Shi Zhaoji.

After years of aligning with Eldest Son against Father, first in China and then in the United States, Fifth Son now recognized that he was wholly dependent on Father. If Fifth Son had felt uplifted by his quest for independence since leaving Shanghai, he now plunged downward into fears of isolation, neglect, even abandonment. Would his parents blame him for his relapse? Would they refuse to pay his expensive medical bills? Living half a world away, would they order him to come home against his will and subject him to inferior care? Struck down by illness far from home, Fifth Son raised these questions in his letters to his parents, and he was devastated by their reply.

Misunderstanding

On December 21, Father received a telegram from Eldest Son and Minister Shi informing him that Fifth Son had relapsed, and he immediately held a family meeting in Shanghai. As soon as the meeting was over, he fired off a telegram to Eldest Son in Philadelphia that was written in English as follows:

> JULIUS AND HANNIBAL [Second and Third Sons] DUE SEATTLE
> JANUARY 22ND MOTHER URGES GEORGE [Fifth Son] RECUPER-
> ATE IN CHINA HANNIBAL WILLING TO ACCOMPANY HIS RETURN
> SPARE NO MONEY ON GEORGE ILLNESS
>
> OSLIEU [Father]

Father's message was intended to reassure Fifth Son that within a month he would have his second and third brothers at his side, that his mother was eager to have him with her in China, and that his father was willing to spend whatever money was needed to make him well. But Fifth Son misconstrued the telegram's dense language, especially the phrase "spare no money," which he interpreted to mean that Father could not spare any money and would not cover the cost of Fifth Son's medical bills in the United States. After receiving a copy of Father's telegram from Eldest Son on December 25, Fifth Son spent Christmas day writing a long, confused, and troubled letter to his parents, admitting that he had not been worthy of them but begging them to reconsider their decision (as he understood it) not to pay for his medical treatment.

In this letter, Fifth Son poured out his feelings of insecurity. "Throughout the past few years," he wrote, "I have proved myself to be the most unworthy child in our family. My result of studying here is a terrible failure." While under his parents' close supervision before coming to America, he had shown promise, but his current collapse had brought his worth to a new low. "Now the child who has been carefully brought [up] and thoroughly nourished," he lamented, had produced "results so unfavorable that he is not to be valued as formerly estimated." Even worse, his parents were justified in lowering their estimation of him because he had behaved contrary to their wishes while he had been in the United States. "I realize too that during the past years I have offended your feelings conspicuously and to the highest degree." Groping for a metaphor to express the full extent of his deterioration, he sadly observed to his parents that he was "like a piece of decaying wood which is impossible to be further put into the original usage"—in all likelihood an allusion to the Confucian saying "Rotten wood cannot be carved."[53]

Yet, even if he considered himself rotten and worthless, he had been shocked by Father's telegram. After sleeping on it, he decided to spend the day after Christmas writing another long letter taking issue with Father's decision to "spare no money." He wrote to Father: "The last sentence is quoted [in Eldest Son's letter to Fifth Son] like this, 'Spare no money on George illness.'" He went on: "From reading your cable, I do not perceive your points that even though having serious sickness, I should have no money to spend as for the present emergency." He admitted that his medical bills at Cragmor would be high. "I need time as well as a lot of money before my health can be recovered." X-rays, the drug numorthorax, doctor's bills, and hospital fees would add up to a total of "a little over two thousand [U.S. dollars] a year, a period, I hope, that will be long enough to recuperate." But even at such a high cost, "I think the amount of money which I am now spending for the emergency may be justifiable and not against your wish."[54]

Building a case for covering the cost of his treatment in the United States, Fifth Son enumerated the reasons why this large expenditure would be worth it. First and foremost, he emphasized that Cragmor was better than any hospital he had seen in China. Second, he noted that he was not the only Chinese at Cragmor. "There are at least more than five Chinese patients whose names have been enlisted in this hospital." Third, he was willing to stay less than a year or even less than six months if his parents would give him at least "a couple of months" at Cragmor. And fourth, if his parents could find no funds for him from any other source, then he urged them to cover his medical bills with the money they had set aside for his future education. These funds, he sadly reflected, "may as well be treated as your final investment in your fifth child."[55]

If his parents would not abandon him and would make this final investment in him, then Fifth Son believed he could recover and lead a reasonably normal life. He had given up his dream for an education comparable to that of his brothers, but he held onto a lesser dream that after recovering from this bout with tuberculosis, he would relieve his parents of any future financial burdens. "With a good healthy physical body, I think I can fulfill my dream," he told them, by becoming "independent [and able] to earn my living." If so, then he would never again put his health at risk. "Dear parents," he vowed, "it is my word of honor that I am not going to ruin myself again."[56]

Reassurance

For nearly a month after writing these letters to his parents, Fifth Son waited for Father's reassurance, and he finally received it, first indirectly through a visit from his two elder brothers and then directly in his father's letters. Second and Third Sons both made the long trip from Shanghai to Colorado Springs and spent the last week of January 1935 with Fifth Son at Cragmor. In their reports home, Second and Third Sons tried to put Father's mind at ease. "I can assure you that under the circumstances you have done all you can for him," Third Son wrote to Father on January 31. "He knows that, and will do everything he can to relieve you of your anxiety as soon as he can."[57]

Even after his brothers' visit, Fifth Son was still eager to receive reassurance in Father's own words, which finally arrived by letter in early February. "Your letter dated December 26th has come to my hand," Father wrote in English to Fifth Son on January 23. "It appears that you have completely misunderstood the purport of my statement— 'spare no money on George's illness' in my cable. If you ask any English-speaking person you will know that 'spare' means save and *not* 'spend.' Therefore 'spare no money on George's illness' means 'spend any amount of money on George's illness.'"[58]

Father went on to express astonishment that Fifth Son had jumped to the conclusion that Father would financially abandon his son. "My dear boy," Father wrote, "I have never in my life either in speech or in deed indicated that money weighs more heavily in my mind than my own flesh and blood." Even for non–family members, Father had made generous contributions to hospitals. Father reminded Fifth Son: "I spend a considerable sum of money each year on hospitals and other charitable institutions because it gives me immense pleasure to see so many lives saved from death and starvation." Given that, Father rhetorically asked, "is it likely that I should hesitate to do the same when the life of my own son is in the balance?" Answering his own question, Father made his unequivocal financial pledge: "You can rest assured that I would forward you $180 a month to cover your expenditure in the sanitarium even if I were driven to the extremity of borrowing."[59]

Two days later Father wrote again to try to reassure Fifth Son. He expressed regret that he had initially urged Fifth Son to return right away to China, and he explained that he would cover Fifth Son's expenses for as long as necessary in the United States as part of a long-term investment in overseas education for all his sons.

> You know it is always so difficult for a parent, especially as I am staying so far away from you, to remain cool and collected when the news of his son's illness reaches his ears. I confess that I was rather over-hasty in suggesting your returning home with Hannibal [Third Son] in my cable. But then I thought you might feel lonely and miserable in America after Franklin [Eldest Son] had left you. You may have my word that any such thought has now been completely banished from my mind. You have my hearty approval to stay at the [Cragmor] Sanitarium as long as the doctor thinks fit.

On the issue of money, Father was equally reassuring. "I wish you would set any consideration about money out of your mind," he wrote. "The business depression in China has certainly struck everyone in the country very hard, but it can not boast of having driven me into financial difficulty. I think I can still keep on investing in you boys for at least another ten years."[60] Within these ten years, Father had no doubt that Fifth Son would have enough time to recover from his illness and complete his education all at Father's expense.

Mother expressed her support for Fifth Son and his care at Cragmor even more emotionally than Father did. "Your mother," Father reported to Fifth Son, "burst out into a torrent of tears when she had your letter read." With her outburst fresh in his mind, Father wrote: "I can quote her exact words as follows: 'My boy must have a complete rest for a year; superior talent and trained ability can be purchased with money. But who can vouchsafe to bring my boy healthy and well back to me once he is down in illness.'" Mother's reaction was to the letter Fifth Son had written on Christmas Day. She did not know that he had written an equally troubled and troubling letter the next day, because Father had chosen to keep it from her. "I am sure," he wrote, "I would have extracted from her a fresh torrent of tears if I had actually told her what you had said about yourself in your last letter."[61]

Once Father had confirmed his and Mother's complete support for Fifth Son's medical care, he expressed his concern for his son's psychological condition. "You must never again have such a depressed outlook on your life as to compare yourself to a piece of decaying wood," Father warned him. "To me all of my children are alike whether in illness or in health, for you are all equally valuable and precious to me. Without any one of you life will not be happy and complete. Therefore I earnestly request you to 'cheer up' and forget that you are an ill man." Father so cherished his children, he maintained, that it would never occur to him to withdraw his support from any of them. "I have never considered for a moment that you in your present state are a burden to me," Father assured Fifth Son. "On the contrary it gives my heart's content to see you fight so courageously to regain your normal health."[62]

As for Fifth Son's future, it still had a secure place in Father's plan. "My dear boy," Father wrote, "do follow my advice and stop worrying about your future." Specifically including Fifth Son along with his brothers, Father reiterated his familiar vision of a Liu business dynasty: "I have the greatest hope to see you and your brothers one of these days carry on my business interests and thus bring honour and wealth not only to our family but to the nation as a whole."[63]

These were the reassuring words Fifth Son had yearned to hear. On February 5, when Father's letter finally arrived (nearly six weeks after the "spare no money" telegram of December 21), he described in his reply how eagerly he had anticipated it. "After speaking face-to-face and at length with Second and Third Brothers," he wrote, "my indescribable bitterness has diminished a great deal. But my hopes for receiving a letter from Father, instead of diminishing the least bit, have greatly increased." Rather than feel grateful to Father for having sent these messengers, Fifth Son was disappointed in him for not sending with them a letter in his own words. "My heart was still full of resentment, and I was thinking about why Father's letter had not arrived. When Second and Third Brothers came, they should have had with them a letter from you."[64] Rarely, if ever, had Fifth Son made a serious accusation against Father, and he felt free to make this one only after Father's letter had arrived, rendering the accusation moot.

Fifth Son attached such profound importance to Father's letter that he took the trouble to describe in his reply the sequence of emotions that ran through him as he received, opened, and read it. "Around ten o'clock this morning, in the midst of my disappointment as I was longing for home, suddenly your letter arrived," he wrote. "At that moment, my heart trembled with joy, sadness, happiness, and fear." At this emotional fever pitch, Fifth Son flew through the letter almost blindly. "I hastily ripped open the envelope and pulled out a two-page letter written in Father's hand," referring to him here, and at other points in this letter, in the third person. "After that I almost felt as though my mental condition was thrown out of balance. If not, why couldn't I understand it after reading it twice?" Finally, on the third reading, Fifth Son began to absorb Father's words and let them sink in, triggering a deep emotional response. "As soon as I finished reading it for the third time, my face was covered with tears. Then the unstoppable tears soaked the corner of the stationary [*sic*] that I was holding in my hand." Thus did Fifth Son's outpouring of emotion literally spill onto the pages of his father's letter.[65]

At that moment, Fifth Son reverted to a complete, childlike dependency on Father. After reading Father's letter, he wrote: "I couldn't help but let my thoughts wander, and I felt that I, already an adult, was suddenly in the embrace of my father as though I were a weak and helpless child." Whatever independence Fifth Son might have sought or achieved by taking a heavier academic load than Father had recommended and transferring to Penn against Father's advice, he was now convinced that he was able to survive in his time of need only by placing his fate entirely in Father's hands. At Penn, "When I was in the *Philadelphia school* [University of Pennsylvania], as I have said to Eldest Brother," Fifth Son wrote to Father, "I faced some threats to my life. Since I was living in the midst of darkness, why wouldn't my spirits and my physical strength be low and weak? Then I found a savior. Who else but you, Father?"[66]

Fifth Son referred to Father as his savior in both the human and spiritual senses. As a human savior, "if you had not come to my rescue, I am afraid that this life of mine would have left this world." As a spiritual savior, Father was able to grant forgiveness and foresee the future. "I saw Father's compassionate face," Fifth Son wrote to him, "and your great and unlimited Fatherly love warmed my heart. I want to beg your forgiveness, and I hope that you will continue to shine your great light to illuminate my future. I know Father will forgive the mistakes that I have made and will forgive this pitiful son of yours as you have done before."[67] Humbling himself like a religious devotee, Fifth Son attributed to Father godlike powers as well as human virtues and expressed his deep filial devotion.

In acknowledging his dependence on Father and expressing his great sense of relief that he had not been abandoned, Fifth Son brought his emotional crisis to an end. In subsequent letters, he apologized for misinterpreting the phrase "spare no money" and continued to plead with his parents not to give up on him, and he repeatedly thanked them for their support, expressing no doubt that they would ever withdraw it.[68]

Meanwhile, Father fulfilled his promise and covered Fifth Son's medical expenses at Cragmor, not only for six months (as he had originally pledged) but for more than a year. Moreover, Father also financed the remainder of Fifth Son's undergraduate education. In 1936, once Fifth Son was finally discharged from Cragmor, rather than returning to Penn, he transferred to Colorado College in Colorado Springs. With Father's approval and financial support, he took his junior and senior years of college there and graduated with his BA in June 1938.[69]

In anticipation of Fifth Son's return to Shanghai, Father cautioned his older sons to be sensitive to his feelings and not demand too much from him at work. As Father put it in a note to Second Son, Fifth Son "is inclined to be sentimental so we have to be careful about what we say so that his feelings will not be hurt. When he does come back, I shall find him some easy and healthy job to do."[70] Once back in Shanghai, Fifth Son seems to have been treated as Father proposed. He was given less taxing and lower level positions than those held by his four older brothers, and in later years, when his brothers were made top executives in the family firm, he did not receive one of these high-level appointments.

From Independence to Dependence

Fifth Son's relationship with Father calls attention to both the pervasiveness and limitations of independence as a goal for children in the Liu family. On the one hand, it shows that Father valued independence even for a son who was not physically strong, not high in the birth order, and not a likely candidate for a position of leadership in the family or the family firm. In fact, it suggests that Father was probably not exaggerating when he told Fifth Son that he wanted all of his sons to become independent thinkers and decision makers who would treat him as a friend and a "democratic leader" of the family, not an autocratic patriarch.

On the other hand, Fifth Son's experience also shows that a son in the Liu family did not necessarily make the transition from dependent child to independent adult once and for all. When he made the decision to transfer from Baldwin-Wallace to Penn contrary to Father's advice, he received Father's congratulations for taking an independent stance. But after he had a medical relapse, he lost this independence and reverted to a state of childlike abject dependence on Father.

Of all the Liu children, Fifth Son was perhaps the most dependent on Father because of his ill health, but his total loss of self-confidence when he thought he was in danger of losing Father's backing raises a question about all of his brothers and sisters: Did any of them ever dare to make a decision that would have jeopardized Father's financial support for them? In Eldest Son's acrimonious arguments with Father, he had not faced this problem because Father had never threatened to cut off funding for his education. For that matter, all of the Liu children had a sense of financial security while abroad because of Father's general practice of depositing lump sums in their names at banks in the countries where they studied. Nonetheless, they all knew that Father could change these arrangements at any time, so whenever they took issue with him about a serious matter, they were well aware that their financial future might ultimately be on the line. Two of them, Third Son and Eldest Daughter, had to decide whether to run this risk in choosing their marriage partners.

6

A Son Who Proposed Marriage
to a Westernized Woman

BESIDES closely monitoring their children's health, education, and careers, Father and Mother set a firm rule for their children's personal lives: Do not marry a foreigner. In 1929, when Father sent off Second, Third, and Fourth Sons—the first of his children to go abroad for their educations—he strongly emphasized this point not only to them but to their English guardian, Alfred Ballard. Father had F. N. Matthews, his British business associate in Shanghai, send a formal letter of instructions to Ballard, who was a senior partner in the London office of the same firm. In this letter, Matthews clearly specified the kind of social life the boys should lead. On the one hand, Father insisted (as reported by Matthews) that his sons "have to enter social life as much as possible," and he set no rules against smoking or drinking: "There is no objection to their indulgences in these things in moderation." On the other hand, Father left no room for negotiation about the ban against marrying Westerners. "A point of utmost importance is that they must not marry European girls; each one had given his word that he will not do so, and it is earnestly hoped that they will escape entanglements."[1] As Father and Mother subsequently sent more children abroad one after another, Father made the same point to each one.[2]

In specifying such a flat rule, Father did not leave room for his children to reach their own independent conclusions and debate with him on the subject of marriage as they had done over business policies, choices of schools, and plans for careers. But when Third Son became the first of the Liu children to make a marriage proposal, he seized the initiative, acted without his parents' approval, and tried to convince them to negotiate with him on this decision too.

The Groom

From an early age, Third Son developed a reputation as a ladies' man. While still a teenager, he became known as "the happy-go-lucky boy of St. Johns [University]" in Shanghai, according to Fourth Son.[3] He grew into a handsome young man—by all accounts the best looking of the Liu boys. He had fine facial features and a disarming grin that made him seem more approachable than his brothers at Cambridge. He also had an attractive physique, slender and graceful, with "long limbs and great height," as Fourth Son characterized him.[4] Over six feet tall, he showed off his lanky frame by wearing fashionable clothes. As may be seen in photographs from 1929–30, his wardrobe included bespoke three-piece suits, tennis whites, and casual sports wear (which seemed even more casual in his photograph because of the cigarette that dangled from his fingertips).

Well aware that members of the opposite sex found him attractive, he freely admitted to Father that he was also attracted to them, including Western as well as Chinese women. "I'll now tell you what we say about women," Third Son announced in a letter to Father on September 27, 1932, after living for three years in England. He acknowledged that "there are exceptional cases, but generally speaking it is unnatural for men not to be fond of women. I am not ashamed to say that I am not one of these exceptions." While openly proclaiming his fondness for women, Third Son admitted that he had little experience with them. At age twenty-one, he acknowledged to Father: "Perhaps I am too young now even to think about women & talk to you like I am doing now. But secret thoughts lead to secret deeds, so I may just as well be frank about it."[5]

He was willing to be even more candid with Father, he said, than with other men. "It is idle to talk about women with other men without being frank in our conversations. But if one is too frank people will think that one is giving oneself away. I always want to be frank to you, and I don't mind even if I do give myself away in my conversations with us, as I know we have a good understanding of each other in all matters."[6] Confident that Father would understand, he revealed his own feelings and frustrations.

Third Son admitted that he had been tempted to take a romantic interest in Western women in England. He acknowledged that Chinese men who did not succumb to this temptation had a moral basis for their resistance, and he reported, with pride, that his fellow Chinese in England had married Western women less often than Chinese in the United States had done. "Compared with Chinese students in America, students in Britain who bring foreign wives back to home are very few. This of course I must attribute to the good morals of the Chinese students in this country." He noted that a few Chinese men lost control of themselves and fell in love with Western women, but he did not summarily condemn them for it. "I must say that not every one of them should be blamed, because there are times when young men of 20 to 26 feel rather lonely alone. Especially in a place like London, the temptation is great."[7] When he wrote these words, he was twenty-one, making him a member of this age group, and readily identified with the ones who succumbed to London's temptations. "Of course," he told Father, "a lot depends on one's self-control, but sometimes the worldly temptations might be beyond one's self-control." Recognizing the depths of their yearnings, he acknowledged: "I really have sympathy for some of them."

While candidly describing his own yearnings to Father, Third Son pledged unequivocally not to violate his parents' ban on marrying foreigners. "There is one thing," he told Father, "of which I can assure you that you need not be afraid of. That is, I am not going to marry a foreign wife." As he saw it, the candidates for a foreign wife fell into two categories. In one category were "cheap girls," who were of no interest to him. In the other category were "nice girls." "There are nice girls in England," he told Father, "but most of them come from good families," and these nice girls kept their distance from Chinese men like himself. "Most of the good class of girls here who are pretty, are as a rule very snobbish and extremely proud." With such snobbish English girls, neither he nor his brothers had any contact. "So," he assured Father, "you need have no fear about us getting too intimate with foreign girls here."[8]

Father was not entirely convinced by such reassurances, especially after rumors reached Shanghai about his sons' romantic involvements with women in England. In early 1933, less than a year after hearing from Third Son about the boys' sexual frustrations, Father went so far as to recruit a Chinese policeman, Yao Zhenmo, to investigate his sons' personal lives. He contacted Yao, an assistant commissioner with the Shanghai Municipal Police, when he heard that Yao was to be sent abroad to conduct a study of police forces in England, the United States, and other Western countries. Father and Yao had been friends since they had been classmates at St. John's University in Shanghai, so it was easy for Father to prevail on Yao to visit his sons in England and look into the rumors about their romances.[9]

In May 1933, Father wrote to his sons, instructing them to greet Yao on his arrival and take him in as a guest. He told Second Son "to meet him at Southampton upon his arrival, to give him accommodation at your house, and to accord him every courtesy and hospitality during his brief sojourn in England, so that he will not find himself a stranger in a foreign country.[10] Following these instructions, the boys welcomed Yao and gave him their full cooperation. They were curious about his work and impressed by his reception in England, where the London newspapers dubbed him "the Chinese Sherlock Holmes."[11]

On their involvement with women, the boys willingly allowed Yao to question them, and they gave direct answers. Fourth Son remarked to Father: "You could not attest a better man than Mr. Yao to discuss with us openly and freely the two major questions which hitherto have troubled your mind, namely the question of our friendship with girls and the question of our returning home. Knowing how sincere and trustworthy he was we disclosed our whole hearts to him on the spot."[12]

The boys were willing to speak freely to Yao because they agreed with Father that they ran the risk of being tempted by women while they were away from home. As Third Son conceded to Father: "No doubt the biggest risk to which we are exposed while out of touch with our parents, is women. We have no one to guide us in this matter while we are in this country and it is only natural that you want to be cautious and are rather inclined to be suspicious after hearing the stories which your friends may have told you about us, no matter how unfounded they are."[13]

While denying that he and his brothers were involved with women, Third Son readily admitted that he had women on his mind. "I am not altogether disinterested in women, in fact I am very fond of them and I am afraid too fond of some of them. But at the same time I wish to think that I have self-respect and some self-control not to lose my head over any woman who may appear to be attractive to me. I know there is little chance for me to make girl friends in this country and am trying, to the best of my abilities, to get them off my mind."[14]

Whether or not Third Son could get women off his mind, he and his brothers convinced Yao that they had not had affairs with women. After Yao's exhaustive interrogation of them, Third Son proudly reported to Father: "We have told him everything you want to know. I think when he returns [from London to Shanghai] he will be able to clear any suspicion that you may have in your mind."[15]

As Third Son anticipated, Father's suspicions were cleared away by Yao's report. As soon as Yao returned to Shanghai, Father invited him to spend an evening in the Lius' home reporting on his investigation of Second, Third, and Fourth Sons, and Father found Yao's report fully satisfying. As Father wrote to Second Son on August 18, Yao "spoke to me very highly of your scholastic achievement, your athletic aptitude, your frugal way of making your living in England, and above all your gentleman-like manner and conduct."[16]

Father was pleased to receive this news about his sons, but he took the occasion to emphasize once again that they must closely confer with Mother and himself about any of their plans for marriage. He delivered this message to each of the three, and he made his most forceful statement to Third Son. "A young man of your age," he wrote to Third Son in August, "may have the freedom to choose his ideal mate among his female acquaintances, but before he commits himself, it is to his own interest to consult his parents" In his references to a young man, Father clearly had Third Son in mind, but to eliminate any possible ambiguity, he gave Third Son a direct order: "Your Mother and I should be fully and frankly informed and consulted before you commit yourself definitely on this matter [of any prospects for matrimony]."[17]

Third Son heeded Father's warnings as he completed his degree in law at Cambridge University in 1934 and went home for six months before returning to Cambridge to take the bar exam in 1935. But his counseling from Father, both by letter during his five years in England and in person during his six months in Shanghai, by no means curtailed his interest in foreign as well as Chinese women. In February 1935, as he traveled via the United States back to England, he became fascinated by sex in America, especially in New York City. "For the last six days before we sailed for England," he wrote to Father on February 16, 1935, from on board S. S. *Berengaria* on the Cunard line, that he and Second

Son "spent practically all our time seeing pictures and shows in this gay city of America. We saw a number of Burlesque shows, where they show nake[d] girls on the stage. This kind of entertainment is not to be seen anywhere else except Paris. After spending so much time seeing shows in New York we shall find the London theatres rather uninteresting."[18]

Third Son was struck not only by the naked girls on stage in New York but also by the American attitude toward sex. "It is amazing," he wrote to Father, "how the Americans exploit the beauty of their females and make a business of it. Sex is so much talked about by every one. The importance of sex is undoubtedly over emphasized in America like in many other western countries, although I must say we Chinese on the whole rather seem to have ignored its quality altogether." Chinese needed to recognize the importance of sex as Americans did, Third Son declared, so that Chinese women would develop more shapely bodies and would make themselves seem more attractive to Chinese men who had seen Western women on their travels abroad. "So few of our girls realise the force of their physical attractiveness," he pointed out to Father. "This is why to most return students from abroad Chinese girls look much less appealing. It is not only the powder and lipsticks which make a woman look beautiful but also a good health and a fine physic [physique]."[19]

Third Son perhaps underestimated the attention that was given to women's bodies in China during the 1930s. In beauty contests, movie magazines, advertisements, and other popular media, women's bodies were on display.[20] But according to Third Son, even in Shanghai, the fashion capital of China, the women generally had not become aware of this need to develop their bodies. "The fashionable girls in Shanghai who do so much to copy the beauty treatment of the West do not seem to realise that." The only "encouraging sign" was "that the schools are now beginning to take games as a part of the training for students."[21]

Third Son realized that his fondness for women and his preoccupation with sex posed a potential problem for his parents. Of all the Liu boys, he was the one most likely to lose his self-control, become involved with a foreign woman, and break the family's rule. As he wrote to Father on February 16, 1935, while en route to England, "you will admit that of all your sons, I am the most restless and wild." Yet, even while he made this admission, which was hardly news to Father, he went on to say in the very next sentence: "Well, I can tell you that even I have a very strong desire to settle down sometimes."[22]

This was news. In fact, it was much bigger news than Father could have imagined, for by then Third Son had already met the woman he intended to marry.

The Bride

In the fall of 1934, during his six-month visit to Shanghai, Third Son met Liane Yen. He was twenty-three, and she was sixteen. At their first meeting, which was arranged and chaperoned by her brother, they went horseback riding. They enjoyed each other's company, but Third Son did not pursue the relationship at that time because his parents did not react favorably to the idea of the match. In particular, Father and Mother had three objections. They considered her and her family too Westernized, too wealthy, and too open to the idea of divorce.

On the first count, Liane was ethnically Chinese, but her mother's natal family (named Huang as pronounced in Mandarin and Oei as pronounced in their native Hokkien dialect) had unquestionably been oriented to the West longer and more fully than the Lius had been. In the mid-nineteenth century, Liane's great-grandfather on her mother's side had taken the family's first step away from China by emigrating from his hometown of Xiamen (Amoy), Fujian Province, in southeastern China, to Java, then a Dutch colony.[23] As a first-generation overseas Chinese, he retained some links with China, but when he died in 1900, his son (Liane's grandfather) decisively reoriented the family to the West. As Liane's aunt later recalled, the death of the elder man "liberated us" because it allowed the family members to make their first trip to Europe. "I doubt if he [Liane's grandfather] would have gone to Europe while his father lived. To my grandfather, China was the world. But my father [Liane's grandfather], now the head of the Oei family, was of a different mind. He visited China, but it held no particular pull for him."[24]

While indifferent toward China, Liane's grandfather embraced European cultural practices and went to great lengths to identify himself and his household with the West. As Lynn Pan has noted, "he dressed himself in European style (always in colonial whites, down to his handmade shoes) and in so doing defied the Dutch ruling that all Chinese in Java wear Chinese clothes. He was the first Chinese in Java to cut off his queue, and by employing the finest lawyer in the colony, a Dutch baron, to argue his case he got the authorities to grant him freedom of residence and to agree to his moving out of the Chinese ghetto and into the European section of town."[25] Affecting a persona as Western as any Westerner, he gave Western educations to his children, especially to his first wife's offspring.

Liane's grandmother was her grandfather's first wife. She came from a Chinese family that had resided in Java for ten generations, and she had been given in marriage to Liane's grandfather as soon as she had turned fifteen. She bore two daughters, Liane's mother and aunt, and no sons. By the time these two daughters were teenagers, Liane's grandmother had become estranged from her husband largely because of his insatiable desire for other women, including eighteen acknowledged concubines, who bore a total of forty-two children.[26] She only continued to live with her husband in Java until she had married her elder daughter (Liane's mother) to the son of a distinguished Chinese family in Indonesia, Kan Ting-liang (Jian Dingliang in Mandarin), who had just returned from completing his education in Holland.[27] Like Liane's mother, Kan spoke English and French as well as Dutch, and when Liane's grandmother packed up her daughter and moved permanently to Europe, he readily went along.

Liane grew up in an even more Western setting than her parents had. Her older brother, Bobby Kan, had been born in Java before his grandmother took him and his parents to Europe, but Liane herself was born in London, and she and her brother were raised there, traveling frequently from their bases in London and Paris (where her parents had a flat) to other European cities. Like her parents, she learned Western languages, including fluent English and French, and in Europe she moved in high social circles. For example, in 1935, China's minister to England presented her, at age seventeen, at the court of King George V and Queen Mary at Buckingham Palace.

In light of Liane's childhood in Europe, Father and Mother had reason to consider her "Westernized," but while such a characterization had some validity, it was an oversimplification. Besides speaking Western languages as a child, Liane also learned Chinese, and she spoke Hokkien, her maternal family's native Chinese dialect, with her grandmother, who never learned more than a few phrases of any European language. Moreover, in 1930, at age eleven, Liane moved with her mother and grandmother to China and lived in Beijing and Shanghai during the early 1930s. So by the time she met Third Son in 1934, she had spent four years in China speaking Chinese and becoming familiar with the country, especially the Lius' hometown, Shanghai.

If the Lius' characterization of Liane as Westernized was overly simple, their characterization of her as extraordinarily wealthy was irrefutable. She and her family were generously financed by their fabulously rich maternal grandfather, known as the Sugar King of Java. According to a recent assessment, he had become "the single richest individual in the Indies."[28] In 1919, shortly before Liane's birth, when Liane's grandmother, with her daughters, son-in-law, and new grandson, moved from Java to London, Liane's grandmother set them all up in lavish quarters. In Lynn Pan's summary, "she bought a mansion in Wimbledon filled with English antique furniture, and a house in Brooke Street, near the celebrated hotel Claridge's. They lived in considerable style, maintaining a Rolls-Royce and a Daimler, and when, every now and then, Mrs. Oei [Liane's grandmother] sent her husband a telegram saying 'Send four,' he would know to remit £4,000."[29]

Drawing on these seemingly inexhaustible resources, Liane and her family grew accustomed to leading lives of luxury. Even after her grandfather died in 1924, they never had to worry about their finances because they were heirs to his estate, which at his death was valued at 200 million Dutch guilders.[30] In 1930, when they first moved to China, they stayed in Beijing at a two-hundred-room imperial palace that Liane's grandfather had bought for Liane's aunt.[31] Moving to Shanghai, they occupied an apartment that was figuratively, if not literally, palatial. Eventually, during the Japanese war and the postwar period, Liane's grandfather's successor—one of his sons—lost control of his business empire, but in the 1930s, when Liane met Third Son, the Oei family's fortune still seemed boundless.

If, according to Third Son's parents' charges, Liane was culturally Westernized and astonishingly wealthy, was she also tainted by divorce? For all her grandfather's eighteen concubines, her grandmother never divorced him, and the Lius expressed no criticisms of her grandparents' marital arrangements. The Lius were concerned about Liane's mother rather than her grandmother. In the early 1930s, Liane's mother divorced her first husband, Kan Ting-liang. Her estrangement began as early as 1930, when Liane and her mother and grandmother were still living in England. Her aunt later recalled: "I knew all was not going well with my sister and her husband, and I had heard rumors she was seeing other men." Apparently giving up on the marriage, Liane's father returned from England to his natal family in Java, and the couple was divorced. Soon thereafter he died.[32]

In the early 1930s, Liane's mother remarried. By that time, she had left England, staying briefly at Liane's aunt's palace in Beijing, and settled in Shanghai, where she met and married Dr. U. Y. Yen. Liane's mother was then in her late thirties, and Yen was in his early fifties. A graduate of St. John's University in Shanghai, class of 1904, Yen had served in Chinese diplomatic delegations in the United States, and after marrying Liane's mother, he became semiretired, spending most of his time on academic pursuits as a private scholar. Once remarried, Liane's mother changed her daughter's name from Liane Kan to Liane Yen.[33]

Born in the West, accustomed to luxurious living, raised by a divorcee—was Liane Yen a suitable bride for Third Son? After mulling over the question for a year, Third Son decided that she was the one for him, and he proposed to her.

The Proposal

After Third Son was first introduced to Liane Yen in Shanghai in August 1934, he heard his parents' objections to her, and he continued for the next year, as always, to assure them that he would not propose marriage to anyone without consulting them. Even when Liane followed him from Shanghai via the United States to England, he gave his parents the impression that he had no special interest in her. On March 31, 1935, two days after she arrived in England, he reported to Father in a matter-of-fact way that "as promised I went to the ship to meet her." Minimizing his connection with her compared to that of others, he pointed out: "She is now in the charge of her cousin and her governess," and he noted that the next day she was visited by Second Son, not himself.[34]

While informing Father that he had greeted Liane merely as a matter of protocol, he went to great lengths to assure Mother that he had no romantic interest in the young woman. "Miss Yen arrived in this country two days ago," he wrote to Mother on the same day. "I have already seen her. You need not worry that there is anything between us. We are just friends and nothing more." If he and Liane had been more than just friends, he would not have hesitated to tell Mother, he said. "You will be informed when I have a love affair. But at present there is no reason to encourage even a suggestion."[35]

In the meantime, he gratefully accepted Mother's offer to find a bride for him. "I want to thank you for your offer to help me to pick a really nice girl to be my wife. I can assure you that I have great respect for your opinion. Don't hesitate to let me know when you have picked your choice." At the same time, he confided to her that he had already spent time with several women of his own choosing. "Of course I welcome your advice and will always give it consideration. But I may tell you that I am not altogether inexperienced in offering my friendship to girls. I regard the problem of my marriage very seriously and will not allow myself to take one wrong step in this matter. So you need not worry about me falling in love with any girl." Without forming any attachments, Third Son was eager to play the field. "I don't see why I shouldn't know as many girls as I like so that I can choose the best."[36]

As Third Son presented it, the question of marriage in his case was entirely hypothetical because it would not be settled until some time in the distant future. While welcoming Mother's advice, he pointed out that with all of her sons still unmarried, she should be more immediately concerned with finding wives for Eldest Son and Second Son because they preceded him in birth order. "You better talk things over with eldest brother first," he recommended, noting that "my turn comes next after second brother." For the foreseeable future, he claimed to be thinking only about general standards for choosing a bride, not about any particular woman. "If you are as particular as I am you will either get no one at all, or get a really first class one, or if you go too far in your demand for the best you will probably be rewarded with a girl of very poor standard."[37]

Still setting standards at this very abstract level, he took the fatalistic position that his prospective bride would appear on her own, and he urged Mother to relax and accept whatever was to come. "There is so much chance and risk in marriage. So it is really no good to worry about it too much. She will either come or not, if she will come, I shall get her one day. If she will not come, I shall lead an independent life until she changes her mind!"[38] Faced with these unpredictable future possibilities, he insisted that neither he nor Mother should worry about his marital prospects.

During the spring of 1935, Third Son replied to his parents' concern about Eldest Son's lack of marital prospects by assuring them that Eldest Son should by all means marry before his younger brothers did. In April, on Eldest Son's return to Shanghai after four years in the United States, Father had written to Second and Third Sons in England: "Our only concern today is with his [Eldest Son's] matrimonial problem. He seems to be very apathetic toward it all. However I think he will be brought to understand the essence of a married life."[39] On June 3, Third Son replied: "At his [Eldest Son's] age [twenty-six] it becomes natural for people to ask the question of his marriage. I wonder if he has already made some new captures. It is high time that he should settle down to be a family man."[40]

Third Son did not claim that finding a wife was easy. He suggested to Father that Eldest Son and other Chinese men of his generation all had to deal with new, even unprecedented, issues. He acknowledged that "these days marriage is a difficult problem to solve and most young men seem to be afraid of facing it. The excuse is usually made on the scarcity of good and sensible young women, in this age. But one should not be so particular," he concluded. "It is better not to make any excuse and face the problem bravely. In a world like this everyone thinks that he or she is too good for the other."[41]

In wrestling with the problem of how to find a spouse, Third Son expressed doubts about whether the modern approach was superior to the traditional one, at least for the purpose of making marriages. "I am not at all sure," he admitted to Father, "whether it is not better to have the matrimonial question decided by the parents as in the olden days." But his double negative suggests that he was at best ambivalent on this issue, and he observed that whether or not marriages arranged by parents were better, "this practice will not work today satisfactorily. Young people have too much to say in this matter today."[42] Taking into account the context of his own time, Third Son adopted the position that Eldest Son and other young people (including himself) should choose their own marriage partners rather than leave the decision to their parents.

Despite Third Son's insistence that his own marriage plans lay in the distant future, well beyond Eldest Son's plans, Mother objected to his relationship with Liane and recommended other candidates to him. Dismissing Liane out of hand, she described for him, among others, one Miss Fong, and compared her favorably with another young woman,

Miss Hong, whom Third Son had met in Europe. "Miss Fong," Mother wrote to him, "is a strong rival to Miss Hong in beauty and grace, though I have not yet seen her myself."[43] Based on hearsay, this recommendation probably had little effect on Third Son, who expressed no interest in Miss Fong. But it shows Mother's determination to divert his attention away from Liane in the spring of 1935 while he was still claiming that he and Liane were just friends.

In August, Third Son announced to his parents that he and Liane had become much more than friends and that he had proposed marriage to her. In maintaining that they had been just friends for nearly a year, he had been telling the truth, he said, because he had spent the year thinking about it before coming to a final decision. "Strange as it may be," he wrote to Father on August 9, "even a little over a month ago I never contemplated this. This does not mean that I have been in any way rash in arriving at my decision, on the contrary I have been slowly making up my mind since I was in Shanghai." During the past year, since he had returned to England from Shanghai, he had harbored doubts, and only recently had his conversations with Liane eliminated them. As he summarized for Father his change of heart since his departure from Shanghai: "I was not sure of my own feeling, at that time. Now things are different. Miss Yen has visited this country [England] twice [in March from China via the United States and in August from Germany] and I met her again. We made sure of our affection for each other."[44] Not until then, after he had proposed to Liane and she had accepted his proposal, did Third Son write to his parents and seek their approval of this decision.

Although his proposal was a fait accompli, Third Son pleaded with his parents for their approval, and he became impatient when it did not come immediately by telegram from Shanghai to England. In August he wrote to Father: "I am now still awaiting your consent with great eagerness as you may well understand. I hope I shall have received your cable before this reaches you." Third Son claimed to have approached his decision exactly as his parents would have wanted, and he thought that he had left them with only one reasonable option—to give their blessing. "My sensibleness, my patience and my precaution deserve every consideration and encouragement. You can hardly refuse to give your approval to my proposal."[45]

If Third Son honestly believed that both his parents could hardly refuse to approve his proposal, he was immediately proven wrong.

From Mother, he received a flat refusal to give her blessing. From Father, he heard nothing directly at first. Indirectly, through Fourth Son (who was living in Shanghai with Father and Mother), he heard that Father approved of his proposal to Liane. But when he received not a word directly from Father, who was a prolific letter writer, he found it unnerving. On August 27, two and a half weeks after he had first informed Father of his proposal to Liane, he wrote to Father that he was "greatly surprised that in spite of the many letters and the cable which I have sent to you, you have not directly expressed to me one word of your opinion on this matter." No longer assuming that he would receive an unqualified endorsement from his parents, he acknowledged that he had heard that members of the Liu family were making arguments against his proposal. "I am not totally blind to the fact that there are many objections in my family to my engagement and I would not say that these objections are entirely without ground from the more conservative point of view." Third Son identified the conservative point of view with Mother rather than Father, and in writing to Father, he did not bother to deal with her position on the issue except to say: "Mother has already expressed her strong objections. I hope you will not allow Mother's objection to come in our way."[46]

Quite apart from Mother's objections, Third Son addressed Father's concern that Liane's rich family members might lure him away from his work in the Liu family business and seduce him into a life of luxury, leisure, and profligacy. In reply to this objection, Third Son was adamant. "As to your fear that after my marriage I might be tempted to move in a circle totally undesirable and different to that which I have been accustomed to," he replied to Father, "I wish to point out to you that I am a very strong minded person and not a man to be easily influenced or changed by circumstances. You can rest assured that much as I care for the girl I am going to marry, I shall still keep my domineering character and lead my own life."[47]

In Third Son's view, Father should set aside his fears about him selling out to Liane's family and should decide whether he was capable of selecting a good wife. "I maintain," he insisted to Father, "that so far [as] Liane is concerned I have not made a mistake in my judgment. You are reasonable and generous enough to credit me with a discretion of my own. I want to assure you that I have exercised my discretion with great care. There are many fine qualities which I see in the girl whom I have chosen to be my future wife. She is sensible, intelligent, well educated, young and healthy." Finding it hard to believe that Father would not trust his judgment and discretion, Third Son pleaded for an answer and came close to resorting to sarcasm. "I trust you will allow me the good sense of knowing what I am doing and hope you will write to me personally at least once to express to me your opinion on this matter."[48] Eventually, as Third Son undoubtedly realized, he would hear from Father on this subject not merely once but many times.

Father sent Third Son a telegram as well as letters. His telegram consisted of only two words: "Consent given."[49] Following up by letter, Father gave his assurance that he trusted Third Son's judgment and held Liane in high regard. "My dear Hannibal," he wrote, using Third Son's English name in a letter written in English, "you must not in any way be offended by what I had said. After all, I am your father and as such I naturally wish to see you marry the best girl in the world. I have stated my objections because I wish to warn you against future unhappiness and inconveniences. That Liane is a good girl I am fully convinced now, having heard so much about her from Julius, Johnson, and yourself [Second, Third, and Fourth Sons]. I shall never regret that I have given you my consent to your engagement with her as long as you two can be blissfully happy together."[50]

Father had refrained from sending his consent to Third Son sooner, he explained, not because he was withholding it but because he was trying to avoid unwanted publicity. "You must have been very much puzzled by my silence," he wrote to Third Son and other sons, "on the subject of Hannibal's proposed engagement with Liane. I have not written to you personally and expressed my opinions because all my private correspondences have to be filed at Lieu Ong Kee [the Liu family's accounts office], and I do not desire the news to leak out prematurely. This explains why I had been talking to you on the subject indirectly through Johnson." Father urged Third Son to avoid publicity too. He and Liane should be discreet about both the proposal and the wedding. "The best thing for you to do," he advised them, "will be to get married quietly in London, thereby you will not only obviate much undesirable publicity but also affect a large economy in the cost of wedding celebrations."[51] As long as their proposal and wedding were kept quiet, Father was willing to give them his blessing.

Mother, by contrast, adamantly refused to approve of Third Son's proposal, much less his wedding. Father took Mother's opposition seriously and conveyed to Third Son how important it was. "Ever since I received the first intimation from you," Father wrote to Third Son, "I have been seriously worrying as to how best to secure your mother's approval and support. You know as well as I do that in an important family event like marriage [the] mother usually plays a much more important part than [the] father. It is really unfortunate that your mother should have been so uncompromising in her views." She was particularly uncompromising, according to Father, on the question of whether Third Son should marry the daughter of a divorced woman. To Mother, "it is nothing short of a crime for any one to marry a girl, whose mother was divorced and got remarried. She told Johnson [Fourth Son] that nothing in the world would induce her to participate in a wedding ceremony when she had to acknowledge a woman like Mrs. Yen and a man like Mr. Yen to be her near relatives."[52]

If Third Son married Liane, Mother would withhold her blessing from the proposal and the wedding ceremony in the immediate future and would never condone the marriage no matter how long it lasted. "She has already intimated," Father wrote to Third Son, "that if ever you two were to get married she would like to wash her hands of the whole thing. So it is futile to argue with her any more."[53] Though refusing to argue with Mother on Third Son's behalf, Father agreed to contact Liane's mother and discuss with her how the Lius and Yens would deal with the couple's engagement.

The Engagement

Neither Father nor Mother was comfortable with the idea of an engagement. They considered it a Western custom that was alien to Chinese culture, and they cited the Yens' acceptance of it as an example of their uncritical adoption of Western practices. Nonetheless, Father was willing to help make arrangements for the engagement as long as the Yen family allowed him to do so on his own terms. To determine whether his and the Yens' attitudes toward the engagement were reconcilable, he convened a meeting in Shanghai with Dr. and Mrs. Yen, Liane's brother, Bobby Kan, and Fourth Son. Mother remained conspicuously absent.

On September 11, Father reported the results of the meeting by letter to Second and Third Sons in England. In Father's view, the occasion was a confrontation between families representing two fundamentally different cultures. "They know as well as we do," he said of the Yens, "that their customs and traditions are essentially different from ours, by reason of their being perpetually in close association with foreign people and their style of living." Separated by a yawning cultural chasm, the two families could not possibly come to any agreement, Father maintained, unless they subordinated all other concerns to Third Son's and Liane's interests as a couple. "I openly told them," Father reported in his conversation with the Yens, "that unless we both choose to ignore minor differences of views and opinions and to keep in mind only the happiness of our children we would inevitably come to an impasse. Both Dr. and Mrs. Yen acquiesced." With the couple's happiness as his focal point, Father made a specific proposal: Third Son and Liane should be married in England. He wanted the wedding to be held there, he said, because "it will serve to avoid much uneasy and awkward feelings which are bound to arise when East and West meet for the first time."[54] In this way, Father argued that holding the wedding in the West would, paradoxically, alleviate the Lius' fears that it might become too Westernized.

In another paradox, holding the wedding in the West would make it less expensive, according to Father. He preferred to have it in England, he told Mrs. Yen, because if it were held in Shanghai, it would grow into an extravaganza that would send the wrong message to the young couple. He reported to Second and Third Sons, "were the wedding to take place in Shanghai it would have to be made elaborate and luxurious." He told Mrs. Yen that it should be held in London so that the parents of the couple could instill "the idea of thrift into the minds of young people prior to their leading their own independent life."[55]

Despite Father's implicit criticisms of the Yens for their conspicuous consumption, Dr. and Mrs. Yen did not confront him or take issue with his proposals. In response to Father, Mrs. Yen made only one additional proposal concerning the engagement. She suggested that two engagement parties be held simultaneously, one in London and one in Shanghai. When Father did not object, Mrs. Yen, Father reported, "proposed that the announcement be made about Christmas time when everybody is bound to feel jolly and happy."[56]

Father felt that this suggestion gave further evidence of Mrs. Yen's orientation to the West rather than China. "As such a procedure is practically unknown to the Chinese people," he remarked, "it is only to be published in the local English Newspapers."[57] Though still troubled by the Yens' preference for Western ways, Father came to a tentative agreement with them about the engagement. Some details remained to be worked out, but Father, Mrs. Yen, and her husband left these to the families' two young representatives: Bobby Kan and Fourth Son.

After the meeting, Father reported to Third Son that he had done his best but confessed that he and Mother still had misgivings about the marriage. "My dear Hannibal," he wrote, "I think that I have done all I can to make things easy for you as well as for our family. You have to realize that to your mother and to some extent myself this marriage is not exactly a perfect and ideal one. I was only persuaded to give you my consent because I knew you have always been sensible and intelligent and that you must have some very sound reasons to have fallen in love with a girl like Liane." Father was willing to put aside his doubts about the marriage because of his faith in Third Son's judgment, but Mother refused to be so accommodating. As Father reminded Third Son on September 11, even after Father and the Yens had agreed to give their approval, "there still remains the question of getting your mother's approval. So far my own and your brother's persuasions have all failed."[58] These failures did not, in Father's estimation, mean that Third Son had no hope of ever winning over Mother, but Third Son's ultimate hope lay in his willingness to make his own appeal to her.

Father repeatedly reminded Third Son that he had never introduced Mother to Liane or consulted her about Liane in person or by letter before announcing his engagement. "I deeply regret," he wrote to Third Son on September 26, that Mother was not "given an opportunity of seeing Liane and getting to know her well when you were all in Shanghai. If I am not mistaken, your mother is one of those people who are easily influenced by insinuating remarks and occasional exhibitions of friendliness or respect coming forth from anyone. You might feel more inclined to excuse her present obduracy if you consider the fact that she had never seen Liane in her life."[59]

Third Son's best chance was to address Mother's objections directly and in detail, Father said. Only in this way could Third Son use his influence with Mother to his full advantage. "I do not believe," Father wrote to Second and Third Sons, "that she is deaf to reasons altogether. If I am not wrong, Hannibal with his ready eloquence and quick wit has had more influence over her than any one else in the family. If he will bring his advantages to bear on her this time he has a great chance to meet with success. Therefore I strongly advise him to write to her directly (preferably in Chinese) and explain to her in details why and how he had fallen in love with Liane." At the same time, Father urged Second Son to write Mother about Third Son's marriage proposal. "I am sure Julius [Second Son]," he told Second and Third Sons, "with his reputation for being steady and sound in his judgment will be able to lend him a useful and effective hand. This is rather a pressing matter and I do hope you will accomplish it before long."[60]

Mother's principal objections to the marriage concerned Liane's presumed attitude toward divorce and money. Although Mother had not met Liane, she was convinced that Liane would be as open to the prospect of divorce as her mother and aunt were. "Judging from her occasional remarks on the subject," Father wrote about Mother to Third Son, "her objections to your marriage with Liane are based more on the dubious matrimonial careers of her aunt and to a less extent her mother than on the character of the girl herself. Of Liane she professed her complete ignorance." Without taking a position on the issue himself, Father wrote to Third Son that Mother, "whether rightly or wrongly, is obsessed with the idea that bad blood runs in the family. She is so afraid that your matrimonial career too might go on the rocks."[61]

In response to Father's suggestion, Second and Third Sons both wrote letters to Mother in Chinese. Each of them addressed one of her major concerns; Second Son discussed Liane's attitude toward divorce, and Third Son described her attitude toward money. Second Son, writing on September 22, urged Mother to distinguish between Liane's mother and Liane herself. He did not deny that Mrs. Yen had done the wrong thing by divorcing one man and marrying another, but "What," he pointedly asked, did Liane "have to do with her mother's marrying for a second time? She was then probably only five years old, and how could she have stopped that?" If, as a little girl, Liane had no way to stop her mother's second marriage, she did find ways to express her opposition to it as a young woman, Second Son reported. "Both Miss Yen and her older brother strongly opposed the second marriage, and have both suffered much because of it. They have never called Mr. Yen 'Daddy.'"[62]

Faced with this family breakdown, Liane deserved Mother's sympathy, not her scorn. "She herself also knows the big mistake her mother has made," Second Son wrote to Mother. This mistake was certainly not Liane's fault, and it probably was no one's fault. "People's fortunes or misfortunes usually come from heaven anyway, and there's nothing anyone could have done for Miss Yen."[63]

Mother needed to judge Liane for who she was, quite apart from her family, Second Son told Mother, and in her own right, she was a fine person. "I myself," Second Son said, "have come to know Miss Yen quite well. According to my observation, she is really a very knowledgeable person and she understands the world well." Second Son reminded Mother how rare it was to find a suitable marriage partner who was as educated and sensitive as Liane. "Proper girls are hard to find, especially those from rich families. Miss Yen is fluent in English, French, and German, and no ordinary female college graduate can begin to compare to what she knows. Due to her unhappy family life, she is very knowledgeable about everything, and is especially sensitive to the feelings of other human beings."[64]

Second Son drove his points home by scolding Mother for her narrow mindedness. "You are conservative in your thinking, and I understand how you feel," he somewhat patronizingly told her. "Most people from Ningbo [the Liu family's native place] think the same way as you do." While identifying Mother with the parochialism of people from Ningbo, he also accused her of having the superficiality of people from Shanghai. "Nowadays you Shanghai people behave worse and worse with every passing day," he said of Mother and everyone else in his hometown. "You only pay attention to people's outward appearances, and you don't know what's inside." If Mother took a closer look at Liane, she would see that "Third Son would be lucky to have her as his wife."

"Dear Mother," Second Son pleaded, becoming less confrontational and more deferential, "please think more about this." He reported to her that her refusal to give her blessing for the engagement had taken a heavy toll on Third Son, and he implored her to relent. "Your opposition to the engagement," he told her, had made Third Brother "deeply unhappy. Why can't you just let it go, so that everyone can be happy for him?"[65] This question Second Son posed on behalf of not only Third Son but the whole Liu family.

If Second Son left any doubt about Mother causing unhappiness, Third Son eliminated it. In his letter to her, he confirmed that he felt a deep need for Mother to give her approval for his engagement. "I know that I should have written earlier and reported everything about this marriage," he wrote to her apologetically on October 24. "But things were rather uncertain at the beginning and so I didn't want to trouble you. Now that you are feeling better about all this, I am writing to report to you and ask that you give your consent to my engagement. If I can have your blessing for my marriage, it will make me very happy."[66] Belatedly but earnestly, he begged for Mother's approval.

Knowing that Second Son had addressed Mother's fear of divorce, Third Son concentrated on her worries about Liane's attitude toward money. He readily agreed with Mother that he should not marry any woman who had been corrupted by her family's great wealth because, however rich any family might be, it could easily suffer from a reversal of fortunes in the unstable economic circumstances of the time. "As China is now undergoing political turmoil and commercial weakness," Third Son wrote, with the Great Depression sweeping through the economies of the world and with the danger of war looming on the horizon in East Asia, "it would certainly be very risky to marry a girl from a rich family who is lazy and self-indulgent. Since childhood, I've always benefited from your instruction and so I've learned about frugality. I will never lose sight of its importance." But in this case Third Son was taking no such risk, because Liane recognized the importance of frugality and was not lazy and self-indulgent. "I have often spoken to Miss Yen about frugality and how important it will be to our future happiness. Although she grew up in a rich family, she possesses innate goodness and understands very well what I mean. Mother, you may not believe this now, but as soon as we return home, you will find out that all this is true."[67]

Third Son admitted that Liane's mother spent money freely without concern for frugality, but he insisted that neither Liane nor he himself would adopt Liane's mother's values. "Miss Yen's way of thinking is very different from that of her mother, so you should not worry. I am my own man and will definitely not be swayed by my future in-laws, and whatever I tell Miss Yen to do, you can rest assured, Mother, that she will do it." Besides learning about frugality from Third Son, Liane had come to appreciate it on the basis of her own observations in the West.

"During her time abroad," Third Son reported, "she has seen many foreign women live a bitter life, spending every day at home, doing domestic chores, and never dreaming of enjoying the comfort that Chinese ladies have. After returning to China, she won't merely be a self-indulgent girl."[68] Liane would not lead a profligate life for all these reasons: her innate good sense, her attentiveness to Third Son's advice, and her awareness of the importance of frugality in the West as well as China.

Third Son wrote this letter to Mother in Chinese as Father suggested, and besides appealing directly to her in it, he devised a devious scheme to appeal to her indirectly. His plan was to involve Mother in his wedding preparations by luring her into picking out Liane's engagement ring. To carry out this plan, he contacted Fourth Son, who was living with Father and Mother in Shanghai, and told him to talk Mother into helping him pick out the ring. As Third Son explained to Fourth Son, the ring needed to be bought in China, not Europe, because "it is Liane's own choice that the ring should be of Chinese jade. She wants a lump of jade of oval shape like a pebble which can be mounted on a ring in England so that you don't have to worry about the size of her finger. I hope you will get a really good stone for this purpose and try to get some people to take some trouble in choosing it."[69]

The search for fine jade might capture Mother's imagination, Third Son pointed out to Fourth Son, and it might even entice her to lend her support to his engagement. "If you can enlist Mother's help it will be all the better. It might be a good move to influence Mother favourably to my side. Our mother is not without a sense of humour, and if you ask her to choose the ring in the same way as you would ask her to give you a piece of cake, you might succeed." To appeal to Mother's sense of humor, Third Son suggested that Fourth Son set a lighthearted tone. "If possible and convenient get the jeweler to come to the house first. Do you remember how I managed to persuade mother to give the Christmas cake over to our younger brothers and sisters? If you don't make your request too seriously, Mother is more likely to concede." Rather than giving instructions that were too specific, Third Son encouraged Fourth Son to devise his own strategy for luring Mother into the hunt for the jade engagement ring. "You are the master of tactics," he told Fourth Son. "I leave you to employ the method that you think is best."[70]

Unfortunately for Third Son, these carefully conceived plans did not persuade Mother to approve his engagement. Neither his direct appeals nor his devious schemes nor his help from Father, Second Son, Fourth Son, and other family members persuaded her to give her blessing. But even without Mother's consent, Third Son prevailed on Father to make arrangements for the couple's engagement party.

Father wanted Third Son and Liane to hold their engagement party at the Chinese embassy in London, and he wrote directly to Ambassador Guo Taiqi (a.k.a. Quo Tai chi and Kuo Tai-chi), China's first diplomat to hold the rank of ambassador in England. (England had raised the status of China's top diplomat there from minister to ambassador in 1933 at the same time Guo had been appointed to the post.)[71] "I am writing," Father explained in a formal request to Ambassador Guo, on September 25, "to entreat the favour of your presence at the engagement of my son Hannibal N. L. Lieu and Miss Liane Yen, the daughter of Mr. and Mrs. U. Y. Yen, on Saturday, December 21st. I shall feel truly grateful if you will be kind enough to be the officiator of the ceremony."[72] Father made this request (quoted here in its entirety) on behalf of Liane's parents and himself. Notably, he made no mention of Mother.

Following Father's lead, Third Son paid a visit to Ambassador Guo and invited him to the engagement party, but contrary to Father's wishes, Third Son did not arrange for the party to be held at the Chinese embassy in London. "I thought," he explained to Father on October 27, "it would be asking too much favour to get him to hold the party at the Embassy as he is an extremely busy man and the Embassy is ill-staffed even for its own work. After a little deliberation with myself I came to the opinion that to invite His Excellency to do me the honour of his presence at the engagement party is as much as I could possibly ask of him."[73] Third Son assured Father that he and Ambassador Guo had had an amicable exchange.

While glad to invite the ambassador, Third Son was content to hold the engagement party in one of London's hotels. His choice of a more modest location for his engagement party was part of his campaign to convince his parents—especially Mother—that he and Liane intended to lead frugal lives. With the same aim in mind, he had declined to accept Father's offer to send 500 British pounds sterling to cover the cost of his engagement. "Remittance unwanted," he cabled back, and then elaborated in a letter that he did not mean to appear ungrateful.[74]

His polite refusal to take the money was meant to persuade his parents that he and Liane would not succumb to the temptation to hold a lavish celebration. He assured Father that Liane felt as strongly as he did not only about making their engagement party modest but more specifically about declining the 500 pounds. "I sent your letter to Paris [where Liane was living in her parents' apartment] for Liane to read," Third Son wrote to Father. "She gave me such a sensible reply that I have a good mind to let you read her letter to prove to you what a nice girl she is. Although I did not tell her about the cable I sent to you, she of her own accord wrote to ask me to stop the remittance, as it is neither her wish nor mine that our engagement should be an expensive affair."[75] Yet, however sensible and frugal Liane might have been, Mother steadfastly refused to give her blessing, and Third Son and Liane hosted their engagement party without it.

The Wedding

Third Son and Liane had no desire for a long engagement. Although their engagement did not become official until their engagement party on December 21, 1935, they announced their plans to be married in early January 1936, only a couple of weeks later. They were well aware that their engagement was extraordinarily short by Western standards, and they defended and explained their decision in letters to their parents. "Liane and I have decided to get married early next year, probably the beginning of January," Third Son wrote to Father. "We fear that the suspense of being an engaged couple would not be conducive to our happiness together and may interfere with my work should I not be able to pass the Bar Final this December."[76]

Third Son and Liane simply could not stand to be apart, they explained. In words that his parents might well have construed as a threat, he added: "We do not wish to stay away from each other even if we are not married." Concerning the English bar examination, he pointed out that in the next six months it would be given only twice, once in December 1935 and again in May 1936. By studying hard, he hoped to pass in December, and if he failed, he would have time for his wedding and honeymoon before preparing to take it again in May. "We shall spend about a month on honeymoon and I shall still have four months in which to prepare for the examination in May."[77]

Little time was needed to prepare for the wedding, Third Son observed, because he and Liane planned to keep it simple. "I do not think it necessary to have an elaborate wedding," he told Father, because the Liu and Yen families would not be there. "As we are not with our own people, personally I do not see the point of having a big wedding in London. Without being in any way boastful, I think I can safely say that Liane will concur with anything I say. She is very wise and sensible."[78]

Confident that Liane would follow his lead, Third Son assumed that only Mrs. Yen would object to a simple ceremony, and he enlisted Father's help with his scheme to deflect her objection. "We shall probably go to a continental country to get married quietly and get someone to testify our marriage," Third Son confided in Father, and he asked Father to contact a prominent Chinese diplomat to vouch for them and serve as a witness. "I wonder if you happen to know the Chinese Ambassador in Germany or in Italy. If we can get one of them to testify the ceremony, probably Mrs. Yen will not object to us having a quiet wedding so much."[79]

While expecting Father to endorse his plan for a simple wedding, Third Son also expected Father to finance it. After declining Father's earlier offer of 500 pounds for engagement expenses, Third Son found himself in need of funds to cover wedding expenses. "Now that we have decided to get married so soon, I am afraid I have to ask you to send me a remittance after all. I know in these difficult and troublous times, it is unfair to ask too much of you. Without imposing too heavy a strain on your finance, you can give any sum you can reasonably afford to send me. I do not want you to go out of your way to gratify your feeling of parental love. I shall be content with whatever sum you give me."[80] Third Son's appeal to parental love implied that he had no doubt that Father would send a remittance, albeit of an unspecified amount of money.

Third Son realized that his reasons for a short engagement might not seem fully compelling, but he was confident that Father would approve of his wedding plans on the same basis that he had approved of his engagement plans. "You may not altogether agree with my reasons [for getting married so soon]," he conceded to Father. "But I trust you to believe that I know what is best for me."[81] In this case, he was right about Father disagreeing with him, and he overestimated Father's confidence in his ability to decide for himself.

Father fired back a reply addressed to both Second Son and Third Son, who were living together in London. "I was rather surprised," Father said, to hear about Third Son's plan "to get married quietly in Europe some time this winter." Whereas Third Son had assumed that only Mrs. Yen would object to such a plan, Father warned him: "I have some very definite views to express." This plan "would not only run counter to the wish of the Yen family but to that of ours as well. Marriage is a very serious event and as such it deserves all the ceremony and solemnity that is commonly attached to it. Although I appreciate Hannibal's good intentions I cannot permit him to resort to the simple and easy way of getting married in a Registrar Office."[82]

Father refused to permit Third Son to hold such a casual wedding ceremony because Mother would have found it mortifying. "Your mother," he told Second and Third Son, "will not even dream of such a thing and it would be a great shock to her to hear it." Apparently, Father did not dare mention Third Son's plan to Mother, but he did discuss it with the Yens. He and Fourth Son (without Mother) accepted an invitation to dinner in the Yens' home, and they found that Mrs. Yen was deeply troubled by the news. "Mrs. Yen," Father wrote to Second and Third Sons, "appeared to feel quite upset, because she had a misgiving that Hannibal and Liane might be so impatient of waiting as to have recourse to elopement. She told me that she had heard practically nothing from Liane regarding the wedding plans. I did my best to calm her down and promised her to write to you and give you the necessary directions."[83]

These included the need to have the wedding later. Mrs. Yen needed until mid-May 1936, four months after the date set by the young couple, to make preparations for the wedding, especially the making of Liane's wedding dress. "Mrs. Yen," Father reported, "pays particular attention to Liane's wedding dress which will be made all of embroidery. She will probably devote all her time up to the wedding to collecting materials and selecting the best designs for this dress."[84] Not until the elaborate gown was completed in Shanghai would Mrs. Yen take it with her to England.

In early December after hearing that Third Son and Liane had refused to wait until May, Mrs. Yen at first seemed to lose all patience with them and dropped her plans for attending their wedding at all. But then she suddenly reversed herself and decided to go. On December 24 she boarded the S. S. *Potsdam,* and all the members of the Yen and Liu families, except Mother, saw her off. She took with her the jade wedding ring Liane had requested. Third Son's devious schemes for luring Mother into helping Fourth Son buy it had all fallen through. Instead Father had arranged for his brother's wife to choose the stone, and he had bought it for $2,500. "Most people who have seen it," Father assured Third Son, "admit that it is the best stone obtainable on the local market today. I hope Liane will really like it."[85] Father's purchase of Liane's jade ring was one of many gestures he made to make the wedding successful. "I fervently hope that the whole thing will come off nicely," he wrote to Second Son on December 12, because Third Son "is the first of the family to get married and as such he deserves all the attentions that are being centered on him and his bride-to-be in Shanghai at the moment."[86]

For all of his efforts to assure the wedding's success, Father was still pessimistic about the prospective marriage. He confided to Second Son: "I must admit that I have been quite troubled by Hannibal's coming marriage with Liane." His fears were deepened by comments he had heard from friends in Shanghai. "Some of the people we know," he told Second Son, thought that the bride would be "a foreign young lady!"[87]

Parental Advice

To allow time for Mrs. Yen's journey, Third Son and Liane postponed their wedding date until mid-February, and as the day approached, Father and Mother each had their final say about the impending marriage.

Father no longer expressed any doubts about Liane herself. "That you have chosen a good girl to be your wife," he assured Third Son, "I do admit now." But he still had grave doubts about Third Son's ability to cope with Liane's wealthy family, and he issued a dire warning. "Everything will hang on what you will do when you come back to China. As I have always said to you and your brothers, to a young man of your age and position a good and noble career counts more than anything else in the world." Such a worthy career might well elude Third Son, Father cautioned, unless he retained a work ethic and rejected a life of leisure. Third Son should take to heart the values of "hard-working and humble-living," Father told him. "We have too often heard of young people who have by a stroke of chance come to fabulous wealth. In the majority of such cases wealth is just an evil in disguise. It weakens their character and kills their ambition. If you still remember, I said to you and Johnson one day that God has blessed you with everything except poverty. Now I wish to repeat those same words to you with greater emphasis."[88]

From the time Third Son had first proposed to Liane, the stark choice between the goodness of a working life and the evil of a life of leisure had begun to loom on Third Son's horizon and disturb Father. "At the inception," Father told Third Son, looking back on the past several months, "my greatest objection to your marriage with Liane has been fear that it might lead you to live a soft and easy life. At times even the strongest-minded young man will have to yield to the temptations of material joys and comforts."[89]

Still not convinced that he should drop this objection, he warned Third Son that only an extraordinary man making a special effort could possibly find a way around it. "If you wish to prove yourself a rare exception you must first of all try to live within the limit of your own earnings, while bearing in mind that it is no shame to live simply and humbly as long as you know you are the master of your own house. You would do yourself an irretrievable wrong were you to live beyond your means and then seek help from ignominious ways." To clarify what he meant by "ignominious ways," Father showed no reluctance to point his finger at who might bring Third Son down. "It is your grave misfortune that you have been married into a rich family like Mrs. Yen's. In spite of their wealth they have not been living a natural and happy life like that which we have been enjoying. As far as I can see they intend to drag you into their world of artifice and superficiality when an opportunity comes." After becoming Liane's husband, Third Son would only be able to assure himself of the natural and happy life of the Lius and avoid the superficiality of the Yens by taking a stand: "It is now up to you to prove to them that you are above their temptations."[90]

Mother's message, like Father's, was highly moral, but she addressed herself to Liane rather than Third Son, and she made demands rather than issuing challenges. As late as December, she had continued to oppose Third Son's marriage to Liane, but by December 12, she had begun to take a less rigid stance. "Your mother," Father wrote to Second Son that day, "has been quite agreeable to the marriage lately, although she still refuses to give it her formal approval. If Liane is really as wise and sensible as Hannibal said, it is quite likely that your mother will get to be fond of her. It is now up to Hannibal to use his influence on both sides so that there will not be any slight misunderstanding between the wife and the mother."[91]

During the last weeks leading up to the wedding, it would be an exaggeration to say that Mother became fond of Liane—a young woman she still had not met—but she finally gave the couple permission to be married, on the condition that Liane would promise to honor nine filial obligations:

1. During the first month, the new wife must serve tea three times daily to Father-in-Law, Mother-in-Law, and other elders in the family.
2. After the new wife gets up each morning, she must proceed to greet Father-in-Law and Mother-in-Law. The same should be done at night before retiring.
3. The new wife must perform kneelings and prostrations when the new wife enters our home for the first time.
4. She must also perform kneelings and prostrations at the time of the Dragon Boat Festival, Mid-Autumn Festival, New Year's Day, and the birthdays of Father-in-Law and Mother-in-Law.
5. She must receive permission every time she leaves the house.
6. She must also receive permission to entertain guests, whether inside or outside the house, and she must not make any decision on her own.
7. The new wife is responsible for administering all household tasks.
8. She must be frugal, not extravagant, and follow the lifestyle of our family.
9. For the time being, the newlyweds will live as part of the big family, and they can move out and form their own family only after permission is granted by Father-in-Law and Mother-in-Law.[92]

In late December, Mother formulated this list and repeatedly urged Father to send it to Liane, but he withheld it because, as he wrote to Third Son in his cover letter with the list, "I wanted time to think about it, so I haven't sent it off to you until today [December 27]."

Mother's insistence on this list and Father's mixed feelings about it suggest how charged the issue of filial piety was for them at the time.

Even though as early as the 1910s and 1920s Chinese modernizing intellectuals in Shanghai and other cities had published scathing critiques of filial piety, denouncing it as a hypocritical cover-up for patriarchal oppression, Chinese families widely continued to base their practices on it in the 1930s.[93] Father showed his awareness of these controversies over filial piety when he pointed out to the young couple that Mother's list of nine filial obligations could be interpreted two different ways. "If considered dispassionately, these obligations are by no means strict as long as they are understood within the context of the old family system with its emphasis on the precepts of the rites. [But] for someone who has received a Western education, it remains to be seen whether these practices would be considered acceptable."[94]

Besides suggesting that Third Son and Liane should read the list from both the old and new viewpoints, Father added a word of pragmatic advice. "Do not act rashly," Father counseled, hoping that the young couple would not angrily and categorically dismiss Mother's list of filial obligations out of hand. "There are still a few months before you come home, so if you find any of the conditions impossible to carry out, write and discuss them with your Mother directly."[95]

The young couple accepted Mother's conditions, and with her conditional consent and Father's and the Yens' unconditional consent, the marriage took place on February 4, 1936. The couple refrained from having a reception because they thought it would be unseemly to do so in London in the immediate aftermath of the death of England's king, George V, who had died on January 20.

In the spring of 1936, Third Son and Liane returned from London to Shanghai as newlyweds, and Liane met Father and Mother for the first time. Almost immediately, Liane began to win over her new in-laws. As she had promised, she honored the nine filial obligations required by Mother, including her performance of the tea ritual for Mother every single day. Once Liane had demonstrated her willingness to fulfill these conditions, she and Third Son finally received Mother's unconditional blessing and had the support of all the members of both the Liu and Yen families as they began their marriage. During the following year, Mother became quite close to Liane and soon relieved her of all onerous household duties—even the ones she later asked other daughters-in-law to do when they married into the Liu family. Subsequently, in the spring of 1937, after Liane moved with Third Son to

Hong Kong, Mother continued to sustain and nurture her relationship with her first daughter-in-law by regularly sending her affectionate letters, and the two women remained on good terms from then on.[96]

The Groom's Independent Actions

In choosing and marrying his spouse, Third Son exercised independence from his parents nearly every step of the way. First, he initiated contact with Liane Yen in Shanghai through her brother without consulting his parents. Next, he secretly courted her in London while giving his parents the impression that he had no romantic interest in her. Then he proposed marriage to her in London and presented his decision to his parents in Shanghai as a fait accompli. Finally, in the following months, he considered his parents' strong and numerous objections to his marriage proposal and sent them his responses, but he continued to carry out his plans right up to the eve of the wedding, when Mother— the last holdout—finally gave her consent on one condition: that Liane perform rituals of obeisance to Father and Mother. The couple's acceptance of this condition was their sole concession to his parents.

Would Third Son have gone ahead with the wedding if Father had withheld his blessing as long and uncompromisingly as Mother did? Would Third Son have married Liane if Father had threatened to disinherit him and ostracize him from the family for doing so? In this first marriage in the Liu family, Third Son's independence was not tested to the extent that he had to face these troubling questions, but in the family's second marriage, Eldest Daughter could not avoid them.

A Daughter Who Spoiled a Marriage Alliance

ELDEST Daughter was the second of the Liu children to be married, and her courtship and marriage stirred even more controversy in the family than Third Son's marriage had. Father, Mother, and Eldest Daughter's older brothers all argued with her and each other about the plans for her marriage. Initially Father took the lead. From the time of her birth, he had doted on her. After he and Mother had produced seven consecutive sons, he was delighted finally to have a daughter, and he became very attached to her. As she grew up, he formulated big plans for her, and in 1934 when she turned seventeen, he devised a scheme for her to become the key link in a major marriage alliance.

The Betrothal

Following Father's plan, Eldest Daughter became engaged to Song Zi'an (T. A. Soong), a member of "republican China's first family," as it has been called.[1] This family was considered politically powerful because he and all of his brothers and sisters occupied prominent positions as high officials or spouses of high officials in Chiang Kai-shek's Nationalist government. His eldest brother, Song Ziwen (T. V. Soong) while serving as minister of finance (1925–1933) became influential as Chiang's chief economic advisor, and the other two brothers, Song Ziliang (T. L. Soong) and Song Zi'an worked alongside him. Their three sisters were all spouses of political leaders: the eldest, Song Ailing, married Kong Xiangxi (H. H. Kung), who succeeded Song Ziwen as minister of finance in 1933; the middle sister, Song Qingling, married Sun Yat-sen, widely known as the Father of the Republic, who had been Chiang Kai-shek's predecessor as leader of the Nationalist Party; and the youngest, Song Meiling, married Chiang Kai-shek himself.

A marriage alliance between the Liu and Song families was potentially advantageous for both sides. After all, if the Songs were considered China's first family in politics, the Lius might well have been considered China's first family in the business world. In addition, the two families had a lot in common because of their strategies for educating their children. In 1934, although Eldest Daughter was too young to have gone to college abroad, her seven older brothers had all done so, and the Song children had done the same. The difference was that while the Lius had been sent to three countries—England, the United States, and Japan—the Songs had all been placed in the United States. The eldest of the Song sons had graduated from Harvard in 1914, the middle one from Vanderbilt in 1921, and Song Zi'an, the youngest, from Harvard in 1928. The three Song daughters had all graduated from American colleges in the 1910s, the first two from Wesleyan College for Women in Macon, Georgia, and the youngest from Wellesley.[2]

All in all, Song Zi'an and Eldest Daughter seemed to Father perfectly suited for a wedding of "matching doors and households," the traditional Chinese expression for a couple well matched for matrimony because of their comparable social backgrounds.[3] Father was well positioned to negotiate the betrothal because he had a long-standing friendship with the Song brothers, especially the middle one, and when he heard that the youngest, Song Zi'an, considered Eldest Daughter a stunning beauty and wanted to marry her, he readily agreed to the match.[4]

The Teenager

The decision to betroth Eldest Daughter to Song Zi'an was made for her, not by her, and she did not readily accept decisions made for her by her parents. Before the question of her betrothal to Song Zi'an was raised, she had chafed under parental supervision and reacted emotionally and even angrily against impositions of parental authority, especially regarding her relations with the opposite sex.

As early as 1932, at age fifteen, Eldest Daughter showed an interest in young men that worried her brothers as well as her parents, and they all discussed her behavior and how they could change it. At that time,

Second Son wrote from Cambridge to Father to express his concern that his sister was "carrying on correspondence with unknown young men and behaves most extraordinarily at home." He had heard about her behavior from Sixth Son (who was then a student in Japan and had recently been home in Shanghai on vacation) and was worried because of his own impression of her: "Judging from what I know of her she is a weak-minded child and liable to go astray under the slightest influence of seducement."[5]

Second Son's reference to Eldest Daughter's weak-mindedness was based on a report on her that had been done in 1930 by the same doctor who had, at the same time, diagnosed Mother's psychiatric condition. In Eldest Daughter's case, "no formal examination was made," the doctor had reported, because Eldest Daughter, at age thirteen, "became antagonistic upon the least direct questioning." But ever since Father had received this report, he had been troubled by the doctor's speculation that Eldest Daughter might have been "a mentally retarded child," and he had repeatedly discussed with his sons the possibility of sending her to a school for children with learning disabilities.[6]

Second Son feared that Eldest Daughter might be seduced or exploited in some other way without realizing what was happening to her, so he urged Father to investigate her friends immediately. "Unless care were taken at the early stage she might do herself serious wrong without our knowledge and to our great regret. I suggest that the person or persons with whom she has been keeping correspondence should be known." If Father did not take action right away, Eldest Daughter might well become involved with the wrong young people behind his back, Second Son warned, and "she may do all sorts of things which you do not approve of and which you will not know before it is too late."[7]

Second Son urged Father to take care of Eldest Daughter more than he had in the past because she could no longer expect her seven older brothers to do so, since they had all gone to college overseas. "Now," he wrote to Father on September 16, 1932, "all brothers being abroad, [Eldest Daughter] is the eldest at home. She has lost the check which she had been under while we were all at home and could keep an eye on her all the time." Second Son maintained that she needed to be held in check by other members of the family, just as he and his brothers were. He noted that at Cambridge, Third and Fourth Sons "have a very valuable check on me and I on them," and he proposed to Father that

Eldest Daughter should have a check on her "in the same way." In the absence of her older brothers, she needed to be put under close parental supervision. "Father," Second Son wrote, "be strict to her and never let her have money to treat her friends and go out very often."[8]

If reducing her allowance did not keep her away from the wrong crowd of friends, then Second Son suggested: "Another way of remedying her bad habits is to send her away somewhere and keep her remote from her friends." Second Son recognized that relocating Eldest Daughter outside Shanghai was a drastic measure, but he thought it was warranted. "I most strongly object to absolute strictness to children," he told Father, "but in this case we must not make light of it." Only by taking Eldest Daughter's current behavior seriously and imagining the worst possible outcome for her could the family do its utmost to prevent such an outcome. "Father," Second Son concluded, trying to anticipate what was to come, "I am not suggesting by any means that [she] is a bad girl, but that we should expect the worst to come in order to avoid any unfortunate happenings in the future."[9]

While Second Son urged Father to be stricter with her, her other brothers suggested that he should be more lenient. Third Son, writing from Cambridge a month later, agreed with his older brother that Eldest Daughter had pulled away from the family and begun to run with the wrong crowd. He had heard from Sixth Son that she "is coming on to a very awkward age. She evades the company of her brothers and sisters and likes to stay with the servants. Moreover she is mixing up with some very undesirable friends outside. She is a very weak-minded girl and can easily be taught to develop foolish ideas and later on to do foolish things." But Third Son advised Father not to intervene unilaterally. Instead, Father should encourage all members of the family (including Third Son) to bring her gradually back into the fold. "Perhaps being a little weak," he pointed out to Father as the head of a family full of strong personalities, "she feels that she is inferior to her brothers and sisters. The thing to do is to treat her kindly and make her enjoy the company of her family. Gradually she may come to realise that we are her best friends after all and forsake her outside acquaintances."[10] To help her realize that her family members were her best friends, Third Son vowed to write to her and persuade her to correspond with him about it.

By contrast with Second and Third Sons, Eldest Son doubted that his father, brothers, or any other man was qualified to advise Eldest

Daughter, and he recommended that Mother should take the lead with her. Writing to Father in 1933, when she was sixteen, he observed that she had "reached an age when she should be spending more and more time with Mother, as there are many things which her father or older brothers would find inconvenient to supervise." Leaving supervision to Mother, he admitted, was risky because of Mother's own mood swings. "Unfortunately, we've always had to be careful about our Mother's mood. When Mother is not feeling good, she can say things which Eighth [Eldest] Sister would resent, and that would hurt their relationship."[11]

Eldest Son was sensitive about the danger that Mother and other family members might say something Eldest Daughter would resent because as a student in the United States he had been reading books on psychology that warned against making such criticism. Writing to Father on the subject in Chinese, he inserted psychological terms in English (italicized here): "[The family should] never say anything or give any indication in front of her that she has a problem because if she becomes *self conscious* this problem will become worse. Recently I borrowed from a friend a book on *Mental Hygiene,* and I found it very interesting. When you have time, I hope that you will buy a copy and read it. Now I'll give you the author and title of the book, and if you can't find it in Shanghai, I can send you a copy. *Inferiority Feeling by Walsh. Publisher E. P. Dutton & Co.*"[12] Eldest Son's reading on self-consciousness and mental hygiene all pointed to the importance of giving Eldest Daughter positive reinforcement. "Whatever the case," he remarked about the various strategies for dealing with her, "I still think that we should all encourage Eighth Sister and not discourage her."[13]

While Eldest Son advised Father to have Mother attend to Eldest Daughter, Fifth Son appealed directly to Mother to do so. In September 1934, after Eldest Daughter had turned seventeen, while he was a student in the United States, he heard about her from Third Son, who had been in Shanghai on vacation from Cambridge, and he interpreted Third Son's description of her behavior as perfectly normal and natural. He reminded Mother that he was "over twenty years old" and noted that while Eldest Daughter might "seem to be very young and immature, she was in fact already in her late teens. At that age, he told Mother, girls have begun to mature. With an eye to Eldest Daughter's future, he pointed out: "When a girl reaches the age of seventeen or eighteen, it is time for the flower to bloom. Their desire to look beautiful increases. This desire is God-given and is theirs to keep."[14] He saw no reason to stifle it. On the contrary, "we should let this desire grow but guide it down the proper path so that the women can enjoy happiness and yet not lose their standing within the family."[15]

He conceded that it was no easy task to guide Eldest Daughter's desire without alienating her, and he was aware that she "was unhappy and had no way of talking about it." But he expressed confidence that Mother would, as always, solve her children's problems. "I know that you, Mother, love all your sons and daughters, and when your sons and daughters feel dissatisfied, you will always want to find ways to eliminate their dissatisfaction."[16] For the moment, Eldest Daughter's dissatisfaction troubled the whole family, he acknowledged, but as soon as Mother found a solution to her problem, "our entire family will be very happy and will move forward together."[17]

After hearing these suggestions from his sons, Father decided that the best course of action was to send Eldest Daughter to Japan for an extended stay under the supervision of Sixth Son.[18] He presented this plan to Eldest Daughter, and to his surprise, she initially rejected it. It took him more than a year to talk her into going.

The Bride-to-Be

In September 1935, Eldest Daughter finally consented to study in Japan. Up to that time, by contrast with her older brothers, who had pleaded with Father to let them travel abroad, she had made no such plea and had evaded Father's attempts to arrange a trip for her. Even though Father had ordered her to study in Japan in 1934, she had refused to go, forcing him to cancel the plans he had made for her.[19] Not until the summer of 1935, when she had graduated from her middle school, Tung Nan Physical Culture School, was she willing to make the trip.[20] By then she had run out of excuses for not going, especially after Father offered to accompany her personally from Shanghai to Tokyo. (He made the trip at this time as one of the Chinese business people and bankers on a monthlong "goodwill mission" touring Japan's industrial centers).[21] On hearing the news that Eldest Daughter had finally acceded to Father's wishes, her brothers breathed a sigh of relief. As Third Son wrote to Father, "I am glad to hear that our eighth sister has at last agreed to go to Japan. I hope the change will prove to be of benefit to her."[22]

Eldest Daughter's reluctance to go to Japan may be partially explained by her objection to what Father intended for her to learn in Japan. As he explained to Fifth Son, he was afraid that she had become too assertive and undisciplined in Shanghai, and he sent her to Japan so that she would take courses in home economics and learn to be a submissive wife. "You see," he wrote to Fifth Son on October 30, 1935, the day after he had returned home from Japan, "Shanghai is not exactly the suitable place for educating young women to be good and dutiful wives. So I persuaded her to complete her education in Japan which is reputed to be the country that produces the best wives."[23]

The best Japanese wives, according to Father, were not only good and dutiful but also educated and self-sacrificing. In reporting on the trip to his sons at Cambridge, he noted: "Nearly all Japanese women have a certain amount of knowledge in domestic science, the essence of which is dietetics, that is how to feed the family enough and not too much, or too little. Another thing that struck me was the ability of Japanese parents to bear sacrifice for the sake of their children. Cases are not few wherein parents starved themselves to death in order to save some money for the education of the young."[24] These qualities—self-discipline and even self-abnegation—were the ones Eldest Daughter would acquire in Japan, Father hoped, and he entrusted responsibility for instilling them in her to Sixth Son, who lived in Tokyo with his Japanese guardians, the Tsuchiya family (whom we will meet again later).[25]

Father's plan for Eldest Daughter in Japan was strongly endorsed by his sons. Even Fifth Son, who had advised his parents to be lenient rather than strict with Eldest Daughter a year earlier, gave his full approval. "It is a very good idea to send [her] to Japan," he wrote to Father and Mother in reply to Father's news of the trip. "Ever since [Sixth Son] went to Japan for study, he has changed remarkably. From reading his letters, I easily find he has become very political and tender. Such qualities coupled with his wisdom and common sense are the best weapons to cure [Eldest Daughter's] nervousness and blindness towards her own welfare."[26] Fifth Son, like his older brothers, had a high regard for Sixth Son, and he spoke for all of them when he expressed the hope that once Sixth Son had Eldest Daughter under his care in Japan, he would succeed in restoring her mental health and setting her straight.

Eldest Daughter lived in Tokyo for four months, September–December 1935, and from the beginning to the end she seemed to Father and Sixth Son to enjoy and benefit from her stay. When she and Father first arrived, he reported to his sons in England, "to my surprise, [she] expressed her liking for Japan and the life of the Japanese."[27] She immediately found it attractive because she was warmly greeted by Sixth Son's Japanese guardian and his family. After Father returned to Shanghai, he instructed Seventh Son, who was also studying in Japan, to convey the Lius' gratitude to the head of the Tsuchiya family for showing her such warm hospitality. "Mr. Tsuchiya has been so kind to [Eldest Daughter]," Father wrote to Seventh Son. "Every detail of her life there has been well taken care of. When you see Mr. Tsuchiya next, be sure to convey my deep appreciation for all that he's done."[28]

Off to a good start, Eldest Daughter was "feeling quite happy" about her time in Japan, according to Sixth Son's reports on her progress.[29] Father forwarded these reports to his sons in England and noted that she followed Sixth Son's orders and performed chores for him as though she were his live-in maidservant. With undisguised satisfaction, Father described the nature of her manual labor as a domestic. "You will be pleased to know," he wrote to Second Son, "that your sister is doing very well in Japan. She does practically all the cooking for your sixth brother, besides having to do a good amount of the house-work. We expect to see her greatly changed for the better."[30] Besides taking care of Sixth Son's personal needs, Eldest Daughter attended classes at a university for about a month, but she did not enroll in a degree program.[31]

By the end of her stay in Japan, Father's prediction that she would be greatly changed for the better seemed to him to have come true. In December 1935 when he welcomed her and Sixth and Seventh Sons back to Shanghai, he was delighted to find that they "are looking terribly fit and well." As he reported to Fifth Son, he was particularly pleased "to notice the change that has come over your sister. She is quite a different girl now." He gave credit for her transformation to Sixth Son because he had taken the trouble "to soothe and admonish [her] throughout her stay in Japan. They got on very well together. Whatever your brother said carried a good deal of weight with your sister. I think [she] is honestly happy now."[32]

Father's portrait of her as "quite a different girl now," "fit and well," and "honestly happy" suggest that she had finally become at age eigh-

teen the young woman he had always wanted her to be. After her rebellious teenage years, she now seemed to fit into the plan for the family
as he had hoped. But his optimism turned out to be premature. While
Father thought that she had been molded into a docile prospective bride
who would form a powerful marriage alliance for the Lius with the
Song family, she was secretly involved with a married man.

The Married Man

In August 1934, a year before her trip to Japan, Eldest Daughter had
met an older man, Xue Diyi. For the rest of her life, she vividly remembered the moment. As she descended the main staircase in the Liu family home, her gaze fell on Xue, and their eyes locked. With rapt attention, she listened to Fourth Son's introduction of Xue and his explanation
that he and Xue had met in England and had traveled home together
as passengers on the S. S. *Conte Verde,* reaching Shanghai August 4.[33]
In response to her brother's introduction, Eldest Daughter made no
more than a small nod to Xue, but it conveyed a message that he took
as her consent for him to pursue her. He was thirty-three and she was
seventeen.[34]

At this first meeting and later ones, Xue was forthcoming about almost everything in his background, especially his lineage and education.
He was born into a wealthy landlord family in Wujin in Changzhou
prefecture, 115 miles northwest of Shanghai, and he was related to the
distinguished industrialist Sheng Xuanhuai (1844–1916), who had also
hailed from Wujin.[35] Orphaned at the age of three, Xue had not benefited from his inherited connections to Sheng's family, but he was left
under the care of an attentive uncle, and throughout his childhood he
was well provided for.[36]

From an early age, Xue began preparation for a career as an engineer, and by the time he met Eldest Daughter, he had completed his education at distinguished institutions. His secondary school was Suzhou
Polytechnic High School (Suzhou gong zhong xue), located halfway
between his hometown and Shanghai. He attended Nanyang University
(renamed Communications University in 1927), which was modeled after MIT and became Shanghai's premier institution for producing an
engineering elite (just as St. John's University, which Father and his sons
attended, was its premier institution for producing a business elite).[37]

For postgraduate study, Xue went to England, where he spent six years, 1928–1934, and earned a master's degree (M.Sc. Tech.) from the Faculty of Technology in 1933 at the University of Manchester.[38] The grim industrial city that provided the setting for Friedrich Engels's classic book on capitalist exploitation of workers, Manchester admittedly had less charm than Cambridge University, where Second, Third, and Fourth Sons were students.[39] But precisely because of its vast cotton mills, Manchester had wealthy industrialists who financed higher education, especially in technical subjects, and by the early twentieth century Manchester University had become a leader in science and engineering. Of all the universities in Britain, it trained the most postgraduate and research students in science, and when Xue was there, he was one of its fifteen Chinese engineering students—more than were enrolled at any other university in Britain.[40] Like all of the schools Xue attended, it had a high reputation in the field of engineering.

Along with his postgraduate degree, Xue brought back from England a wardrobe and a set of mannerisms that earned him the nickname "The English Gentleman." Wearing white linen suits and a fedora, carrying a polished wooden cane, and walking with a spring in his step, he cut a striking figure in Eldest Daughter's eyes. At their first meeting and ever after, she considered him a very stylish and handsome man.[41]

The one major feature in his background Xue neglected to mention to Eldest Daughter and the rest of the Liu family was his marriage. He had been betrothed at a young age to his first cousin in his hometown, Wujin, and they had married and produced one child, a daughter, before he had gone to England in 1928. During his six years abroad he had lost interest in this family, and now that he had returned to China, he had set up his residence in Shanghai, leaving his wife and child in Wujin. But even if he had not lived with them for a long time and had lost his emotional attachment to them, he was still a married man and a father.[42]

The Affair

Eldest Daughter became attracted to Xue Diyi without knowing that he was married. She was impressed when he drove up in a car and offered her a ride as she emerged from Tung Nan Physical Culture School, and she was amused to hear him boast about successfully tracking her down without consulting her family. As she eventually learned, he had borrowed the car, and he continued to borrow it so that he could whisk her away from school on a regular basis. Between their first meeting in August 1934 and her departure for Japan in September 1935, they kept their romance a secret from the Liu family, and Eldest Daughter's desire to see Xue at this time explains why she postponed going to Japan—evading Father's insistent orders—for as long as she did. Not until after she returned from Japan to Shanghai at the end of 1935 did their families become aware of their affair.

The first person to discover that Eldest Daughter and Xue were having an affair was Xue's wife. She caught them together in his Shanghai house, and in a fury, she went straight to Father and threatened to reveal the story to the press. Father was shocked to hear of the affair, and he took immediate action to avoid a public scandal. He offered Xue's wife 30,000 yuan to keep quiet, and she accepted this hush money, but she did not immediately grant Xue a divorce.[43]

From Eldest Daughter, Father learned still more shocking news: she was pregnant. She and Xue had conceived a child in September 1935 on the eve of her trip to Japan, and she had kept her pregnancy a secret on her return to Shanghai in December (when Father, showing no awareness of it, had pronounced her "quite a different girl now," "fit and well," and "honestly happy"). But as she entered her third trimester in the spring of 1936, she could no longer conceal her pregnancy. When Father became aware of it, he uncharacteristically lost his temper and accused her of disgracing the whole family. Considering her behavior outrageous on all counts, Father immediately disowned her and subsequently instructed the family lawyer, Xu Shihao, to make her disinheritance legal and official.[44] To spare Mother's feelings, Father sent Eldest Daughter to Japan for the duration of her pregnancy and ordered her not to tell Mother about it until after the baby had been born.[45]

Father kept the news of Eldest Daughter's pregnancy within the family as much as possible, but he could not avoid telling her fiancé, Song Zi'an.[46] To Father's astonishment, he found that after Song heard this news, he wanted to marry Eldest Daughter anyway. Despite her affair with Xue and her pregnancy, Song said that he still loved her and was willing to proceed with the wedding. When Father insisted that he could not permit his daughter to marry Song in light of her misbehavior, Song became distraught and withdrew into a Buddhist monastery.

Shaving his head, he announced that he would become a monk and never marry. But his dramatic gesture did not cause Father to change his decision. Seeing that Father was unmoved, Song emerged from the monastery within two weeks. He later married another woman.[47]

On May 27, 1936, at age nineteen, Eldest Daughter gave birth to a son in Tokyo. She had gone there following Father's orders, and she had taken her best girl friend with her as a traveling companion. She was hosted and looked after by Sixth Son, who made all of the local arrangements. At first Xue Diyi was not with her, because Father and the other Lius refused to tell him where she had gone, but eventually he found out from her classmates, followed her to Tokyo, and made contact with her through her traveling companion. Once he finally reached her, he assured her that he loved her and would marry her as soon as he was divorced from his first wife. Even though he was still married, Eldest Daughter promised to wait for him to extricate himself from his marriage and marry her. In the meantime, she moved with her new baby from Tokyo to Nanchang, 485 miles southwest of Shanghai, where Xue Diyi held a job in local bureau for highway construction.[48]

The Reconciliation with Mother

Father's disinheritance of Eldest Daughter legally ostracized her from the family and cut her off from the Lius permanently and definitively. But as soon as Mother heard what had happened, she began reaching out to Eldest Daughter in hopes of bringing her back into the family. As a first step, she sent Third Son from Shanghai to Nanchang to investigate Eldest Daughter's circumstances.[49] When he reported back that he considered her living conditions to be wretched—far below the standard to which the Lius were accustomed—Mother immediately contacted Eldest Daughter and convinced her to come back to Shanghai. Mother's handling of her daughter under these tense and potentially disastrous circumstances made a deep and lasting impression on her children. As Fourth Son reminded his brothers several years later, "from the way she [Mother] treated Eighth [Eldest] Sister, we know how great she is. She beat and scolded her, but at the same time she wholeheartedly helped her."[50]

While Mother welcomed Eldest Daughter and her infant son, Mother's first grandchild, into her home, she tried to keep Xue Diyi away from Eldest Daughter at least until his divorce from his first wife was final. If she delayed the couple's reunion, she certainly did not prevent it. In October 1936 they were married.[51]

On September 5, 1937, just sixteen months after the birth of Eldest Daughter's first child, she delivered her second one, a girl, in Shanghai, and this time Mother was directly involved. She had not even known about the first child until after its birth, but for the delivery of the second child, she made all the arrangements and stayed at her daughter's side every step of the way. When she was ready to deliver, Mother took her to Bethel Hospital in Shanghai, where she carefully monitored all the care Eldest Daughter received. On September 14, a little over a week after the baby was born, Mother proudly reported to Third Son's wife that Eldest Daughter "had a remarkably easy and speedy delivery. She has been out of bed since yesterday and is now feeling very well."[52] Mother was so pleased with Eldest Daughter's treatment that she sent the hospital a donation of 100 yuan and a thank-you note expressing her appreciation to the staff for giving Eldest Daughter "good care in every respect."[53]

After Eldest Daughter left the hospital, Mother continued to look after her and her children in the Liu family home. On October 11, five weeks after Eldest Daughter had given birth to her second child, Mother sent a progress report to Third Son's wife. "My daughter has grown plumper. In fact, she is feeling as strong as ever now. Her baby is fine and I am very fond of her."[54] Mother was impressed with not only Eldest Daughter's strength but also her ability to care for her children without the benefit of a wet nurse and other servants. "She nurses her children and bathes them each day," she told Third Son's wife on December 5, four months after the younger child's birth.[55]

As the months went by, Mother took great pleasure in keeping Eldest Daughter and her two grandchildren in her home, and she felt sure that they were pleased to be there. She wrote to Sixth Son on February 14, 1938, when Eldest Daughter's son was twenty-one months old and her daughter was six months old, "I believe that your eighth sister and her little family are happy here with us. The children are growing beautifully and they are all feeling remarkably well."[56] Over the next six months Mother sent equally positive reports to other members of the family, always emphasizing how pleased Eldest Daughter and her family were to be with Mother and never making any mention of Xue Diyi.[57]

Not until August 1938, after Eldest Daughter's son was two and a half years old and her daughter nearly a year old, did Mother approve of her daughter and grandchildren starting their own household with Xue Diyi. By then the Japanese had invaded Shanghai and Father had fled to Hong Kong. Mother wrote to him: "If he [Xue Diyi] wants to fetch [Eighth Daughter] away I think we ought to let her go." She was willing to hand over her daughter and her grandson to Xue, but she hoped to hang onto the granddaughter still longer. "It is best that they themselves should keep watch over the little boy," she told Father. "I wonder whether we are to keep the little girl with us for some time. However, we will see to that later."[58] At that time and for the foreseeable future, Mother claimed her daughter and her grandchildren, if not her son-in-law, as her own.

Independence, Estrangement, and Reunion

Before reconciling with Mother, Eldest Daughter took an even more independent stance in choosing her spouse than Third Son had done in choosing his. Like him, she initiated contact with her mate without consulting Father or Mother, kept her courtship secret from them, and remained committed to her choice despite their objections. But in defending her choice, she acted on her own more than Third Son had done.

From her brothers, Eldest Daughter did not receive strong support of the kind given to Third Son. In his case, he rallied his brothers to his side, so while Second Son wrote from England to help win over Father and Mother by letter, Fourth Son lobbied on Third Son's behalf in person in Shanghai. In Eldest Daughter's case, all of her older brothers sent advice by letter to Father and Mother about how to counsel her on her relations with the opposite sex, and Sixth Son took personal responsibility for supervising her in Japan during her four-month stay in the fall of 1935 and her brief visit to give birth to her first child in the spring of 1936. As Second Son pointed out, if the seven eldest sons had not been overseas, they would have paid even more attention to her, providing a face-to-face "check" on her behavior throughout her upbringing in Shanghai (just as they provided a check on each other at home or wherever else they lived together), and from abroad they tried to do the same by letter. But when she revealed that she was pregnant and would marry her child's father, who was already married to another woman, she received no support from any of her seven older brothers.

In relation to Father, Eldest Daughter also acted on her own more than Third Son had done. Whereas Third Son ultimately received Father's begrudging consent to marry Liane Yen, Eldest Daughter never did receive Father's consent to marry Xue Diyi. Yet she remained committed to Xue even though Father disinherited her. Running the risk of becoming totally estranged from her family, she did not reverse her decision.

Only from Mother did Eldest Daughter receive support comparable to the kind given to Third Son. Eldest Daughter did not try to persuade Mother to approve of her behavior or pretend that her pregnancy had not caused a scandal and disgraced the family. In 1941, five years after her affair with Xue had come to light, Mother still withheld her approval of this behavior, remarking in a letter to Fourth Son: "I always regret what eighth sister has done."[59] Moreover, Mother continued to harbor doubts about Xue, whom she tried to keep away from Eldest Daughter for three years (1936–1939) after the birth of their first child, until she felt confident that their marriage would last. But if Eldest Daughter had strained her emotional bond with Mother, she fully restored it during the three years they spent together raising her first child, Mother's first grandson. At this time, Eldest Daughter became one of Mother's two favorite children, second only to Eldest Son, according to other members of the family.[60]

Thanks to her reconciliation with Mother, Eldest Daughter settled into the family home before the Japanese military invasion in the summer of 1937, the beginning of the Sino-Japanese War. By then, almost all of the Liu children who had left home between 1929 and 1936 had returned to Shanghai and taken jobs in accordance with their parents' wishes. Eldest Son had finally received his MBA from the University of Pennsylvania and become the head of Liu Hong Ji, the Lius' accounts house. Second, Third, and Fourth Sons, their BA degrees from Cambridge University in hand, had become managers in some of the Lius' biggest businesses—Second Son in the match factories, Third Son in the cement works, and Fourth Son on the wharves supervising shipping. Fifth Son, after recovering his health at Cragmor Sanatorium, had earned his BA at Colorado College and come home to take a job in a bank that helped finance the Lius' enterprises. Even Eldest Daughter, who had taken the most radical stance against her parents of all, was living with her child in the family home.

On the eve of the Sino-Japanese War, after all of these children's passionate arguments with their parents and declarations of independence from their parents, they seemed to be back on track and poised to follow their parents' plan for establishing a business dynasty based in Shanghai. But they had expected to carry out this plan in peacetime, and once the war began, they found themselves forced into making unforeseen decisions in the family and the family firm.

III

REACTING TO WAR
1938–1945

8

⇒◆⇐

Sons Who Became Leaders in Wartime

IN LATE June 1938, a year after the Japanese military invasion of China, Father fled Shanghai. Pulling his hat down and his scarf up to cover his face, he slipped onto the Canadian ship *Empress of Russia*, bound for Hong Kong, 760 miles southwest of Shanghai, where he arrived June 30. He left behind in Shanghai his business, his wife, and most of his children.[1] By then, he had lost control of parts of his business (his match mills, cement plant, enamel factory, and wharves) because these had been seized by the Japanese forces under their occupation of Shanghai. But he still retained control over a considerable amount of property (his eight-story headquarters building, bank, insurance firm, and real estate agency) because these were located in the British-dominated International Settlement, which the Japanese left untouched until December 1941—the time of Pearl Harbor and the beginning of the Pacific War against Britain, the United States, and other Western countries.[2] With his family and these assets in Shanghai, he had good personal and professional reasons to remain in his hometown.

Father left his family and his family firm behind and fled Shanghai because he was afraid of being assassinated by combatants on both sides of the Sino-Japanese War. From the Japanese side, a military official named Ueda Jiichiro had personally threatened Father. In a series of four or five meetings with Father and Second and Fourth Sons during June, Ueda had offered Father the presidency of the Japanese-sponsored Shanghai Chamber of Commerce and ominously declared that if Father declined the offer, Ueda could not guarantee the safety of the Liu family. From the Chinese side, pro–Chiang Kai-shek agents had posed a less direct but equally dangerous threat to Father because they had already begun assassinating Chinese for accepting Japanese offers of posts exactly like this one. Caught in a crossfire, Father feared putting his family and himself in harm's way whether he accepted or declined Ueda's offer, so he avoided the issue by fleeing to the British colony of Hong Kong, which the Japanese refrained from invading between 1937 and 1941.[3]

When the war forced Father to leave Shanghai, it marked a key turning point in the history of the Liu family. As he left, he expressed the hope that he would soon return. Contrary to his hopes, he did not come back until the end of the long war in 1945, seven years later. He did not leave the family entirely headless, because he tried to maintain his authority over it from a distance by regularly writing letters and periodically arranging for family members to visit and work with him. But his long absence had profound effects on decision making in the Liu family. During this time he was no longer available to provide face-to-face consultation and supervision in Shanghai, leaving far more responsibility for decision making in the hands of his wife and children there.

In the family firm, his four eldest sons were directly affected by his absence because they were catapulted into top executive positions. Before the war Father had warned them that they would need to spend several years learning about the business and working their way up the managerial ladder. In the wartime emergency, he waived this requirement and excused them from making further preparations. Though the four eldest sons were all still in their twenties, he gave them full responsibility for presiding over the family firm. He recognized that their youthfulness would spare them from the dilemma that drove him out of Shanghai because the Japanese authorities would never appoint such young men to high official positions under the occupation. But with their lack of experience, would his sons make sound business decisions, and in his absence, would they follow his orders? These questions arose as Father delegated authority to them, and each son seized the opportunity to take the initiative in his assigned sector of the family firm.

Eldest Son and Finance in Shanghai

After fleeing, Father recognized that his life was at risk, and while not relinquishing his authority over the family firm, he took steps to shift it all into his sons' hands in the event of his death. Within a week of his arrival in Hong Kong, he sent his sons in Shanghai legal documents that would, if necessary, grant them power of attorney. As he wrote in a cover note to Eldest Son and his other sons on July 6, 1938, "I have signed 12 copies of powers of attorney & witnessed by 2 friends. I did it simply against any emergency. Nobody can be too careful. Please keep them locked & only use them when it is necessary."[4] Although straightforward and matter-of-fact, Father's handwritten note was a grim reminder that "any emergency" might well include an attempt to assassinate him. Even if he were to die, he believed that the family firm would live on because his sons had become mature adults and potential leaders. As he wrote from Hong Kong to Fourth Son in Shanghai on September 24: "I have grown up sons, whose minds have developed & matured, therefore I am always ready to take your opinions into consideration. In fact I have more faith in you boys than anybody else including myself."[5]

If, as he claimed, Father really did have greater faith in his sons than himself, this faith was severely tested during the war. Within the first year after Father had fled to Hong Kong, he clashed with Eldest Son over the handling of the family firm's finances in Shanghai. In May 1937, just two years after Eldest Son had returned from his studies at Harvard and University of Pennsylvania and only a few months before the war broke out, Father had appointed Eldest Son as the general overseer and head of Liu Hong Ji, the family's accounts office. In Eldest Son's first year at this post, Father had closely supervised him both in person and indirectly through senior managers whom Father assigned to work with him.[6] But after Father left for Hong Kong, Eldest Son did not heed his warnings or follow his senior managers' advice as closely as he had when Father was in Shanghai. Instead, he began appropriating funds from Liu Hong Ji for real estate speculation and making decisions on his own.[7]

When Eldest Son first neglected to consult Father about financial decisions, Father tried to reason with him. In April 1939, less than a year after Father had left Shanghai, he became annoyed with Eldest Son for putting the Liu family home up for sale without mentioning it to him, and he mildly chastised him and his brothers for it. Explaining to them that he had learned what they had done from the buyer, whom he had met by chance on a business trip, Father wrote from Hong Kong to his sons in Shanghai on April 23: "I didn't have any idea of this until he told me this time. I hope you can let me know of things like this next time before they are put into effect."[8] But Eldest Son and his brothers did not take this admonition to heart.

In June, Eldest Son made another financial decision without considering advice from Father and the business's senior managers, and this time Father lost his temper. Eldest Son made the mistake of keeping Liu Hong Ji's funds largely in Chinese currency and buying only US$10,000 in foreign currency just before the value of Chinese currency suddenly dropped. Other senior managers of the family's businesses, notably Xu Shihao, a lawyer and accountant at the Lius' Great China Match Company in Shanghai, had followed Father's orders to buy large amounts of foreign currency and had made substantial financial gains as a result of its rising value in relation to the fall in the value of Chinese currency. But Eldest Son and his brothers had gone their own way, bought too little foreign currency, and suffered heavy losses.

When Father learned that his sons had ignored his advice on currency exchange, he came down hard on them. Barely containing his anger, he reminded them that he had deliberately loosened their leash and allowed them to play a greater role in the decision-making process in Shanghai during his year in Hong Kong. Now, he declared, he would no longer grant them such latitude. "You are aware," he wrote to his sons on June 25, "that in spite of the complexities in the affairs of my various companies in Shanghai, all along I have been endeavoring to keep things as quiet as possible, at least on the surface, by [the] method of compromise. Circumstances have convinced me however that I have now to take a more firm attitude."[9]

In these unequivocal words, Father ordered Eldest Son and his other sons to relinquish their authority over financial decision making to Xu Shihao. "Whatever development may come in future," Father told them, "Mr. Hsu [Xu] will have full power to deal with it as he likes." His sons, by contrast, were to play a strictly subordinate role. "I cannot emphasize to you too strongly," Father told them, "that in all matters you should listen to his advice and not be too independent and do things on your own account. It is my wish that in case of any difference in opinions Mr. Hsu's views shall prevail."[10]

Father made clear that he did not want Eldest Son and his other sons to become too independent until they had acquired more experience. "While you boys may be of some assistance to him in his work, you must bear in mind that in many respects you are as yet still entirely inexperienced."[11] In Father's absence, all of his sons—even Eldest Son, who had held a high position longest—should conduct the business not on their own but under the tutelage of his senior business associates, like Xu.

In light of their financial losses, Eldest Son and his brothers could not deny that they had failed in this case. In fact, Third Son admitted in a letter to his brothers that Father was right about the mistakes they had made. At the time of Father's tirade against them, Third Son was working with him in Hong Kong, and after hearing Father's complaints in person, he conveyed them to his brothers in Shanghai. "This time," he wrote, implicitly reminding them that it was not the first time, "Father is really justified in making his complaint as he has been asking us to buy foreign currency all the time and we did not carry out his instructions. From now on I hope you will read his letters carefully and give a little thought to his instructions."[12]

In making this criticism and recommendation, Third Son took his share of the blame, acknowledging that he, along with his brothers, had been wrong not to take Father's advice seriously. "Please," he told them, "do not think that I am shifting the blame on you. In fact I was in Shanghai myself at the time when his letters came and consider myself equally responsible. I think the practice of passing father's letters along is not very good. Next time if he gives any specific instructions we must," he emphasized, "consider what action we should take."[13] But even as Third Son took the blame in this case and proposed to his brothers that they should be more attentive in the future, it is notable that he assumed that he, Eldest Son, and his other brothers would continue to hold ultimate decision-making authority in their own hands, as he implied in saying that they would be the ones to "consider what action we should take." Despite the bad outcome in this one case in 1939, Third Son and his brothers had no intention of relinquishing their newly acquired authority in the family business at Shanghai for the foreseeable future.

These exchanges between Father in Hong Kong and Eldest Son and his brothers in Shanghai underscore the difficulty in wartime China of managing a business from a remote location. On the surface, it might appear that from his new base in Hong Kong Father could have easily managed his finances in Shanghai simply by relying on Eldest Son to do his bidding. In fact, Father could not exercise authority or supervise his sons as closely as he had done face-to-face in prewar Shanghai. Marooned in Hong Kong as an absentee father and manager, he had a difficult time persuading his sons to take his advice or even give him their attention. In Shanghai he had left a leadership vacuum, and his sons readily filled it.

Second Son and Industry in Shanghai

Just as Eldest Son took new authority over the Lius' finances, Second Son took new authority over their biggest industrial enterprise. In June 1938, when Father refused to collaborate with the Japanese and fled Shanghai, he resigned as general manager of his biggest industrial enterprise, Great China Match Company, and left Second Son in charge of it. For the next two years, Second Son did not have official authority over the company because it was located in Zhabei, a district of Shanghai under Japanese occupation, and the Japanese military authorities designated it "enemy property" and seized control. In May 1940, Second Son and the other members of Great China Match's board of directors were notified that they might be able to regain control of the company if they would cooperate with a new Chinese regime that had been founded with Japanese approval under Wang Jingwei, a former member of Chiang Kai-shek's government. Intrigued by this possibility, Second Son tried to talk Father into pursuing it.

In the summer of 1940, Second Son traveled to Hong Kong and had a series of meetings with Father face-to-face to present his proposal for regaining control of Great China Match Company in Shanghai by cooperating with Wang Jingwei's collaborationist government. By then, Second Son no longer espoused ardent anti-Japanese nationalism as he had done during the Shanghai Incident of 1932, when he and his brothers had rejected Father's proposal that they become British citizens. But in 1940, after returning to Shanghai, assuming a position of authority in the family business, and living under Japanese rule, Second Son was frustrated to discover that Father was more nationalistic than he was.

On his visit, Second Son was unable to talk Father into approving his ideas for cooperation with the Japanese, and he accused Father of allowing a nationalistic political bias to cloud his judgment as a businessman. On August 5, as he prepared to return to Shanghai after spending a month with Father, he vented his frustration. "While I had no intention of driving into your mind the wisdom of your early return to Shanghai," he wrote to Father, "I must confess that your view on this matter has been a very great disappointment to me. While you are considering political complications of your return I stick 100% to business and industry."[14] By sticking strictly to business and industry, Second Son felt that he had set well-defined goals that were free of nationalism and other ideologies.

Second Son considered his own position pragmatic and flexible, and he complained that Father was being politically rigid. Confronting Father more directly by letter than he had allowed himself to do in person, he wrote: "I have found your own views so often totally contradictory that I completely gave up the idea of any personal persuasion on my part. It has been difficult for me as a son to express my inner feelings so I have deliberately avoided discussing this matter [with] you too often. I shall go back to Shanghai with renewed courage though somewhat puzzled and disappointed."[15]

Second Son was disappointed not only with Father but with the other émigré Shanghai business people who, in his estimation, were wasting their time remaining idle in Hong Kong merely for the sake of fleeing from the Japanese occupation rather than returning home now that they had the opportunity to regain control of their businesses under Japanese or Japanese-sponsored Chinese governments. "I can now only laugh," he wrote sardonically to Father. "We are now in the process of making a great decision. We all take our respective chances. It puzzles me how so many big shots in Hong Kong can solve their dilemma by staying on and remaining inactive there."[16] He was unable to fathom why any Shanghai businessman would choose to waste time this way in Hong Kong.

Back in Shanghai, he tried to outmaneuver the Japanese controllers at Great China Match Company. "As the Japanese control over our company gets tighter and tighter, we have resorted to keeping a second set of books," he wrote to Father on November 6. "So far, they haven't been to our company to check our books."[17] Besides hiding financial records in a secret set of books, Second Son searched for other ways to keep funds out of the Japanese controllers' hands. "I have been in close touch with our attorney about possible ways of protecting our money," he wrote to Father.[18] Under his management, this money had increased, he reported to Father on December 28. "The future of Great China Match Company is difficult to predict, but it is now doing quite well. Profit for this year will be 2,000,000 yuan. Please keep this a secret."[19]

Second Son took pride in his success at not merely preserving Great China Match Company but making it profitable under the Japanese occupation during his first years in charge, 1938–1940. Under Japanese restrictions, he could not take profits, give bonuses, or distribute dividends at the company, but he believed that he could overcome these restrictions if only Father would allow him to cooperate with Wang Jingwei's government and the Japanese authorities in Shanghai. While Second Son favored this policy of cooperation, he could not pursue it without Father's approval, which he was not likely to receive unless he won the support of others in the family not only in Shanghai but also in Hong Kong.

Third Son and Industry in Hong Kong

In the first years after Father's flight from Shanghai in 1938, Third Son worked with him more closely than any of his other sons did. In 1939, at Father's request, Third Son and his young bride, Liane, joined Father in Hong Kong, and in 1940 he became the manager of a new venture Father had founded, Great China Match Company of Hong Kong. Between the Lius' registration of the company in June 1940 and the Japanese invasion of Hong Kong in December 1941, Third Son made a promising start with the new business. Initially capitalized at HK$300,000, it earned between HK$500,000 and HK$600,000 in 1940 and 1941.[20] In these years, Third Son was pleased to be working with Father and supporting the family firm through the new branch in Hong Kong, and he fully aligned himself with Father's policies for Shanghai as well as Hong Kong. Before the Japanese occupation of Hong Kong, he became the intermediary for conveying Father's views—including his criticisms—to the rest of the family in Shanghai.

After hearing Father grumble about his sons' lack of cooperation in Shanghai, Third Son told them that he thought this criticism was valid. "Now that I have been away," he wrote from his post in Hong Kong to his brothers in Shanghai on July 22, 1941, "I can see more clearly the necessity of cooperation among us brothers more than ever. Unless we work hard and cooperate smoothly we shall not stand a chance against others." They needed to cooperate, he pointed out to them, to justify Father's decision to delegate authority to them during the war. "There must be perfect cooperation and understanding among us brothers before we can expect Father to have faith in us. He will simply say how can you expect to get on well with other people if you cannot get on well with each other."[21] If they were cooperating perfectly, Third Son implied, Second Son and the others in Shanghai would undeviatingly follow Father's orders as Third Son himself was doing in Hong Kong.

He also passed along Father's criticism of them for not working hard. "We must show complete devotion to our work before we can expect Father to look on us with approval," Third Son told them. Father "has the impression that we are all having an easy and comfortable time in Shanghai and ought to work much harder," and, Third Son had to admit, he had the same impression. "When I think that in Shanghai everybody leaves the office at 4 P.M. this is really not hard enough work for young men." In Hong Kong, Third Son himself put in much longer days. "Without any exaggeration, I now work from 9 A.M. to 1 P.M. and from 2 to 6 or 7 P.M." He added: "Father works even harder."[22]

Failing to rise to Father's standards would cause the brothers to suffer in the long run, Third Son warned them. Even if Father had been forced to elevate them to high positions because of the war, they would be wrong to assume that he would pardon them or make exceptions for them merely because they were his sons. Third Son admitted that Chinese businessmen commonly practiced nepotism, but he reminded his brothers that Father did not. "There are two schools of thought among the leading businessmen of China. One will trust blindly everything in the hands of members of the family and relatives. The other will go out of his way to prove his fairness by not allowing members and relatives of the family to hold key posts unless they have really proved their worth. The latter school is comparatively rare, but our father belongs to that school."[23]

As an opponent of nepotism, Father would hold his sons to a high standard, and in Third Son's estimation, even while Father was based outside Shanghai, he still retained the ultimate authority to determine all of the posts his sons would hold throughout the family firm. "I am telling you this," Third Son wrote, "because I want you to realise that

we cannot expect father to lift us to any high post unless we can convince him of our ability to be able to do the job better than anyone
else."[24] As Third Son envisioned the future in July 1941, five months
before Japan's invasion of Hong Kong, no matter where the family's assets might be dispersed, Father would always have the authority to
hire, promote, and fire the family firm's managers.

Up to this point in the war, Third Son was aligned with Father and
against his brothers, but after Japan's invasion of Hong Kong in December 1941, his sympathies began to shift. By then Father had established
a residence in Chongqing and was paying fewer visits to Hong Kong,
and when Third Son had to face the prospect of a Japanese takeover of
Great China Match Company in Hong Kong, he began to identify less
with his father and more with his brothers in Shanghai on the issue of
whether to cooperate with the Japanese and Wang Jingwei's Japanese-
approved Chinese regime.

In June 1942, after living under the Japanese occupation of Hong
Kong for six months, Japanese business associates representing Mitsui
Company in Hong Kong approached Third Son. He listened to their
proposals, and he began to reconsider Father's wartime policy of dividing the family business between Shanghai and Hong Kong. "The Mitsui
Company here," he wrote to Eldest and Second Sons on June 22, "has
repeatedly invited us to return to Shanghai to revive our old enterprises there." He urged his brothers to take this proposal seriously, and
he assumed that they would react favorably to it, as long as it was carefully carried out after "making sufficient preparations" to avoid "any
rash decision so that we'll have no regrets in the future."[25]

On the same day, Third Son sent Father a version of the same proposal and admitted in his cover letter that he was apprehensive about
Father's reaction to it. "We are afraid that you will not approve our request," he wrote, "and then there will be a deadlock." He pleaded with
Father to consider the proposal carefully, give approval, and avoid a
deadlock because the time was right for a change in the family's policy.
Third Son warned Father that if the Lius did not accept the Japanese
invitation to move from Hong Kong back to Shanghai and form new
Sino-Japanese joint ventures immediately, they would miss their
chance. Referring to conversations with his Japanese business associates at Mitsui, he wrote: "Now that they have already shown an interest in us, it would be easy for us to push the boat in the direction that

the current is flowing. If we don't accept, they will certainly find others [who would take advantage of the Japanese invitation to cooperate]. After they succeed in finding others, it will be impossible for us to put our hand in." With a sense of urgency, he told Father: "Time is not on our side, and the opportunity mustn't be lost. It is apparent that we should carefully consider this matter from all sides and come to a decision soon."[26]

While calling for action in the immediate present, Third Son noted the long-term significance of this decision for the future. He predicted: "There are only two possible outcomes in the future. Either A [Japan] wins, and if that's the case, our making a move now will not cause any problems. Or B [the Nationalist government of Chiang Kai-shek] wins, and as it's now going, that won't happen for several years." In case the Japanese won, the Lius should begin cooperating with them as soon as possible. Even if the Nationalists were to win, it would take so long for them to do so that the Liu family would not benefit from having allied with them. "By then," Third Son lamented to Father, "it would be impossible for us even to begin a revival of our business." So the Lius should accept the invitation to cooperate with the Japanese in either case.[27]

Anticipating Father's political objection to this plan, Third Son addressed the question whether it was unpatriotic. He dismissed as hypocrites those Shanghai business people currently based in Hong Kong who now claimed that they refused to form Sino-Japanese joint ventures in Shanghai because of their patriotic principles. "Those big shots owning property in Hong Kong and Shanghai may sing sweet melodies to please the ears in public," he told Father, "but in private they are doing everything in their power to protect their enterprises." Privately, if not publicly, these Shanghai capitalists had already set precedents for cooperating with the Japanese. "Many others have done so before us, and no one will criticize us for it."[28]

In resisting the temptation to collaborate with the Japanese, the Lius had held out longer and adopted a more principled position than any of the other Shanghai business people, Third Son maintained. "We have suffered great pain and made great sacrifices during the past five years," he reminded Father in 1942. "We can honestly face Heaven in good conscience." If one viewed their decision in strictly nationalistic terms, he admitted, the Lius faced a difficult choice "between the bad and the worse," but he claimed that his proposal for cooperating with the Japanese was not devoid of patriotic value. "Saving the enterprises," he wrote to Father, "would mean preserving the national spirit."[29]

In June 1942 Third Son placed his proposal in the hands of a trusted business associate whom Father had sent from Chongqing to Hong Kong to serve as a personal envoy and courier. Third Son also sent a copy to his two eldest brothers in Shanghai and urged them to bring it to the attention of other members of the family and senior managers in the family firm. Confident that they would support the idea, he deferred to their judgment. "We have been away from Shanghai for a long time," he wrote to Eldest and Second Sons in 1942, three years after he had left Shanghai and four years after Father had done so. "You brothers have been there, and what you have seen and heard must be closer to the truth."[30] Now fully aligned with his elder brothers in Shanghai, he did all that he could to win Father over to their side.

By the end of 1942, Third Son and his brothers in Shanghai finally had their way. On December 1, the Lius' Great China Match Company and the Japanese Central China Match Company signed a formal agreement creating a joint venture. On paper the Chinese side held a majority of the stock, but the Japanese side, which was a subsidiary of a huge Japanese holding company known as the Central China Development Corporation, retained control over raw materials and sales of matches. Second Son served on the joint venture's board of directors, and by giving it two of Great China Match's plants, he became free to make use of profits from the firm's other four operations in Shanghai.[31]

While Third Son's proposal for forming joint ventures in Shanghai was carried out, his plan for disposing of the family's Hong Kong match company and moving back to Shanghai was not. The Lius retained ownership of it, and Third Son stayed on as its manager in Hong Kong. After the Japanese occupied Hong Kong, he kept control of it for eleven months, from December 1941 to November 1942, and when he lost control of it, he tried to regain it by petitioning Japanese officials not only in Hong Kong but also through his family's contacts in Shanghai. He notified his uncle (Father's brother) in Shanghai that the Japanese authorities in Hong Kong "strongly believe that our factory has hostile connections and have handed our case over to the enemy properties committee." He explained that "hostile connections" meant "Chongqing colors"—loyalty to the Nationalist government of Chiang Kai-shek, whose wartime capital was in Chongqing.[32] To exonerate the Hong Kong company from these charges, Third Son had his family members in Shanghai apply to the Wang Jingwei government for certificates indicating that he and Father "were merely merchants without any connection to hostile forces."[33]

With help from his family in Shanghai and his Japanese business associates in Hong Kong, Third Son regained control of Great China Match Company of Hong Kong in August 1943. His success at resuming control so quickly—only ten months after he had lost it—was attributable to his and his brothers' improved relations with the Japanese authorities in Shanghai since they had formed their first Sino-Japanese joint venture in December 1942.

In retrospect, it is clear that Third Son preserved the family business in Hong Kong by following a precedent that had been set by Second Son in Shanghai. Second Son had initially joined with Father in rejecting the policy of cooperation with the Japanese in Shanghai in 1938 and 1939 and then had begun to urge Father to approve this policy beginning in 1940. Taking the same steps slightly later, Third Son initially joined with Father in rejecting the policy of cooperation with the Japanese in Hong Kong in 1940 and 1941 and then began to urge Father to approve this policy in 1942. Both sons came to the conclusion that only by adopting this policy could they regain control over the family business and keep it operating under the Japanese occupation.

Second Son and Third Son both had difficulty persuading Father that cooperation with the Japanese authorities and Wang Jingwei's government would bring control over management, profits, dividends, and bonuses back into the family's hands and would cause the family businesses in Shanghai and Hong Kong to prosper. He refused to adopt this policy while he resided in Shanghai in 1937–1938 and Hong Kong in 1938–1940, and he only acquiesced to it after he had left his sons in charge in those cities. Fleeing first from Shanghai to Hong Kong in 1938 and then from Hong Kong to Chongqing at the end of 1940, he was not physically present to preside over any of the family businesses in these cities under the Japanese occupation. But in Chongqing, which was never occupied by Japan, he did personally establish new enterprises as part of the family business, and he recruited Fourth Son to help him there.

Fourth Son and Industrial Equipment for Chongqing

In December 1940, Father moved to Chongqing and dispersed the Lius'
investments over a much larger geographical area. After maintaining
his base in Hong Kong for two and a half years, from June 1938 to December 1940, he was invited to Chongqing by Chiang Kai-shek, who
promised to help him finance new business ventures there.[34] In 1938,
after being forced to flee the Japanese occupation of Shanghai, Father
had devised a strategy for moving a modest amount of his Shanghai-
based assets to Hong Kong. Now, in 1940, he broadened this strategy
to include the transfer of far more personnel and equipment from
Shanghai to Chongqing, and he recruited Fourth Son to carry out this
transfer.

Just as Father had assigned Eldest and Second Sons to high posts in
the family's businesses in Shanghai and Third Son to a high post in
Hong Kong, he assigned Fourth Son to a high post, second only to his
own, in Chongqing. But Fourth Son played a somewhat different role
in preserving and utilizing the Lius' assets in Chongqing from the role
his brothers played in Shanghai and Hong Kong. Before the war, he had
never been as outspoken as his older brothers in arguing with Father
during the Shanghai Incident of 1932 or any other time, and throughout the war, he continued to defer unequivocally to Father as leader of
the family business. As Father's right-hand man, he followed orders
and did not devise plans or make decisions on his own. Moreover, he
did not deal with Japanese occupying forces in Chongqing because it
was never occupied. His contribution was to rescue the Lius' technicians and machinery from Japanese-occupied Shanghai and arrange
for their transfer to Chongqing and other inland cities, which had been
virtually unindustrialized before the war.

Between 1937 and 1939, the Lius had protected some of their industrial equipment by moving it from their factories in the Japanese-
occupied part of Shanghai into the city's Western-controlled International Settlement (which the Japanese did not occupy until December
1941), and they had sent a small fraction of the same equipment to Hong
Kong.[35] But these operations were simple and straightforward compared
to the logistical nightmare of transporting equipment from Shanghai
across enemy lines to distant Chongqing, a thousand miles from Shanghai and hundreds of miles from any coastal port or major railway line.

Father warned Fourth Son that this job would require him to carry out dangerous missions across enemy lines, and Fourth Son, whose young wife had recently given birth to their first child, declared that he was willing to take the risks.

Fourth Son's first Chongqing-related assignment was a clandestine operation in Shanghai. In 1939, a year before Father moved his residence from Hong Kong to Chongqing, he anticipated the move and gave Fourth Son the task of transporting machinery from the Lius' China Wool Manufacturing Company in Shanghai to Chongqing. At first Fourth Son could not lay his hands on the spindles, looms, dyeing equipment, and other machinery in the Lius' mill because it was located in Pudong, a district of Shanghai that had been under Japanese occupation since the invasion of 1937. Before he could ship this machinery out of Shanghai, he had to smuggle it from Pudong into the British-dominated International Settlement, the so-called solitary island, which was spared from Japanese occupation until Japan went to war with the Western powers in late 1941.

Lacking experience as a smuggler, Fourth Son sought help from a Swiss adventurer named Widler. At a series of meetings, Fourth Son plotted strategy with Widler, who always held a pistol in his hand while they talked. Fourth Son was alarmed when he first saw the gun, so Widler explained that he would never use it on Fourth Son and kept it handy strictly to protect himself whenever he undertook a dangerous mission. Widler accomplished the mission by bribing a major general in the Japanese army's headquarters at Shanghai and working nights under the cover of darkness. Over a period of six months in late 1939 and early 1940, he smuggled five hundred tons of equipment by boat across the Huangpu River from Pudong into the International Settlement. For his work, Fourth Son paid him 500,000 yuan.[36]

Once Fourth Son had moved this equipment into the International Settlement, he used some of it in newly built factories there and shipped the rest out of Shanghai. His original plan was to send the portion destined to go overseas via the port of Haiphong in the French colony of Vietnam, where it could travel first by rail to Kunming in southwest China and then by truck to Father in Chongqing. But by the time the ships approached Haiphong, France had been defeated by Germany in Europe and had yielded to demands from Germany's ally, Japan, for limiting supplies carried north on this railroad. The Japanese took this action to cut off all the supply lines to their enemy, Chiang Kai-shek's Nationalist government in west China.

Fortunately for Fourth Son, he had one other option because a new supply line, the Burma Road, had been opened in late 1938. It ran through rugged mountains for 715 miles (115 in Burma and 600 in China) from Mandalay in the British colony of Burma to Kunming in southwest China. To take advantage of it, Fourth Son devised a plan for sending his equipment by ship westward via Burma's capital of Rangoon to Mandalay and then northward by truck over the Burma Road to Kunming and over roads in China from Kunming to Chongqing. But despite his efforts for more than a year in 1939 and 1940, he was able to get the equipment only as far as Rangoon.

Exasperated, Father summoned Fourth Son to Chongqing. When he received this message, Fourth Son had already set out with his wife and daughter from Shanghai to Hong Kong, and on December 2, 1940, at Father's urging, he promptly left his family behind and flew to Chongqing. On arrival, he received a warm greeting from Father at the airport. "Son," Fourth Son recalled Father saying, "I am very touched by your willingness to give up your comfortable life in Shanghai and Hong Kong and come to work with me in such an impoverished place. I really need your help now."[37]

In Chongqing, Fourth Son became Father's second in command and took on the task of delivering to Chongqing the equipment he had already shipped from Shanghai to Rangoon. For months Father had appealed to the Nationalist government's Southwest Transportation Bureau to carry the cargo from Rangoon to Chongqing, and he had even enclosed with his requests Chiang Kai-shek's own official endorsements, "Generalissimo Chiang's Written Orders," but all to no avail. Finally in August 1941, eight months after Fourth Son's arrival in Chongqing, Father sent him to Rangoon to handle the matter in person.

As soon as Fourth Son's plane landed in Rangoon, he went directly to the Southwest Transportation Bureau and found the equipment from Shanghai piled up in an obscure warehouse with no prospect of leaving on government transportation. After fruitless negotiations, he recognized that he could not expect this badly managed bureaucratic agency to transport his goods, so he decided to make the delivery himself. With Father's backing, he bought five Dodge trucks from an American dealer and used them to make the twenty-five-hundred-mile round trip over winding roads between Mandalay and Chongqing—five times. On these arduous journeys over mountainous terrain, he and his truck drivers encountered bad weather, treacherous conditions, and numerous outposts and bureaus that imposed both official and unofficial taxes.[38]

Fourth Son overcame some of these obstacles by taking advantage of his past experience as a student in England. Since English was an official language in the British colony of Burma, he was able to make good use of his ability to speak it there. On the Chinese portion of the Burma Road, he also took advantage of his Western education. As a graduate of Cambridge University, he had become a member of the Renshe Chinese Alumni Association for returned students from the United Kingdom and United States, and he used this membership to make contact with many fellow members who were serving as officials along the Burma Road. For six months he continued to make these trips, and he succeeded in delivering all of the equipment to Chongqing before the Japanese military occupied Burma and closed the Burma Road in early 1942.[39]

With this equipment in hand, Father and Fourth Son opened three woolen mills in inland China outside the Japanese occupation. The two largest were the China Woolen Company in Sichuan and the Northwest Woolen Manufacturing Company in Lanzhou. In these businesses, the Lius took advantage of locally available raw materials, especially cheap and plentiful supplies of raw wool, and built factories in which they relied on their capital, machinery, and technicians from Shanghai to transform the raw materials into finished products.[40]

Father and Fourth Son also opened factories in several other cities. Besides founding three woolen mills, they established ten other major industrial enterprises in Chongqing, Guiyang, Kunming, Guilin, Lanzhou, and Baibu—all cities not under Japanese occupation—between 1940 and 1945. These enterprises included eight match factories, two cement plants, and ancillary units. As Fourth Son reported, Father was frustrated to discover that officials siphoned off large shares of the profits from firms that were partially state financed, but all of these new businesses took hold and generated profits, especially in the match industry, where the company had a virtual monopoly on the sale of safety matches.[41]

In all these ventures, Fourth Son invariably followed Father's lead and carried out his orders. As he wrote from Chongqing to his brothers in Shanghai on October 30, 1943: "Father and I haven't ever had a confrontation. Especially in business, the two of us as father and son are always in harmony. I respect and worship Father for his great personality and great fortitude. Therefore I am willing to work for him. He also trusts me very much, and whenever there is trouble, he always discusses it with me. Over these past three years, we have never had a single argument." Fourth Son was so in awe of Father's accomplishments that he could not imagine questioning his business decisions. "In all honesty," he told his brothers in Shanghai, "I can't even begin to fully appreciate all of Father's ideas and experiences, so how can I take issue with him?"[42]

Fourth Son's claim that he unquestioningly served Father in the family business was confirmed by both his parents. At the time, Father held up Fourth Son as a model for his other sons. Writing from Chongqing to the members of the family in Shanghai, he proudly reported that Fourth Son had done "wonderful work."[43] In reply, Mother heartily agreed and expressed her belief that Fourth Son's dedication to Father's work was inseparable from his devotion to Father as a parent. She wrote to Father on May 6, 1942: "It was to come help you that our fourth son left his wife and child behind. His filiality is indeed praiseworthy."[44] Mother also lavished praise on Fourth Son in letters to him, and she told him that everyone in Shanghai who knew him lauded him for his efforts. "The year before last you unhesitatingly left Shanghai and traveled a thousand miles to help Father," she recalled in a letter to Fourth Son on July 17, 1943. "Your actions have won praise from all our relatives and friends. I, especially, have great respect for you."[45] In hailing Fourth Son's filiality and devotion to Father, Mother bestowed on him her highest possible accolade. Even though she made no invidious comparisons between his wartime achievements and those of his older brothers, she did not praise them in the same terms.

Wartime Separation and Individual Initiative

These examples of Father's relations with his four eldest sons show how the war altered decision making in the Lius' family firm. After Father fled first from Shanghai to Hong Kong and then from Hong Kong to

Chongqing, he left the family business in the hands of his three eldest sons in these cities, and he tried to retain control over the entire family firm by writing them letters, but he soon discovered that they had seized the initiative and begun making decisions on their own. He clashed with them over financial issues, which he preferred to leave in the hands of his more experienced senior managers, and political issues, particularly the question whether to cooperate with the Japanese authorities. As the war wore on, he found that his sons resolved these issues less and less in consultation with him and more and more by themselves. As long as the war kept him away from them, each of the three eldest sons took individual initiative and acted autonomously rather than following Father's orders as closely as they had previously done when he had personally supervised them in Shanghai before the war.

While Father lost a measure of his authority over his three eldest sons during the war, he retained authority over Fourth Son by bringing him from Shanghai to Chongqing and ending their wartime separation. As long as they lived in the same city and consulted with each other face-to-face on a regular basis as the two top executives in the Chongqing branch of the family firm, Fourth Son did not challenge Father's business policies or vie with him for the authority to make decisions.

If the war had not occurred and Father and his children had all resided continuously in Shanghai during the 1930s and 1940s, would the four eldest sons all have conformed with Father's wishes for the family firm as closely as Fourth Son did in wartime Chongqing? Such an unhistorical question is difficult to answer, but it is safe to say that the war convinced Father to give his three eldest sons opportunities for leadership in the family firm at Shanghai and Hong Kong when they were still very young—much younger than he would have preferred. From Father's point of view, the war forced him to make this move even though it put the family firm at risk. From his three eldest sons' point of view, the war kept Father at a distance from them and left a leadership vacuum for them to fill as rising young executives. In other words, what loomed as a wartime threat for Father proved to be a wartime opportunity for his sons.

Younger sons in the Liu family also faced wartime threats and opportunities. They did not have opportunities to become top leaders in the family firm because their older brothers had already filled these positions. But like their brothers, they also reacted to the war's loosening of family ties and creation of opportunities for individual thought and actions. Of all the Lius, the one who entertained the most radical ideas and took the most radical actions was Sixth Son. Propelled by the war, he tried taking several different paths before ultimately choosing the road to Communism.

9

A Son Who Joined the Communists

THE WAR with Japan had a traumatic effect on Sixth Son, plunging him into despair, introspection, and a quest for a new identity. While his four eldest brothers responded to the war by accepting and taking advantage of their roles as leaders in the family firm, his initial reaction to it was to separate himself from the firm and question his most fundamental beliefs about religion, politics, and life in general. As he groped for a philosophical position that would guide his actions in wartime, he retained his belief in his family but at the same time considered committing himself to a range of other ideas and institutions: nationalism, Christianity, marriage, Communism. In retrospect, some of these possible commitments seem mutually contradictory, but Sixth Son took all of them seriously. He gave them careful thought and took actions to pursue each one—all within the first two years of the Sino-Japanese War, July 1937–July 1939. During a period of great upheaval for China and himself, Sixth Son discussed these ideas in correspondence with his parents, but he made decisions about whether to commit himself to each course of action on his own. Only in retrospect, after he had already made each commitment, did he seek his parents' approval for the action he had taken.

Making Japan a Second Homeland

Sixth Son took the war very personally and was deeply affected by it because it pitted his original homeland against his second homeland. During the six years leading up to the war, 1931–1937, he lived in Japan.

In January 1931, he had gone there as a student at age fifteen, the youngest age at which any of the Lius ever went abroad.[1] The timing of his arrival turned out to be critical: nine months before a key moment in Sino-Japanese relations, the Japanese seizure of Manchuria (northeast China) in September 1931. This action provoked angry anti-imperialist protests in China, especially at Shanghai, and caused many Chinese students to leave Japan, dropping the number there from 590 in 1930 to 83 by the end of 1931.[2] If Sixth Son had not already been in Japan before this incident, he might not have been allowed to go there at all. Father wrote to Eldest Son in November 1931: "had I not made arrangements for him to go to Japan before September 18, the black day whereon the Manchurian Affair began, he might have come to the U.S. with you [in the summer of 1931]."[3]

In the immediate aftermath of the Manchurian Incident, Sixth Son allowed for the possibility that he would cut short his stay in Japan and return home once and for all. On September 23, 1931, five days after the Manchurian Incident and one day after the Japanese military took control of all the cities in Manchuria, he sent home this telegram: "ALL WELL WILL QUIT IF NECESSARY."[4] When he did not quit, his brothers studying in the West repeatedly urged Father to force him to leave Japan. On November 19, Eldest Son proposed that Father should transfer him to a university in the United States or Germany,[5] and on February 10, 1932, Second Son pleaded with Father for an explanation as to why Sixth Son had not left Japan. "I cannot understand," Second Son wrote, how Sixth Son "can remain in Japan when the trouble is at its acutest point."[6] But Father accepted Sixth Son's decision to stay in Japan and told his other sons not to worry. On July 29, 1932, nine months after the Manchurian Incident, Father wrote to Eldest Son in the United States that Sixth Son "had an unperturbed time in Tokyo in spite of the troublous times we have to go through here."[7]

Sixth Son was reluctant to leave Japan because he had felt at home there since he had first arrived. At the outset, Father had prepared the way for him through contacts at Mitsui Trading Company, Japan's biggest international corporation, which had operated in China since 1877.[8] In response to Father's request for help, his business associate at Mitsui, Onoda Satoshi, in consultation with the head of Mitsui's worldwide operations, had worked out a plan in three phases. First, Sixth Son would move into the home of his new Japanese guardian, Tsuchiya

Masazo, a Mitsui employee who was familiar with Chinese because he had previously managed the company's office at the city of Dalian, which at the time was a Japanese-controlled leased territory in Manchuria. Second, Sixth Son would devote his first year to intensive study of the Japanese language. Third, he would enter Tokyo Institute of Technology (Tokyo Kogyo Daigaku), which had been elevated to a degree-conferring university in 1929 and was widely regarded as Japan's equivalent to MIT. "We have not yet made the final arrangements," Onoda telegraphed Father on August 17, 1931, "but if you have no objection to this proposal, we are going to make an offer to [Tsuchiya]."[9] Father fully approved this arrangement, which bore a close resemblance to the one he had made with Lowe, Bingham and Matthews to appoint their employee Alfred Ballard as the guardian for Second, Third, and Fourth Sons in England.

Sixth Son accepted his Japanese guardian even more readily than his older brothers had accepted their English one. Soon after he moved into Tsuchiya's home, he became very attached to his Japanese host family. In July 1932, eighteen months after he had arrived in Japan and nine months after the Manchurian Incident, Father reported to his elder sons in England that Sixth Son "has made himself a great favorite with the people of whose home he is inmate." Based on Sixth Son's letters, Father concluded, "In fact, the whole household there are good to him. Consequently he is finding himself very much at home there."[10] Throughout his years in Japan, Sixth Son regarded Japan as a second homeland, and even during the war after he had returned to China, he continued to speak fondly of his Japanese host family.[11]

He plunged into the study of Japanese and achieved good results. Father reported with great satisfaction to Eldest Son in early 1932: "Reports are constantly coming in to the effect that he [Sixth Son] is making remarkable progress in the mastery of the new language. He is devoting almost his whole attention and time to the learning of the Japanese tongue, and it is hoped that by next spring he will be able to take entrance examinations into college."[12] By July, Sixth Son fulfilled Father's hopes by passing the entrance examinations at Tokyo Institute of Technology. His "command of the Japanese language is remarkable," Father wrote to Eldest Son. "He can now carry on a conversation fluently in that tongue. I think it is not at all easy for one to pass entrance examinations into a school after having only such a brief preparation."[13]

Once Sixth Son had passed these entrance examinations, he agreed to follow Father's plan that he should learn all he could about the cement industry. Just as Father had assigned to Eldest Son the task of concentrating on one of the family firm's commodities, coal, he now assigned to Sixth Son another of its commodities, cement.[14] Never losing sight of cement, Sixth Son eventually majored in chemical engineering with a focus on ceramics.[15]

After his first year at Tokyo Institute of Technology, 1932–33, Sixth Son took an apprenticeship in a Japanese cement factory during his summer vacation. His letters to his brothers about it led them to conclude that he "seemed to be quite keen on his work in the factory."[16] His enthusiasm for his apprenticeship by no means diminished his enthusiasm for his studies. Returning to the classroom in 1933–34, he completed the year successfully and made his parents proud. "We are exceedingly glad to see the good report on your work at school," Father wrote to him at the end of the academic year on May 28, 1934. "I am glad that you are finding life at school very pleasant and enjoyable."[17] Sixth Son's academic achievements also impressed his older brothers, who almost all sent high evaluations of him to Father. "Sixth Brother is, I think, very clear minded, and he also takes great care in whatever he does," Eldest Son wrote in 1933.[18] "A clever boy like Nyan Dee [Sixth Son] should have advanced studies abroad," Second Son added in 1935.[19]

Between 1931 and 1937, as Sixth Son achieved one success after another—with language study, at university, in his apprenticeships—he chose to live and study in Japan despite the deterioration of Sino-Japanese relations. Along the way, he always had the options of returning to China or transferring to universities in the West, as Father reminded him whenever Sino-Japanese relations took a turn for the worse. Once in 1933 when his parents were particularly worried, Father "wrote very earnestly to your sixth brother," he told his sons in England. "I brought up every unfavourable side of studying in Japan that I could think of. And I insisted on his prompt decision whether to return or to remain. I left everything to him and would gladly send him elsewhere to study should he decide to come home. I was particularly ardent on the matter myself, because I wanted to have your sixth brother's whole future made as bright and promising as ever possible."[20] But Sixth Son had embraced Japan as his second homeland, and he assumed that he would remain there until he earned his bachelor's degree.

By the summer of 1937, he had finished all his course work, leaving only the writing of his senior thesis as his last requirement.[21]

Suddenly, to Sixth Son's horror, while he was home in Shanghai for summer vacation in 1937, Japan invaded China. In July Japan made its initial thrust into north China with the focus on Beijing and Tianjin and in August shifted to Shanghai after Chiang Kai-shek's forces launched an attack on the Japanese warships anchored there. During the next few months, hundreds of thousands of Chinese and Japanese troops were mobilized to fight the Battle of Shanghai, making it the second most intense military engagement up to that point in world history, surpassed only by the Battle of Verdun in Europe during World War I.[22]

For the people in Shanghai, the battle was a catastrophe, and for Sixth Son, it had especially deep significance because of his past six years in Japan. His original homeland was now at war with his second homeland, and the military forces of the two countries had taken their stand in a titanic struggle right in his own hometown. As he later put it, "at that moment I felt that the fire of war had burned its way to the front door of my own home."[23] Recoiling from the violence, he immediately ruled out the possibility of returning to Japan (where, as it turned out, he never again set foot), and he began to argue with his family about what he should do during the war.

Serving Family and Nation

During the first week of the Battle of Shanghai, Father and his eldest sons formulated a plan in which Sixth and Eighth Sons would pursue their studies in the West—Sixth Son in Germany and Eighth Son in the United States. Father was apparently unconcerned about the rise of Adolf Hitler and the Nazi Party in Germany, but when he announced the plan, while Eighth Son gladly agreed to go the United States, Sixth Son adamantly refused to go to Germany. He later recalled: "Suddenly I felt that 'every ordinary person' bears responsibility for the rise and fall of our nation, and I should not continue my studies."[24]

Father was surprised by Sixth Son's decision to stay in China and contribute to the war effort against Japan, but he accepted it and agreed to find a job for Sixth Son at the newly opened Sichuan Cement Company in Chongqing, 900 miles west of Shanghai. Father was able to arrange this appointment because he had made contacts and investments in the company and had sent technicians from his own cement company in Shanghai to work there.[25] As Father pointed out, if Sixth Son accepted this position, besides serving his country in an area not occupied by Japan, he would gain valuable experience in preparation for his future work on cement production in Shanghai. Emphasizing that opportunity above all, Father told Sixth Son: "To acquire some practical knowledge both intensively and extensively is the real object of your coming [to Chongqing]."[26]

Sixth Son was satisfied with this alternate plan, and he left Shanghai with Eighth Son on September 6, 1937, three weeks after the Battle of Shanghai had begun. With Chinese refugees clamoring for space on ships departing from Shanghai, even the influential Liu family could not lay hands on the most desirable tickets for this trip. The best they could do was make reservations for the boys on a ship to Hong Kong in fourth-class steerage, which did not permit them to take any luggage. Arriving in Hong Kong with little more than the shirts on their backs, they were met by Third Son, who had preceded them there, and helped them arrange the remainders of their two journeys, Sixth Son inland to Chongqing and Eighth Son overseas to the United States.[27]

On September 9, the day after their arrival in Hong Kong, Sixth Son sent his parents a thank-you note in which he ranked as his two top priorities filial piety and service to the nation. "During this time of national crisis," he earnestly wrote on behalf of Eighth Son as well as himself, "we, your sons, are fortunate to have had the opportunity to study abroad and to travel inland. We shall always remember to do our best and to take care of our health so that your hopes and the hopes for the nation that you have placed on us will not be in vain."[28] Taking this pledge of allegiance to his family and his country, Sixth Son began his long journey inland from Hong Kong.

Along the way, he reaffirmed his vow to serve his family and nation. On September 14, he took a four-and-a-half-hour flight from Hong Kong to Wuhan (not to be occupied by Japan until a year later) and from there wrote to his parents and brother in Shanghai: "I shall bear your words in mind always and try my very best to honour the glorifying name of our family."[29] As he then proceeded by ship up the Yangzi River, stopping in several ports, he observed with satisfaction that he was finally seeing his own country firsthand. "I was young when I went abroad," he wrote to his parents on the night of September 25, after his ship had made its last stop before reaching Chongqing, "and I stayed there for several years. I had not known anything about the situation in our country. What I have seen and heard during this trip has helped me to get to know my fatherland."[30] Discovering that China had great needs, he became eager to make his contribution to it.

Within a week of his arrival at Chongqing, he went to work as a technician at the Sichuan Cement Company, and from the beginning he approached his job as an opportunity to serve his country. To demonstrate this commitment in actions as well as words, he put his entire first paycheck into the war effort. "My first month's salary," he wrote to his family, "all went into Liberty Bonds [literally, the National Salvation Fund]. In this way I have contributed my entire first paycheck to our country."[31]

On hearing that Sixth Son had begun work soon after his arrival in Chongqing, Father showed his appreciation for his work ethic and patriotism. "It is exceedingly nice," Father wrote to him in November, that he "so quickly got into the factory. You are our first boy to work on the outside [that is, for a business other than the family firm]."[32] But a few weeks later, after finding out how Sixth Son had disposed of his salary, Father cautioned him against overzealously retaining nothing to meet his own needs. "My dear boy," Father wrote, "if I were you I should not spend any more money on buying Liberty Bonds. Not that I disapprove your fine expression of patriotism but that I do not see the necessity at the moment. It will please you to know that our family has more than done its share in this period of national crisis."[33] Father was not exaggerating about the Liu family's contribution to the war effort. He gave generously of his own time and money as director of the Shanghai Commission to Aid Wounded Soldiers (Shanghai shangbing jiuhu weiyuanhui), which transported injured men to hospitals, and he helped to provide five thousand beds for wounded soldiers in Shanghai.[34]

Father suggested to Sixth Son that if he was determined to be self-supporting on his low pay as an entry-level technician, he would be wise to save the money or spend it on himself. "Your own earning does not amount to very much. It is barely sufficient to pay for your monthly expenses on clothing, food, and lodging. Any saving which you may effect is sure to be useful to you in the future." Sixth Son should not only spend his salary on himself but should also supplement it by asking Father for money at any time. "I must particularly request that you write to me when you are in need of money," he insisted. "My financial conditions while not too bright at the moment are more than sufficient to support my family in its present needs."[35]

After making this generous offer, the last thing Father expected was that Sixth Son would then send money to him, but Sixth Son surprised him. Having given his first paycheck to the nation, Sixth Son gave his second one to his parents. In an emotionally charged declaration of filial devotion, he wrote at the end of November to his family: "I'd like to present the paycheck my second month to Father and Mother. I don't know why, but as I'm writing now, my tears are flowing. What you have given me since my birth is a debt that I can never repay in full. Although this is a very small amount, I hope that Father and Mother will willingly accept it."[36]

Sixth Son was well aware that this was largely a symbolic gesture, and he made it even though he initially sent only a receipt for his salary, not a remittance of the salary itself. "I am not sure if I can mail the money to you," he told his parents, "so I am now just sending you the receipt of my salary. I'll go downtown on my day off to find out [about how to send you the money]. Whether or not I can send you the actual money, I feel certain that Father and Mother will be just as happy as if they had actually received it."[37]

Once he had gone to the trouble of making all the arrangements to send a remittance across enemy lines from Chongqing to Shanghai, it eventually reached his parents, and it deeply moved them. In thanking him for it on January 3, 1938, they made this extraordinary statement: "You are the first child to show your filial love for us."[38] They confirmed Sixth Son's point that the gesture was almost purely symbolic and deeply meaningful. "Your remittance of $60 [in Chinese currency] has safely arrived," they acknowledged. "We are not at all in need of money, but we shall always treasure your expression of love in our heart." While gratefully accepting this money, they once again urged Sixth Son to spend his income on himself. "Remittance these days is difficult to make," they reminded him. "Hence we strongly advise you not to remit any more money to us. It will please us greatly if you are to spend your future earnings in Chungching [Chongqing] on nourishing foods and warm clothing."[39] Following their advice, Sixth Son sent no more paychecks to his parents in Shanghai, but he remained unwaveringly devoted to them.

His long-standing devotion to his parents and relatively new commitment to his country's defense continued to sustain him throughout the war, but he apparently felt the need for additional sustenance and guidance, and he sought to meet this need by turning to Christianity. Just as he had made up his own mind to stay in China contrary to Father's proposal for him to study in Germany, he made up his own mind to become a Christian before he announced his conversion to his parents.

Converting to Christianity

"Have I not told you that I decided to be a true Christian?" Sixth Son asked in a letter he wrote from Chongqing to his father, mother, brothers, and sisters in Shanghai on November 19, 1937.[40] His posing of this question in a casual form (when he knew full well that the answer was no) suggests that he was apprehensive about broaching the subject. As he went on, he made clear that he assumed his family would not welcome the news of his conversion to Christianity, and he defended his decision by anticipating and countering their objections in advance.

He forthrightly admitted to his family that it was his despair about the war with Japan that had caused him to seek solace from Christianity, and he pleaded with his family to recognize that he had been right to make this commitment. "[Converting to Christianity] may sound absurd to you as it did to me before I had converted myself," he acknowledged. Yet it was not absurd, because "I have always been unhappy since the war, but I am profoundly happy now." He overcame despair and achieved happiness because he came to believe that God would save not only himself but also his country. He explained this linkage between his own salvation and his country's salvation: "My absolute trust and faith in God, we call it complete surrender to God, has brought forth the trust and faith in myself as well as in our final victory over Japan."[41]

This religiously inspired confidence in the certainty of China's victory over Japan did not, Sixth Son assured his family, undermine or weaken his resolve to defend his country. "No, not at all, contrarily, I have decided to sacrifice myself more and more for the sake of our fatherland. The Gospel has taught me to do so." While Sixth Son valued words from the Bible in themselves, he was also convinced that these words inspired him and other Christians to take action, especially in wartime. "I am not presenting you beautiful words only. I believe it is utterly possible to get hold on ourselves even in this critical climax only if we have faith and trust in ourselves."[42] As the war moved toward its climax, he tried to realize this possibility of getting hold of himself through Christianity.

He had embraced this way of thinking and decided to convert to Christianity after hearing sermons and lectures in Chongqing by the American Methodist missionary Dr. E. Stanley Jones, who was a prominent figure. *Time* went so far as to characterize him as "the world's greatest Christian missionary."[43] In the first four decades of the twentieth century, he took India as the principal field for his missionary activity, but in 1937 he made a tour of China. Originally he had intended to campaign in China strictly as a Christian evangelist. After personally witnessing Japanese bombing in Shanghai when the city was engulfed by war in August 1937, he began to protest against the war. On August 15, the day after the fighting had begun in Shanghai, he preached a sermon at the city's Community Church in which he called for Japan and China to lay down their arms. "To us Christians," Jones told the congregation, "the method of war for the settlement of international differences is abhorrent. It seems not only inhuman but futile. The history of modern wars demonstrates indisputably that in the end everybody loses."[44] When the fighting intensified during the next few days, Jones fled China and spent six weeks in the Philippines, where the Japanese invasion had not yet reached. Still incensed, he denounced Japanese aggression in China, and he returned there in October 1937 for two months of public speaking in cities not under the Japanese occupation—Hong Kong, Wuhan, Changsha, Chengdu, and Chongqing.[45] In Chongqing, Sixth Son heard Jones speak.

Sixth Son was deeply moved by Jones's Christian message, especially as it applied to China's war with Japan. Jones's crucial words, as Sixth Son quoted them to his family, were these: "God often uses calamities to test us."[46] From this Christian perspective, Sixth Son imagined himself and his compatriots rising to the test in the war with Japan. According to Jones's optimistic prediction, once the Chinese people passed this test, China not only would defeat Japan but also would turn its wartime suffering to its postwar advantage. "I believe in what Dr. Jones has said," Sixth Son wrote to his family on November

19; "that China will come out through the flame, in which she is now falling, as a purified new nation. China will be able to reconstruct herself far more quickly, her progress will be many times more remarkable than her big achievement during the last five years."[47] In this vision of the future, China's baptism by fire would carry it first to victory over Japan and then to rapid postwar progress.

Sixth Son also drew inspiration from the wartime message delivered by the Chinese Christian Dr. Zhang Boling, founder and president of Nankai University in Tianjin. Zhang had risen above despair, even though the war might have driven him into it for both personal and professional reasons. On July 29–30, during the first month of the Japanese invasion of China, Japanese planes had bombed the Nankai University campus, reducing Zhang's life's work to rubble, and shortly thereafter, Zhang's son was killed when his plane crashed during a bombing mission in Shanghai.[48]

Describing these tragic events to the Liu family, Sixth Son attributed Zhang's avoidance of wartime despair to his Christianity, which shielded him because, paradoxically, it had originated in prewar despair. Ten years before the war, Zhang had been so depressed by corruption in China that he had joined with his like-minded friends in a suicide pact. "He thought he had no other way out," Sixth Son told his family. "He thought by his and his friends' suicides the government's officials and the people might be alarmed and wake up." Zhang would have committed suicide at that time, Sixth Son explained, if he had not turned to the Bible. "Before he and his friends were going to carry through the plan, he took the New Testament into his hands and read it," and miraculously he was saved. "God had got hold of him, lifted him up and his friends! He was born again."[49] It was this rebirth before the war that gave Zhang the strength to endure the destruction of his university and the death of his son during the war. "Was he discouraged? Has he decided to commit suicide again?" Sixth Son asked. "No," he answered, "not at all." Once reborn, "nothing could discourage him any more. He sees his new life and the life of China through his faith and trust in God."

Hailing this as an example of regaining hope through Christianity, Sixth Son reported to his family that Zhang had now founded another academic institution and was beginning to rebuild his life in Chongqing.[50] Sixth Son made no mention of whether he himself had contemplated suicide, but he clearly stated his belief that just as Christian faith had prevented Zhang from committing suicide, it would prevent anyone from doing so.

Sixth Son's reference to Zhang was meant to remind his family that Chinese as well as Westerners had become genuine Christians, and he exhorted his family to consider Christianity a valid option for any Chinese. He admitted that "a lot of people laugh at Christianity as I did without having the least understanding of it," and he urged his family members to take it seriously. If they believed that Christianity was laughable from a Chinese point of view, then they should think of Christ and his teachings in relation to great Chinese thinkers and their teachings. They should "take it as a teaching just as you do the teaching of Confucius or Mencius."[51]

In comparing these thinkers, Sixth Son saw close similarities. "Many of the teachings of our great teachers such as Confucius, Mencius, are very much the same as the teaching of Jesus Christ." But he also saw one major difference: "simply that they are not as inclusive and as great a teaching [as that of Christ]." Fully convinced of the superiority of Christian teachings, Sixth Son closed by offering his prayer for his family: "I pray that you may be blessed and relieved of despair for Jesus' sake."[52]

On November 19, after Sixth Son dramatically revealed to his family that he had converted to Christianity, he was disappointed not to receive an immediate reply. In early December he wrote again, and as before, he anticipated that his family would not welcome the news of his conversion. "You should not bear any hostility to Christianity based simply on your prejudice," he warned his family. He then shifted from a defensive to an offensive approach. "I don't mean to preach to all of you," he said, before he then began to preach, "but I really want to share with others the blessings that I have already received. In particular, for those of you in my family who have cared for me so long and so deeply, how can I not tell you all about blessings that can be received so easily?"[53] This rhetorical question conveyed Sixth Son's eagerness for exchanges with his family on the subject of Christianity.

When a reply from Father and Mother finally reached Chongqing, it did not include a single objection to Sixth Son's decision to convert to Christianity. Contrary to his apprehensive expectations, Father gave him nothing but encouragement and explained why the whole family was receptive to the idea. "It was a perfect sermonette," Father remarked, referring to Sixth Son's letter of November 19 (quoted above). "We were not at all dazed by your dramatic conversion, though. You are aware that the spirit of perfect tolerance prevails in our family. Each and every one of us is left to the dictates of his or her own conscience. In this respect, at least, we think that we are on a par with any progressive family today."[54]

Showing his own tolerance, Father not only accepted but found favorable the news of Sixth Son's conversion. He noted that religion was a perfectly valid means of dispelling the kind of doubt and despair that had brought down Sixth Son's spirits during the war. In Father's words, "religion becomes an inevitable power when everything around fades into impotency and ineffectiveness." Far from objecting to Sixth Son's turn toward religion, Father applauded it. "We are glad," he wrote, "that you have already found such a source of unfailing strength even at such an early stage of life [Sixth Son was twenty-one]. More effective than anything else Religion can emancipate you from brooding over despairing thoughts and sights."[55]

Father approved of Sixth Son seeking relief not only through religion in general but also through Christianity in particular. "And of all religions you have wisely chosen Christianity. The strength or superiority of this religion lies in its universality and all-inclusiveness. Christianity has become a universal religion because its truth or principle is universally valid." In praising Christianity's inclusiveness, Father echoed Sixth Son's evaluation of it—even using Sixth Son's word. Father did not go so far as to announce that he or other family members were prepared to convert to Christianity too, but he readily endorsed Sixth Son's own decision to do so. "Well, dear boy," Father wrote on December 6, accepting his son's decision as final, "we expect to see you take big strides in Christianity."[56]

After receiving Father's approval, Sixth Son did take big strides in Christianity. First and foremost, he was baptized at Chongqing on Christmas Eve, 1937. His announcement of his baptism brought a response from his parents that conveyed the same equanimity that they had shown on hearing the news of his conversion. "It is splendid," they told him on January 3, 1938. "We have not the least doubt that you will get the very best happiness and comfort out of the religion."[57] As they were all painfully aware, this happiness and comfort were not common at the time in China because of the latest news of the war. In November 1937 Japanese troops had won the Battle of Shanghai, and in December they had begun to commit the seven weeks of atrocities that became known as the Rape of Nanking (Nanjing). As Chiang Kai-shek retreated from his capital at Nanjing and the battlefront moved westward toward Chongqing, Sixth Son sought comfort not only from religion but also from female companionship.

Proposing Marriage

In early November 1937, at the same time that Sixth Son converted to Christianity, he sent a proposal of marriage to Wu Yuying, a Christian, whose father, Wu Qingtai (T. T. Woo), had been Father's business associate since the 1920s.[58] With her, as with Christianity, he felt that the war was a crucial determinant of his thinking. But whereas the war brought him and Christianity together, the war drove him and Wu apart.

Sixth Son made the decision to ask Wu to marry him while he was in a hospital suffering from a case of malaria. During bed rest in Chongqing, he assumed that his parents would approve of his choice, and he wrote to Father and asked him to convey the marriage proposal to Wu, who was living with her family in Shanghai. A few weeks later, at the end of November, after being released from the hospital, Sixth Son had second thoughts about having resorted to this approach. "While in the hospital," he reminded his family, "I wrote to you to ask you to propose to Miss Wu on my behalf. After thinking about it for the past few days, I feel that it was foolish of me. Maybe I was not exactly myself when I was in the hospital. Without God's help, if she refuses my presumptuous request, I'll certainly feel that I have lost face."[59] Since he had barely met Wu, he would not have made such a premature move, he noted, had the war not put so much distance between him in Chongqing and her in Shanghai, keeping them literally across enemy lines from each other.

He believed that the war also stood between him and any prospect of marrying Wu because it required him to give priority to national concerns over personal ones. "I long to be comforted by the opposite sex," he confided to his family, "but at this time of national crisis, I must assign lower priority to personal issues." Not until the war was over and Sixth Son had taken a well-paying job should he be married, he decided. "I believe the time for me to get married is when my financial independence is achieved, the national crisis is resolved, and my personal income has reached over one hundred dollars [in Chinese currency per month]. At the moment, no one can tell when that time will be."[60]

With no end to the war in sight, he regretted that he had asked Wu to wait for him, because she had not fallen in love with him. "Of course," he wrote hopefully to his family, "if Miss Wu and I had love between us and she was willing to wait, then it would have been all right [for me to have proposed to her]." But in this case, "I trust that she understands my present circumstances, and I believe that she will not agree to such a seemingly hopeless marriage prospect—one that lies in such a distant future." If they were together, the war would still prevent them from becoming married. "Even if she accepts my proposal," he pointed out to his family, "I can still only agree to a spiritual union until the national crisis is resolved and my financial situation has improved."[61]

While emphasizing that the war forced him to postpone marriage, he expressed pessimism about his prospects with Wu even after the war ended. He questioned whether she would ever be willing to join him in a less lavish life than the one to which she was accustomed in her wealthy family. "Miss Wu has led such an extremely comfortable life," he reminded his family, that "she will lead a bitter life if she marries someone like me, who will not only be poor but won't even want to get rich."[62]

Sixth Son was relieved to hear from his parents that even though he had been correct in assuming that they approved of his choice of spouse, they had not proceeded to make the proposal to Wu as bluntly and prematurely as he had feared they might do. On receiving his letter containing his proposal to Wu, Father and Mother had not delivered it to her or even contacted her about it. They had held it back, as Father explained to Sixth Son, because "we realized that the affair was a delicate one. A hasty or indecorous approach might do injustice to the dignity of the matter. Hence I went to Mr. Woo [Wu] merely for his assent that you have the happy privilege of setting up a line of correspondence with his second daughter as you desired."[63]

Father was delighted with Mr. Wu's enthusiastic approval for this opening of correspondence between his daughter and Sixth Son. "Mr.

Woo beamed," Father reported to Sixth Son. "The radiance on his face was the reflection of joy from his heart. He was all willingness. We assure you that we can count on Mr. Woo as potentate spokesman [sovereign representative] both for his wife and his daughter in question." Despite Mr. Wu's eagerness, Father did not broach the subject of marriage with him. "We will not and cannot approach the Woo family for your betrothal," he wrote to Sixth Son on December 15, "until you have definitely made known your decision to us. Meanwhile we leave you a free hand to work out the problem. We will remain inactive as far as we can."[64] Subsequently, even as Father and Mother gave their blessing to this match, they honored their pledge not to interfere.

In December Sixth Son and Wu Yuying began corresponding with each other. Their letters were sent via his parents, but the parents on both sides refrained from conducting marriage negotiations. "We have so far only set up a sort of post office for you," Father and Mother informed Sixth Son on January 3, 1938. "Further than that we have not yet gone, though our intention is by no means unknown to the Woo family."[65] When Sixth Son and Wu began to make use of this personal post office, his parents were pleased. "Of course you could not expect everything out of that first letter," Father and Mother assured him on March 7. "But the start has been made. The ball is now set rolling. And you have scored your maiden victory. We trust that you will apply yourself to writing with ever-increasing diligence and that your new correspondent will soon turn into great joy and blessing to you."[66] It was only a matter of time, Mother and Father imagined, before he achieved his ultimate triumph and claimed his bride.

Contrary to their expectations, time conspired against this marriage. In April, as heavy fighting between Chinese and Japanese troops continued in central China, Sixth Son felt overwhelmed by the war and began to doubt whether he should contemplate marriage or stand by any of the other commitments that he had made. By April, his brooding reached the point where he lost control of his emotions. "The troubles burning inside my chest, after being suppressed by my simply ignoring them, have finally rebelled," he wrote to his family. "During this process of bitter struggle, I lost an entire week of sleep as I found myself increasingly troubled by unsolved problems."

Totally exhausted, he could not hide his depression at work from his boss, Xu Zongxu, the head of the Sichuan Cement Company's engineering division, who suggested that he should take some time off and go to Beipei, an industrial park, intellectual community, and resort that had been developed by a Chinese capitalist about forty miles northwest of Chongqing. In the serene atmosphere of this bucolic setting, he finally got some sleep and pulled his thoughts together.[67]

"At about 2:30 this morning," he wrote from Beipei to his family in Shanghai, "I woke up and found myself ready to seek solutions to the rest of my problems." Within thirty minutes, 2:30–3:00 A.M., he made this breakthrough. "I began writing this letter at three o'clock in the morning (as you can all probably guess)," he wrote to his family in the opening paragraph of a letter he labored over for the next four days, April 22–26, 1938.[68] He explained to them that he had reconsidered not only his marriage proposal to Wu Yuying but all of the major commitments he had recently made, and he was prepared to break some of the most significant ones.

Unloading Burdens

During the intense first year of the war, Sixth Son had responded to it by making three major decisions that might well have led to lifelong commitments. First, he had come to the Sichuan Cement Company and taken a job that seemed appropriate to groom him for a long-term position as the cement specialist in the Liu family business. Second, he had converted to Christianity as his religion for life. Third, he had proposed marriage to a woman who was expected to be his one and only wife. If the language in his letters is any indication, he was a sensitive and sincere young man who had not made these commitments lightly. Nonetheless, in writing this long letter, he reevaluated all of these commitments and presented each one in a new light.

Concerning his job and future career, he unveiled a radically new plan. He was on the verge of leaving his job. His dissatisfaction with it had been growing for months, but up to this point he had been reluctant to reveal his feelings to his family. "In your letters," he acknowledged, "you have repeatedly asked about my work in the factory. I was afraid that if I dealt with this subject, I would explode and would worry all of you. So I haven't dared to talk about it in my letters before now."[69]

The trouble at work had begun soon after he had arrived in Chongqing, and before long it had demoralized him. "During the first month here, I was busy familiarizing myself with the situation in the factory, and I didn't think much about it. But later I began to feel that things were meaningless." He blamed this meaninglessness not on his boss, Xu Zongxu, who was Father's friend, but rather on Kong Chengyu, the head of the company's manufacturing division—"the person who holds the real power." Kong clung to his power by refusing to share it with Sixth Son or anyone else who proposed to reorganize low-level workers on the shop floor for the sake of raising efficiency. "Why," Sixth Son angrily asked, posing a rhetorical question for his family, did Kong and his cronies "pay no attention to efficiency in the factory? Why have those who are essential to the factory become so discontent?"[70]

Convinced that the problems were traceable to Kong's abuse of his authority, Sixth Son could find no way to solve them without incurring Kong's wrath. Within his first month at Chongqing, "I began to feel depressed. Very early on, I realized that if the situation continued, I would only sink to the bottom." While putting up with the situation for the next six months, he could not bring himself to complain about it to Xu Zongxu.

Not until Sixth Son had begun to write the letter to his family at the end of April 1938 did he finally lodge his complaint. Halfway through his writing of the letter, he ended his retreat, returned from Beipei to Chongqing, and appealed directly to Xu Zongxu. "I went to see Director Xu," he reported as he resumed his long letter, "and I spoke frankly about issues at the factory and my own lack of interest in my work. He seemed to be open to my ideas, and he promised that he would fulfill my hopes and wishes." Sixth Son drew some satisfaction from this exchange, but he was not optimistic about his future with the company. "Things cannot change overnight," he noted, "so I don't expect any major change in the near future." For the next few months he was willing to stay at the company to see whether the manufacturing division would undergo serious reorganization, but "in the end perhaps I won't want to stay on at the factory due to my lack of interest in this job."[71]

Besides announcing to his family his decision to quit his job in the immediate future, he made another startling revelation about his long-term plans for his career. He reminded Father and his brothers that before he left Shanghai as the war broke out, they had instructed him to go to Germany and the United States for further education, and they had acquiesced to his idea of going to Chongqing for a factory job only on the condition that he would go to Germany and the United States later. Now he informed them that he had decided not to go to Germany and the United States at all because he had found a more qualified person to go in his place. He had met this person, Wang Jingci, at the Sichuan Cement Company, and he had been impressed by Wang's achievements and potential. A graduate of Hebei Normal College and Beiyang University, Wang had worked in the Engineering Department at Beiyang and Qinghua University, and he had made important discoveries there and in the laboratory of the Sichuan Cement Company. "He aspires to model himself after Newton and recent winners of Nobel prizes in the sciences," Sixth Son observed. "I am especially impressed by his creativity." This creativity, Sixth Son claimed, made Wang superior to himself as a candidate for further study: "he has a fine personality and an ability to think creatively (both of which I lack)."

Sixth Son recognized that the family customarily sent abroad its own members, not nonkin, but he insisted that this extraordinary step needed to be taken because of the challenge posed by the war. "Even though he is not Father's son," he assured his family, Wang "can attain a goal that none of Father's sons or anyone else can, so surely Father will be willing to support him." In peacetime, the family might have had the luxury of providing overseas study exclusively for its own members, but in wartime, the family should finance Wang's overseas education for the sake of the nation. "If we can use money to help nourish a talent on behalf of China, I am certain that the money will be worth several tens of times what is spent," he wrote. "In the end, I feel that during our national crisis, the most important thing is to put the interest of the majority before anything else. So we should all be seeking first and foremost to benefit the general public."

If Sixth Son would quit his job and not go to Germany or the United States, what would he do instead? "At times," he told his family in the same letter, "I've thought of going to join the [Communist] Eighth Route Army in northern Shaanxi Province. The Chinese Communist Party under Mao Zedong had recently established a soviet base area there with its capital at Yan'an." Sixth Son saw reasons both for and against making this move. "Life over there may be a hundred times more bitter than it is here, but at least I could find satisfactions of other kinds." He was willing to endure bitter conditions, but he held back because he was not prepared to make the ultimate sacrifice. "The reason why I have not gone to northern Shaanxi is that I, as an educated person, might end up sacrificing my life, like any little soldier, by taking a bullet. This would seem to be a loss to our nation." Uncomfortable claiming an elite status for himself as "an educated person" and "a loss to our nation," he tried to deny that he was doing so: "I am not saying that I am too privileged to go to the battlefront. I simply think that I am not yet needed by our nation at this point."[72]

He did not specify for his family members at what point he thought he would be needed in the Eighth Route Army, but he warned them that it might be soon. "Although you have asked me [about my politics] repeatedly in your letters, I have not given you any concrete answers," he acknowledged, and then he gave an answer. "To be straightforward and frank: my thinking leans to the left. At any moment I might drop everything and go to northern Shaanxi to lead a bitter life."[73] Thus did he put his family on notice that he might soon join the Communists.

While he believed that joining the Communist movement would require him to quit his job and forgo his studies in Germany and the United States, he also thought it would cause him to drop his plans for marrying Wu Yuying. If he went to Yan'an, he would, as he put it, "eat two-cent meals and earn a one-dollar monthly wage—even the commander of the Eighth Route Army makes only five dollars a month."[74] If he was leading this life of poverty, he would not be attractive to Wu, he predicted. "In light of her background and upbringing, I don't think Miss Wu would be able to stand an impoverished husband such as myself."

Despite this doubt, he had not quite given up on Wu. As with his job at the factory, he still held out some small amount of hope. "If Miss Wu doesn't care about material comfort and has the fortitude to endure a bitter life, I would like to continue the relationship," he assured his parents. But he was convinced that she did care about material comfort. From the beginning of their correspondence he had been candid with her about his own indifference to acquiring wealth, and after taking into account her responses (and lack of responses), he had run out of things to say. "To tell the truth, I really don't know what I can write in my letters," he admitted. Even if he could think of something to say, he would not compromise his leftist principles, which seem to have kept her cool toward him throughout their correspondence. "In her letters she has agreed only to be my friend," Sixth Son reported to his family in the same letter, and he noted that she had not written to him since January 18. In April, after her long silence, he "now suddenly began to feel cold" toward her, and he concluded: "there's little hope for Miss Wu and myself."[75]

Backing away from these recently made commitments—to his job, his education in the West, and his prospective bride—he clung tenaciously to his belief in Christianity. In fact, he gave his Christian God credit for showing him how to unburden himself of his other commitments. In this letter, announcing to his family that he was relinquishing these burdens, he wrote: "My dear God, I thank you for sweeping away all those troubling thoughts that I had on my chest during the past several months."[76]

Sixth Son was able to retain his faith in Christianity as he contemplated going to Yan'an because he considered Christianity compatible with Communism. At the time of his conversion, he thought about Christianity's relationship to Communism and concluded that the two had the same goal. "[The] Communist idea is thought to be a very new idea, but it has been the idea of Jesus Christ. They are of course in many respects different as to the means of acquiring the same end."[77]

When he converted to Christianity, he declared that he had faith in it above all else, even Communism, but he saw no reason why he could not believe in both. "I had faith in communism, and still have it," he wrote to his family when he became a Christian, "but I have the greatest faith in God."[78] This faith did not stand in his way as he made his decision to go to Yan'an. He felt the need to bring his job, his plans for study abroad, and his marriage prospects to an end, but he remained a Christian as he resolved to join the Communists.

This final decision to join them was triggered by their victory over Japanese troops in the battle at Pingxing Pass in north China. In the first year of the war, Japan's forces from north China had moved easily westward and southward from Beijing and Tianjin and had routed Chinese troops along the way, except in this one case.[79] In May, Sixth Son heard that the Eighth Route Army had annihilated a brigade of Japanese soldiers in this battle, and the news convinced him that the Communists were effective militarily as well as politically. "Initially I had thought of joining the Nationalist Army," he later recalled. But he objected to the Nationalist officers' brutal treatment of their recruits in Chongqing. Only after reading pamphlets published by the Communists did he, according to his later recollection, discover "for the first time that there is an army in our country actually fighting the Japanese."[80]

As word leaked out at the Sichuan Cement Company that Sixth Son was contemplating a move to Yan'an, Xu Zongxu heard about it and summoned Sixth Son to his office. "You are already twenty-four years old [by Chinese reckoning], and I imagine even your father wouldn't be able to talk you out of it," Xu said after hearing Sixth Son out. Accepting Sixth Son's decision as final, Xu wrote a letter of introduction for him to Zhang Boling, the Christian leader and social reformer whom Sixth Son admired, and urged Sixth Son to see Zhang before setting out from Chongqing.

As Xu Zongxu expected, Sixth Son found Zhang eager to help. "Liu Hongsheng's son has decided to go to Yan'an," Zhang announced with great pleasure to his staff after greeting Sixth Son and reading Xu's letter. He then picked up his writing brush and dashed off letters of introduction for Sixth Son to Zhou Enlai and Wang Ming, both members of the Central Committee of the Chinese Communist Party and based at Yan'an.[81]

With these letters in hand, Sixth Son made the twelve-hundred-mile journey from Chongqing to Yan'an via Wuhan and Xi'an. Along the way, he stopped to check in at the offices of the Communist army in each city. He realized that he was making a move that reflected his politics and might transform his life, and to commemorate this decision, he adopted a new name for himself, as did many other young people who joined the Communists. Whereas his parents had chosen for him the birth name Liu Nianti (Remember Brotherliness Liu), he chose for himself the new name Liu Gongcheng (Sincerely Public Spirited Liu).[82] Over his old name, not his new one, he sent a telegram to Father before leaving Xi'an in which he notified Father that he was departing on the last leg of his journey to Yan'an, but he gave no explanation for his decision to take this step.[83]

Joining the Communists

On July 15, he reached Yan'an and presented Zhang Boling's letters to the Communist leaders.[84] He was exhausted by the arduous 175-mile trip from Xi'an to Yan'an. "It took a whole week to make a two-day trip," he wrote to his family and friends on July 17, his third day in

Yan'an. "The road has not been repaired for some time, and it's been raining very hard, so the automobile got stuck all the time." Other material conditions also struck him as poor. "In the northwest, life is really hard, and we have hardly anything to eat." Local peasants had an even harder time, suffering from low wages and inadequate hygiene, among other things. "Material life here is really rough," he wrote on a postcard in Chinese for all to see. "I can't begin to tell you what our food is like."[85]

Yet, he chose to stay despite these uncomfortable conditions. He remained at Yan'an not because he discovered new ideas there but because he became convinced that the Communists were acting in accordance with principles he had espoused for a long time. "Throughout my life, I have all along been sympathetic to communism," he had written to Father from Japan as early as February 1937, more than a year before he made his decision to become part of Mao's Communist movement in Yan'an.[86] He was, to be sure, exaggerating, but in fact his interests in Communism did date back to his teenage years.

Like many young Chinese in the early twentieth century, he became politically radicalized as a student in prewar Japan. While there, he read the Japanese Marxist Kawakami Hajime, who had published a Japanese translation of Marx's work *Das Kapital* in 1927. Sixth Son was attracted to Communism as a loosely defined, eclectic set of theories that provided solutions to the problem of mass poverty.[87] At the same time, even before Japan's invasion of China, he had anticipated the coming of the war and had decided that his country would only win if its leadership remained in the hands of Chiang Kai-shek and his Nationalist government. So before going to Yan'an, he believed that postwar China should be governed by the Communists but wartime China should be led by the Nationalists.

In the months before Japan's invasion of China, he spelled out this political position in correspondence with Father. In advocating Communism for the long-term solutions to China's problems, he was unequivocal. "I am convinced that communism offers the best way to realize the people's livelihood in the Three People's Principles [of nationalism, democracy, and people's livelihood, as formulated by Sun Yat-sen]," he wrote from Tokyo to Father in Shanghai on February 26, 1937. "I sincerely hope that China will one day adopt communism so that the common masses will attain real happiness." Anyone doubting that these principles would work in China needed only to consider the example of the Soviet Union, where, Sixth Son claimed, Communism had already been put into practice with good effect. "The equality that exists among the people and the social welfare benefits enjoyed by the working class in Russia are the envy of other nations."[88] Despite this firm commitment to Communism, Sixth Son was receptive to Father's suggestion that Chiang Kai-shek, the anti-Communist leader of China's Nationalist government, deserved his support.

Sixth Son told Father that he was willing to support Chiang Kai-shek after reading a copy of Chiang's journal on the Xi'an Incident, which Father had sent to him in Japan in February 1937. This incident had occurred in Xi'an two months earlier. On December 12, 1936, Chiang had been kidnapped by the Chinese warlord Zhang Xueliang, who had attempted to force him to agree to a Nationalist-Communist united front against the Japanese military forces in China. Chiang had been held captive until negotiations between the Nationalists and the Chinese Communist Party (represented by Zhou Enlai) had resulted in his release on Christmas Day. After his release, he had published his journal chronicling the events at Xi'an.

Sixth Son was deeply moved by this journal and was fully persuaded that Chiang—not Mao or any other Communist—should be China's leader. He wrote to Father: "Generalissimo Chiang's character is indeed worthy of our admiration. I have learned a lot about Generalissimo Chiang from reading Japanese newspapers. (Japanese people respect Generalissimo Chiang very much). Now that I've also read his journal, I have a deeper understanding of him. He is indeed well qualified to be our national leader." Sixth Son's reading of the Xi'an journal convinced him not only that China needed Chiang as its leader but also that the country could do without Communism, at least temporarily. "Since reading Generalissimo Chiang's journal, I firmly believe that there is no need for China to adopt communism—at least not at the present moment. If China needed communism, Generalissimo Chiang would not be so opposed to it."[89] So as early as early as February 1937— six months before the war began and eighteen months before Sixth Son went to Yan'an—he had advocated the policy of short-term support for Chiang and the Nationalists and long-term support for the Communists.

During Sixth Son's year at Yan'an, from July 1938 to July 1939, he continued to advocate the same policy, and he found that it coincided with the Communists' official policy of forming a united front with Chiang and the Nationalists in the war against Japan. Sixth Son was one of many young urban Chinese who were attracted to Yan'an after the Communists announced their united front policy in 1935. According to one estimate, between 1937 and 1940, one hundred thousand immigrants, about half of them students, teachers, writers, and intellectuals, arrived at Mao's base.[90] Like many others, Sixth Son was relieved to find on his arrival that he was encouraged to express his advocacy of the united front and other ideas he had brought with him to Yan'an. On his third day there, he wrote to his family and friends: "Although we have not been here long, all of us newcomers are very impressed by ideas of equality and democracy. The biggest surprise to me is the freedom of political thought that is allowed. Last night the university's president gave a speech guaranteeing it."[91]

At Yan'an, Sixth Son was first assigned to the Department of Military Affairs at Resist Japan University (Kang Ri Daxue) and then appointed as a Japanese-language teacher in the Enemy-Work Training Corps. At the university, Communist leaders presented their views and prepared young people to become party cadres. With great excitement, Sixth Son attended lectures by Mao Zedong and other leaders, and he was impressed by their commitment to maintaining a united front with Chiang Kai-shek against Japan. On May 6, 1939, after spending ten months at Yan'an, he wrote to his parents: "One strength of the education at Resist Japan University is that there are lectures given regularly by famous people. Our most recent lecture was entitled 'Political Activities of the Japanese Thugs and How We Deal with Them.' The lecture revealed in graphic detail the enemy's evil conspiracy of 'Overthrowing Chiang Kai-shek and Opposing the Communists.'"[92]

Such an evil conspiracy would be overcome, Sixth Son pointed out, only if China prevented Japan from both overthrowing Chiang and opposing the Communists. "We'll only defeat our evil enemy," he told Father and Mother, "if national unity is strengthened, cooperation between the Nationalist Party and the Communist Party is lasting, the enemy's trap is avoided, and the Resistance War under the leadership of Generalissimo Chiang Kai-shek is carried out."[93]

In substance, this endorsement of the united front strategy, written to his parents from Yan'an in May 1939, was almost identical to the one he had sent them from Japan more than two years earlier. But in

tone, his message was different. Before going to Yan'an, he had fallen
into despair about his and his country's ability to cope with the war,
and even when he had found comfort for himself in Christianity, he
had not discovered any way to mobilize the Chinese people against Japan. At Yan'an, by contrast, he came to believe that the Communists
were fully capable of mobilizing the masses. "Fortunately," he wrote,
"the majority of the Chinese people see through the enemy's evil con-
spiring. Guerrilla warfare is already spreading within the [Japanese]
occupied areas." It spread partly because it went hand in hand with the
Communists' production campaigns, which attracted popular support
and raised the morale of all the participants, he claimed, including
himself. During one such campaign, he reported, "I was selected as
one of the labor heroes. Father and Mother, I hope you are both proud
of me."[94]

Sixth Son was undoubtedly proud of himself, but his parents were
not proud of his decision to go to Yan'an—at least not as long as he remained there far beyond their reach.

Calming Father's and Mother's Fears

On the eve of Sixth Son's departure from Chongqing in July 1938, his
parents had showed no awareness that he would be going to Yan'an.
"We have been exceedingly happy that you have been getting along
very well in Chungching [Chongqing]," they wrote to him, apparently
oblivious to his mounting frustration with his life there. "One of our
biggest wishes is that when you come back to us we may find you still
plumper and healthier."[95] When they received from him the news that
he was leaving for Yan'an, it came in a brief telegram with no explanation.[96] To be sure, his parents had been receiving letters for years showing his sympathy for Communism (as quoted above), but when he
made this move to Yan'an, they had not expected it, and both of them
reacted sharply to it.

At first, Mother refused to believe that he would have made this
decision without consulting Father and herself. On July 11, 1938 (while
Sixth Son was en route from Chongqing to Yan'an), Mother reported to
Father in Hong Kong that Sixth Son had stopped writing to her—a
lapse in his correspondence that was completely out of character, she
pointed out. "I am very sorry that of late we have not received any

news from our sixth son. I do not at all understand why he did not come directly home after leaving Chungking [Chongqing]. He used to be a sensible boy. I thought he would not do anything or go to any-where without first obtaining our permission."[97]

Mother had no explanation from Sixth Son as to why he would have made a rash decision without consulting his parents, but she sus-pected he might have been upset because Wu Yuying had not accepted his marriage proposal. "I am afraid that some terrible disappointment must have weighted his heart down or else he would not have taken any step without our consent. Perhaps love has been the great deter-mining force in what he is now doing. Youth is ever full of romance."[98] Mother did not rule out the possibility that he might have had some political motivation—"I know he is fired by a genuine spirit of patrio-tism." But she did not attempt to speculate about it. Whatever his rea-sons for going to Yan'an, Mother desperately wanted him back, and in letter after letter she pleaded with Father to deliver him to her.[99]

On August 14, a month after Sixth Son reached Yan'an, Mother received two postcards from him, and she was somewhat relieved by his attitude toward his new home. "Physically he is going through great hardships," she told Father in her summary of the cards' contents. "Still he seems happy in the spiritual and conscientious sense."[100] But his claim that he was happy in spirit and conscience by no means satisfied her. After hearing from him, she repeated over and over her demand that Father bring him home. On August 25, she wrote to Father in Hong Kong: "I want you to make every possible effort there to have him come back to me. You must tell him that I will always feel miserable if he does not come back to me. Indeed, I will not be happy so long as he is away from me. Hence do your utmost to persuade him to come back to me."[101]

Father reacted to the news of Sixth Son's move to Yan'an by taking action even before Mother asked him to. He learned of Sixth Son's de-parture for Yan'an just after his own escape from Japanese-occupied Shanghai for Hong Kong. On July 2, Father's second day in Hong Kong, he sent an urgent telegram to Fourth Son in Shanghai requesting cop-ies of Sixth Son's letters and addresses so that his exact whereabouts could be ascertained, and in a follow-up letter the same day, Father unveiled his plan to bring Sixth Son back from Yan'an.

The previous night, July 1, Father had met with Zhu Jiahua, a high official in Chiang Kai-shek's Nationalist government, at a dinner hosted by Third Son's in-laws, members of his wife's rich overseas Chinese family.[102] Over dinner, Father had discussed Sixth Son's move to Yan'an with Zhu and appealed to him for help.

Zhu was ideally positioned to track down Sixth Son and talk him out of staying in Yan'an. In fact, it is difficult to imagine a Chinese leader with better political and academic credentials as an anti-Communist protector of Chinese youth. Zhu had great influence at the highest levels of the Nationalist Party, especially its apparatus for recruiting and training young party workers. He had first entered politics in 1927 at the time of the so-called party purification movement in Shanghai, and he had demonstrated his anti-Communism in several different official capacities—as minister of education (1932–1933), minister of communications (1933–1935), and a member of the Nationalists' Central Executive Committee and Central Political Council directly under Chiang Kai-shek. In March 1938, only a few months before his conversation with Father, he had been present at the Extraordinary Conference of the Nationalist Party when Chiang Kai-shek had been proclaimed party leader, and in April 1938, Zhu had been named secretary general of the Nationalists' central headquarters and acting chief secretary of its new youth corps.[103]

At the dinner, Father found that Zhu was sympathetic and eager to intervene on Sixth Son's behalf. Father reported to Fourth Son that Zhu believes the Communists "have spoiled many a useful youth and they cannot give young men any useful training except propaganda. They can talk but not act."[104] Troubled by this description of Sixth Son's prospective indoctrination, Father pressed Zhu to come to his aid, but Zhu responded by giving only qualified reassurances. "He [Zhu] promised me," Father told Fourth Son, "that he will help us to get Nyandi [Sixth Son] out of the area, but he cannot promise that he will be successful because they [the Communists] are very short of engineers of all kinds [and therefore value Sixth Son's training]." Recognizing that this approach by no means guaranteed success, Father nonetheless decided to submit an official request for Zhu's help.[105]

Over the next few months Father found that working through Zhu did not get Sixth Son out of Yan'an, so he adopted a direct approach. On September 23, he wrote a letter to Sixth Son summoning him to Hong Kong.[106] This letter to Sixth Son and Sixth Son's reply as written are not available, but more than forty years later, Sixth Son recalled that "at that time I refused to meet with him and reported orally to my leaders about this."[107]

Not until Sixth Son and the leaders at Yan'an decided that he should leave did he do so. Writing in 1981, he explained how this decision was made. "In the summer of 1939," he recalled, "I returned to Chongqing because the Natural Science Institute at Yan'an wanted to send people to Chongqing to purchase equipment and raise money. I considered my social background to be appropriate for this assignment, so I applied and received permission from my leader to go to Chongqing. At the time my father did not write me to summon me to Chongqing nor did he even know that I had plans to go to Chongqing."[108] But if Sixth Son decided to leave Yan'an on his own initiative—not Father's—he was nonetheless in touch with Father, and he began to appeal to Father for financial aid on the eve of his departure from Yan'an for Chongqing.

In May 1939, Sixth Son had been notified of his transfer from Resist Japan University to the newly opened Natural Science Research Institute at Yan'an, and at that time he had informed his parents of the need for financial support of this new venture. "The government [of the Communists' base area] is welcoming outside investment," he wrote to them, hinting broadly that Father and other Chinese capitalists should make this investment.[109]

In June, as soon as the Natural Science Research Institute opened, Sixth Son was transferred into it, and he accepted an assignment to go to Chongqing to raise funds for it. The newly founded institute was desperate. One of Sixth Son's coworkers there later recalled:

> We did not have any modern scientific apparatuses or equipment, let alone spacious and well-lit classrooms. The conditions of school life were even harder. Classes were conducted and meals taken in open air. Bricks and tree stumps were our stools, and our knees served as desks. Walls were smeared with soot and used as blackboards. When the ground was leveled, a raised portion was left to serve as a platform. The students had no paper to write on, and so they did their exercises on the ground. They had no pens to write with, and so they tied nibs onto goose feathers or twigs.[110]

Faced with these primitive conditions, the Communist leadership gave Sixth Son the task of acquiring resources to finance improvements in the institute.

On his fund-raising mission, Sixth Son traveled by truck to Chongqing and on his arrival there had a warm reunion with Father. But as he
proceeded to make appeals for money he began to try Father's patience.
Sixth Son's propagandizing for the Communists' cause with Shanghai
capitalists in Chongqing was politically risky, Father pointed out. If
Sixth Son provoked an anti-Communist reaction, he would endanger
not only himself but the entire Liu family. To avoid the risk, Father was
willing to hand over the money himself, as long as the amount was not
unreasonably high. Father asked how much more money was needed,
and when Sixth Son said 10,000 yuan, Father promised to cover the
whole amount, on the condition that Sixth Son bring his fundraising in
Chongqing to an end.

At first he was upset by Father's seemingly abrupt change of attitude. "Up until then," he later recalled, "Father had never expressed any
objection to my going to Yan'an and coming to Chongqing, and I had
never heard him say anything critical about the Communists. When he
suddenly issued this 'cease and desist order,' I was naturally shocked
and resentful." But he gratefully accepted Father's offer. "In the end, I
deeply appreciated whatever he gave because he had never spent freely
on himself, was running short of cash at the time, and made no complaint about giving an amount that was by no means small."[111] Before
leaving Chongqing for Shanghai, Sixth Son asked Father for more money,
saying that he needed it for the trip, but in fact he used this along with
his other funds to buy equipment for the Natural Sciences Research
Institute.[112]

Once Sixth Son had carried out his fundraising mission in Chongqing, he gave the impression that he had finished the Communist phase
of his life and was reclaiming his place as a budding young business
executive in the family firm. He accepted a managerial position at a
newly opened match factory Father had built in Chongqing, and before
taking up his new job, he had a two-day reunion with Mother in
Shanghai. His safe arrival there and return to the family business came
as a great relief for her. As she wrote to Eighth Son on October 20, 1939,
Sixth Son's "visit has given me a world of happiness and comfort. He is
now in business with your father. I am very glad that they can be together, for each is to be of incalculable help and value to the other."[113]
As she predicted, Sixth Son retained a position in the family business
and was helpful to Father at the Lius' match and cement factories in

Chongqing, Kunming, Guizhou, Lanzhou, and other cities outside Japanese-occupied China during the remaining years of the war.[114]

Yet Sixth Son had not in fact set aside his experience at Yan'an, unburdened himself of his Communism, and returned to the business world as readily or as fully as his parents supposed. While resuming his place in the family business, he did not reveal to them that during his year at Yan'an he had joined the Chinese Communist Party and that after leaving Yan'an, he secretly continued to serve the party. In fact, he kept his party membership a secret from his family, friends, and everyone else outside the party for more than thirty years, not making it public until the 1970s.[115]

Fighting Wartime Despair

Why was Sixth Son attracted to Communism more than his brothers and sisters were? Some scholars have argued that sons in Chinese families have been more likely to espouse Communism the more brothers they have had and the more junior they have been in the birth order.[116] This description fits Sixth Son insofar as he had no fewer than eight brothers and had a relatively junior place among them. Perhaps he would not have been inclined to espouse Communism if Father had sent him to a university in the West as expensive and prestigious as the ones the eldest sons attended or if Father had given him one of the family firm's top executive positions that went instead to the four eldest sons. But this interpretation has its limitations. After all, Sixth Son was not the most junior son in the Liu family, and his younger brothers, unlike him, did not become Communists or show any particular sympathy for left-wing politics.

A more plausible explanation for Sixth Son's decision to become a Communist may be found in his despair over the effects of the Japanese war and his search for a means of coping with it. Before the war, while studying in Japan, he became attracted to Communism but showed no interest in joining the Chinese Communist Party. Even after the war began, he did not immediately commit himself to the Communist cause. Only after he experimented with other possibilities and found them wanting as guides for personal fulfillment and wartime action did he finally resolve to make the trek to Mao Zedong's soviet base at Yan'an.

During his struggles with his wartime predicament, Sixth Son achieved a high degree of personal independence. He did not cut himself off from his parents, but while physically separated from them, he made major decisions on his own without consulting them or anyone else in advance. He followed this pattern in all of the decisions described here: to stay in China and work in a factory rather than going to the West for further education; to convert to Christianity; to choose a mate and propose marriage to her; to set out for Yan'an and join the Chinese Communist Party. Not until he had already made up his mind to take these actions did he inform his parents of them and seek their approval of his decisions.

In making these decisions, Sixth Son took initiatives as an independent individual. After grappling with the issues, he built up his confidence to the point where he felt prepared to make commitments whether or not they were at odds with the religious and political beliefs of his family. But during a long wartime separation like this one, what if a son felt compelled to act on his own not because of his growing self-confidence but rather because of his isolation from the members of his family? This was the question that haunted Eighth Son. As noted, Sixth and Eighth Sons escaped together from Shanghai to Hong Kong on September 6, 1937, three weeks after the Battle of Shanghai had begun. Within a week after their arrival in Hong Kong, they parted company, Sixth Son flying north to inland China and Eighth Son setting sail across the Pacific. As the war spread, while Sixth Son worked through one set of personal issues in China, Eighth Son worked through another set in the United States.

Father, late 1920s. *(Courtesy of the Shanghai Academy of Social Sciences)*

Mother, late 1920s. *(Courtesy of the Shanghai Academy of Social Sciences)*

The first eleven Liu children, late 1920s. *(Courtesy of the Shanghai Academy of Social Sciences)*

Second Son ready for the hunt in England, 1929. *(Courtesy of the Shanghai Academy of Social Sciences)*

Third, Second, and Fourth Sons (from left) at Cambridge University, early
1930s. *(Courtesy of the Shanghai Academy of Social Sciences)*

Eldest Son on the eve of his departure from Shanghai for the United States, c. 1931. *(Courtesy of the Shanghai Academy of Social Sciences)*

Fifth Son at the University of Pennsylvania, 1934. *(Courtesy of the University of Pennsylvania Archives)*

Third Son at Cambridge University, 1930. *(Courtesy of the Shanghai Academy of Social Sciences)*

Third Son with Minister Shi in London, 1931. *(Courtesy of the Shanghai Academy of Social Sciences)*

Liane Yen in 1935, shortly after she first met Third Son. Photograph taken when the Chinese minister to England presented her at the court of George V and Queen Mary. *(Courtesy of Liane Lieu)*

Eldest Son, Father, and Second Son in Shanghai after the boys returned from abroad and entered the family business, c. 1938. *(Courtesy of the Shanghai Academy of Social Sciences)*

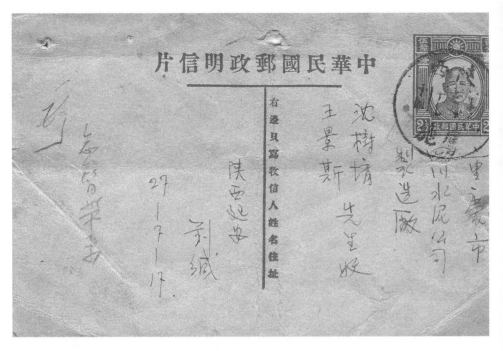

Sixth Son's postcard from Yan'an, 1938. *(Courtesy of the Shanghai Academy of Social Sciences)*

Fourth Son and his wife, standing, with Sixth and Eighth Sons (right to left), while Father sits in front with the couple's daughter on his lap, Chongqing, 1943. *(Courtesy of Shanghai Tan)*

Eldest Daughter and Xue Diyi in Hong Kong, c. 1960. *(Courtesy of Lee S. Hsueh)*

Mother at home in Shanghai with her photo of Father, who was in
Chongqing, early 1940s. *(Courtesy of Frank Lieu)*

Father and Mother reunited in postwar Shanghai. *(Courtesy of the Shanghai Academy of Social Sciences)*

Youngest Daughter in her early teens in wartime Shanghai, 1939. *(Courtesy of Linda Chang)*

Youngest Daughter and Zhang Qinshi in Beijing, 1951. *(Courtesy of Linda Chang)*

Eighth Son at his MIT graduation, June 1947. *(Courtesy of the Shanghai Academy of Social Sciences)*

Father with factory workers, early 1950s. *(Courtesy of Shanghai Tan)*

10

A Son Who Battled Depression

WHEN Eighth Son was sent to the United States, he was sixteen, the youngest age at which any member of the Liu family went to the West for a college education. He was also the last of the Liu sons to be given this opportunity. He left home at this tender age even though Fourth Son opposed the idea. Having gone to England at seventeen in 1929, Fourth Son was back in Shanghai at the time of Eighth Son's departure, and he expressed the belief that anyone so young would not be emotionally mature enough to adjust to student life at a Western college or university.[1] But in September 1937, within weeks after the war broke out, Eighth Son sailed off to the United States.

Did Father take an ill-advised risk in letting a young son go abroad so early in life? In a family of independent-minded individuals, why would anyone in good physical health not relish and benefit from the opportunity to be on his own? Eighth Son's first year in the United States went smoothly, leaving the impression that he had not begun his studies abroad prematurely. In the fall of 1937 he matriculated at Colorado College, where Fifth Son was entering his senior year after recovering from tuberculosis in the Cragmor Sanatorium. Eighth Son wrote to his parents that Fifth Son showed him "kind affection" during the one year they spent together as classmates.[2] But as it turned out, this was the only satisfying year of Eighth Son's four-year visit to the United States. In the fall of 1938, he transferred to MIT, and after taking intensive summer courses there in preparation for admission, he began classes at there as a sophomore. From then on, he had no family members with him there or anywhere else in the United States or Europe.

By letter, he revealed to the members of his family in China that he desperately missed them, and he warned them that if he could not depend on them to come to his aid, he was afraid he would suffer from a psychological breakdown in the United States.

Suffering without Friends

In his first year at MIT, 1938–39, Eighth Son began to describe himself in letters to his parents as "emotionally unstable" and suffering from a "truly nerve-cracking" state of mind. He felt that he had many of the talents needed to achieve academic success, but he was afraid that these would not be enough because of his psychological weaknesses. "It needs more than courage, determination, and intelligence to study abroad," he wrote Father and Mother at the end of his first semester at MIT on January 9, 1939. "My love of life and hopes for the future seem dimmed by the dull and cruel way everything is going on here."[3] Dullness, he believed, was the key trait of his American classmates, and cruelty was evident in the behavior of his Chinese classmates.

Potential American friends, he found, were too different from him to form deep relationships with him. "They share their sympathy and talk loud," he wrote to his parents, "but never are a hospitable people." At best, they provided him with an occasional diversion. "I sometimes talk together with them to forget myself for a while, but seldom since they live differently than I do which I perfectly understand. They consider us as different." Eighth Son felt that Americans differed from himself not only in the way they lived but also in their experience. In particular, they had never had the unhappy experience of living abroad at a great distance from their families. "They at this point," he reported to Father and Mother, "are truly innocent—they do not understand. They themselves have actually never experienced any real difficulties." Unable to identify with Eighth Son, American students did not realize how deeply depressed he was, and they offered him only superficial advice. "American students' advice," he told his parents, has often been to "stop worrying and have a nice time. I may be [should] get a couple of girls according to them."[4]

If Eighth Son felt distant from his American classmates at MIT, he nonetheless preferred them to his Chinese classmates. Even if Americans had no more than a superficial understanding of him, they still "understand me much better than my Chinese friends [do]." When he asked Chinese classmates for their interpretation of his emotional difficulties, he discovered: "The Chinese students' version (many of them) is vicious if you permit me to say. They think all my trouble is that I have been only worrying about the grades. Their remarks are often insulting and jealous with little consideration that I am considerably younger than they are and should need some words of encouragement and some willing help from them."[5] Of the forty-six Chinese students at MIT at the time, the vicious ones gave him no encouragement, so he turned to a small fringe group that he characterized as "care-free goers."[6] He found that they were easygoing, and at first he could not understand how they could be so cavalier about their studies. Then, he discovered, some of them soon dropped out of school. "Certainly," he observed, reflecting on their fate, "M.I.T. can never allow any slackening on the part of the students."[7]

Finding Parents Unhelpful

With no American or Chinese friend to comfort him at MIT, he sought solace from his parents in China, but they did not take his emotional problems seriously either. Just as he was transferring to MIT in the summer of 1938, Father was fleeing from Japanese-occupied Shanghai, and when Father subsequently began to establish new enterprises in Hong Kong and Chongqing, he wrote fewer letters to Eighth Son than he had sent to his older sons when they had been students abroad.

Preoccupied with the war in China, Father appointed an American local guardian and depended on him to advise Eighth Son. As he had done for his older sons, Father recruited a guardian abroad through a business associate he knew in China, in this case, William P. Hunt, president of Hunt Engineering Corporation, who had worked closely with Father on construction projects in Shanghai and Hong Kong. Hunt, in turn, assigned his New York–based vice president, C. C. Frick, to be Eighth Son's guardian. But Eighth Son received little advice or even attention from Frick. As he later observed near the end of his stay in Cambridge, Frick "is an extremely busy man, and I don't know him very well."[8]

Father's failure to pay close attention to Eighth Son was not lost on Mother, and she tried to cover for her husband. "I wonder," she wrote to Eighth Son on January 20, 1939, "whether your father has written you from Hong Kong. If not, then you will have to understand that he is busily occupied with business. He is very strong and well and so you need not take any thought about him."[9] For her part, Mother wrote regularly to Eighth Son, on whom she had doted since he was a small child, but he found that her advice to him concerning his emotional problems was very simple, consisting of little more than bland reassurances. "You are a good and brave boy and I trust that you can get along all by yourself there just as well," she told him.[10] She was more concerned about his physical appearance than his psychological well-being and did not see a direct connection between the two. After receiving from him a photograph of himself in February 1939, she remarked: "You look rather thin in the picture to me. I am afraid that you are working too hard at school. You [must] always bear in mind not to overexert yourself in anything. You ought always to have plenty of nutritional food. I expect to see you plumper in the next picture."[11]

Mother did not entirely ignore Eighth Son's obsessive worrying, but she advised him simply to stop it. On the eve of Eighth Son's final examinations at the end of his first year at MIT, she wrote to him: "I hope you are taking everything easy. You yourself know very well that nervousness is extremely detrimental to the working of the brain. It is something which should be eliminated for all time."[12] After he passed these examinations, Mother was aware that his success on them did not bring an end to his nervousness, and in her letter of congratulations on the examinations she remarked: "I never have any doubt in your ability. You need to have a great deal more of cheerfulness and social spirit, though."[13]

Mother's solution for ending loneliness was as simple as the one for eliminating worrying. In dealing with either of these sources of unhappiness, Eighth Son should stop dwelling on the problem, which generated dark thoughts, and concentrate on the solution, which would show him the brighter side. In the fall of 1939, after Eighth Son had been writing home about his depression for a year, Mother offered him her antidote for loneliness. "I certainly sympathize with you for the loneliness you have to endure in America," she acknowledged. But, she insisted, "Loneliness is none other than a mere sense which one gets if he sets his mind to it. What you have to reflect upon now is that you are lucky to have the chance to study abroad." By concentrating on his good fortune, he could overcome loneliness. "If you but think about the bright or sunny side of things you will not find time to brood over solitude."[14] Eighth Son's brighter side should be especially bright, according to Mother, because of his privilege of studying abroad.

This rare opportunity for studying abroad, Mother reminded him, had been fully exploited by his elder brothers. Second, Third, and Fourth Sons, she conceded, went to England as a threesome, so none of them had to live alone. But whenever any of them or Eighth Son's other elder brothers had to be by himself while abroad, "he would feel that home was right behind and with him." In addition, she cited the examples of sons who had preceded Eighth Son to the United States. "Just think of how your eldest and fifth brothers fought their good fight alone— singlehanded. You are no less brave than any of your brothers."[15]

It is doubtful that Eighth Son found as much assurance in Eldest and Fifth Sons' good fight in the United States as Mother thought that he should. After all, each of them had suffered through his own frustrations. But Eighth Son was well aware—perhaps painfully aware—of Mother's point that most of his brothers had risen to the challenge of coping with life abroad and had set high standards for the family to use in measuring his personal and academic success.

This advice from Mother did not ease Eighth Son's emotional pain. Her call for him to lift himself out of his depression was unhelpful; in his condition, he did not feel capable of such a sheer act of will. Meanwhile, Father's inattentiveness left him feeling cut off and afraid to raise emotional issues with Father. As Eighth Son wrote to Fifth Son in the fall of 1939, a year after he first attempted to broach these issues with Father, "there have been many times when I have wanted to speak with Father straightforwardly about these problems and ask him to help me solve them. But in the end I didn't dare to."[16] With Father unavailable and Mother unhelpful, Eighth Son sought advice from his older brothers.

Feeling Guilty toward Brothers

On March 19, 1939, a few months after confiding in his parents about his emotional instability, Eighth Son expressed to Eldest Son his fear of a nervous breakdown. He made this revelation in a letter written in Chinese, but in the passages on his psychology he inserted English words (italicized here and in other quotations below). "Sometimes," he wrote to Eldest Son in Shanghai, "I do get very *discouraged*. Whenever I have pessimistic thoughts, I even think to myself that *I will probably end my career with breakdown my health*."[17] He insisted that he had not always been prone to pessimism, let alone a breakdown. "Eldest Brother, I had lots of *confidence* before coming abroad," he recalled. In China, he admitted, his confidence had been based on an education that had not been very challenging. "Looking back on the days in China, the *training* I received was in fact too little." By contrast, his work at MIT was extremely demanding—so demanding that he had become afraid to leave his desk. "My academic work has kept me so busy," he confided to Eldest Son, "that I seldom go out (and I am afraid to go out)."

In advising Eighth Son, Eldest Son showed little awareness of his brother's psychological needs. Like Mother (whom he saw almost every day in Shanghai), he urged Eighth Son to recognize his own talents, which he insisted would automatically raise his level of self-confidence. "You are bright and able," Eldest Son wrote to Eighth Son, "and I can visualize the brilliant successes you will achieve. The essential thing is that you must all the time have full confidence in yourself."[18]

Eldest Son also reiterated Mother's point that Eighth Son should stop worrying, but he cited the example of Eighth Son's brothers for a different purpose than hers. Whereas she had praised them as young men who had bravely spent time abroad without worrying, Eldest Son identified them as sources of support who made it unnecessary for Eighth Son to worry. "Above all," Eldest Son told him, "you must free your mind from the least worry, for your other brothers and I will always see to it you are adequately provided for."[19] Eldest Son seemed to assume that Eighth Son's anxiety was all attributable to his concerns about financial rather than psychological security.

Eldest Son brushed aside Eighth Son's complaints about his demanding courses and busy schedule and proposed that he should increase his academic load by enrolling in a dual degree program. Thinking back to his year at Harvard Business School, 1932–33, Eldest Son recalled hearing about a "Cooperation Course" in which an MIT undergraduate could enter Harvard Business School at the end of junior year and finish both a BS at MIT and an MBA at Harvard in five years rather than the usual six.

Eighth Son was appalled by this proposal, and he wrote to Fourth Son to seek help in talking Eldest Son out of recommending it or any

course of study like it. It was out of the question to take this course because it had been canceled ten years earlier—five years before Eldest
Son had been a student at Harvard. It was possible for Eighth Son to
enter Harvard Business School after completing his bachelor's degree at
MIT, but he adamantly opposed this idea too. He objected to it on both
practical and personal grounds. In practical terms, *"I think it costs too
much time and money,"* he wrote, using English for this statement. Personally, he opposed the idea of going to Harvard because he did not feel
up to it. He would not be prepared, he said, because "courses taken at
MIT are completely different from the *requirements* at Harvard."[20]

He did not want to consider going on to Harvard in the future when
he already felt inadequate at MIT in the present. "Fourth Brother," he
observed, "I don't believe that I am unintelligent, but when it comes to
my *capacity for solving engineering problems,* I am a *100 percent dumb guy.*"
His intelligence was actually decreasing at MIT, he said, because he felt
overwhelmed by the engineering curriculum, especially in mathematics and physics. Under emotional stress, the more he threw himself into
his work, the more he lost his ability to reason, analyze, even speak.
"When my mind is not clear *(bad mood),* I make mistakes in *simple addition.* When I am working on *math and physics problems,* I lack analytical
power and am at a loss *to find a method of attack.* I am absent minded all
the time. Recently I have found myself unable to speak correctly."[21]
Suffering from these diminished capacities, he was in no mood to lay
plans for extending his education beyond MIT to Harvard Business
School. He was desperately groping for a way to survive in the present
and the immediate future.

On June 4, as Eighth Son prepared for final examinations at the
end of his first year at MIT (and second year in the United States), he
replied to Eldest Son about his suggestions. After politely thanking
him, Eighth Son tried once again to convey how deeply depressed he
felt. Desperately homesick, he pleaded with ·Eldest Son to write him
more often and to persuade his other brothers to do the same. "Here
abroad," Eighth Son wrote from Cambridge to Eldest Son in Shanghai,
"encouragement is hard to come by. Only if no one *discourages* me am I
satisfied. So every time I receive a letter from home, the letters from all
of you always make me feel better. Eldest Brother, if you and other
elder brothers can find time to write me a few lines from your *office
desk,* I'll greatly appreciate it. If you can't, I'll understand, of course,

since all of you are the *men of the hour* in our family, and you are busy all the time."[22]

Already feeling guilty about imposing on Eldest Son, Eighth Son also felt guilty toward his other brothers and sisters because he had the privilege of studying at a high-priced institution abroad while they suffered under the hardship of wartime conditions in China. "I am always very self-conscious," he wrote to his brothers and sisters, "and have long felt guilty in studying in such an expensive school." He was well aware that they, by contrast, were all enduring "a sort of ordeal at home."[23] By comparing himself to each of his brothers, Eighth Son found more than one reason to feel guilty.

In relation to Fourth Son, Eighth Son felt guilty because he had not overcome the disadvantages of beginning his studies at a young age in a Western university, as Fourth Son had done. Whereas Fourth Son had responded to Cambridge University maturely, Eighth Son lamented that he was unable to do the same at MIT. "Fourth Brother, although I am not that young any more," he wrote in 1939 at age eighteen, "I am still *immature* and in many ways I can't even measure up to a ten year old."[24]

Toward Sixth Son he felt guilty because he believed that he occupied a place at MIT that should rightfully have gone to Sixth Son. He recalled sailing with Sixth Son from Shanghai to Hong Kong in September 1937, and he couldn't help thinking that he should have stayed home and let his brother go to the United States because he was "much more brilliant than I am" and better qualified to attend MIT."[25]

Toward Eldest and Fifth Sons, Eighth Son felt guilty because he had not risen to the challenge of studying in the United States as they had done before him. "I very much hope that you and Eldest Brother will understand me," he wrote to Fifth Son in the fall of 1939. "I envy you and Eldest Brother because both of you were able to *pull through*." He, by contrast, was not pulling through. "I always stay in my room. This kind of life is cold as ice. It'll really *drive me* [to a] *nervous breakdown*."[26]

Diagnosing Himself to His Family

After writing this letter in Chinese and inserting the term "nervous breakdown" in English, Eighth Son decided that the only way to avoid suffering from this affliction was to figure out exactly what a nervous breakdown was. During the fall of his junior year at MIT, he began to discuss his state of mind in the language of psychology. It is not clear how he learned this terminology. He did not mention seeing a therapist, taking a psychology course, or reading psychology books. In his letters home he occasionally referred to conversations with friends at MIT, but by the fall of 1939 he had given up on them. "Some friends' advice has given me comfort," he wrote to Fifth Son, "but many intentionally ridicule me and even treat me as a coward. So I no longer seek friends out."[27] Wherever he had learned psychological terms, he began to incorporate them into his vocabulary. Writing his letters in Chinese, he inserted these terms in English (along with all other English words from his letters, they are italicized in the following quotations).

Eighth Son first tried out his medical self-diagnosis on Fifth Brother, who had learned a lot about American medicine during his long hospitalization for tuberculosis in the United States. "Fifth Brother," Eighth Son wrote in the fall of 1939, "I now suffer from some kind of depression. Or maybe it's some other kind of illness. I simply cannot study. I've spent lots of time trying to *analyse* it."[28] According to his analysis, the key question was how to regain his powers of concentration. "I'm puzzled," he wrote to Fifth Son, "as to why I cannot study. I had once figured out that it's because the academic work is not *interesting*, and maybe I have chosen the wrong path. First, I am not very bright. Second, I have little idea about engineering. Up until now, I've spent almost all of my time on it, not caring about anything else, even my friends. Sometimes, I've even neglected my friends because of my academic work. And now I am all by myself, feeling lonely and not *secure* at all. So I can't do any studying."[29] Isolated and insecure, he concluded that his only hope for avoiding a nervous breakdown and resuming his studies would be found either if he could return to dependence on his family as a son and brother or if he could master independence on his own as a mature adult.

In Eighth Son's estimation, dependence on his family had given him ample motivation to pursue his studies before he came to America. "I've always thought," he wrote to Fifth Son, "that in the past the reason why I was willing to work hard, *a shame to say*, was entirely because of *encouragement*. Since coming here, I haven't gotten to know a single soul, and no one has given me a single piece of advice."[30]

He yearned nostalgically for a return to his place in the world of his siblings as a little brother. "At home, all my elder brothers spoke to

me in a straightforward way and sometimes even beat me up, but I felt
several hundred times better then. I have always longed for a friend
who would treat me like my elder brothers treated me. But how would
that be possible." At MIT, it was not possible to recreate even an ap-
proximation of the brotherly relationships that had existed within his
family, because "No one teaches me, scolds me, or corrects me. By now,
I have made a heap of mistakes and repeated the same ones over and
over. I don't have any *confidence* whatsoever."[31] Cut off from his family
and lacking a surrogate family or even a close friend, how could he rebuild his confidence?

In theory, he imagined that it was possible for him to become confident as a mature and independent adult, but in practice, he could not
find a way to achieve this goal without help. "In my view," he wrote to
Fifth Son, "everything that has happened is simply because I am not
yet *mature in thought*. If I were *mature,* I would have the ability to 'distinguish' and *build* my confidence and *independence*. But during this *period,*
there should be someone to *encourage* and advise me. Yet, I don't have a
single good friend with whom I can discuss things. Neither is there
anyone *outside of school* willing to give me advice."[32]

No longer able to depend on his family but still not capable of becoming mature and independent on his own, Eighth Son felt that he was
caught in a dreadful bind. "I have lost my dependence on you," he wrote
to Fifth Son (using "you" in the plural in Chinese to refer to all of the
members of the family), "and I have experienced much *discouragement*.
I am *afraid to face realistic world* and have become very *pessimistic*. As I am
all by myself, I often feel as though *someday before long* I'll have a *nervous-
breakdown*. Ai! Fifth Brother, I don't know how to describe for you my
bitter predicament."[33] Teetering on the brink of a collapse, Eighth Son
urged his brothers to appeal on his behalf to Father. He asked Eldest
and Fifth Sons to do him the favor of asking Father to "introduce me to
one of his friends to give me advice or take care of me so that I can study
with ease." To underscore the desperate nature of his request, he ominously added: "I'll never forget such a favor even until my death."[34]

Writing separately to Eldest Son in the spring of 1940, Eighth Son
seemed even more desperate and preoccupied with death. He again
drew the distinction between dependence on his family at home and
loss of this dependence abroad, but now he described his life as utterly
bleak. "In a foreign country," he wrote to Eldest Son, "where no one

deals with you lovingly like a family member and where everything is based entirely on '*business,*' I've found my existence in this world meaningless."[35]

In this meaningless world, Eighth Son attended to business as though he was not going to survive at MIT. On the subject of finances, he asked Eldest Son to manage his accounts in Shanghai and pay his bills for him in the United States rather than sending an annual lump sum, as Eldest Brother had done up to that time. If Eighth Son continued to have a large sum entrusted to him, he was afraid that it would be lost. "I have a condition of *emotional,*" he once again reminded Eldest Son, who presided over the family's accounts office in Shanghai. "I am alone in a foreign country, and I am not familiar with the legal procedures here. I am afraid that my classmates will find out about it. I often worry about this. Sometimes I am afraid and wonder, *if something happens to me what can I do?*"[36] In posing this question, he implied that he fully expected some disaster was about to befall to him.

As usual in his letters home, he assured Eldest Son that he realized that it was impossible for family members in China to solve his emotional problems in America. "I know that you can't find a way to *sooth my troubling soul,*" he wrote to Eldest Son in the spring of 1940, near the end of his junior year.[37] By then he was at least looking forward to the summer. After attending summer school during both of his first two years in the United States, 1938 and 1939, he finally had the opportunity in the summer of 1940 to hold an internship at an American factory.

Following Father's Advice

When Eighth Son had first complained about his nervousness in the United States, Father had made one of his few suggestions to him, recommending that he should get away from MIT during the summer vacations and hold an internship at an American factory.[38] In the summer of 1939, his application for internships had been denied on the grounds that he was an alien, but in 1940, at the end of his junior year, he landed an internship with America's second biggest power company, Westinghouse. (Only General Electric was bigger.)

During his two months as an intern, July and August 1940, he worked at Westinghouse's biggest plant, in East Pittsburgh, Pennsylvania, and he found by the end of the summer that his spirits had risen sharply. Initially he was afraid that he would suffer from discrimination against him as a foreigner, and he was pleasantly surprised to discover that he was at least tacitly accepted. "I am well liked here," he wrote to Fourth Son on August 21, near the end of his internship. "At least they pretend to like me. Knowing that I am no spy and quite amiable if they treat me right—they are very good to me sometimes."[39]

Eighth Son found himself particularly at ease with ordinary working people. "In here," he wrote, referring to the factory, "I have varied experience and meet different people from a common workman to company officials. It is surprising that the working class is much easier to talk with than the high officials." After getting to know his fellow workers, he received an unforeseen benefit from his internship. Initially he expected to confine himself to learning about the job, but once he got to know other workers, he observed: "I come here not only to receive practical experience but also how to influence people and make friends."[40]

Besides enjoying the company of his fellow workers, he got along with the one MIT student he saw at Westinghouse—Yao Jun, a Chinese student on the same internship. He attributed their relatively good relationship to the fact that they were both not merely from China but from the same native place there. "He is also a Ningbo native-place associate," Eighth Son reported. "We knew each other when we were both studying at M.I.T., and we were good friends, as all Ningbonese are when they are out of their country." He found Yao less appealing than other people at Westinghouse but more appealing than others at MIT. "We can get along fairly well," he said of Yao and himself, "at least better than most of the Chinese students I know at Tech. Yao has a quick temper though—a little bit quicker than my own, I am afraid."[41] If Eighth Son got along fairly well with Yao, he got along much better with others.

As a result, he was moved to describe his mood at Westinghouse in language unlike any he had ever used at MIT: "I find myself quite happy lately," he wrote, "because I am beginning to make friends."[42] "Happy" was a word that had rarely, if ever, appeared in his letters home since his arrival in the United States.

Pleased with his friendships, he also began to sort out his professional plans. Ever since arriving at MIT, he had been in a quandary about whether he should major in mechanical engineering (his de-clared choice), chemical engineering, or engineering administration, and characteristically, he had brooded at length over this decision.[43] But now that he had followed Father's advice and gotten away from MIT by taking an internship at Westinghouse, he began to envision a clearly defined career path for himself. "You probably know," he wrote to Fourth Son, "that Father would like me to enter 'Power Engineer-ing.'" In this case, "the proper place for me to go next year if I enter the Westinghouse Graduate Training Course is their plant in South Phila-delphia."[44] Eager to please Father and also pleased with himself, he now knew what his next step would be after completing his senior year and graduating from MIT in June 1941.

As Eighth Son's happy summer internship came to a close and his postgraduate plans for the future took shape, he dreaded returning to MIT for his senior year. "I really hate to go back to school," he wrote, "honestly because of my experience in my last two years at Tech, al-though I foresee that I will like it better this time when I go back."[45] Unfortunately for Eighth Son, his prediction for his senior year did not come true. He did not like it better. In fact, it turned out to be a per-sonal disaster.

Rebelling against Hospitalization

On October 18, 1940, Eighth Son was taken from the MIT campus to McLean Hospital, a widely known psychiatric hospital, in Watertown, Massachusetts, three miles away. According to his recollection three months later, he was tricked into allowing himself to be admitted to McLean. "I don't know why the M.I.T. authorities, using deception, brought me to *McLean Hospital*," he wrote to Mother on January 21, 1941, while still under confinement there. This whole episode, he claimed, "was arranged by a doctor and a nurse, *Miss Newton* of the *Homerberg Infirmary* at *Technology*. The physician here is *Dr. Chamberlain*. I have protested numerous times against their reasons for sending me here. They said that it was because I have had a *nervous breakdown.*"[46]

Throughout his stay at McLean, he denied that he had ever had a nervous breakdown. "I asked why I was sent here," he wrote to Mother. "They said I *work* too hard. It was the beginning of the school year. It is my last year. I wanted to have a good start. The last year, though very busy, is not as difficult as earlier years. I am not a lawyer, but sending people into a mental hospital on the basis of no evidence is a violation of the law. I have not done anything wrong. The strategy of the hospital has been *a series* [of] *intimidation.*"[47] As a hardworking, law-abiding student, he had given McLean no justification for incarcerating him or intimidating him, he insisted.

In retrospect, he could imagine only one possible explanation for the doctor's and nurse's decision to confine him. Perhaps one of his Chinese classmates at MIT had misinformed them about him for political reasons. As he later recalled, this classmate, who later became an anti-Communist military officer in the Nationalist government, once noticed a book in Eighth Son's room at MIT that had come from Sixth Son and showed a return address in Yan'an. From that point on, the classmate suspected Eighth Son of having pro-Communist sympathies and sought to undermine his credibility—perhaps even going so far as to convince Miss Newton and Dr. Chamberlain that Eighth Son had had a nervous breakdown.

Eighth Son's explanations for his admission to McLean were not reliable, according to his psychiatrist, Dr. Oscar Raeder. Throughout the first four months of Eighth Son's confinement, October 1940 to January 1941, Raeder noted in a letter to C. C. Frick, he "worries about the fact he cannot recall various incidents that occurred at the time of his great excitement. This is natural, because he is too confused at the time for most things to register on his mind." In his diagnosis of Eighth Son's condition, Raeder avoided the vague term "nervous breakdown" in favor of more scientific language. "His mental condition is not of a malignant (dementia praecox-type), but rather of a maniac depressive type that gets well."[48] Providing a reason for hope, Raeder maintained that Eighth Son was not suffering from schizophrenia, which was thought to be lifelong and incurable, and was instead a victim of manic depression, which was considered to be episodic.[49]

Whatever his exact condition, Eighth Son objected to his confinement from beginning to end. As soon as he realized that he had been admitted to a mental hospital, he began protesting violently, and he was placed under restraints—strapped to his bed day and night for the first few weeks and then at night for the next few. He insisted that he should be released from the hospital, and he harangued the staff at first entirely in English and later entirely in Chinese. His doctors characterized his first few weeks at McLean as "the violent stage of his illness." After three weeks, he was allowed to see visitors representing the Liu family, and they reported that the medical staff had seen him act violently, but these visitors did not witness any violence with their own eyes.

During his first months in the hospital, Eighth Son's visitors were all struck by his lack of lucidity. One of the first visitors, a Chinese friend who worked for the YMCA in New York and visited him at the request of the Liu family in Shanghai, saw him on November 13, 1940, less than a month after he had been admitted. "He did not seem to recognize who I was," this friend reported, after spending half an hour with Eighth Son,

> but when I gave him my visiting card he read the name and seemed to remember me. Of course he and I have met quite a number of times, and the last time I saw him was at the International House, New York, at the end of September [two months earlier], when he was driving back to Boston for the registration of the fall term. I could not get him to answer my questions, as his mind was not clear. Most of the time he laughed and he mentioned the name of this and that, and asked me whether I knew them.[50]

In mid-November, Eighth Son began to have "increasing periods of lucidity" according to C. C. Frick, "although they are still of short duration."[51] By December, he had made additional improvements but was still not clear-minded. On December 7, a Chinese American scientist who had known Eighth Son at MIT paid him a visit and sent a report through a mutual friend to the Liu family. "Of course, he talked all nonsense in the main," this professor noted. "Yet he could formulate his own arguments and did not seem as bad as other people suspected."[52] On December 12, the hospital indicated that he still spoke gibberish but noted substantial improvements since his admission two months earlier. Eighth Son "is showing considerable improvement over the rather excited condition he was in when he was admitted. He is still rather erratic and at times rather too talkative and it is impossible for him to stay on the subject for any length of time. There is a certain playfulness in his condition but he seems to show much more improvement than he did previously."[53]

Even if Eighth Son had moments of lucidity, he was given little opportunity to communicate his thoughts during the first phase of his
stay at McLean. During his first two months, the hospital had a policy
of isolating him from all those who knew him, other than representatives of the Liu family. "So far," McLean's staff told potential visitors on
December 12, "we have not encouraged any of his friends to visit him.
Unless you find it necessary to see him in order to report on his condition to his family we would not advise your coming up just yet."[54] During his first month, McLean also withheld Eighth Son's mail from him.
His Chinese friend who worked for the YMCA in New York discovered
that even letters written by Eighth Son's family had not reached him.
"I told him," this young man reported to the Lius through an official at
the YMCA in Shanghai on November 14, "that his parents asked me to
come to see him. He seemed to be glad of that. When I asked him
whether he had any messages for me to forward to his parents, he said,
'Ask them to write me.' Then one of the doctors who was present told
me they had not let him read letters from his home in China yet."[55]

Eighth Son had no respect for the treatment he was given at McLean.
"Treatment in a *mental hospital* is not much better than that in a *German
Concentration Camp*," he told Mother on May 14, 1941, in the midst of the
Allies' war against Hitler. He particularly resented the hospital's policy
of isolating him. "It was truly very painful," he wrote Mother, "being
locked up all day and having no communication with anyone that I
know. Also, they've treated me in a way that I'll never forget until the
day I die."[56]

Instead of giving Eighth Son treatment, the hospital subjected him
to threats, he charged. "The policy here depends entirely on *threatening*," he told Eldest Son. In a letter written almost all in Chinese, he
added a postscript in uncharacteristically broken English: *"They have no
right to lock me here. Moreover they are keeping my passport and most of item. I
am also no even allow to call on the phone."*[57]

In his letters home, Eighth Son pleaded with his family to secure
his release and take legal action against McLean and MIT. "Eldest
Brother," he wrote from McLean on January 21, 1941, "Please take legal action immediately against the M.I.T. authorities for having brought
me to *McLH*. McLH is almost no different than a prison. I don't know
what the *treatment* is." But his calls for action did not persuade his family to seek his release, let alone bring a lawsuit against McLean. Instead

the Lius responded by sending one of their family members to pay a visit to him in person.

In early January 1941, he had a visit from his father's brother, Uncle Liu Jisheng, who had made the trip all the way from Hong Kong. He was the first family member Eighth Son had seen since Fifth Son had returned to China from Colorado two and a half years earlier. After observing his nephew, Uncle Jisheng confirmed to the family that he was capable of conducting a coherent conversation. "He is on the road to recovery," Uncle Jisheng wrote to Eldest Son on January 18, one week after his meeting with Eighth Son. "I had about one hour and a half talk with him and most of his talk is very rational."[58]

On the basis of conversations with McLean's staff, Uncle Jisheng discounted Eighth Son's charges that the hospital had imprisoned and mistreated him. While Eighth Son "is complaining for being taken to that hospital, the doctor explained to me that this is simply a phase of his illness and will pass in time." Uncle Jisheng accepted the doctor's account because "I am pleased to let you know that he is under safe and capable hands and is very well taken care of."[59] Although Uncle Jisheng's visit lasted less than one day, he was favorably impressed with McLean, and Eighth Son's other visitors (not to mention other observers) generally shared his positive view of it.[60]

Eighth Son did not share his uncle's favorable assessment of McLean. Even on the eve of his release four months after his uncle's visit, he still had not one good word for his treatment at McLean, except that it had become better during his last four months than it had been during his first four. "They are treating me much better than before," he told Mother in May 1941, eight months after he had first been admitted. He was no longer isolated and was even allowed to leave the hospital in Watertown and go to Boston. But such trips were closely monitored. "Everything here is under close surveillance," he told Mother. "Even when I go to Boston, I am being watched. I don't know why they won't just let me go."[61]

He attributed his improvement not to any treatment at McLean but rather to the suspension of its treatment, especially the end of his isolation and the policy of allowing Uncle Jisheng to pay a visit. "My condition has been improving," he explained to Mother on May 14, 1941, "ever since Uncle's first visit [in January 1941]. The reason is that I began to relax as soon as I saw Uncle."[62]

A family member, not a mental institution, had been Eighth Son's salvation, he believed, and he could hardly wait for his reunion with the rest of his family. He was particularly pleased to have heard from Father, who was then residing in Chongqing. "Father has written to say," he wrote to Mother, "that after my return home he will help me feel comfortable and will put me at ease." Eighth Son was eager to be comforted by Father and by everyone else in the family. "My only hope now," he wrote to Mother, "is to leave America and to see family members that I haven't seen in four years."[63]

Returning to China

On July 10, Eighth Son left the United States, departing from San Francisco on the S.S. *Matsonia*. He traveled alone. In preparation for his trip, Father had gone so far as to instruct his eldest sons to decide which of them should go from China to the United States to accompany Eighth Son home. On April 7, Father had written from Chongqing to his sons in Shanghai that he did not want to take "even the slightest risk" with Eighth Son. "Now I want you boys to seriously consider the matter among yourselves to make an eventual decision as to which one among you is best suited for taking the trip to the States to bring your younger brother back."[64] In reply, Eldest Son offered to go to the United States and bring Eighth Son home, but ultimately no one went. Father eventually became convinced that Eighth Son needed no escort for the trans-Pacific journey because of assurances from C. C. Frick, who had not been very attentive to Eighth Son during his two years at MIT but had efficiently managed his affairs during his eight months at McLean.[65] With Frick's and Father's approval, Eighth Son made the trip home on his own.[66]

On the night of July 25, after two weeks at sea, Eighth Son's ship arrived in Hong Kong. Its passengers were kept on board until they could be examined by a physician the next morning, and on July 26, after waiting anxiously all night, Eighth Son finally began the first phase of his family reunion. Third Son "came to meet me and I met Father in his office," Eighth Son wrote on the same day to his brothers and sisters in Shanghai. "The whole reunion is so happy for me since I haven't seen them both for almost four years."[67]

While pleased and relieved to rejoin his family, Eighth Son still harbored bitter feelings about his experience at McLean. "I am so glad that I am now back from the States," he went on, "especially out of hospital in which I was almost confined nine months against my will." Still angry about his confinement, he also had regrets about failing to complete his studies and earn his degree from MIT. "I feel so sorry," he wrote, "that I could not finish my school in the States due to the misfortune of my illness. I would have gotten my degree you know, if I was not put into a hospital. The whole thing still seems screwy and misty to me."[68]

Falling between Dependence and Independence

Eighth Son's choice of these vague words, "screwy and misty," suggests that he did not have a precise diagnosis of his condition or that he had one and preferred not to share it with his family after his hospitalization. As mentioned earlier, before he was hospitalized, he had diagnosed himself as descending into depression because he had no solid ground on which to lead a stable life: on the one hand, he felt cut off from his family, on whom he had been heavily dependent; on the other, he believed that he had not matured to the point where he was prepared to become fully independent. Insofar as these were his only alternatives, he considered himself incapable of carrying out the latter one as an independent adult, so his only option was to take the former one by returning home and resuming his role as a dependent member of his family.

Father came to approximately the same conclusion about him. On April 7, 1941, two months before he had been discharged from McLean and started his journey home, Father made his diagnosis and described his plans for Eighth Son's treatment. "Since the root cause of his illness is mental depression arising from loneliness and homesickness," Father wrote to Frick, "it is my intention that my son should stay close to me after his return from the States, so that I may give him some interesting work to do to divert his mind from all worry and care and at the same time enable him to enjoy the bliss and happiness of his home."[69]

It was typical of Father to take personal responsibility for his child's problem, as he proposed to do here. But if Father recognized that the cause of Eighth Son's depression was loneliness and homesickness and if he believed that he could solve the problem by making his own intervention, then why hadn't he intervened earlier and cut short Eighth Son's agonizing three years at MIT and McLean?

To be sure, it was difficult for Father and Eighth Son to stay in close touch while one was in China and the other was in the United States. Yet Father had overcome comparable geographical distances between himself and his other sons in earlier years. When Second, Third, and Fourth Sons initially been denied admission to Cambridge University between 1929 and 1930 and later brooded over the shocking news of the Japanese bombing of Shanghai in 1932, Father gave them his attention and calmed their fears much more effectively in England than he calmed Eighth Son's fears in the United States. While Eldest Son wrestled with academic difficulties at Harvard in 1932–33, Father monitored him closely and corresponded with him much more intensively than he did with Eighth Son at MIT. When Fifth Son fell ill in the United States in 1934–35, Father wrote numerous letters and telegrams to him and sent other sons and China's ambassador to his aid—a far more impressive effort than the one Father made to alleviate Eighth Son's suffering. When Sixth Son sought guidance about how to approach his education in Japan, 1931–1937, Father advised him much more closely than he did Eighth Son in the United States.

Why was Father less attentive to Eighth Son abroad than he had been to his other sons earlier? Any explanation should begin with the war and its effects on him. Some of these effects were the result of his flight from Shanghai and his relocations in Hong Kong and later Chongqing, where he became preoccupied with his wartime work, leaving him physically and psychologically distant from his wife and youngest children. But during Father's wartime separation from them, his work was not his only preoccupation. He also became deeply involved in starting a new family and building a new life quite apart from the one he had previously had with Mother.

11

━━➤◆◆◆━━

Mother's Struggle to Save Her Marriage

OF ALL the threats Father's wartime separation posed for the Liu family, none had such far-reaching implications as the danger that it would end his marriage to Mother. Other wars that have kept husbands away from their wives for long periods of time have commonly strained or terminated marriages, and the Sino-Japanese War seems to have been no exception.[1] During their long wartime separation, Mother began to fear that Father might abandon her in favor of another woman, especially in light of his prewar philandering.

Throughout her marriage, Mother had never approved of Father taking another sexual partner. She had not selected a concubine for her husband in their household or encouraged him to choose his own concubine, as many Chinese women in wealthy families had done in late imperial China and continued to do up to her own time in the early twentieth century. She had never posed for him the question that the grand dame of an elite eighteenth-century family had asked of her husband in China's greatest novel, *The Dream of the Red Chamber:* "Other distinguished people can have several concubines, why can't we?"[2] Nor had Mother given her consent for Father to set up a permanent relationship with a mistress outside their household in the 1920s and 1930s. If she had done so, then under Nationalist law at the time, she would have been granting to any children he had by his mistress all of the legal rights that Mother's own children possessed.[3]

Yet, despite Mother's desire to be Father's only wife and her success at bearing sons (thus eliminating the most common rationale for a Chinese man to take a concubine or mistress), she had found that his attentions had shifted to other women. It is not clear when she first became aware of his sexual liaisons, but by the mid-1920s, when she was in her late thirties, she had incontestable proof of them.

Fighting Back against Father's Philandering

On December 8, 1926, Father had a child by his mistress, Bao Shuzhen.[4] He had met Bao in a courtesan house that ranked at the top of the elaborate hierarchy of prostitution in Shanghai, where she was reputed to be the number one beauty. Like many other Chinese women in her profession at the time, she claimed to be a sixteen-year-old virgin from Suzhou, a city sixty-five miles east of Shanghai that was the hometown of the renowned "Suzhou beauties." She may have hailed from Suzhou, but by the time she met Father she was in her early twenties, and when she bore his child she was twenty-six.[5] Be that as it may, she was considered by her madam to be of great value. Not until Father paid a considerable sum for her buyout was she allowed to leave the courtesan house. Only then was he able to set her up in a separate house, where she raised their son, Liu Nianci, who bore not only Father's surname (Liu) but also the same middle or generational name as all of Father's other sons (Nian).[6]

When Mother heard about the birth of Father's son by another woman, she was furious. She did not direct her anger at Father or propose to separate from him, let alone divorce him, and she did not avenge herself on Liu Nianci; according to one in-law, Mother received Liu Nianci in her home and treated him "as though he were her own son."[7] Mother took as her sole target Bao Shuzhen. She descended on Bao's house, confronted her, and slapped her across the face. Then with the help of several servants, she smashed Bao's furniture and destroyed her other belongings. Having reduced the place to rubble, she warned Bao never to see Father again.[8]

Mother's attack on Bao apparently had the desired effect, because Bao and Father ended their intimate relationship once and for all. He continued to give Bao financial support, and he eventually covered all the costs of their son's education, including college at St. John's University—the same school his other sons attended in Shanghai. But Bao was intimidated and shaken, and she no longer served as Father's mistress or had any more children by him.

Mother's angry protest won the sympathy of her children and caused Father to take the blame for what had gone wrong between them in the 1920s and early 1930s. In 1934, when Sixth Son (then a student in Japan) wrote to him expressing concern about Mother's unhappiness and discord in the Liu household, Father replied, "The fault is mine. I ought to have devoted more time to her. I should talk to and with her all the more and do my best to follow the line of her thought and thinking. And I ought to have more patience to hear her out and through whenever necessary."[9]

Besides making this self-criticism, Father praised Mother's virtues, especially her competence in the domestic domain. "Really, she is possessed of a nice temperament, that is, when it is rightly understood. And she is also a competent manager of home affairs. Though existing circumstances have made things appear otherwise yet we have all the qualities that are essential to the happiness of a home. All that we need now is a little more polishing or cultivating."[10]

At the same time, Father implicitly placed a share of the blame on Mother by noting that she did not join him in the social life that was part of his business world. In other parts of China, businessmen might not expect their wives to come with them on evenings out, but in Shanghai, according to Father, it was common practice. "You see," he explained to Sixth Son,

> social life has almost all the time been making heavy demands upon my leisure moments. My day has not consisted of office duties only. Friendly invitations, business meetings, and social engagements of various descriptions have all to be met outside of office hours. One day simply speeds upon the heel of another when one gets thus occupied. If your mother could bear my company on most of the occasions, both her life and mine could have been made all the easier and happier.[11]

While regretting Mother's unwillingness to accompany him to social occasions, he found her attitude understandable in light of her background. "I do not at all feel blue or discontented over something which cannot be helped. Your mother is by no means at any fault when her schooling and present addiction are taken into consideration."[12] Mother's schooling, as Sixth Son well knew, had been minimal, leaving her virtually illiterate, and her addiction to opium had been acquired in her search for relief from depression, which had plagued her intermittently all her life.

Father's characterization of his relationship with Mother made the gap between them sound unbridgeable, but he assured Sixth Son that he had already formulated a plan for bringing them back together. "I have begun to deny myself a part of my club life and come home as early as I ever can. So, my dear boy, you may as well spare yourself of any worry as far as my attempt to make our home a happy one is concerned. I will do everything I can to make everyone happy."[13]

Whether or not Father carried out this promise to deny himself a part of his "club life," he did not deny himself a mistress. In 1933, even before Father wrote so reassuringly to Sixth Son in the letters quoted above, he found a new mistress, He Guiying. Like Bao Shuzhen, she was regarded as the most beautiful woman in a high-class courtesan house in Shanghai, and she claimed to be a sixteen-year-old from Suzhou. (Father was then forty-five). But unlike Bao Shuzhen, He Guiying really was a sixteen-year-old from Suzhou, and she offered Father more than her youthfulness and beauty. Although born into an impoverished family and sold into prostitution by her father, an itinerant Suzhou bean curd peddler, she had become literate by converting to Christianity and receiving an education, and she had mastered the courtesan's arts of reading poetry and telling stories. In all these respects, she provided Father with a contrast to Mother. Whereas Mother came from a wealthy family, received little education, and devoted herself to producing and raising a big family, He Guiying came from a poor family, acquired literacy, and had no children. Making a life for himself with both women, Father continued to live at home with Mother and their children on Jessfield Road to the west of the International Settlement, and he discreetly set up He with her own house in the Hongkou district, across town in the eastern part of the city.[14]

By all accounts, Mother did not know about Father's relationship with He Guiying. If she did suspect that Father had this mistress, then it is possible, as one of her daughters-in-law later recalled, "that she just had to take it."[15] Putting up with a mistress or concubine would not have made her unique among Chinese women in her generation who were married to Chinese leaders—not only wealthy capitalists like Father but also leaders in politics and cultural life. "In the end," as the historian Lynn Pan has remarked about the fate of the wife of one these leaders, "it came down to the same old Chinese pattern: her husband found himself another woman, a concubine—was there not always a concubine?"[16] But it seems likely that Mother did not know about He Guiying, because if she had known, she would probably have taken action as aggressively against He as she had against Bao Shuzhen.

Yet, even if Mother was capable of driving every one of Father's mistresses away from him as long as he was living with her in their home in Shanghai, would she be able to do the same when he had left her behind in Shanghai and had moved to a distant place where he could maintain a separate household and start a new family? Mother had to face this dreaded possibility with the coming of the Sino-Japanese War.

Writing Father Wartime Love Letters

When Father fled Japanese-occupied Shanghai in 1938, he left secretly and did not even let Mother know he was going. Despite his departure without a goodbye and his earlier affairs with other women, Mother still seemed to trust him and wrote him a series of love letters. She and everyone in the Liu family assumed that he would be gone only briefly and would return to Shanghai as soon as the danger of an assassination attempt on his life had passed.

With this prospect of reuniting in mind, Father wrote as warmly to her as she did to him. As soon as he reached Hong Kong on June 30, he reassured her and urged their children to comfort her and help her avoid loneliness. By then, she and other members of her family no longer lived together at the Liu family home on Jessfield Road. They had escaped from it because it was outside the British-controlled International Settlement and French Concession, the only two parts of Shanghai not occupied by Japan since 1937. Mother now lived with only one member of their family, Youngest Daughter, in her new home, an apartment in a fashionable new high-rise building, Grosvenor House, which had been constructed in the French Concession in 1934.[17] "Please do come home as much as you can to accompany your mother as she will feel very miserable," he instructed all of his sons, daughters, son-in-law, and daughters-in-law in Shanghai.[18]

Within his first ten days away from Shanghai, he wrote three more letters to Mother. Since she read poorly, he sent these letters via Fourth Son, with instructions for him to read them aloud to her. "Please do read carefully and thoroughly to her," Father told Fourth Son in an enclosure with the fourth letter on July 9, 1938. "I want to give a good impression to her in order to avoid trouble on my return. It is my earnest desire that your mother and I must spend the rest of our life happily. I am willing to do the best I can to make her feel happy."[19]

In reply, Mother expressed her relief that Father was safe and her hope that he would hurry back to her. "Your letters came constantly," she gratefully acknowledged six weeks after he had left Shanghai, "and they gave me a lot of comfort concerning your personal safety." For him to remain safe, she had to admit that he would be ill advised to come back quite yet. On August 14, she cautioned him against returning immediately as he had proposed to do in a telegram on the previous day. Apparently encoding her language to escape the wartime wrath of Japanese censors and Nationalist Chinese agents, she wrote: "Our boys will tell you when it gets pleasant and cool for you to come home. Just now it seems pretty hot yet. Most probably the heat wave will go away with the present month."[20]

While urging him to postpone his return, Mother was delighted that he was eager to come back, and she let him know that she was equally eager to see him. "No wonder that your yearning for home has run up to the boiling point. I do also desire that you will come back soon. I hope you will be home again the coming of September at the latest."[21] Yet, however ardent their feelings, they did not immediately reunite.

As the summer of 1938 came and went, Mother began to realize that Father would not return to Shanghai soon, and when he invited her to visit him in Hong Kong, at first she was reluctant to go. She reminded him: "you know that I do not like to go about and that travel is such a hard undertaking for me." In addition, she was busy presiding over their family in Shanghai. "To whom," she asked him rhetorically, "can I entrust the management of our home here during my stay with you in Hong Kong?" Besides, she would not be able to travel alone, and if she brought along a son and servant, the trip would be expensive. "It cuts [to] the quick for me to waste any of the money which you have so painstakingly earned. We should especially be sparing at such hard and unproductive times."[22]

By mid-September 1938, Mother was willing to put aside these reservations because she had begun to miss Father dreadfully. A month earlier, she had bravely written to him: "I want to assure you that I am far from feeling lonely," because her sons and daughters-in-laws and other relatives had come to see her almost every day.[23] But on September 14, she confided to him that his absence had been devastating to her. "Since you went away I seem to have lost interest in everything. I can hardly enjoy more than two hours' sleep each day. My appetite has not been sharp and I have not even the stomach to go out shopping. Since you left home I had only been prevailed upon or persuaded to see our married children at their respective homes. Outwardly I do not at all seem lonely but at heart I really feel deserted. So in spite of everything I am now zealously looking forward to coming to you."[24] Although she undoubtedly had trouble openly expressing her affection in letters dictated to a scribe, she conveyed how desperately she missed Father. In this and all of her letters to Father at this time she addressed him as "My dear Daddy" and signed them "Your loving Haomei [Little Darling]."

After equivocating, she told Father that she ultimately decided to make the trip to Hong Kong not only to reunite with him but also to talk him into withdrawing from his new business ventures in Hong Kong and elsewhere in China outside Shanghai. His ambitions along these lines would be detrimental to him and his children, not to mention herself, she told him. "As a businessman and industrialist you have, I think, already done enough," she declared. At age fifty, if he took on too much new work, he would put his health at risk. Being the same age, Mother compared herself with Father and noted: "I, on my part, have already felt the decline of advanced years. The faculty of my senses are getting feebler every day." Anticipating Father's response, she acknowledged: "You may say that you are much stronger and tougher and can therefore still bear the buffet and strain of work. Perhaps you are right. But you cannot deny that physically you have already left youth and prime behind."[25]

If Father's strenuous work was hazardous to his health, it was also contrary to his children's wishes, she claimed. Their adult children "may not like what you do. You have already started enough lines here [in Shanghai] for them to follow and succeed." Meanwhile, their youngest children, aged nine and fifteen, would not be properly raised without their Father, Mother warned. "You must bear clearly in mind that our little son and daughter are too young and incapable yet to fight the battles of life without us. This is why I am so anxious that you should not attempt anything further there or elsewhere to run yourself down."[26]

In making this emotionally charged appeal, Mother clearly distinguished between two spheres, the domestic domain and the business
world. She admitted that she was no expert on the latter realm, but in
this case she insisted that no matter what Father's business prospects
were in Hong Kong or China, he should turn his back on them and
come home to fulfill his domestic obligations to his family in Shanghai.

> What I am saying to you here I say out of the very bottom of my heart.
> As your life partner I mean you no harm but good. You may think that
> as a woman I know nothing about business and that I should not inter-
> fere with you in what you contemplate doing. But you ought to know
> that it is [not only] for myself that I speak. It is for your dear sake as
> well as for the cause and interests of our children that I write this here
> to you.[27]

So even if Father did not come back to Shanghai for her sake (as she
had previously urged him to do), then he must come back for the sake
of his health and his children.

In reply, Father conceded Mother's point that he was no longer in
the prime of life. On September 24, he wrote from Hong Kong to her: "I
have been feeling the effects of advancing age for some time. At age 37,
I had to begin wearing bifocal eyeglasses. In recent years, my teeth
have become troublesome. At every meal, I have problems with chew-
ing hard food. I am not as strong as before, either mentally or physically. I feel that my brain and my ideas have both fallen behind."[28] Admitting that he had these physical and mental deficiencies, he could see
why Mother thought he should retire, but he refused to do so until he
put himself to at least one last test.

Now that he was cut off from his business enterprises in Shanghai,
he decided to launch two new ventures in western China, which was
under Chiang Kai-shek's rule and not occupied by Japan. He was determined to do all he could for these two businesses, the Huaye Match
Factory and the Sichuan Woolen Mill. He claimed that then, if they
were not successful, he would take Mother's advice and end his career
in business. "I will definitely not take risks in my old age and do things
that I'll regret later. Please don't worry. I'm afraid that you might misunderstand all this, so I have given you these details."[29] After describing his plans for the new businesses, he promised: "If any of the above
fails, I will stop." But his businesses did not fail, and his career did not
stop.

Allying with Family Members

When Mother failed to talk Father into giving up his new business ventures and returning to Shanghai, she began appealing to him to establish a permanent residence for them as a couple in Hong Kong. In the spring of 1939, after nearly a yearlong separation, she spent the months of March and April with him in Hong Kong, and from then on she wrote more insistent letters from Shanghai not only to her husband but also to his brother, Liu Jisheng, who had moved from Shanghai to Hong Kong and begun working in Father's new match factory there.

In October 1939, six months after her visit, Mother wrote to her brother-in-law that "having once come to Hong Kong and seen what a hard life your brother is leading, I am more than anxious to join him." She had heard from Father and others in the family that he frequently traveled from Hong Kong to western China where his new factories were located, but she saw no reason why she could not accompany him on these trips. Recalling a trip around the world that she and Father had taken together twelve years earlier, she posed this rhetorical question: "If I could go round the globe with your brother, why can't I make trips with him now?" Frustrated by her husband's opposition to her plan to move from Shanghai to Hong Kong, she sought the support of her brother-in-law for this plan, because "I am in burning fervor to be with your brother."[30]

By early 1940, Mother's campaign succeeded to the extent that Father accommodated her by renting a new house in Hong Kong and inviting her to reside in it. But she still did not achieve her goal of reuniting with him, because by then he was traveling often to Chongqing, Kunming, Guiyang, and other cities in western China, and he had no intention of residing with her in Hong Kong or taking her with him to China.

Uncertain whether to leave Shanghai or not, she sought advice from her children, who gave her conflicting opinions. On one side were those who opposed the move because Mother disliked travel, especially the expense of it, and would face the prospect of further frustrations in Hong Kong as a result of Father's frequent business trips away from there. On the other side were those who favored the move because Mother yearned to be with Father. Writing from Hong Kong to his brothers and sisters in Shanghai, Sixth Son took the latter position.

"Most important of all," he emphasized, "is that if Mother comes to live with Father in Hong Kong, it'll make her one hundred percent happier and healthier." He sympathized with Mother's plight. "Recently, Mother has had more sorrow than happiness. She also has been feeling weak because of having given birth so many times. On top of that, she doesn't know how to enjoy life. While we may not be able to help her live a really happy life, we should definitely do our best to help her recover her health."[31] During the following year, 1940, Mother remained caught between these two positions—eager to reunite with Father but fearful that if she left Shanghai for Hong Kong, she would find that he had left Hong Kong for Chongqing.

In mid-1940, when Father began to spend more time in Chongqing than Hong Kong, Mother pleaded with him to let her join him in both places. Receiving no encouragement from him, she once again turned for support to his brother, who was still in Hong Kong, and she proposed both a plan and a contingency plan. "My heart's dearest wish is to come to your brother in Hong Kong. I have already written him about my scheme." Her reasons for these latest plans were more for her own emotional well-being than for her family. "Now," she told her brother-in-law, "I feel all the more strongly that we ought to be separated no longer. I feel that he is the only one who really understands me. On my own part, I know that I am the only one who has him closest to heart and who can really take the best care of him. So I have fully set my mind and heart upon going to Chungking to join him in the fall." After baring her heart to her husband's brother as well as her husband, she implored her brother-in-law "to take this matter up for me with your brother to the effect that I may go to stay with him for good."[32]

In response to Mother's proposals, Father continued to take care of her financially but became more and more distant from her physically and emotionally. As noted, he rented a house in Hong Kong and invited her to occupy it, and he provided for her personal and financial security in Shanghai by opening a special account for her at the Liu family accounts office. But rather than have her with him in Hong Kong or Chongqing, he formally and legally established a family rule that one married son and his wife must live in Mother's house with her at all times in Shanghai. If Eldest Son was available, he and his wife were to live with Mother in Shanghai. If not, then Second Son and his wife were to live with her. If not them, then Third Son and his wife were to live with her. And so the obligation passed from one son to the next in their birth order.[33]

In 1940–1941, as he moved his household from Hong Kong to Chongqing, Father became less and less responsive to Mother. On March 15, 1941, now fully ensconced in Chongqing, he explained in a letter to Eldest Son in Shanghai that he was too busy to solve Mother's personal and emotional problems, and he called on his sons in Shanghai to serve as her principal caregivers. Alluding to Mother's earlier psychiatric difficulties, he told Eldest Son:

> Your mother apparently is experiencing another period of mental depression. I hope you and your brothers will do your best to cheer her up. I am now giving my whole time to developing industry in the interior of China; therefore I find it very hard to find out a solution to various problems given me by your mother. However, I have written to her telling her that she can have everything she wishes for after the conclusion of the Sino-Japanese hostilities. We have a great future ahead of us if we will only pull ourselves together through this crisis.[34]

If only Mother would leave him alone and let him complete his work in wartime Chongqing, then Father promised that he would reunite with her in Shanghai as soon as the war was over and give her his full attention there.

Conspiring with Fourth Son

Mother refused to accept Father's claim that he had no time for her, and she sought help from Fourth Son, who had been summoned from Shanghai to become Father's right-hand man in Chongqing. Writing to Fourth Son on April 5, 1941, she took the position that Father would surely rescue her from Shanghai and welcome her to Chongqing as soon as he came to realize the extent of her physical deprivation and emotional disintegration. To bring Father to this realization, she instructed Fourth Son to set him straight. "Your father, on his part, may have the wrong impression that we are spending so much money and are enjoying gay life here. He does not know that I still have to spend most part of my miserable day without even thinking of what delicious things to eat or any fine clothes to wear."[35]

This deterioration of economic conditions was only a small part of her problem. The psychological effects of wartime chaos were even more

devastating. She wrote to Fourth Son: "Then you know that I am subject to nervousness. I feel anxious, especially, about you all who are
dear to my heart. Whenever your brothers here go out on social occasions my heart is burdened with worry till I am fully assured that they
have come safely back home. Conditions in general here, as you know,
are becoming worse and worse. Thugs and gangsters are at almost every turn of the road. I have always wanted to get away from Shanghai
because the place is full of danger."[36] Noting the danger of kidnapping
in Shanghai, Mother warned Fourth Son that his baby daughter might
become the next target.

In desperation, she asked him: "How can you expect such a person
of fine nerves as me to remain contented here in Shanghai? My top
desire is to come with your youngest brother and sister as well as your
wife and daughter to Chungking right away. You must settle us in a
place where we can have safety and peace. Get it promptly done or you
might find it is too late and regret [it]."[37]

In this letter and especially in this last passage, Mother resorted
to strong language in pleading for help. She still seemed to assume
that Father would heed her plea and bring her to Chongqing if only
she could convey to him the gravity of her predicament. Not until she
heard back from Fourth Son that Father had rejected this latest proposal did she threaten to adopt a more drastic strategy: the breakup of
the Liu household.

Threatening to Split the Family

After Mother heard from Father that he had decided to stop dealing
directly with her and her problems, she adopted a new strategy for handling him. She did not give up on her marriage, but she began to investigate Father's life in Chongqing, and she threatened to split the Liu
family if he did not reaffirm her position as his wife.

On May 9, 1941, Mother conveyed these ideas in a long letter to
Fourth Son. Although not addressing it to Father, Mother left no doubt
that her proposals were meant for him. "I do not write to your Father as
he is busy there and has to go away much of the time," she told Fourth
Son. "I have therefore to write to you. My letter for you is really for you
three"—Father, Fourth Son, and Sixth Son, who were all working to-

gether in Chongqing. Fourth Son, Mother emphasized, was to serve not merely as her messenger but also as her private investigator, coconspirator, and advocate with Father. "Tell everything to me," she instructed Fourth Son, "so that we may scheme together."[38]

Mother resorted to this scheming, she reminded Fourth Son, only because Father had abandoned her. "Your Father has left me for years now and I have begun to lose interest in everything," she lamented. Trying to bring back memories of a happy family, "I often see the photographs of you boys and girls. Your Father's picture is also on my dressing table."[39]

To some extent, she attributed the change in Father to their wartime separation: "Since your Father went away he does not seem to have me truly in his heart." At the same time, she recognized that his wartime withdrawal was a culmination of tendencies he had shown earlier. "In heart your Father has given me up for more than ten years. There were times when he was still true to me. But since the outbreak of the present trouble he has completely abandoned me."[40]

Before posing any threat to family solidarity, Mother once again declared that she would make no trouble at all if only Father would allow her to join him in Chongqing. "About my coming I wonder what you two boys [Fourth and Sixth Sons] are going to say to your Father and what reception is he to give me. I wonder why your Father only looks to business and does not care about home. Does he think he [at age 54] will have another 54 years to live?"[41]

In earlier letters Mother had made this point to Father, urging him to retire from business and spend his last years with her and their youngest children, but in this letter, she called for a showdown for the first time. "I wonder whether it is his notion to imprison me here to death," she asked, referring to her confinement in Shanghai. "My wanting to come to Chungking this time is the very last step I ever wish to take. Because you two boys are there I want to take this last step to come and see exactly how your Father is to treat me."[42]

If Father did not allow Mother to take even this "very last step," then what was left for her to do? She did not spell out a plan of action, but she did pose a veiled threat. "If your Father does not want me to stay long with him," she told Fourth Son in the same letter, "then I think I will go to stay with my brother, your uncle, who seems to behave much better now. I shall then get a nice girl for him so that he may have a home wherein my own ancestors may be 'fed.' I have all the time been following the precepts of my own parents and grandma. I have never done anything good to repay my own people. My Yih [Ye] family was originally a good family. Now it has declined. It ought to be restored to its former position, that is, if ever possible."[43]

As Mother reflected on her need to repay her birth family, she recalled that the Lius had gained from her marriage at the Ye family's expense. "You may ask your Father how much have I suffered since I married him," she told Fourth Son, and she noted an apparent causal relationship between the rise of the Lius and the decline of the Ye family since then. "It seems quite mysterious to me that you Lieu [Liu] people had to get a lift from Yih people. Now my own house has gone to pieces and all Yih people have become dependent upon you Lieu people."[44]

Sharply separating herself and "my own house" from "you Lieu people," Mother proposed that she should be the one to reverse the fortunes of the Ye family and bring it back to prominence. "Now, of all Yih people I am the only one who is in a substantial position. I think there is no difference between boy or girl. There is no reason why I should not do something to restore my own house into some position. I should not stand by and do nothing because I am a girl. Though a woman I ought to do what I should to rebuild my Yih family in a way so that my ancestors may perpetually have their 'meals.' "[45]

While emphasizing that there was no reason why she as a woman should not restore her family, she did not say exactly how she would do it. She only hinted that her sons might have to choose between aligning with Father and the Lius on the one hand or herself and the Ye family on the other. "If he [Father] does not have me in mind now I have to think of restoring my Yih family. You boys should all listen to what I say to you so that the world may become better and really fit for people and your descendants to live in."[46] Her sons, she suggested here, needed to side with her and against Father if they wanted to set a moral standard that would make the world worth raising their families in.

This letter from Mother to Fourth Son was one Father could not ignore, and he sent a reply that convinced Mother she finally had his attention. "A few statements in your letter," she wrote back to Father on June 19, 1941, "have touched my heart deeply. We have been together for long years and I realize that in this whole world you are the only one who understands me best. And I think you have also realized that it is I who really care for you most in heart."[47]

Feeling emotionally restored, Mother once again laid plans to rejoin Father and live with him. "My desire to come and see you is as strong as ever. We are now both getting well advanced in years and I feel stronger than ever that my rightful place is to be with you."[48] Ready to take action, Mother urged Father to send a telegram approving her plan to close down her house in Shanghai, meet him in Hong Kong, and move with him to Chongqing as soon as her belongings had been shipped there.

Mother persuaded Father to let her meet with him in Hong Kong but not to let her live with him permanently in Hong Kong or Chongqing. In July 1941 she made the voyage from Shanghai and moved in with him at the Repulse Bay Hotel in Hong Kong. Once she finally saw him face-to-face in the privacy of their suite, she vented her fury. "Mother raised hell for a few days as expected," Third Son reported from Hong Kong (where he was then working with Father) to his brothers in Shanghai. "She kept father awake until 3 in the morning one day and father said he had better go to Chungking as soon as possible." She only backed off when Father's doctor "came to father's rescue and explained to mother that unless father is given a complete rest he will not regain his health and be fit for work in Chungking or anywhere else." Father was obliged to stay with Mother in Hong Kong for a few weeks before escaping to Chongqing on August 25. Once he had left Hong Kong without her, she sailed back to Shanghai.[49]

In her exchange with Father at Hong Kong, Mother thought that she had convinced him to let her join him in Chongqing, and she wrote to Fourth Son and his wife saying she would see them there "in the near future."[50] But after weeks went by without Father making any arrangements for her to come, she began to investigate his life at Chongqing more closely.

In October 1941, Mother became suspicious about Father's allocation of funds for his private use in Chongqing and confronted him about it. In response, he dismissed out of hand her suggestion that he had a secret bank account. He wrote from Chongqing to his children in Shanghai: "Your mother has the impression that I am keeping a separate reserve for somebody else but God only knows what makes her to think so."[51]

To show that Mother's charges were groundless, Father explained that his sons and his accountant kept track of all his finances. "All my investments and interests in Hongkong are known to Hannibal [Third Son] & he looks after them during my absence & all accounts are kept by Mr. Chang, the accountant of Great China [Match Company of Hong Kong, which Father had recently founded]. The only money under my care is restricted to couple of hundred dollars or less in the bank under my own name. Johnson [Fourth Son] has the same control of my investments and interests here [in Chongqing]. My accounts with the bank here is only about C.N.$720 & no more." Thanks to this financial transparency, he told his children: "Now you can see that I have nothing hidden from my family."[52]

The real problem, according to Father, was not his finances but Mother's dissatisfaction with any living arrangements that he might make for her. He told his children that he would welcome the prospect of living with her, but he pointed out that she would need to make use of three residences—one in Hong Kong and another in Chongqing, plus the one in Shanghai—and he thought that she would find the arrangements frustrating. Never eager to travel, she would be bothered by the expense and difficulty of securing passage across enemy lines as she shuttled from one of these cities to another, he predicted. Worse yet, Father admitted that he would not be available to assist her. "Being busy in solving National and Company's problems and overloaded with difficult tasks," he explained to his children, "I am sorry to say that not much attention and energy can be spared from me to comply with all her wishes."[53]

Yet Father recognized that no matter how busy he was, he would run a serious risk if he ignored Mother's complaints or did not deal directly with her. He wrote to his children: "I have no intention to evade or dodge the responsibility & I cannot pass it on to any member of the family, even if he or she is willing to take it from me, because Mother cannot be satisfied by so doing. I suppose that I have made the case clear to you and in fact you know it without my saying."[54] His children knew that he had to deal with Mother directly because they had seen the failure of his earlier attempt to deal with her indirectly through Fourth Son. Troubled by their parents' seemingly irreconcilable differences, they began to consider the unnerving possibility that Mother might split not only the family but also the family firm.

Triggering a Debate over the Family Business

While telling his wife and children otherwise, Father did, in fact, secretly set aside money for his mistresses. Even before he moved to Chongqing, he lived with other women in Hong Kong. If Mother did not know about them, her children certainly did. In January 1940, Sixth Son (who, as noted earlier, had questioned Father as early as 1934 about his inattentiveness to Mother) reported from Hong Kong about Father's active sex life there. "You probably all know," he wrote to his brothers and sisters in Shanghai, *"Father never lives alone even during Mother's absence"* (English words italicized here; this letter otherwise written in Chinese).[55]

In late 1940, after Father had settled in Chongqing, he heard from He Guiying, his mistress in Shanghai, that she had given birth to his son, Liu Nianliang. This news took Father by surprise, but he immediately invited He and their son to come live with him, instructing Fourth Son to arrange for their passage from Shanghai to Chongqing. On their arrival, they settled with Father into housing in the compound at Father's Huaye Match Factory in the Danzhishi district, and he financed their household by drawing funds from the accounts office of the Liu family enterprises.[56]

So even while Father claimed that Mother should not join him in Chongqing because it would be too expensive and too difficult to arrange, he secretly arranged for He to join him and maintained a separate household with her there. While he purported to be too busy to attend to Mother because he was serving his country and building up his business, he was not too busy to attend to He in Chongqing and take her with him on trips to Kunming and other parts of China outside the Japanese occupation.[57]

As Father became more and more deeply committed to his new family in Chongqing, Fourth Son became critical of him for his treatment of Mother. In 1943, Fourth Son began discussing with his brothers the danger that by antagonizing her, Father might cause her to tear apart the family and the family firm. After living in Chongqing and working closely with Father between 1940 and 1943, Fourth Son concluded unequivocally that Father bore all the blame for his marital differences with Mother. Fourth Son wrote to his brothers in Shanghai: "After coming to Chongqing and living with Father for three years, I can now see that it is not Mother's fault that Father and Mother differ with each other. It's all a matter of Father's unfaithfulness. When Father is clear-headed, he always says to me, 'Fourth Son, your mother is a person who truly loves me. I am an idiot, and women make me especially idiotic.' "[58]

Just as Fourth Son had observed Father's unfaithfulness, he had also come to appreciate Mother's greatness as a pillar of family solidarity. "I have not realized until now that Mother is also a great woman. We must all love and protect her. With her alive in this world, we in the Liu family will certainly never be torn asunder."[59] Apparently alluding to Mother's earlier threat to withdraw from the Liu family and return to her birth family, Fourth Son paid tribute to her in this letter for refraining from carrying out this threat.

Mother had ample reasons for giving up on Father, according to Fourth Son, and he urged his brothers in Shanghai to sympathize with her. "Mother must have felt lonely and abandoned in Shanghai. She is over fifty years old, and she has had too little opportunity to be with Father. She has been longing for Father but how about Father? He has for a long time had a new love. I wrote the [earlier] letter [to his brothers criticizing Father] because I pity Mother so much and I hate Father's unfaithfulness." While Father was able to enjoy his new love in the present and foreseeable future, Mother had only bleak prospects. "She has already lost her husband's love. If she loses her children's love, what will she have to live for?"[60]

Fourth Son questioned whether Mother had anything to live for, but he by no means regarded her as powerless. On the contrary, he suggested to his brothers that her power was the key to the family's future solidarity. Reminding them of their family's history, he asked: "Do you remember when Grandmother was alive and our branch was very close to Third Uncle's branch [of the Liu family]? Since Grandmother died, haven't we become distant? In the future, Mother's power will be even greater than Grandmother's. She truly is a fair and unselfish mother, never liking this son and disliking that son. In her eyes, children are all the same."[61] In her hands, Fourth Son implied, Mother had the power to pull the family together or tear it apart.

In writing these criticisms of Father and tributes to Mother, Fourth Son conveyed not only his own sentiments but also those of Sixth and Eighth Son, who were working with him and Father in Chongqing in

1943. "Whenever Sixth and Eighth Brothers and I talk about how pitiful Mother is, we are always reduced to tears," he confided. He asked
that his letters be shown to all five of his brothers who were in Shanghai, and he made what he thought was an uncontroversial proposal for
dividing their filial responsibilities: "We three brothers here ask that
you all take care of Mother, and we will take care of Father."[62]

Of Fourth Son's points, his brothers found it much easier to endorse the one about Mother than the one about Father. They had never
doubted Mother's dedication and long suffering. "Mother has devoted
most of her life to bringing up her children and has suffered through all
kinds of hardships," they reaffirmed. "For several decades, she has
managed our household with diligence and frugality, and she has never
violated these principles under any circumstances. Her spirit unquestionably deserves our deep respect. Her conservative way of thinking
has to do with her age, education, and lack of contact with the outside
world."[63] But no matter how much they sympathized with Mother,
they saw no justification for criticizing Father.

Fourth Son's brothers insisted that even as Mother had been un-
waveringly dedicated and long-suffering in the domestic domain, Father had done the same in the realm of business. "Most of his life," they
reminded Fourth Son, "Father has worked hard for his enterprises. Although he has aged and weakened, he has not shirked responsibility for
his enterprises, and he has not retreated from his duties. His dedication
is truly admirable, and all of us have benefited greatly from his work."[64]
In light of Father's exemplary record, why would Fourth Son find fault
with him?

Some, if not all, of Fourth Son's brothers and his uncle in Shanghai suspected that his moralistic condemnation of Father's unfaithfulness as a husband was merely a cover for a scheme Fourth Son had
concocted to withdraw from the family firm and go into business for
himself. "In your recent letters," Fourth Son's eldest brothers wrote to
him on behalf of their uncle and their younger brothers in Shanghai
in the summer of 1943, "we can read between the lines subtle words of
disapproval that you have inserted regarding Father's personal ethics.
All your brothers and our uncle have read them here, and they have
jumped to a perhaps mistaken conclusion that you may have had a falling out with Father and that you may be setting out to establish your
own separate business."[65]

Their uncle's and brothers' conclusion was perhaps mistaken, Fourth Son's eldest brothers believed, because they doubted that he was capable of such cynical manipulation. "We are fully convinced that no such thing is going on. We know you very well. You have always put the interests of Father's enterprises above all else, and you would never change your earlier way of thinking so abruptly. But if his eldest brothers expressed confidence in Fourth Son's character, they still thought he had made a mistake. They told him: "What you said in your letters was perhaps the result of some sort of oversight or carelessness. You will regret it later."[66]

According to them, he was wrong to have raised the subject of Father's personal ethics at all.

> As for Father's personal ethics, if he has minor flaws, these flaws will not overshadow his greatness. Our point is that we, as his children, should not comment on or be critical of whatever flaws he has. He was born with a quick temper and a tendency to become angry and scold people. But he never harbors any ill will. We all need to be patient with him. If those who have worked with him realize this, how much more should we as his own children accommodate him and make him happy.[67]

Leaving no room for further debate, they closed the subject with finality: "We think you will agree with us about this."

Fourth Son did not agree. "You have all misunderstood the events that I described about Father in my letter," he wrote back to his brothers in Shanghai. They had missed his point because they had failed to see his crucial distinction between Father's failure as a husband and his success as a father and businessman. "I must declare," he said forcefully, "that Father is a great man in this world and a great father to us, but he is an unfaithful husband."[68]

As a great man in this world, Father remained the leader of the family business, and Fourth Son assured his brothers that he had a working relationship with him that was free of any friction, "so you all must stop worrying about this."[69] In addition, Fourth Son revered him as a father. "Please don't misunderstand. In the end, Father is still the person that I worship the most. His great personality is something that we as his sons should take as our model."[70] On Father's affection for his children, Fourth Son was particularly emphatic. He had no doubt that

Father "loves his children very much, and he is very forgiving toward his children. I consider myself to be an obedient son to him and a son willing to make sacrifices for him."[71]

Fourth Son went to great pains to draw this distinction between Father as a peerless business leader and loving father and as an unfaithful husband, and he closed a long letter to his brothers on the subject by asking: "Have I made myself clear to you now?"[72]

Yet it is easy to imagine why his distinction was not clear to his brothers. After considering Father the head of both the Liu family and the Liu family enterprises all their lives, they understandably found it difficult to draw a sharp distinction between his roles as head of the family and as head of the family firm. Moreover, in light of Mother's earlier threat to split the family, it seems likely that Fourth Son's brothers in Shanghai feared that he and their two other brothers in Chongqing might encourage Mother to carry out her threat if they aligned themselves with her and against Father.

Avoiding a Wartime Breakup

Of all the war's effects on the Lius, its separation of Father from Mother had the greatest potential for not merely loosening but destroying family ties. During the four years Father and Mother did not see each other in person, 1941–1945, both of them were victims of this wartime separation, but each had the power to save their marriage. Father risked ending their marriage by leaving Mother in Shanghai and living with his mistress and infant son in Chongqing, and he tried to preserve it by not telling Mother about them. At the same time, Mother did not passively accept his decision to forbid her to join him in Chongqing. She acted on her fears and suspicions by forming alliances with her brother-in-law in Hong Kong and Fourth Son in Chongqing and by warning Fourth Son that she would split the family and the family firm if she found that Father had replaced her with another woman. Just as she had ended Father's relationship with Bao Shuzhen before the war, so she vowed to end his relationship with any other mistress in Chongqing during the war.[73]

Fearful that Mother would exercise her power, Father and his sons and others who knew that he had He Guiying and her son with him in

Chongqing all kept Father's second family a secret from Mother throughout the war. With her suspicions still unconfirmed in her own mind,
Mother continued to plead with Father to let her join him in wartime
Chongqing, and he continued to postpone their reunion until the war
came to an end.

12

⟫⬥⟪

The Family's Postwar Disunion and Reunion

"FINALLY victory is here, and the whole world is celebrating," Father wrote from Chongqing to his younger brother in Shanghai on August 15, 1945, the day after Japan surrendered, bringing an end to the Pacific War. Immediately he added: "I am anxious to know about my family in Shanghai." In the same letter he expressed his concern about the fate of the family business. Like almost everyone else, he had not anticipated the United States ending the war so abruptly during the previous week by dropping atomic bombs on Japan, and now he was eager to plot strategy to reclaim his business and save his family from possible postwar threats. "I have yet to set my departure date," he wrote. "When I arrive [in Shanghai], I will take the opportunity to discuss with you the best strategy for dealing with our business matters."[1]

Father had good reasons for his anxiety over his postwar prospects. It had been more than seven years since he had set foot in his hometown, Shanghai, and nearly four years since he had seen any of the Shanghai-based members of his family. In Chongqing, he had worked closely with Fourth, Sixth, and Eighth Sons and had tentatively resumed contact with his estranged eldest daughter. With Father as the head, these people had formed a distinct Chongqing branch of the Liu family during the war. Now all of the Lius would soon come together and resume their lives in their hometown, Shanghai. But had the long wartime separation between these two branches prepared them to come together in a spirit of reunion or disunion?

On his return to Shanghai, Father immediately reconciled with Mother while keeping his relationship with He Guiying secret from her. He succeeded in maintaining this deception, but he faced a dilemma: how to divide his time between He, with whom he had lived in wartime Chongqing, and Mother, now that he and Mother were both living in Shanghai? He resolved this dilemma by reverting to his prewar pattern. He moved He and their son back into the house he had bought for them before the war—a plain, nineteenth-century place tucked into a lane off Henan Road in Shanghai's Hongkou district, at a discreet distance from the Liu family residence in the French Concession—and he visited them there regularly.[2] He took the Liu family home as his principal residence and conducted daily life there with Mother and their youngest daughter, now a teenager.

This attempt to balance a Chongqing commitment against a Shanghai commitment was typical of Father's approach to the problems he faced in the postwar era. Again and again, he sought to resolve potential conflicts between commitments that he had made in wartime Chongqing and commitments his family expected him to make in postwar Shanghai. In his relations with his eldest sons, who had stayed in Shanghai during the war, Father found this dilemma especially acute.

Chongqing Protectors and Shanghai Sons

The postwar Nationalist government brought charges that Second and Third Sons in Shanghai had committed treason during the war. Father thought the official connections he had formed in Chongqing during the war, when he had worked closely with the Nationalist government there, would protect his sons. He had originally gone to Chongqing at the personal invitation of Chiang Kai-shek in 1940, and while founding industrial enterprises there between 1940 and 1945 he had also accepted official positions, notably in 1942 as head of the National Match Monopoly and in 1944 as head of the National Monopoly Bureau (the same agency but reformed to include responsibility for cigarettes as well as matches).[3] In Chongqing, he had met regularly with the minister of finance, Kong Xiangxi (H. H. Kung), and as he wrote from Chongqing to his brother in Shanghai at the end of the war, he had "worked closely with all levels of the bureaucracy under the ministry of finance."[4]

With these extensive connections, Father took steps in Chongqing as soon as the war ended to recruit Nationalist officials as protectors for his sons in Shanghai. Since he knew the Nationalist government had already begun to appoint local officials who were still in Chongqing to posts they would take up in the Shanghai area, he sought protection for his sons from two of them: Xuan Tiewu, who was slated to become chief of police in Shanghai, and Zhou Xiangxian, who was to resume his post as mayor of Hangzhou, a position he had held for nearly twenty years under a series of provincial governors before the war.[5] Father had solidified his relationships with these men in wartime Chongqing on the basis of hometown and native-place ties. With Xuan he shared a hometown tie because both had lived and known each other in prewar Shanghai, and with Zhou he shared a native-place tie because both men's families hailed from Dinghai County in Ningbo Prefecture.

As soon as Father heard that Xuan and Zhou had been appointed, he invited them to a farewell dinner in Chongqing and unveiled his plan to them. According to the recollections of Fourth Son (who also attended the dinner), Father told Xuan and Zhou: "I have two boys in Shanghai. Second Son is called Nianyi, and Third Son is called Nianli. They are both graduates of Cambridge University in England. Second Son studied economics, and Third Son studied law. They have some knowledge about the world. They can help both of you smooth relations with the Allied forces. I hope that the two of you will look after them and give them appointments as commissioners."[6]

In reply, Xuan and Zhou readily agreed to find jobs for both sons. Within a few days, Father received official letters appointing Second Son as a commissioner in the Special Commission's Office of Zhejiang Province and Third Son as commissioner for foreign affairs in the headquarters of the Shanghai Police. As Fourth Son commented, "once they were commissioners, naturally they would have no further problem [with charges against them for treason]."[7]

Relieved to have made these arrangements, Father insisted that his sons carry out his plan. Writing from Chongqing on August 15, the day after Japan's surrender, he assured them in Shanghai that he had firm commitments from their future bosses. "Both Xuan and Zhou have promised [your appointments] to me in person," he told them. He directly ordered them to accept the appointments and go to work with Xuan and Zhou. "I hope that you, my two sons, will do as I say. This is very important."[8] To guarantee that his sons would follow these orders, Father wrote another letter on the same day to his brother in Shanghai instructing him to deliver the same message to Second and Third Sons face-to-face. He explained that he had "personally recommended" Second Son to Mayor Zhou and Third Son to Police Chief Xuan and that his sons must without fail take these jobs for their own protection. "Please tell my sons to do as I say," he emphasized to his brother. "Tell them not to be concerned about either title or pay. This is very important."[9]

For the next six weeks, Father was not able to rush in person to the rescue of his sons in Shanghai because he could not extricate himself from his obligations in Chongqing. Still stuck there when Fourth Son left on September 28, Father told him that on his arrival in Shanghai he should visit his elder brothers and arrange for their protection before doing anything else. Following these orders, Fourth Son proceeded directly from the Shanghai airport to pick up his uncle and go to Second Son's home, where he presented appointment letters to Second and Third Sons, officially confirming their jobs with Zhou and Xuan.

To Fourth Son's astonishment, his brothers in Shanghai not only declined these job offers but literally laughed at Father's effort to protect them from charges of treason. "You're a little late," Second Son told Fourth Son, chuckling to himself. "I already have a powerful man protecting me."[10] Second Son went on to explain that they had found their own protector in General Dai Li, the head of the Nationalist government security forces, who held ultimate responsibility for identifying and incarcerating wartime traitors in postwar China. In Second Son's words (as quoted by Fourth Son): "As soon as General Dai Li arrived in Shanghai, our uncle proposed that I should host his visit, so he has already lived in my house for more than two weeks and we have now become old friends. He likes my house because it is quiet and safe."[11]

Second Son had apparently won the trust of the usually reclusive head of security to the extent that he was willing to socialize with Second Son's Chinese and American friends. "He asked me to organize a couple of dancing parties," Second Son reported to Fourth Son, and urged Second Son "to invite all of Shanghai's celebrities and their wives to get together with our American friends to show our gratitude to our allies for their wartime contribution."[12] Second Son's relationship with Dai Li was all the protection he needed, he assured Fourth Son. Father's arrangement based on his connections with local officials was fine, Second Son acknowledged, but his own arrangement based on his personal connections with Dai Li as security chief was even better. "Now that I have Dai Li as my personal bodyguard," Second Son wryly observed, "what do I have to be afraid of?"[13]

If Father had any lingering doubt about the strength and dependability of these ties with Dai Li, Second Son soon eliminated it. In October Second Son flew with Dai Li to Chongqing to pick Father up and fly him back to Shanghai. Ironically, Dai Li made the flight to escort Chinese prisoners who had been accused of treason, but the Lius traveled as Dai Li's privileged guests.

In this case as in others, Father discovered the difficulties of making the transition from wartime Chongqing to postwar Shanghai. From his eldest sons' viewpoint, his actions on their behalf in Chongqing were redundant in Shanghai because they had built up their own network of connections for protecting themselves. After Father arrived in Shanghai on October 2, he teamed up with his eldest sons in appealing to the Nationalist government to return the family's businesses to them, and on December 15 they submitted their official petition to the Enemy and Puppet Property Office of the Shanghai District, arguing that their family members had only signed the agreements and formed joint ventures with the Japanese and Wang Jingwei's Japanese-sponsored government because the Japanese military had coerced them into it. Once the Nationalist government approved this petition, the Lius acquired an even greater share of the stock in their joint stock companies than they had held in prewar Shanghai.[14]

Father's name was on this petition, but in the aftermath of the war he did not exercise authority as the sole head of the family firm in Shanghai. Instead he left decision making for daily operations largely in the hands of the eldest sons, who continued to preside over the family's businesses as they had during the war. For his part, Father complemented what his eldest sons were doing by making use of his official contacts from wartime Chongqing in postwar Shanghai.[15]

Chongqing Connections and Shanghai Agencies

If the eldest Liu sons considered Father's Chongqing contacts irrelevant in official relations in Shanghai, Fourth Son considered them vital for this purpose. He had worked closely with Father in Chongqing for four years, from 1941 to 1945, and he continued to work closely with him in postwar Shanghai. While leaving the daily operation of the family business to the eldest sons, he and Father concentrated on rehabilitating it by taking advantage of new industrial equipment and raw materials that were exported to Shanghai by two official agencies: the United Nations Relief and Rehabilitation Administration (UNRRA) and the China National Relief and Rehabilitation Administration (CNRRA), the Nationalist government's counterpart to UNRRA. In these organizations, which both had China headquarters in postwar Shanghai, Father and Fourth Son landed prominent positions because of their contacts in wartime Chongqing.

In the fall of 1945, after the end of the war and before the Lius' return from Chongqing to Shanghai, Father urged Fourth Son to socialize with young American intelligence officers in the U.S. Office of Strategic Services (OSS). With this aim in mind, under the sponsorship of a Nationalist official and a manager of one of Father's factories, Fourth Son joined the Masonic Lodge in Chongqing and began attending lavish banquets the lodge held every week. Of its more than two hundred members, 70 percent were high-ranking U.S. military officers. As one of the few Chinese members, Fourth Son attracted considerable attention and received more than one job offer; for example, the American manager of Standard Oil Company's China office recruited him to become the agent responsible for Chongqing and the sales territory in southwestern China. But Father talked Fourth Son out of considering any of these prospective jobs until one was proposed by the head of the Chongqing office of the OSS, Lieutenant Colonel Munroe. At Munroe's invitation, Fourth Son met with him for a series of lunches at the U.S. army command in Chongqing, where they discussed the prospects for postwar Sino-American cooperation.[16]

As the time for their departure from Chongqing drew near, Munroe raised the possibility that he and Fourth Son might work together in Shanghai. He explained that he and his fellow officers in the OSS would be managing UNRRA in Shanghai, and he assured Fourth Son that at UNRRA they would prefer to deal with Chinese capitalists rather than Chiang Kai-shek and other officials from the Nationalist government. As Fourth Son later recalled, Munroe told him over lunch: "We Americans don't trust many of the officials serving under Mr. Chiang. They are self-seeking, corrupt, and lacking in organizational skills. What we need are people like you who come from big capitalist families, have been educated in the West for many years, and know Western countries well."[17]

From his standpoint as a U.S. military officer, Munroe saw lots of advantages in working with Fourth Son. "You have many qualifications that have led us to select you," he told Fourth Son. "First, you are a member of a fabulously rich family, so you don't need to make money through corruption. Second, you are young, strong, intelligent, and capable. Third, you've studied in England, have an excellent command of the English language, and have a big social circle. You are a rare talent. We need you, and you also need us. Since we have mutual needs, let's cooperate for a long time to come."[18] In response, Fourth Son agreed to cooperate, and he soon had his chance to do so.

In early September, while Father and Fourth Son were still in Chongqing, they both received appointments by the Nationalist government to serve as officials responsible for distributing U.S. aid in Shanghai. Father became head of CNRRA's China Water Transportation, the agency in charge of shipping UNRRA's supplies into and out of Shanghai, and Fourth Son served under him there. They were appointed by Song Ziwen (T. V. Soong), chief of the Nationalist government's executive council, and their official letters of appointment were delivered in person by Song's advisor, Liu Gongyun. As this emissary handed over the letters, he explained why the Lius were receiving them: "The Americans recommended you directly to Mr. Song." In other words, as Father observed at the time, he and Fourth Son would not have received these appointments without recommendations from Munroe.[19] Even though these jobs were unpaid, Father and Fourth Son eagerly accepted them and resigned from all their other official posts in the Nationalist government before returning to Shanghai.

On their return to Shanghai, Fourth Son (arriving September 28) and Father (arriving October 2) immediately took up their posts at CNRRA and set out to gain the confidence of their American supervisors. Within his first ten days in Shanghai, Fourth Son won over Colonel George Olmstead, the U.S. army officer in charge of distributing relief supplies for UNRRA in China. Olmstead was predisposed to admire effective businessmen because he had been one himself. After graduating from the United States Military Academy at West Point, he had entered American civilian life during the prewar period and had risen to the position of chairman of the board of an insurance company.[20]

With this background, Colonel Olmstead was immediately impressed by Fourth Son's businesslike efficiency. He began by asking
Fourth Son to conduct a survey of Shanghai's harbor, and since Fourth
Son had worked on his father's docks before the war, he was able to produce a comprehensive and accurate report for Olmstead almost overnight. Without hesitation, Olmstead then gave Fourth Son two American
assistants, both veteran U.S. army officers, and granted him considerable latitude in his relations with his American counterparts.[21]

On the job Fourth Son and Father took advantage of their positions
at UNRRA and CNRRA to rehabilitate their family's businesses. As
they shrewdly anticipated, these agencies operated on a vast scale in
the postwar period, supplying in 1946 and 1947 hundreds of shiploads
of aid valued at US$313 million—nearly one-third of the amount of
China's total commercial imports in these years.[22] As the ships arrived
in Shanghai, Fourth Son guided ships that he selected to his family's
docks and warehouses. As he described the process, "one freighter after
another loaded with relief supplies arrived in Shanghai's harbor. I
used my power to give priority to the three docks and warehouses of
the Chung Hwa Wharf Company [owned by the Lius] as the receiving
point for relief goods. I generated a lot of business that made a lot of
money for the Chung Hwa Wharf Company from storing and shipping
these goods." For Fourth Son, his interests in the relief agencies and his
interests in his family's business were fully intertwined. "Serving simultaneously as a merchant and an official, I found that my work went
very smoothly."[23]

Between 1945 and 1947, Father and Fourth Son continued to serve
in these positions without pay. But if the Lius received no direct remu-
neration from CNRRA during these three years, they earned handsome profits indirectly by gaining access to relief supplies and equipment and diverting these into their businesses. As Father remarked to
Fourth Son, "though we worked for this agency gratis, we nevertheless
got the advantage of being in a favored position. As you know, because
of our powerful positions we got a whole set of cement-making equipment for our Shanghai Cement Works, coal mining equipment and
generators for our East China Coal Mining Company, wool from Aus-
tralia for our China Wool Manufacturing Company, as well as spare
parts needed to repair the warehouse of our Chung Hwa Wharf Company. So, all in all, it still paid off for us."[24]

Even though the Lius found that the technology coming in from the United States was not up to date by American standards, they made full use of it in their postwar rehabilitation of their Shanghai factories.[25] At first they had a relatively narrow range of industrial materials to choose from because in the immediate aftermath of the war UNRRA was more concerned about supplying daily necessities (rice, wheat, flour, clothing, medicine) than industrial materials. But in 1947, the Lius had a wider selection of chemicals, equipment and tools as UNRRA shifted its emphasis from relief to rehabilitation and began exporting more industrial materials than consumer goods to China.[26] Since UNRRA funneled about 75 percent of all its China-bound supplies through Shanghai, the Lius were perfectly positioned to take what they wanted for the duration of UNRRA's aid program, which lasted until the end of 1947.[27]

In arranging to hold these positions at UNRRA and CNRRA, Father and Fourth Son showed that in postwar Shanghai they could put to good use their Chongqing contacts, especially the ones with Americans. As at Chongqing, Father continued to work with Fourth Son in these dealings with Americans, and he had plans for deploying the other two sons who had worked with him in Chongqing, Sixth and Eighth Sons, in developing another kind of relations with the United States.

A Chongqing Team Member Away from Shanghai

In the spring of 1945, Father had seized an opportunity in Chongqing to send two of his sons to the United States. The opportunity arose when the Nationalist government's minister of economics, Weng Wen-hao, negotiated an agreement with the U.S. government for sending three hundred Chinese students to do one-year internships with industrial enterprises in America.[28] On hearing about this program, Father immediately recognized that two of his sons who had been working with him in Chongqing and other inland cities had ideal educational backgrounds for it: Sixth Son because of his studies at the Tokyo Institute of Technology and Eighth Son because of his studies at MIT. Citing these credentials, Father had little difficulty reserving positions for both of them. He found Minister Weng receptive not least because he and Weng had a lot in common: their age, their Ningbo native-place tie, and their experience working together at the ministries of economics and finance in wartime Chongqing.[29] Once Sixth and Eighth Sons were accepted into the program, they left China directly from the cities where they had been working—Sixth Son from Chongqing and Eighth Son from Kunming. Meeting in Calcutta, they traveled the rest of the way to the United States together.[30]

In Sixth Son's case, Father had political as well as business reasons for sending him abroad. Just as Father had anticipated before the end of the war that the Nationalist government would charge his eldest sons with treason, he also feared that it would accuse Sixth Son of being a Communist or at least a Communist sympathizer. Sixth Son had never publicly revealed that he had become a member of the Chinese Communist Party or even disclosed this fact to his family, but his year in the Communist base area at Yan'an, 1938–1939, was no secret. During the latter part of the war, from 1940 to 1945, he had served as a manager in the Liu family's businesses, especially the match materials factory in Chongqing, and on the surface his work for these capitalist enterprises had no connection with Communism. But in this period he had continued to work for the Communist cause behind the scenes, and his Communist sympathies were not easy to conceal. Several times during the war, Dai Li, the leader of the Nationalist government's campaign against Communism, warned Father that Sixth Son would be arrested if he persisted in working through Communist contacts at the New China (Xinhua) News Agency. As Father mentioned to Fourth Son, "Dai Li sent me a message to warn Sixth Son not to have contact with the Communists. Otherwise Dai Li will show him no mercy."[31]

When Father said goodbye to Sixth Son in Chongqing in June 1945 (two months before the war ended), he was relieved that his son would be out of the Nationalist government's reach, but after Father returned to Shanghai in the fall of 1945, he came to the conclusion that Sixth Son was not in immediate danger from anti-Communist campaigns there. No longer worried about this political threat to Sixth Son, he was eager to have by his side in Shanghai the sons who had worked closely with him in Chongqing. He was pleased that Fourth Son continued to team up with him in Shanghai, and he wanted Sixth Son to do the same.

As early as December 1945, six months after Sixth Son had gone to the United States, Father began to urge him to come home as soon as possible. He complained about his own heavy workload, and he told

Sixth Son that it was time for him to assume his share of responsibility for the family firm. "Since I came to Shanghai, I have not been able to take one day off for rest," Father wrote to Sixth Son on December 3, two months after his return from Chongqing. "I am old and I need my sons to look after my various factories." The factory Father had in mind for Sixth Son was the cement plant, for which he had been grooming him since the early 1930s. "The Shanghai Portland Cement Works will soon resume its operations, and therefore I hope you can return after your training to give us some help."[32] To meet this urgent need, Sixth Son was expected to come home as soon as his one-year internship ended in June—no later.

As the end of Sixth Son's internship drew near, Father was disappointed to receive from him a request for an extension of at least six months. As Sixth Son explained to Father, he had personal as well as professional reasons for wanting to stay in the United States. "Besides my desire to be with my girl friend," he wrote to Father on May 27, 1946, "I also wish to complete my study and investigation on cement which would take me at least 6 months more."[33] When Father finally granted this extension, Sixth Son thanked him and Mother profusely. On June 18, speaking for Eighth Son as well as himself, he expressed "our most profound gratitude for your having endorsed our request for an extension of our stay in this country, and for having remitted to each of us the sum of $900.00. We feel the added responsibility to avail ourselves of your generosity and the opportunity to achieve to the best we can during the following extension period."[34] In the end, Sixth Son took not one but two six-month extensions, stretching his original one-year internship into a two-year visit to the United States and postponing his return home until July 1947.

Father was frustrated by Sixth Son's delay of his return home not because he believed Sixth Son was simply wasting time in the United States but because he was eager to reassemble in Shanghai the team of three sons who had served him well in Chongqing. Of the three—Fourth, Sixth, and Eighth Sons—only Fourth Son returned to Shanghai as soon as the war ended. When Father sent the other two to the United States, he had no way of knowing how soon the war would be over, and he did not imagine that Sixth Son would be away for the first two years of the postwar period, much less that Eighth Son would be gone even longer.

Another Chongqing Team Member Away from Shanghai

Before allowing Eighth Son to take an internship in the United States, Father made clear to him that he, like Sixth Son, should remain abroad no more than one year. He sensed that Eighth Son, after his failure to complete his senior year at MIT, 1940–41, would want to vindicate himself by finishing his college education at MIT or some other American university after his internship in 1945–46. But Father wanted Eighth Son to join him and his other sons in the Liu family business before returning to school, so he specifically instructed Eighth Son to come directly home after completing his internship rather than remaining abroad to continue his education at MIT or any other American university.

Father and Eighth Son confirmed this point in an exchange of letters three months before Eighth Son left China for his internship in the United States. On March 19, 1945, Father wrote to Eighth Son: "Since the internship will last as little as one year, I hope that you will take full advantage of the opportunity to learn as much as you possibly can. If you wish to continue with your university education after you return to China, this can serve as a very useful credential for you."[35]

In reply, Eighth Son confirmed that he understood Father's terms. He expressed interest in taking examinations in China for studying abroad, but he gladly accepted Father's proviso that he should come home after his internship before entering a school abroad. "I am very pleased to find in your last letter," he wrote to Father on March 27, "that you think I can continue my education after coming home from the internship."[36] Not until Father had allowed Eighth and Sixth Sons to extend their stay in the United States for a second year did Eighth Son reveal his intention to resume his college education abroad without coming home first.

In the summer of 1946, Eighth Son disclosed to his family that he had applied to American schools in hopes of finishing his bachelor's degree during the following academic year, 1946–47. "I hope to get back to school this fall," he wrote from his assigned post as an intern in Cleveland to his brothers in Shanghai on June 29, 1946. "But enrollments in all colleges are very heavy due to returned veterans."[37] Despite this competition from American war veterans, he was soon able to gain admission at leading engineering schools because of his past academic record at MIT. "I have practically succeeded in getting back into M.I.T. this fall," he wrote to Eldest Son on August 4. "Case School of Applied Mechanics [at Case Western Reserve University in Cleveland] has already admitted me as a first-term senior student this fall. I probably will return to M.I.T. though, if I have the choice."[38] As he expected, he was readmitted to MIT, and he took his senior year there in 1946–47.

While studying at there, Eighth Son heard from his parents that they eagerly anticipated his return home and expected him to leave the United States for China as soon as he graduated in June 1947. Ruling out any additional extensions, Mother wrote to him and Sixth Son on February 15, 1947: "When summer comes you will be through with what you are doing there now. You should set your mind on coming back home then. We have been earnestly expecting your return, you know." Mother was eager to have them return because they were the last remaining members of the family who had not come back to live in Shanghai since the end of the war. "Now we look only for your company," she wrote to her two sons in the United States. "When you are home we shall have our truly grand family reunion. Every heart will be full of true happiness then. So you both must come back home as soon as you can."[39]

In response, when Sixth Son made plans for his trip home, Eighth Son gave his family the impression that he would follow not far behind. As late as April 27, 1947, he wrote to Father that Sixth Son "told me that he is ready to sail for China on May 16. You all must be joyously expecting him. Let's hope that I shall soon follow suit." But Eighth Son had applied to Harvard Business School, and after he was admitted on May 28, he convinced Father to let him take the two-year course of study for an MBA.[40]

Eighth Son's insistence on staying abroad marked him as a unique holdout—the only member of the Liu family who had not returned to Shanghai by 1947. But he was not the only one who felt distant from Father. While Eighth Son was geographically separated from Father, Eldest Daughter remained personally separated from him. Even though she had not lived far from him most of the time since he had disinherited her in 1936, they had not fully reconciled before, during, or in the immediate aftermath of the war.

Eldest Daughter's Return from Chongqing to Shanghai

In December 1945, Eldest Daughter and her family returned from Chongqing to Shanghai. After living with Mother in Shanghai from 1936 to 1939, she had moved with her husband and two children to Chongqing (via Hong Kong and Rangoon), and she had resided there for the duration of the war, from 1940 to 1945—the same years Father had been there. But she had not joined Fourth, Sixth, and Eighth Sons on Father's team of family members in Chongqing. Nor had her husband, Xue Diyi, ever held a job in any of Father's businesses. During these years in Chongqing, Eldest Daughter had received loving and solicitous letters from Mother, and she had benefited from help given to her by Fourth, Sixth, and Eighth Sons, especially during her pregnancies leading to the births of her third child, a girl, in 1941, and her fourth, a boy, in 1943.[41] But her relationship with Father still suffered from the damage that had been done when she had revealed her premarital affair and pregnancy to him in 1936.

During the war, with no help from Father, Eldest Daughter and Xue Diyi set out to prove that they could succeed in business on their own. In Chongqing they had begun with little capital and had endured hardships, but eventually they had managed to finance and start two firms, Qingli Iron Works and China United Engineering Company. In these enterprises, they had worked together, effectively combining Eldest Daughter's acute business sense as a manager with Xue's technical training as an engineer. By the war's end, they had built up these businesses to the point where they had accumulated assets valued at 400 ounces of gold.[42]

On their return to Shanghai, Eldest Daughter and Xue Diyi brought their companies with them from Chongqing, and they risked their wartime savings on a bid for the construction project of their dreams: the expansion and renovation of Shanghai's Longhua Airport. In the immediate aftermath of the war, the Nationalist government had retained this airport for military use by both the Chinese and American armed forces. But a few months later in early 1946 the government arranged for the Chinese Air Force and U.S. Air Force to move their planes to another of Shanghai airport, Jiangwan, and laid plans for converting Longhua into China's biggest and most important commercial airport. On October 11, 1946, the government's Ministry of Transportation allocated 9 billion yuan for the construction of long concrete runways where planes weighing up to seventy tons could safely land. At the same time, the government appointed the Committee on Engineering for Longhua Airport, which consisted of officials from the Ministry of Transportation, Ministry of Defense, Shanghai municipal government, China Airlines (Zhonghang), Central Airlines (Yanghang), and Zitai Engineering Company, the designer of the project. As soon as it was formed, this committee began to take bids from construction companies.[43]

Xue and Eldest Daughter recognized that this was the opportunity they had been waiting for, and they initially made an ambitious bid on behalf of their China United Engineering Company based on greater financing than they had ever previously arranged. They were bidding against well-endowed rivals—notably Tao Guiji Construction Company, capitalized at 5 million yuan, and Baohua Construction Company, capitalized at 6 million yuan—and they aggressively vied with these competitors for the job.[44] When the results of the bidding were announced, Eldest Daughter and Xue Diyi were informed that the Committee on Engineering for Longhua Airport had decided to accept their bid, but only if their financing would be guaranteed by major investors.

Despite their best efforts, Eldest Daughter and Xue Diyi could find no one—neither Father nor any other qualified guarantor—who would back their proposal as it stood. Only after they scaled it down to one-third of its original size did they find a backer, Xu Guanqun, a successful pharmaceutical manufacturer based in Shanghai. Xue Diyi knew Xu because both hailed from Wujin, and Xue used this native-place tie in appealing to Xu for help. In 1946 Xue's timing was right, for Xu's businesses were booming, and he had recently formed the New Asia Enterprise Group (Xinya qiye jituan), whose diversified holdings were capitalized at more than a billion yuan.[45] With Xu's backing, Xue and Eldest Daughter succeeded in persuading the Committee on Engineering for Longhua Airport to accept their bid, and their China United Engineering Company became one of the three companies (along with Tao Guiji and Baohua) responsible for the construction work on this large-scale project.[46]

When construction began at Longhua Airport on December 19, Eldest Daughter suddenly found that she had to take sole responsibility for managing the work of China United Engineering Company because her husband was stricken with tuberculosis and confined to bed.

Operating on a tight schedule, she took command as supervisor of more than two thousand subcontractors and workers. On March 7, 1947, her company began to pour concrete, laying down runways that were 6,000 feet long, 165 feet wide, and eleven to sixteen inches thick. At the peak of the construction, she had thirty-four trucks hauling building materials, including cement from Father's Longhua Cement Company, which was located near the site of the airport.[47] On June 2, the runways were completed, and on June 23, they were officially opened.[48]

After the successful completion of the job at Longhua Airport, Eldest Daughter's subcontractors showed their respect and admiration for her handling of the project by hosting a party in her honor on her thirtieth birthday. They held it at a temple and conducted it on a lavish scale. For food they served an array of Shanghai delicacies, and for entertainment they had live performances of Chinese opera. They presented expensive gifts to all the Xues and their servants, who each received a traditional-style red envelope containing a twenty-five-carat gold bracelet.[49]

Father was invited to this festive occasion, and he took advantage of it to reconcile with Eldest Daughter. For the first time since he had disinherited her more than a decade earlier, he had a serious talk with her about their relationship.[50] He was favorably impressed, he told her, by how she had raised her family and managed her family business. Surveying the crowd of subcontractors at the party, he took note of the extensiveness of her contacts and congratulated her on her financial success. Her huge new house for her family, he pointed out, was even bigger than his own. While his other children had all taken positions in his businesses, only she had achieved success without his help. Because of her singular accomplishments, even though he had lost his respect for her at the time of the scandal, he now assured her that she had earned it back.[51]

Postwar Reunification

Father's reconciliation with Eldest Daughter in 1947 brought the Liu family to a peak of postwar unity. In 1945, when the war had ended, the family had been divided between the branch that had lived and worked in wartime Chongqing and the branch that had remained in wartime Shanghai. Between 1945 and 1947, the two branches had continued to differ on some issues, but they had eventually worked out a division of labor: those from the Chongqing branch held official positions in U.S.-sponsored international relief organizations or pursued studies in the United States, and those from the Shanghai branch continued to manage the family's factories in Shanghai. Under this arrangement, the family drew almost all of its members into the family business. By 1947, Father and all of his sons except Eighth Son lived in Shanghai, and of the eight sons there, all except the youngest held jobs in or related to the family business.[52] Mother and all three of the Lius' daughters were in Shanghai too. While Eldest Daughter engaged in the construction business there, Youngest Daughter attended a Shanghai middle school, and Middle Daughter was married to a professor of English at St. John's University and stayed at home raising her sons.

All of these children saw Father and Mother on a regular basis. "At ordinary times," Mother wrote to Eighth Son on February 15, 1947, "your brothers and sisters-in-law come here with us by turn." For festivals and other special occasions, the family gatherings grew to a grand scale. In the same letter, Mother reported a recent example: "And as your Father is now back great crowds of people came to see us during the first days of the lunar year. We are very happy to find ourselves so warmly remembered."[53]

In holding these reunions, the family celebrated the ending of its wartime policy of dispersing its family members and business assets. Like many other Chinese capitalists, they had only resorted to this policy as a survival strategy during the war.[54] Now that all of them except Eighth Son lived and worked in Shanghai, they seemed to be back on track to resume their prewar quest for establishing an enduring business dynasty.

All too soon, they once again faced wartime conditions, as Chiang Kai-shek's Nationalist government battled with Mao Zedong's Communist forces in the civil war that led to the Communist Revolution of 1949. In coping with this new challenge, the Lius again grappled with the decision whether they would continue to concentrate their family and resources in Shanghai or disperse them elsewhere—even possibly abroad.

IV

ADAPTING TO REVOLUTION
1946–1956

Father's Decision to Live in the People's Republic

DURING the civil war between Chiang Kai-shek's Nationalist government and Mao Zedong's Communist forces (1945–1949), Father once
again faced the dilemma of whether to move away from Shanghai and,
if so, whether to take his wife and family with him or leave them behind
as he had done during the Sino-Japanese War. As he followed the news
of clashes between the two rival armies and brooded about whether to
relocate his family and his assets, he was aggressively courted by
leaders from both sides.

Moving the Family to Taiwan

Right up to the last year of the civil war, 1949, Father remained
aligned with the Nationalists. Even after the Communists mounted their
decisive offensive in the fall of 1948 and the Nationalist forces began to
retreat southward in China and then flee to Taiwan, Father seemed prepared to continue to follow Chiang Kai-shek. Since the 1930s he had
known Chiang as a fellow native-place associate from Ningbo, and he
had accepted official appointments to posts in the prewar, wartime,
and postwar Nationalist governments. After following Chiang from
Shanghai to Chongqing in the early 1940s and then back to Shanghai in
the mid-1940s, why wouldn't Father follow him from Shanghai to Taiwan in 1948 and 1949?

   In 1948 Father took steps that seemed to commit him and his entire family irrevocably to a future in Taiwan. In January, before making this commitment, he traveled to Taiwan. Writing to Eighth Son in

the United States on February 23, he characterized his visit as "brief but very pleasant." At that point he was tentative about moving to Taiwan because he was still optimistic about his prospects for remaining in Shanghai under Nationalist rule. "It's true that the political situation has not been stabilized," he wrote to Eighth Son about conditions in Shanghai, "but no young person should worry about it to the point of ignoring reality and becoming pessimistic."[1]

In the course of the spring and summer of 1948, as the Communist forces took control of north and northeast China, Father became more pessimistic about the future in Shanghai and decided to open "a back way out" for his family and businesses to Taiwan. He sent Eldest and Fourth Sons on separate trips to prepare the way, and before going, these two sons collected gold, silver, and jewelry from his parents, brothers, and sisters and shipped these valuables to Taiwan on a boat belonging to the Zhongxing Navigation Company. Once there, they invested in real estate and made preparations to open two new factories, a candy mill in Taipei and a chemical plant in Kaohsiung. By the end of the summer, while Father and Mother remained in Shanghai, most of their children and grandchildren had already moved to Taipei and established residences there, giving the distinct impression that the family was emigrating.[2]

Father had barely sent off his children and grandchildren and made these substantial investments in Taiwan before he began to reconsider transferring his headquarters there. His doubts arose because of his experience with the Nationalist government's currency reform in Shanghai during the fall of 1948. Chiang Kai-shek introduced this reform as an attempt to halt runaway inflation and raise tax revenue, and in Shanghai it was carried out by Chiang's son, Chiang Ching-kuo. For two and a half months from August 19 to October 31, 1948, Chiang Ching-kuo froze prices and appealed to Shanghai's capitalists to submit not only their old Chinese currency but also their gold, silver, and foreign currency in exchange for a new Chinese currency, the gold yuan.

Initially Chiang Ching-kuo tried to win Father's support for the gold yuan reform by using a soft sell. He invited Father to the Huizhong Hotel on Nanjing Road in Shanghai's Central District, addressed him as "uncle," and coaxed him into volunteering to turn over his gold, silver, and foreign currency for the sake of recovering stability and financing the war against Communism. When Father did not comply within the next day or two, Chiang took a hard line. He claimed to know what

Father's holdings were, and he threatened to punish him under martial law if his precious metals and foreign currency were not delivered to the Bank of China within three days. Meanwhile, Chiang publicly attacked all of Shanghai's wealthy capitalists, whom he referred to as "traitorous merchants." As he put it on the third day of his anticapitalist crusade, "those who disturb the financial market are not the small merchants, but the big capitalists and big merchants." After his meetings with the Lius and other Shanghai capitalists, he concluded that they were friendly to his face, "but behind one's back there is no evil that they do not commit."[3]

Chiang's threats scared Father, especially after the Nationalist government began carrying them out. Within the next few weeks, several uncooperative capitalists were arrested, with bail set for each as high as US$300,000 or even US$1 million, and one of them was sentenced to death. According to Fourth Son, Father was frightened into redeeming eight hundred gold bars, several thousand silver dollars, and US$2.3 million in exchange for the new gold yuan currency at the Bank of China. Within the next few weeks the Lius and Shanghai's other capitalists were appalled by the outcome of the reform, as the gold yuan currency became virtually worthless.[4]

On October 31, the Nationalist government admitted that the gold yuan reform had failed and revoked the price controls that had been introduced two and a half months earlier. Chiang Ching-kuo publicly apologized to the people of Shanghai, although even then, as a parting shot at Chinese capitalists, he expressed the hope that the people would "not again allow traitorous merchant-speculators, bureaucratic politicians and ruffians and scoundrels to come and control Shanghai."[5]

Father was deeply disturbed by the failure of the gold yuan reform and Chiang Ching-kuo's treatment of Chinese capitalists, and he was not alone. According to Lloyd Eastman, "most people thereafter abandoned all hope for economic recovery; the failure of the reform seemed to demonstrate that the National Government was totally without resources to control the inflation."[6] Though disturbed, Father did not immediately abandon all hope or withdraw all of the family's assets from Taiwan. As late as November 25, Second Son made a four-day trip from Shanghai to Taiwan to survey the Lius' investments in Taipei and Kaohsiung, and Seventh Son continued to reside and work in Taipei, as he had done since 1947.[7] But before the end of 1948, all of the Lius except Seventh Son had moved back to Shanghai. By then Father had ceased to consider transferring the headquarters of the family business to Taiwan. Under the Nationalist government, he soberly told his children at a family meeting in Shanghai, "Taiwan would not be a safe place."[8]

Leaving China

If they did not follow Chiang to Taiwan, would Father and the rest of the Liu family remain in China under Communist rule? In early 1949, as the People's Liberation Army swept southward from the northeast and descended on Shanghai, Father and his family began to receive assurances from the Chinese Communist Party. If the Lius would stay in Shanghai, they were told, then after the People's Liberation Army took over the city, their safety would be guaranteed and their factories would be protected. The Lius first heard this message from one of their own family members, Sixth Son.

Sixth Son insisted that all members of the family should remain in Shanghai and become committed to the Communist cause, but he did not reveal to them that he had become a member of the Chinese Communist Party ten years earlier during his days in Yan'an. Instead, in March 1949 he brought a classmate to a family meeting, explaining that this man was a party member who could speak authoritatively about the party's policies and plans. Previously known to the family as Wang, this agent's real name was Dai De, and after Sixth Son revealed his identity, Dai explained in detail the party's policy of "promoting production, achieving economic prosperity, taking care of both state and private enterprises, and benefiting both employees and employers." He urged all of the Lius to stay in Shanghai, and he promised that the People's Liberation Army would guarantee the Lius' safety and factories as soon as it took over the city. He followed up by visiting Fourth Son three times and urging him to work with the Communists to protect the Liu family's factories from sabotage by retreating Nationalist troops. During these last months before the People's Liberation Army took over Shanghai, the Communists repeatedly urged the Lius to stay there in radio broadcasts to the city.[9]

Father was not won over by the Communists' campaign. He had met and chatted with Zhou Enlai twice in Chongqing during the Sino-Japanese War, and had been favorably impressed with him, Mao Ze-

dong, and other Communists as approachable and self-confident leaders, but he was still wary of the Chinese Communist Party and its
policies toward capitalists. In the spring of 1949, after hearing Sixth
Son and Dai De present the case in favor of Communist rule, he told his
family: "The Communists will never be our real friends."[10]

In the spring of 1949 on the eve of Communist takeover of Shanghai, Father weighed his options. In light of the abysmal outcome of the
Nationalist government's gold yuan reform, he ruled out emigration to
Taiwan, and despite Sixth Son's assurances, he remained skeptical about
keeping the entire family and all of its assets in Shanghai under Communist rule. As a third alternative, he proposed to move part of the family and its business to the British colony of Hong Kong and leave the rest
in Shanghai. According to Fourth Son, all family members except Sixth
Son endorsed this decision, and they took as their motto one of Father's
favorite English sayings: "Don't put all of your eggs in one basket."[11]

As Father and his family deliberated over the decision whether to
leave or stay, they came under close surveillance from Nationalist
government officials who became suspicious of them for not leaving
Shanghai for Taiwan sooner. In March 1949, Chiang Kai-shek ordered
the Shanghai city government to organize the Committee for the Defense of Shanghai, and Father was appointed to it. From then on, according to Fourth Son's memoirs, Father was monitored closely by
Chen Baotai, the head of the Shanghai Social Bureau. In May, during
the last days before the People's Liberation Army reached Shanghai,
Father received a telephone call from Chen every hour of every day.
Then on May 22, three days before the Communists' Third Field Army
took over the city, Father was ordered to attend an emergency meeting
in Guangzhou with Chiang Kai-shek. Given no prior notice, he was
picked up by Chen Baotai and three armed men who drove him to the
airport and escorted him onto a private plane that was chartered for
this flight. As recounted by Fourth Son, this sequence of events was
"like a kidnapping" by the Nationalist secret police. Only after he was
forced to fly out of Shanghai and held against his will in Guangzhou
was he able to escape from the Nationalists and flee to Hong Kong.[12]

In light of Father's preparations for his trip to Hong Kong, it seems
unlikely that he left Shanghai as involuntarily as Fourth Son indicated
in the account given above. As early as April, more than a month before he was supposedly forced to fly from Shanghai to Guangzhou, he

had corresponded with the Central Air Transportation Company about arranging his own flight between these two cities.[13] Also in April, his top business associates outside the family, two cousins named Cheng Nianpeng and Hua Erkang, had smuggled foreign currency, finished products, and raw materials valued at US$5 million to Hong Kong, and in early May, Cheng and Hua themselves had boarded a plane in Shanghai that was bound for Hong Kong. When workers from the Lius' China Wool Manufacturing Company had tried to stop Cheng and Hua from leaving Shanghai, Father had calmed down the crowd by promising that Cheng and Hua would not remain in Hong Kong for long. As it turned out, Father joined his two business associates in Hong Kong only a few weeks later on May 24, and Cheng and Hua never returned to Shanghai.[14] Whether Father was coerced by Chiang Kai-shek into leaving Shanghai or not, he seems to have severed his ties with the Nationalist government, and he did not visit Taiwan at this time or ever again.[15]

Father's decisions in May 1949 not to leave Shanghai for Taiwan under Nationalist rule and not to stay in Shanghai under Communist rule indicate the range of his options and the volatility of his situation. At this time, other Chinese capitalists also fled or contemplated fleeing Shanghai, and compared to them, Father had as much or more financial and cultural resources to secure a future for himself and his family anywhere in Asia or the West.[16] Yet even with his money, technology, Western- and Japanese-educated children, and other movable assets, Father had great difficulty deciding where to go in 1949. His arrival in Hong Kong on May 24 still did not settle the issue, for he continued to wrestle with the question whether he should stay in Hong Kong or return to China.

Receiving Appeals from Shanghai and Beijing

During six months in Hong Kong, from May to November 1949, Father was caught in a tug-of-war. His business associates who had fled Shanghai with him urged him to stay in Hong Kong and go into business with them there. His family members who remained in Shanghai insisted that he must come home. In Fourth Son's words, "Father had his legs pulled apart" by these two groups until he finally reached a decision about where to live.[17]

Despite the civil war, revolution, and turmoil, the Liu family in Shanghai never lost touch with Father during his six months in Hong Kong and never ceased to plead with him to return home. As early as June 4, only two weeks after Father had left Shanghai, Second Son indicated that the coast was clear and he should come right back. "Well, Father," he wrote in a letter to Hong Kong, "I am glad to learn that you've managed to tear yourself away from the politicians in Canton [Guangzhou]." During the Communist takeover of Shanghai, Second Son had expected the city to suffer, but he was relieved to report to Father that it had been "through the crisis with little damage." What little damage did occur he blamed squarely on the Nationalists. "It is indeed painful to think of the wanton destruction of properties preceding the general retreat and withdrawal of the Nationalist troops. Our glue factory is a typical example." But according to Second Son, the wild and destructive Nationalist forces had now been replaced by well-disciplined Communist troops who were as good for Shanghai as the Nationalist troops had been bad. "It won't be even fair to compare these troops with that of the Liberation Army. They are just two different groups of men altogether."[18]

Within two short weeks following the People's Liberation Army's march into Shanghai, the new government had already won over the people of the city, Second Son wrote. "The new government is lenient, reasonable, dead honest, hardworking, practical, patriotic, humble and they certainly mean well. Of course, we have yet to see how they will behave in the future but they have been perfect so far." Second Son said that the new government's perfect performance had converted him from a pessimist into an optimist about China's prospects for the future. "At one time I was thoroughly depressed by what was going on since the V-J day [August 15, 1945], but I have now changed my outlook. In the People's Government I have found new hope which will give me courage to go through all kinds of hardship and privation which may lie in my way."[19]

While speaking for himself, Second Son reported that he was not the only one who had undergone this kind of conversion. He claimed that former anti-Communists had also quickly come around to a favorable view of the new government. "Even the most severe critics of Communists now agree that the destiny of our country has never been handled more efficiently than it is today. In the present People's Government lies the hope of turning China into a strong nation. The process will be a long one and accompanied by personal hardship and privation of all kinds. Nevertheless, it will be in the right direction."[20]

Now that the new government had proven itself, Second Son told Father, it was time for him to come home. "Your home is definitely right here, where you will be able to do greater things and where your ability will be better appreciated." In case Second Son's letter was not enough to persuade Father, he announced that he would come to Hong Kong and make his case to Father in person. "As soon as I get the permission of the authority I will take a trip to Hongkong," he wrote. "I do most sincerely urge you to get prepared and return to Shanghai with me."[21]

In July, Second Son kept his promise. Nine years earlier, in the summer of 1940, he had made the same trip to try to persuade Father to come home from Hong Kong and resume business under the Japanese occupation of Shanghai. At that time he had argued that the Lius should keep business wholly separate from politics—sticking "100% to business and industry"—and he had failed to persuade Father to come back. In 1949, Second Son again went to Hong Kong and urged Father to return and resume business—this time under Chinese Communist rule. Now the practice of business would undeniably become directly dependent on politics, but Second Son believed that the Communists were creating a more favorable political context for business than the Japanese, the Nationalists, or any other previous government had ever done in Shanghai.

In the summer of 1949, despite his best efforts, Second Son failed to convince Father to return from Hong Kong to Shanghai. According to Fourth Son (who did not go to Hong Kong but heard Second Son's report on his return to Shanghai), Father chose to stay in Hong Kong at that time because "my father was somewhat influenced by the Nationalists' anti-Communist propaganda. Some friends also told him that the Communists might have been good at other things, but definitely not at economic matters. My father thought that this assessment sounded plausible."[22] Father's "friends" included his business associates who had fled Shanghai and decided to remain in Hong Kong permanently, and he found their arguments more persuasive than the ones Second Son made. In August, Second Son returned to Shanghai without Father.[23]

During the summer of 1949 other members of Father's family besides Second Son also begged him to come home. Sounding desperate,

Mother reminded Father that "you and I are already old" (one year after they had both turned sixty), and she posed this question: "If you don't come to reunite with me now, when will we ever see each other again?" Recalling their long years apart during the war, she found it depressing to contemplate the prospect of another separation. "It's sad that you and I have been separated so often even in our old age. The nights are long and are filled with too many dreams. I hope you will find a way to return to Shanghai soon."[24]

Mother's appeal to Father was reinforced by appeals from their children. "All of us have been missing you very much since you left," Sixth Son wrote on behalf of the whole family on June 9, less than three weeks after Father's departure for Hong Kong. He assured Father "that your return to this port shall be welcomed by all persons concerned"—a phrase he might well have intended for Father to interpret as including not only family members but also officials in the new government.[25]

Father's mistress, He Guiying, also wrote to him from Shanghai. Like the Lius, she expressed hopes for an early reunion, but she did not implore him to come home for the sake of his family or business. A lifelong Christian, she conveyed her concern in a religious idiom. "Under God," she wrote to Father in Hong Kong, "I know that our Heavenly Father will look after you, and I hope that God will let us see each other again soon." Writing on June 30, she described prayers that seemed to imply she would be willing to follow him to Hong Kong. "In our prayers," she wrote, speaking for their son as well as herself, "sometimes we ask God to give each of us two wings so that we can fly to you."[26] But when Father subsequently asked her to join him in Hong Kong (as she had done in wartime Chongqing), she declined his invitation, saying that she cherished the home he had bought for her in the Hongkou District of Shanghai and that she did not want to give it up. In the end, she never did go to Hong Kong.[27]

In the fall, Father continued to be bombarded by telephone calls and letters from his family and mistress, but he remained in Hong Kong as long as he considered the family business to be vulnerable to threats from the Chinese Communists' takeover of Shanghai. He only began to rethink his position after he heard directly from representatives of the Communist leadership.

Shortly after the People's Republic of China was founded on October 1, Zhou Enlai, as premier of the new national government at its capital in Beijing, dispatched emissaries to Hong Kong to persuade Chinese capitalists to come back to China. These emissaries emphasized to Father and others in Hong Kong that they had nothing to fear from the new government in China. As long as they were patriotic, they would be welcomed back, given protection for their families and property, and offered opportunities to serve as leaders.[28]

Zhou Enlai's emissaries apparently persuaded Father that he would find more promising business opportunities in Shanghai than he had discovered in Hong Kong. The riskiness of his Hong Kong ventures was evident in one he had pursued in vain: an attempt to purchase wool in northwest China and sell it to a leading U.S. carpet manufacturer, Bigelow Sanford, in the United States. He had conceived the idea before leaving Shanghai, and after reaching Hong Kong in the summer of 1949, he had founded China Trading Corporation exclusively to purchase wool in China. He had flown from Hong Kong to Lanzhou in northwest China in August—three months before it was taken over by the People's Liberation Army—and had arranged the purchase of wool in person. But after racing against oncoming Communist military forces in China, he had not been able to negotiate a profitable bargain with Bigelow Sanford, so the entire deal had fallen through.[29]

Father's disappointment with the outcome of this and his other business ventures in Hong Kong made him receptive to the message he heard from Zhou Enlai's emissaries. Even before hearing assurances from the new government, he had been tempted to return home as his family had urged him to do. Now that he had done poorly at business in Hong Kong and received assurance from Beijing that his family firm would survive in Shanghai, he let his family know that he was ready to return.

Returning to China

On November 1, Second Son made another trip to visit Father in Hong Kong. As soon as he arrived, Father explained to him why he had decided to go back (in words that were later repeated to the family in Shanghai): "I am an old man already over sixty. All of my enterprises are in China, so I'll go back and not stay abroad as a white Chinese [referring to Chinese at the time who were said to be comparable to white Russian exiles from the Russian Revolution]. All of you are expecting me to return home. What's the point of my living alone in exile. I've decided to come home."[30] Father's emphasis on his family members' expectations as the decisive determinant in his thinking suggests that he might well have preferred to live in Hong Kong if they had joined him there and that he returned Shanghai because they would not or could not do so.

As soon as Second Son joined Father in Hong Kong, they made arrangements for a clandestine departure to avoid possible interference by agents of the Nationalist government. At midnight on November 2, they sneaked onto a steamship belonging to the British trading company Butterfield and Swire and took it from Hong Kong to the north China port of Tianjin.[31] Greeted at the docks by newspaper reporters on November 3, Father gave them three reasons why he and other Chinese capitalists would return to China from Hong Kong: all of their enterprises were in Shanghai, all of the funds they had taken to Hong Kong would soon be used up, and all of their fears that their property would be confiscated in China were now allayed. Others like himself, he predicted, would soon come back from Hong Kong, and he mentioned the example of Wu Yunchu, "the MSG King," who in fact did return to China soon thereafter.[32]

From the moment Father's ship docked in Tianjin, he found that officials in the new government made good on their promises to give him opportunities as a leader. On disembarking, he was handed a telegram from Premier Zhou Enlai inviting him and Second Son to Beijing. Proceeding directly to the capital, he had a two-and-a-half-hour lunch with Zhou on the same day, and Zhou assured him that he would have protection for his enterprises and other property and could retain the lifestyle to which he was accustomed. He was also urged to set an example for other Chinese industrialists and businessmen by cooperating with the new government.

When Father heard Zhou say that he was a "national capitalist," as distinct from a "comprador bureaucratic capitalist," he was suspicious and expressed doubts about the term's applicability to himself. As he pointed out, he had previously held a post as a comprador for the Kailuan Mining Administration under British ownership, and he had served as an official managing the state-owned China Merchants Steam Navigation Company, state monopolies on matches and cigarettes, and the state-sponsored China National Relief and Rehabilitation Administration—

all under Chiang Kai-shek's Nationalist government. He accepted Zhou's designation only after he heard Zhou's explanation that the Chinese Communist Party used the term to express its approval of one group of capitalists (the "national" ones) and its disapproval of another group (the "comprador bureaucratic" ones).[33] More confident, Father then asked whether his East China Coal Mining Company would be returned to him along with his other enterprises, and he discovered that his new status did not automatically bring all of his property back into his hands. Zhou explained that Father could have back all of his other enterprises, because they were in light industry, but not East China, because it supplied coal to heavy industry, which was all under the ownership and management of the state, according to the new government's policy. The most Zhou could promise was that Father would eventually be compensated for his loss of East China.[34]

The next day, November 4, on his return to Shanghai, Father received another official welcome from Chen Yi, the city's new mayor. Over dinner at Chen's home, he was warmly received and encouraged to come directly to Chen if he had any questions or difficulties. Almost overnight Father found himself appointed to influential committees along with high-ranking Communists. On December 18, he became a member of the Shanghai Political Consultative Committee, which was chaired by Mayor Chen Yi and included Deputy Mayor Pan Hannian, the key liaison between the city's new political leaders and its capitalists.[35] Besides serving on this and other committees in Shanghai, Father was appointed to regional organizations, such as the East China Military and Political Council, and he gave speeches on national and international issues as well as local ones.[36]

In his speeches (which were reprinted in newspapers), Father endorsed the new government's proposed policies for regulating entrepreneurs like him under Communist rule. On December 17, speaking as a member of the Shanghai People's Congress, he recalled that Shanghai had previously been "a semicolonial city" in which Chinese people like himself in industry and commerce "were heavily oppressed by imperialism, feudalism, and bureaucratic capitalism. . . . We couldn't even breathe." But now "the liberation of Shanghai has opened up a free, glorious new world for industrialists, creating a new environment in which to shake off our chains." He admitted that even in this new world Chinese entrepreneurs faced many difficulties, and he urged them to prepare themselves by adopting the Communist Party's spirit of hard work and struggle. In this spirit, "we must eat bitterness at first so that we can enjoy happiness later."[37]

While urging his fellow Chinese entrepreneurs to take their inspiration from the Communist Party, Father also made practical proposals for reforming Chinese industry to capture the export trade. In these proposals he anticipated the export strategy that was eventually adopted and ultimately helped to produce the "economic miracle" beginning in Hong Kong and Taiwan in the 1950s and 1960s and the People's Republic of China in the 1980s. The aim, he said, should be to generate an economic cycle to raise the quantity and quality of consumer goods for export. In phase 1, Chinese entrepreneurs should use domestically grown raw materials to manufacture consumer goods for export; in return for these goods, they would receive foreign exchange. In phase 2, entrepreneurs should use foreign exchange to buy needed foreign-made producer goods (especially machinery and chemicals)—never foreign-made consumer goods. In phase 3, entrepreneurs should use these imported producer goods in conjunction with domestically grown raw materials to raise the sophistication of their products for export. And so the cycle was to continue, with the products growing in quantity, rising in quality, and garnering more and more foreign exchange. Meanwhile, as the demand for consumer goods in China's domestic market rose, Chinese entrepreneurs would satisfy it not by importing foreign-made consumer products but by distributing Chinese-made ones. While producing high-quality consumer goods for export abroad, Father proposed, "we can distribute lower quality goods at a lower price to lessen the burden on our fellow countrymen."[38]

In outlining this scheme, Father cited the example of his own woolen mills, implying that the government should authorize him to put his principles into practice in this specific case. He proposed to carry out phase 1 by procuring wool from northwest China, exactly as he had unsuccessfully tried to do when he was in Hong Kong a few months earlier. The only difference was that now he planned to manufacture woolen fabric with it in his China Wool Manufacturing Company in Shanghai rather than exporting the raw wool abroad. In phase 2 he would then export these woolens as finished products abroad, selling them primarily in the accessible markets of Asia, Africa, and Latin America and secondarily in the less accessible markets of Europe and the United States, thus earning foreign exchange. In phase 3, he would complete the cycle by using the foreign exchange to buy foreign-made producer goods, particularly chemicals that were needed to manufacture matches in his Great China Match Company at Shanghai.[39]

While giving these speeches publicly, Father confided to Fourth Son privately that he expected state planning agencies to carry out his ideas by giving government contracts to state-owned enterprises, not privately owned ones like his. Accordingly, he was pleasantly surprised when the Economic Planning Committee of the People's Republic ordered woolen uniforms for government officials from his mills rather than state-owned ones. He took this decision to mean that he was accepted as a capitalist under Communism not only in theory but also in practice.[40]

As shown here, Father's rationale for choosing to live in China shifted after he returned home. Before leaving Hong Kong and even during his first days back in China, his reasons for returning were strikingly personal, pragmatic, and nonnationalistic. On the eve of his return to Shanghai from Hong Kong, he said that he was making the move because of his awareness of his Shanghai-based family members' expectations, his desire to be near his family firm, and his concern for his advanced age—considerations that seem to have been paramount in the minds of many Chinese capitalists at the time as they decided whether to live in Shanghai or Hong Kong.[41] On his arrival in China at a press conference, Father cited for newspaper reporters slightly different but equally apolitical reasons for coming back: the location of his factories in Shanghai, the danger of exhausting his resources in Hong Kong, and the government's assurances that he could retain his property in the People's Republic. In his first meeting with Zhou Enlai, he was suspicious of ideological designations and questioned Zhou's characterization of him as a "national capitalist" until Zhou patiently explained that the term was used by the Chinese Communist Party to express approval of some capitalists as distinct from the rest.

These examples all suggest that while he was still in Hong Kong Father made his decision to return to China primarily because of his concern for his family and his family firm—not because he held the ideological orientation of a national capitalist (as opposed to a comprador bureaucratic capitalist) or because he was a nationalist (as distinct from a pragmatist). Only after he had returned to Shanghai and become fully engaged in life and work in the People's Republic did he begin to take strong nationalistic positions.

Supporting the Nation

Although the speeches quoted above contain critiques of foreign imperialism, Father did not begin to take pride in the achievements of the People's Republic of China as a nation until late 1950 when it became involved in the Korean War against American-led United Nations troops. Ever since he had been a schoolboy at St. John's Middle School and St. John's University (both founded in Shanghai by the American Episcopal Mission), he had been in awe of U.S. power. Even after the fighting began in Korea, he was initially dubious about China's campaign to Resist America and Aid Korea. In September and October 1950, when the Americans pushed North Korean troops out of South Korea and captured the North Korean capital, Pyongyang, he was afraid that they would drop an atomic bomb on his hometown, Shanghai.[42] But in December 1950, after the Chinese "Volunteer Army" crossed into North Korea and pushed the United Nations troops once again south of the thirty-eighth parallel, he took patriotic pride in this achievement and began to participate ardently in the Resist America and Aid Korea campaign.

Father was not the only capitalist to make philanthropic donations to the war effort, but among Shanghai's entrepreneurs he took the lead.[43] His enterprises gave funds to help cover the cost of acquiring airplanes and artillery, and he delivered speeches exhorting his employees and other entrepreneurs to make contributions too. In a substantive and symbolic gesture, he donated one thousand sets of woolen uniforms to troops at the front and personally wrote letters to another thousand veterans who had been wounded there. These patriotic actions inspired an editorial in the Shanghai newspaper *Wenhui bao* that hailed him as a model for all the Chinese people.[44]

Following Father's lead, Second Son also became personally involved in the Korean War. In the spring of 1951, he served as a member of the First Chinese People's Delegation to Give Comfort in Korea. On its trip to Korea, he visited Chinese soldiers from the Volunteer Army on the front lines and talked with American prisoners of war in English, which he had learned as a student at Cambridge University in

the 1930s. In 1952 he also served as a member of the second such delegation. Listening to Second Son's stories about Korea, Father said that
he was deeply moved by the bravery of the Chinese soldiers. In 1952
he told the family: "For the first time in my life, I am proud to be a
Chinese."[45]

Surviving Anticapitalist Campaigns

If the Korean War gave Father new nationalistic reasons for staying in
China and keeping his family there, then an anticapitalist campaign
added political reasons because it elevated him to a position of national
leadership. As a result of it, first he became a representative from Shanghai to the People's Congress, and then he was designated a member of
the National Committee of the Chinese People's Political Consultative
Conference. But he only acquired these high-ranking positions after
paying a heavy price.

In the first months of 1952, Father and other capitalists in Shanghai and China's other major cities became targets of the Chinese Communist Party's Five Anti campaign, so named because it aimed to
eliminate five kinds of wrongdoing: bribery, tax evasion, theft of state
property, cheating on government contracts, and robbery of economic
information. Between January and May 1952, thousands of capitalists
in Shanghai were denounced by workers, fellow capitalists, and even
members of their own families. While demonstrators paraded in the
streets and shouted their names over loudspeakers, capitalists had to
open their factories and account books to inspection teams and in many
cases were forced to give confessions of their crimes. Some capitalists
suffered more than others from the Five Anti campaign, but even those
who did not confess to any crimes seem to have felt socially violated
and personally humiliated by the experience.[46]

Father, perhaps more than any other Chinese capitalist, was in a
position to be spared during the Five Anti campaign. Two years before
the campaign began, when the government had first introduced laws
against tax evasion and other economic crimes, he had immediately
and publicly endorsed these new laws. "It is important for merchants to
have credibility," he had said, representing capitalists at a meeting of
Shanghai's People's Political Consultative Conference in 1950. "Those
who have evaded taxes have no credibility and are scum. We should

have nothing to do with them." Thus anticipating the Five Anti campaign long before it began, he had advocated punishing violators of the new laws "severely and without concern for giving them face."[47]

Even though Father had taken the moral high ground and urged fellow capitalists to obey new laws against economic crimes before the Five Anti campaign, he was not spared during the campaign. When party cadres made him their target in early 1952, he was physically sickened by the experience. At age sixty-four, he fell ill from a heart condition and stayed at home to recuperate. At the height of the campaign, he expressed to his family the fear that the campaign marked the end for capitalists in the People's Republic. "Now that the Chinese Communist Party has put the country on the right track," Fourth Son later recalled him telling his sons at his sickbed, "it no longer needs the capitalist class as its friend. You boys go find your own path and come up with your own way."[48]

Fourth Son, at age forty, was more vigorous than Father, but he too collapsed under the intense psychological pressures of the Five Anti campaign. In a 1958 interview with a Japanese journalist, he remarked:

> As a capitalist I would like to forget the Five Anti campaign forever. In 1952, the workers came to criticize me to my face and the class struggle became sharper day by day. The workers hung the label "leading capitalist" on me, and I suffered humiliations. In the struggle, hidden wealth was to be brought out into the open, and although it was hard for me to endure, I resisted strongly almost to the very end. But ultimately I had to quit resisting and go along because a high-level employee that I had been counting on took the workers' side. I lost 11 percent of my body weight at this time.

At the height of the Five Anti campaign, Fourth Son reached the breaking point and was ready to flee the country. "One night after returning home from a particularly vehement meeting with workers, I confronted my father and told him I wanted to go to Hong Kong, but Father just held his head in his hands and said that he hadn't thought it would get so bad."[49]

At that moment, like Father, Fourth Son had begun to think that the Chinese Communist Party regarded him as redundant. "I had no idea what would happen to me and was afraid and suspicious of the Chinese Communist Party. I wondered how long the Communist Party would find any need for me."[50] Preparing to escape from Shanghai to

Hong Kong, he might have gone if the Five Anti campaign had not come to an end just then in May 1952.

Yet after all their suffering, when the results of the Five Anti investigations were announced late in 1952, Father and his family found that they had not only survived but greatly benefited from the outcome. They were fully exonerated and declared to be "law abiding." In fact, they were hailed as model national capitalists, and they were rewarded with 2.5 million yuan in special financing plus 2.8 million yuan in goods that had been confiscated from the warehouses of capitalists who had been found guilty of economic crimes. Father was invited to go to Beijing to dine with Mao Zedong, and when he returned to Shanghai, he assured his family that the Chinese Communist Party had not changed its favorable policy toward national capitalists after all. More than ever, he told a Japanese journalist, he was enthusiastic about "taking the socialist path," as a representative to the National People's Congress and a member of the National Committee of Chinese People's Political Consultative Conference.[51]

Continuing Family Debates

Father's decision to return to Shanghai after his six months in Hong Kong was made in the context of long-standing debates among members of the Liu family. All of the Lius in Shanghai wanted Father to come home for reasons they derived from their past experiences dating back to pre-1949, the Sino-Japanese War, or even earlier, but these reasons were by no means identical. Second and Fourth Sons, as top executives in the family firm, appealed to him to come back and join them in managing their business. Sixth Son, who secretly belonged to the Chinese Communist Party, was determined to bring him home so that he would cooperate with the party and build socialism under the newly founded government. Mother wanted him to help her preside over their family. He Guiying, his mistress, hoped he would give his attention to herself and their young son.

It is not clear what priority Father gave to each of these rationales. But it is clear that he made his decision to return to China on the basis of these and other expectations from his family more than his ideological attachment to China as his country. After he settled in Shanghai and became active in Chinese political life, he began to participate in patriotic campaigns and attribute his actions to his nationalism. But earlier, on the eve of his departure from Hong Kong in November 1949, he had emphasized to his family that he had decided to return because of their expectations for him and because of the Chinese government's assurance that the Lius could retain their family firm. In fact, at that time Father was so unmotivated by nationalism that when he and Second Son first arrived in China and met with Premier Zhou Enlai, he did not understand Zhou's attempt to label him a "national capitalist" as opposed to a "comprador and bureaucratic capitalist," and he frankly reminded Zhou that before the revolution he had been a bureaucrat in the Nationalist government and a comprador in a British-owned coal-mining corporation.

In Father's debate with members of his family over his return from Hong Kong to Shanghai, as in his previous debates with them, he argued vigorously with them over a period of time and then ultimately accommodated them. If he had refused to compromise, he could have remained in Hong Kong permanently. Once based there, he might have been able to bring some or all of his family members from Shanghai to Hong Kong, and if not, he would have found it logistically simpler to gather around him in Hong Kong those of his children who were already outside China. But these children had their own dilemmas in relation to the revolution and worked out their own political positions wherever they chose to live. On this issue, even Youngest Daughter, theoretically the most disadvantaged of all the Liu children in terms of gender and seniority, took her own independent stance in the family.

14

❖

A Daughter Who Forged Family Alliances

IN NOVEMBER 1949, when Father returned from Hong Kong to the People's Republic, his youngest daughter had been a student in the United States for more than a year—since the fall of 1948. She did not go back to Shanghai with him. In fact, even after Father reached Shanghai and ordered his sons to join him there in the spring of 1950, Youngest Daughter remained in school in the United States. Her continuation of her overseas education for three academic years, 1948–1951, broke precedent for daughters in her family. Her eldest sister had been given only one semester in Japan, and her middle sister had spent less than a year in England. Moreover, while abroad, Youngest Daughter's costs for her education were high—roughly equivalent to those of her brothers. As shown earlier, Father had invested heavily in her brothers' overseas educations because they were expected to become his successors as leaders in the family's firm and perpetuators of its business dynasty. But Father had no such rationale for supporting Youngest Daughter's education because she, like her sisters, was expected to marry into her future husband's family and have no opportunity to serve the family firm directly—only, if at all, indirectly through a marriage alliance (like the one Father had had in mind for Eldest Daughter).

As a woman and the youngest member of her family, why was Youngest Daughter given the privilege of this expensive education? Between 1949 and 1951, with the coming of the revolution, how was she able to continue her studies abroad? Did she seek independence for herself in the Liu family just as her brothers did? She won approval for her education not by acting strictly on her own as an individual but rather by aligning herself with some members of the Liu family and against others. Only twenty years old when the revolution occurred in 1949, by then she had already decided who would be her allies and her enemies in the family, and she made these decisions based on her reactions to various family members' attempts to exercise authority over her as the youngest daughter.

With Father and Mother in Prewar and Wartime Shanghai

In the first years of her life, Youngest Daughter's family unit consisted almost exclusively of Father, Mother, and herself. She was born in 1929, the year three of her older brothers left Shanghai for England, and during her girlhood her other older siblings almost all attended colleges overseas or boarding schools outside the home. "All your brothers and sisters are now at school," Father wrote to Eldest Son in the United States on October 2, 1931, when Youngest Daughter was two years old. "Your youngest sister is the only comfort your mother and I now have at home."[1] She was the baby of the family by a good margin— six years younger than the second youngest child—and Father took great pleasure in doting on her and extolling her virtues to his older children abroad. "Your youngest sister is growing beautifully," he wrote to Sixth and Seventh Sons in Japan on November 30, 1932, when she was three. "She can talk or rather prattle very well now and she likes to use her tongue a great deal. I want her to get out into the park [Jessfield Park near the Liu family home in the northwestern part of Shanghai] often so that she can grow all the more healthy and robust."[2]

Year after year, Father lovingly charted the growth of her powers of observation and intelligence as though astonished by every phase of her development. On June 22, 1935, when she was six, he wrote to Fifth Son in the United States: "Your baby sister knows the ins and outs of the park as well as anyone else in the family. Before long she will be able to tell us the number of birds and animals in the zoo! She has grown to be quite a big girl and very intelligent too."[3] Utterly captivated, Father indulged Youngest Daughter from the time she was born until she reached the age of nine. At that point, in 1938, when he fled Japanese-occupied Shanghai, she was suddenly deprived of his indulgent care and left entirely in Mother's hands.

Youngest Daughter did not see Father for the duration of the war, 1938–1945, and throughout these seven long years her relationship with Mother was stormy. A few years after the war, while still in her

teens, Youngest Daughter bitterly recalled this unhappy period in a letter to her brothers and sisters and their spouses. She admitted that at
the time she had "fits of bad temper," and she blamed her behavior on
Mother's failures as a parent. "I have been denied Mother's love since
childhood," she lamented. "A mother's love is especially important for
girls. But we have all been denied Mother's love. Not every rich person
is entitled to that kind of love, and not all poor people are denied it, either. Don't you agree?"[4] Youngest Daughter expected her brothers and
sisters to agree with her, and she thought they would join her in attributing Mother's actions to the worst possible motives. "I know," she told
them, "that all of the children in our family recognize that our mother's actions are vicious and her intentions are cruel."

As an example of Mother's ill-tempered outbursts, Youngest Daughter reminded Eldest Son of "that day in Lieu Hong Kee [the family
firm's accounts office] when Mother smashed cups in public and made
a scene." In light of Mother's abominable behavior, Youngest Daughter
was amazed that Eldest Son had handled the episode so gracefully. "You
kept everything to yourself," she told him with admiration. "That's
something none of my other older brothers could have done." His high
level of tolerance for Mother's outrages made him Mother's favorite,
Youngest Daughter pointed out. Then, careful not to leave the impression that he or anyone else should want to be Mother's favorite, Youngest Daughter added: "It isn't really an honor to be so loved by our
mother."[5]

Denied her mother's love or unwilling to accept it, Youngest
Daughter reciprocated by giving Mother nothing more than pity in return. As she pointed out to her brothers and sisters, the only limit she
placed on her hatred for Mother was based on the fact that she "is our
mother after all," at least to the extent that she had "direct blood relations with us." So rather than hate Mother without qualification, "I
can't help but pity her."[6] Whether her pity was any better for their relationship than her hatred, Youngest Daughter clearly found living with
Mother intolerable.

From Mother's side, the relationship also became intolerable. She
was strict with Youngest Daughter because she was determined to prevent a repetition of the family's earlier traumatic experience with Eldest Daughter. As Mother explained, writing from Shanghai to Fourth
Son in Chongqing on May 9, 1941, "I always regret what your eighth

[eldest] sister has done." In light of Eldest Daughter's bad precedent, Mother kept Youngest Daughter under "a watchful eye," she told Fourth Son, so that she could monitor her every movement.[7]

After residing together without Father for three years during the war, 1938–1941, Mother and Youngest Daughter reached the breaking point, and Mother allowed her daughter, then twelve, to move out. Mother acknowledged at the time that she took this action because her own nervous anxiety had kept them both awake at night. "You know that your youngest sister and I share [a] room together," she wrote, referring to their apartment at Grosvenor House in the French Concession, "and when 'things' came up I could not sleep and your youngest sister too could not get sleep."[8] For her daughter's sake as well as her own, in 1941 Mother moved her out of their apartment and into the home of Second Son and his wife.

Mother had no trouble persuading her daughter to make this move. In fact, she jumped at the chance. Since Father's departure in 1938, she had missed his parental indulgence and resented Mother's strict discipline. She had also become painfully conscious of the age gap between her mother and herself. Her parents had been in their early forties when she was born and were in their early fifties by this time. Without hesitation, she seized the opportunity to escape her fifty-three-year-old mother and embrace her fashionable brother and his wife.

With Second Son and His Wife in Wartime Shanghai

Between 1941 and 1945 Youngest Daughter aligned with Second Son and his wife, Xia Tianjin (Mitze), against Mother. Her new surrogate parents were much closer to her in age; Second Son, at thirty-one, was nineteen years older, and Mitze, at twenty-one, was only nine years older. Unlike Father and Mother, Second Son and Mitze had no children, so Youngest Daughter did not have to compete with brothers or sisters for attention. Even before she moved in they had taken a keen avuncular interest in her, and when Mother asked them to take Youngest Daughter, they eagerly welcomed her into their home.

From Mother's point of view, Second Son and Mitze were ideally suited to serve as parents for Youngest Daughter—better suited than Mother herself was. "Our youngest daughter has now arrived at an important stage of life," Mother wrote to Father on March 23, 1942, when

Youngest Daughter was thirteen and still in her first year with Second Son and Mitze. "She needs someone to guide and look after her especially at this time. I am occupied with other things, you know, and I cannot take this great care into my own hand." For Youngest Daughter's guide, Mother regarded Second Son's wife Mitze as the ideal candidate. "To undertake this task," Mother wrote to Father, "none of our daughters-in-law is so fit and qualified as Mitzie. Besides being a capable manager of home affairs Mitzie is outspoken and resourceful. She will correct what is not right with our youngest daughter in every and all ways."[9] While capable in her own right, Mitze could also call on her mother to step in when needed. "Whenever Mitze has to go out," Mother wrote to Fourth Son, "she has her mother there to look after your sister."[10]

With Mitze and her mother monitoring Youngest Daughter's behavior, Second Son took responsibility for her education. As Mother told Father, "he is an affectionate brother. He helps her in studies."[11] When Youngest Daughter encountered academic difficulties, Second Son hired a tutor for her. As Mother reported to Father, he "secured a girl-teacher to coach our youngest daughter in her studies."[12] With Youngest Daughter in this young couple's capable hands, Mother was finally able to relax. "So my mind is at perfect ease to let our girl stay with her brother and sister-in-law," she wrote to Father. "You can readily agree with me that our daughter is now being well looked after and cared for."[13]

From Youngest Daughter's point of view, she had escaped Mother's clutches and become liberated. On weekdays she remained at Wai Foong, her boarding school in Shanghai. Every weekend she paid Mother a token visit and then spent nearly all of the rest of the time with Second Son and Mitze.[14] As a teenager, she was thrilled to be in the company of these young socialites. She attended their exciting parties, met their dashing friends, and kept late hours along with them. She became close to both Second Son and Mitze—closer to him than to any of her other brothers and closer to her than to any of her own sisters, not to mention her other sisters-in-law. During her four years of living with this couple, 1941–1945, Youngest Daughter forged strong and lasting ties that continued to bind her to them in a separate family unit even after she moved back in with Father and Mother at the end of the war.

With Father in Postwar Shanghai

When the war abruptly ended in August 1945, Father took six weeks to wind up his business dealings in Chongqing before he returned to Shanghai, and during this period Youngest Daughter wrote to him from the Grosvenor apartment where she had moved back in with Mother. Then age sixteen, she eagerly looked forward to her reunion with Father and began pleading with him to join her in an alliance against Mother.

In her letters to Father in Chongqing, she complained that Mother was treating her outrageously. She had agreed to "stay home quietly" only after she had fought with Mother and had found that Mother was rigid and uncompromising. She wrote to Father that Mother "is so fixed in her own ideas. You know about that. I am not diplomatic in my language and worry that I may make her angry, so I seldom speak with her." She could not understand why Mother was so angry. "Ai! Mother just can't let go of things. She gets angry almost every day. She is now at an age when she should be enjoying life. The bitterness in life should be left for us young people to swallow. Wouldn't you agree?" Youngest Daughter assumed that Father would agree and would side with her against Mother on all issues. "Father," she wrote, "you are indeed my dearest person in the world." Despite his long absence, she assured him that she continued to adore him. "Since you are not in Shanghai, I am so unhappy. I envy my classmates, who all have their fathers accompany them every week to ride bicycles or to pass the time. When I think about my own father, I haven't seen him for seven whole years. Father, do you sometimes think about this daughter of yours?" Showing eager anticipation, Youngest Daughter could hardly wait for Father to come home. "My dear Father, when can you come back? Your daughter is waiting here for you every day. When you return, how happy we all will be!"[15]

On October 2, when Father finally did arrive back in Shanghai, she was overjoyed to see him, and she tried to solidify her father-daughter alliance by moving into his wing of the house, leaving Mother in her own separate wing. Under these living arrangements, Youngest Daughter personally took care of Father and brought all of her questions to him, never to Mother.

Of all her questions for Father, her request to study abroad was the one she pressed most urgently and persistently. Ultimately, with help from her wartime surrogate parents Second Son and Mitze, she wore down his resistance. As early as January 1947, she persuaded Father to give his consent for her to study abroad, but he was not able to secure a passport for her until mid-1948.[16] By then the time seemed right, because she had completed her secondary education and had begun taking courses at Aurora College, a Catholic postsecondary school in Shanghai.[17] The time was also right because Father had scheduled a trip to the United States for himself in the fall of 1948, so after preceding her to San Francisco, he would be there to greet her when she arrived.

Father's official reason for traveling to the United States at this time was to attend the annual meeting of the International Labor Organization as China's "employers' delegate" in San Francisco in July 1948.[18] But after doing so, he extended his trip partly to prepare the way for Youngest Daughter in advance of her arrival in the United States. Traveling across the continent, he paid a visit to Dr. C. E. Mullin, a chemist who was introduced to him by a Chinese business associate, and he interviewed Dr. Mullin and his wife in their home in Huntingdon, Pennsylvania, before recruiting them to serve as a host family for Youngest Daughter.[19] After making this arrangement, Father once again crossed the United States so that he reached San Francisco in time to meet her as her flight arrived from Shanghai.

On August 19, Youngest Daughter was relieved to find Father waiting to greet her at the San Francisco airport. Forty hours earlier, she had reacted emotionally to the send-off she was given by the rest of the Liu family in Shanghai. "I was quite upset," she wrote a few weeks later to her brothers, sister-in-law, sisters, and brothers-in-law, "when the boarding announcement came so suddenly and there wasn't time to say good-bye to you each individually. As I was watching you waving your hands through the window, it broke my heart. When the airplane took off and all of you slowly disappeared, I finally broke down and cried."[20]

On board this flight and subsequent ones, she remained tense. She traveled with her friend Bessie Sze (Shi), the daughter of the Lius' longtime friend Shi Zhaoji, former ambassador from China to England and the United States, but Bessie's attempts to humor her did not raise her spirits. "Though Bessie has been kind to me, this time she could not make me laugh." Youngest Daughter found nothing exciting or even pleasant about the long trip. "We were in the plane for over forty hours, and the food was simply awful. I didn't eat a thing. First stop was Tokyo, then Okinawa, Honolulu, and San Francisco."[21] Not until the end of the ordeal when she arrived safely in San Francisco and saw Father waiting did her mood swing from sadness to joy.

She wrote home that she had not expected Father to meet her plane, and in describing the moment when their eyes met, she added a humorous touch. Seeing Father was a pleasant surprise, she told her siblings and their spouses, "but I was naturally disappointed that President Truman didn't show up. Third Brother, you must have forgotten to cable him about my arrival." She talked with Father for six hours between her flight's arrival and his flight's departure for Shanghai (on the same plane that had brought her to San Francisco), and in his presence she regained her poise. But when he boarded his flight, she once again lost control of her emotions. "As I watched the plane take off," she wrote, "I was thinking to myself that I was doing what you did on the day that I left, and I broke down again." For her, sending off Father was a poignant and memorable moment. A year later she still recalled the details. She wrote to him: "Around eight o'clock the plane took you away. I still remember the white handkerchief that you waved from the window. It broke my heart."[22]

Once Father had departed, Youngest Daughter was left in the United States without him or Second Son or Mitze, her closest family members. But Father had assured her that after her transcontinental journey from San Francisco to the East Coast, she would be looked after by other family members: Eighth Son, a student at Harvard Business School, would meet her plane on her arrival in New York, and the Mullins of Huntingdon, Pennsylvania, would serve as her American host family.

With the Mullins in Huntingdon

On August 22, after resting for a few days in San Francisco, Youngest Daughter and Bessie Sze took a flight to New York, and Youngest Daughter found this trip as unpleasant as the one across the Pacific. "I was really uncomfortable because the flight was bumpy," she wrote home. "I almost threw up."[23] They were met by Bessie's family, whose home was in New York, and Eighth Son, who took Youngest Daughter sightseeing

and treated her to meals in Chinese restaurants in New York before ac-
companying her by plane to Huntingdon on the night of August 24.

On arrival in Huntingdon, Youngest Daughter discovered right away
that the Mullins welcomed her with open arms, and she readily hugged
them back. On August 24, from the moment Youngest Daughter first
saw Dr. Mullin, she was favorably impressed because he met her plane
from New York even though it arrived at two o'clock in the morning.

Although grateful to the Mullins for their warm welcome, Youngest Daughter initially suffered from homesickness. For a few weeks
after August 27, when Eighth Son returned to Boston, leaving her with
the Mullins, she was particularly lonely and frightened. She wrote home:
"poor me, I was left alone in this new and strange place. The only comfort I had was climbing into bed at night and crying." Her homesickness
worsened whenever she received letters from her siblings and their
spouses. "While living at home," she wrote to them, "I didn't know
how lucky I was. Only now do I appreciate the happiness of home. Every
time I get a letter from home, I cry." She also missed Shanghai's food.
As she summarized the Mullins's meals, "the breakfast consists only of
fruit. Lunch is at 11:00 and dinner at 5:00. There is never much to eat,
so at night I often wake up hungry. My mouth waters whenever I think
about the steamed chicken and the salted fish served at the Xinya
Restaurant."[24]

Yet even when hungry or upset, she maintained good relations
with the Mullins by hiding her feelings. "In front of them," she confided to her family, "I always show a smile. That's because I don't want
to worry them since they have been so kind to me." Similarly, she did
not let the Mullins know that she thought they had faults. In fact,
rather than criticize them to their faces, she manipulated them, taking
actions they would find appealing because of their weaknesses. As she
wrote home, "the one thing I can't get used to is their wastefulness.
They are not careful in their work either. For example, when washing
dishes, they put lots of soap in the water, let the dishes soak in the water for a little while, and then take them out. So, I always fight for my
chance to do the dishes. That makes Mrs. Mullin like me even more."[25]

Within a few weeks, Youngest Daughter began to recover from her
homesickness and bask in the warm reception her host parents were
giving her. Whatever faults the Mullins might have had, she felt they
were outweighed by their generous displays of affection toward her.

Writing home a few weeks after she had first met them, she reported that they literally embraced her. "Mrs. Mullin often hugs me and kisses my cheek and calls me 'darling sweetheart.' I feel very close to them, too. Even Dr. Mullin has recently started kissing me good night. He was a little uneasy about it at first, because he had heard all along that in China, men and women always stay apart."[26]

She found that Mrs. Mullin doted on her all day, and she reveled in this attention. "Mrs. Mullin is quite talkative. She walks with a limp. I can never be out of her sight. Otherwise she will cry out '*Linda, Linda* [Youngest Daughter's Western name].'"[27] Youngest Daughter did not exaggerate the amount of attention and affection the Mullins lavished on her, according to Eighth Son. "They just adore Linda," he confirmed in a letter to his parents on September 9.[28]

In late September she had to go to the Boston area to start school at Pine Manor Junior College, but she gladly returned to Huntingdon for her first Christmas in the United States, when she once again enjoyed a warm reception from the Mullins. To express his affection, Dr. Mullin joked with her that he had a romantic attachment to her. He "comforts me," she wrote home to her parents. "He loves Chinese a lot. He always says that I am his Chinese girl friend." At age nineteen, she attributed no ulterior motives to him and had only good words to say about him: "Dr. Mullin can't be nicer to me. He cares a great deal about me." Grateful to him and his wife, she wrote home: "I hope that Father will write to Dr. Mullin to thank him for being so kind to me."[29]

Youngest Daughter's only problem with Dr. and Mrs. Mullin was that they found her too attractive. After spending a little over a week with them at Christmas, she began to sense that their own daughter had become envious of her. Staying with the family during the holidays had made her "very uncomfortable," she confided in a letter to her parents, "because Mrs. Mullin likes me so much that her daughter has become quite jealous of me." Originally she had planned to spend the entire Christmas vacation with the Mullins, but she cut her visit short by a few days "because I hate to see their daughter so upset."[30]

By this time, December 29, Youngest Daughter had readily adapted to her host family. Since leaving Shanghai in September, she had relocated in the United States, recovered from homesickness, and built an alliance with Dr. and Mrs. Mullin not unlike the one she had with Father, Second Son, and Mitze. On her last day with the Mullins at

Christmas, she described for Mother her relationship with Mrs. Mullin and conveyed the clear impression that it was preferable to her relationship with Mother. "Dear Mother," she wrote, "I often speak about you to Mrs. Mullin. She really likes me very much, and she certainly lets me know it. They have given me lots of gifts this Christmas. I'll hate to leave here."[31]

Youngest Daughter's reluctance to leave the Mullins' household implied that she could imagine becoming part of this family and residing in America on a permanent basis. But in the fall and winter of 1948, she did not have this option. If she was to remain in the United States on her student visa, she had to attend college. Eighth Son had selected Pine Manor Junior College.

With Eighth Son in the Boston Area

In placing her near an older brother, Eighth Son, who was supposed to serve as her guardian, Father was following a pattern set by her two older sisters. Just as Eldest Daughter had Sixth Son nearby as her guardian while she was in Japan in 1935 and Middle Daughter had Second Son nearby as her guardian while she was in England in 1935–1936, Youngest Daughter had Eighth Son nearby as her guardian when she went to the United States in 1948. In each case, the sister was younger than her brother-guardian and was supposed to depend on him to advise her, manage her finances, protect her from harm, and give her a sense of security. Eldest Daughter and Middle Daughter and their older brothers followed this pattern throughout their time abroad. Initially, Youngest Daughter and Eighth Son followed it too.

In July 1948 on the eve of Youngest Daughter's arrival in the United States, Eighth Son eagerly assumed his role as her guardian. Father had the idea that she would stay on the West Coast—far from Eighth Son at Harvard—and would bring with her from China her own guardian, an older woman who had been the principal of the girls' school Father had founded in his native place, Ningbo. But Eighth Son intervened and volunteered to be her guardian. He did not want her staying on the West Coast at International House, as Father had proposed, because he was determined to protect her from sexual dangers. "It is not that I do not trust Linda to live by herself," he told his brothers on July 15, "but according to what I have witnessed, girls of Linda's age very often feel lonesome in a strange land especially after seeing the loose moral[s] of the American and other foreign girls. [Sixth Son] can tell you [about] the night scenes in the International House where boys and girls fondled each other."[32]

Eighth Son would protect Youngest Daughter from these loose American morals, he said, if he could locate her near him so that he could see her on a regular basis. "What I had hoped," he told his brothers, "was to have her entering a good girls college in the East, even as a Freshman, learning the American ways of doing things and enjoying a wholesome school life. I could see her on weekends."[33] As he had hoped, Youngest Daughter's plans were changed so that she entered a school near him rather than one in the western United States. After surveying the possibilities, he chose for her Pine Manor, a junior college he did not regard as academically impressive but preferred because it was only about ten miles from his residence in Cambridge.

At first Youngest Daughter depended heavily on Eighth Son, and they managed to cooperate even though they had previously spent very little time together.[34] A few weeks after her arrival in the United States, she assured her family in Shanghai that he, despite his nervousness, took good care of her. On September 15, she wrote to them: "Eighth Brother treats me very well. He looks a little thin and seems to worry too much. He can't sleep well whenever he has things on his mind. He and I are not too far from each other."[35] Eighth Son found her willing to accept help, but from the beginning he sensed that she yearned for independence from him. As he wrote to his parents, she "has been very cooperative. In fact, in many places, I have been too attentive to her which makes her feel that she is not having an opportunity to learn her independence. Since she is already a big girl, I have to let her have her own ways."[36] Soon he discovered that she wanted to have her own way whether he approved or not.

Within her first month in the United States, she clashed with Eighth Son over his choice of Pine Manor for her. Even before she started classes there, she expressed her doubts about it. She was pleased with its location near Boston and Cambridge, but she was disappointed to learn from him that Pine Manor did not offer home economics, which, according to her plan, was supposed to be her major. On September 15, writing to Shanghai from the Mullins' home before registering at Pine Manor, she complained to her family that "Pine Manor does not have

Home Economics, so I'll only go there for half a year. All of the schools have started, and it's too late to do anything else."[37]

At Pine Manor she took only nine credits, and she disliked all her courses. She dismissed her course in European history saying, "I don't even like Chinese history, let alone the history of foreign countries." For her speech class, she had to write an essay every week. As a result, she felt that she had too little time to devote to her most important subject, English. "I have not had time to study English," she complained to her parents, "and I seem to have set my goals all wrong."[38]

Her numerous complaints to her parents about Pine Manor prompted Mother to ask why she was so negative. "Mother," she replied, "you ask me why I keep complaining. My dear Mother, I am not complaining because I am too busy with my schoolwork. First, since my preparation was poor, I have not been able to complete the teachers' assigned readings no matter how hard I've tried. Second, this is the first time I've left home, so I am finding it rough. Most of all I am afraid of not passing all my courses."[39]

Her fears of failure were not borne out, but she was disappointed with her grades. "Although I passed all my subjects in my recent exams," she wrote to her parents in November, "my grades were not great. Maybe I can do better next time." She was so upset with her grades that she telephoned Eighth Son and asked him to persuade the president of Pine Manor to let her transfer to another school. As Eighth Son reported to Father and Mother, she told him that "it will be difficult to continue at Pine Manor because despite her hard work day in and day out, she sees no progress."[40]

Representing Youngest Daughter, Eighth Son met with Pine Manor's president, presented her case, and asked for permission to let her transfer. But the president disagreed with Youngest Daughter's self-evaluation and opposed her proposal to transfer. As Eighth Son reported to Father and Mother, the president said "that Little Sister is too ambitious, that she has in fact made very fine progress, and that she should be able to handle all three of her courses." In response, Eighth Son raised the possibility that Youngest Daughter might transfer in the spring semester to the Garland School, another women's junior college, in Boston. The president disagreed. According to Eighth Son, he "does not think that she will do well if she transfers to Garland School next semester, and he believes that she should improve her English first and then transfer."[41]

The president's assessment, Eighth Son told his parents, coincided with his own. "I, too, am of the opinion that if Little Sister is too busy with only nine units now, then imagine how much busier she would be at Garland, where she will have to take twenty-four units each semester. Even though most of the work at Garland is done in the lab, there will still be books to read." He also reminded Father that Youngest Daughter's transfer would have adverse financial consequences. "Father," he said, "I don't know if you remember that it is stated in the document you signed on her behalf that you will be 'responsible for one year tuition of $1,800.' If she transfers during this first half of the year, the tuition for the next half year still needs to be paid."[42]

On the question of her transfer, Youngest Daughter took issue with Eighth Son and appealed to Father to overrule him. She thought that she should leave Pine Manor no matter what the cost, and she expressed disdain for it and its students. "Most students at Pine Manor," she wrote to her parents, "come from very rich families. Girls living in this house are fine, but they are very lazy. There are sixteen of us, and only six managed to pass every subject." Completely disaffected, she explained, "I originally started thinking about changing to another school next semester because I have absolutely no interest in Pine Manor."[43] Youngest Daughter complained so much that Eighth Son became exasperated with her. "She is no longer the little girl I remembered," Eighth Son wrote to Father and Mother on November 18. "She is already a grown-up. I really cannot make any decision on her behalf. She also changes her mind quite often."[44]

Near the end of Youngest Daughter's first semester in late 1948, she sent Father her proposal for leaving Pine Manor, and after weighing it against Eighth Son's counterproposal for keeping her there, Father decided in Youngest Daughter's favor. He allowed her to transfer from Pine Manor to the Garland School in time for the spring semester of 1949. As Eighth Son had warned, Father was required to cover her spring semester tuition for both schools, which, as Eighth Son pointed out, was higher than the tuition for Wellesley College, a prestigious four-year liberal arts institution.[45]

In Youngest Daughter's disagreements with Eighth Son over transferring and other matters, she became such a trial for him that he urged his parents to replace him with one of his brothers as her guardian, even though he was the only one of the Liu boys in the United States at the time. "I have tried my best to make her happy," he wrote to his parents on November 18, 1948. "I have been visiting her at least once a week, and I have done as she wishes. But I often feel that I am not up to the task. And I am the type of person who gets disturbed easily. Maybe she would respond better to an older brother who is stricter and more imposing."[46] This request did not result in any formal announcement of a new guardian, but in practice Second Son became her principal advisor.

With Second Son by Letter

After Youngest Daughter left Shanghai for the United States, she continued to seek advice from Second Son, just as she had done since he and his wife had taken her in and raised her during the war. She loved him like a second father, and she wrote adoring letters to him in Shanghai (while she fought with Eighth Son in Boston) comparable to the adoring letters she had earlier written to Father in Chongqing (while she had fought with Mother in Shanghai). Even though Second Son was not physically present in the United States, she preferred to write to him for advice rather than consult Eighth Son in person (just as she had preferred to write to Father in Chongqing rather than consult Mother in person during the war).

As early as November 1948, her third month in the United States, she informed Father and Mother that she was accepting advice from Second Son. "I am now following instructions from Second Brother," she wrote to her parents on November 20, and in subsequent correspondence with her parents she referred repeatedly to the letters Second Son had written her.[47]

By the late spring of 1949, with a mixture of envy and relief, Eighth Son recognized that Second Son was much closer to Youngest Daughter than he was. "Little Sister has strong opinions of her own, and she listens only to Second Brother," he wrote to Eldest Son, "I am sure that Second Brother cares about her a great deal, and I want to avoid any misunderstanding, so I seldom give her any suggestions." To avoid tension between himself and Second Son, he proposed that all responsibility for Youngest Daughter be placed unambiguously in Second Son's hands. "My dear Eldest Brother," he wrote on April 21, "since Second Brother obviously cares a great deal about Little Sister, and since bonds among all of us brothers are very important, wouldn't it be better to have Second Brother fully in charge of Little Sister's planning for the future? Having anyone else make a suggestion would only lead to unnecessary confusion."[48] Wanting neither to offend Second Son nor to spar any more with Youngest Daughter, Eighth Son was eager to bring his tenure as her guardian to an end.

Once all agreed that Youngest Daughter did not have to consider Eighth Son her guardian any longer, she took full responsibility for her finances and took pride in her careful accounting. In the spring of 1949, as she neared the end of her academic year in the United States, she wrote to Second Son: "Every single penny is recorded." She also assured him that she did not take for granted the funds her family had sent to her to finance her education. "I know that foreign exchange is hard to come by these days, and I am very careful with money," she wrote to him in Shanghai, as the People's Liberation Army was on the verge of taking the city. "I also know that I need to save as much as possible during these unstable and difficult times."[49]

Fortunately for Youngest Daughter, her family had anticipated the dangers posed by unstable times and provided her with ample financing. She had arrived in the fall of 1948 with US$2,000 available to her, plus another US$1,500 in an emergency fund. She and Eighth Son estimated the cost of her education (including tuition, room, and board) at Pine Manor in the fall of 1948 at about US$1,000 per semester, which used up the US$2,000 that had been sent to her in the fall of 1948.[50] In May 1949, she received US$2,000 from Eldest Son to cover the expenses for the coming academic year of 1949–50. In addition, she was given another US$1,000 by Second Son, plus US$2,250—half of the US$4,500 that Eldest Son sent to Eighth Son at the same time.[51]

With a grand total of US$6,750 in hand, she was well funded for the academic year of 1949–50. For that matter, she was capable of stretching her funds over more than one year because she had learned to manage her money; as Eighth Son observed to Eldest Son, "normally she is quite thrifty."[52] As she faced the decision whether to return to China, with the coming of the Communist military victories and revolution in 1949, she was not forced to go home for financial reasons.

As she pondered whether to return to Shanghai, she very deliberately decided not to go with Eighth Son to Hong Kong. His departure from New York was scheduled for July 27, a month after his graduation from Harvard Business School, and by then the two of them had become more antagonistic toward each other than ever. From Eighth Son's viewpoint, Youngest Daughter had turned their relationship as advisor and advisee on its head. "My advice is no longer considered by her," he wrote to Father in June. "On the contrary, she likes to give advice."[53]

Six weeks before he parted company with her, he looked back on their year together in the United States and summed it up for Father. "Linda has always been difficult to please," he wrote on June 12. "In many ways, she wants to make things difficult for me. We seldom have a meeting of the minds." Her manner so grated on his nerves that he found her "really irksome." Out of a sense of obligation to the family, he saw her during his last days in the United States, but on these occasions he felt that she continued to be insensitive to his needs. "I try not to leave her alone because I feel it is more or less my duty to look after her," he wrote. "But now [having undergone a recent appendectomy] I am not well. She has little consideration."[54]

When Youngest Daughter finally saw Eighth Son off, their contrasting perceptions of the moment of parting suggest how differently they viewed each other's attitudes and actions. Writing from shipboard on July 30, three days after he had put out to sea, Eighth Son told Father that Youngest Daughter had "cried bitterly on bidding me farewell."[55] By contrast, she reported rather dryly to Father on the day after her brother's departure: "We shook hands to say good-bye."[56]

Eighth Son recognized that communication had broken down between his sister and himself, and as he sailed away from her, he admitted to Father that she would be better off in the United States without him. "I believe that she will profit much in her next year after my departure, more than her first year while she was with me," he ruefully predicted. "Her sharp tongue will be tempered as time goes along." By the same token, he expected to be better off without her too, because "she has caused me many headaches and unnecessary worries."[57] This sister and brother made no plans for any future reunion in Hong Kong or anywhere else.

In the summer of 1949, as throughout the previous year, Youngest Daughter continued to write to Second Son and rely for advice more on him than on Eighth Son. But after the People's Liberation Army took Shanghai in May 1949, she had begun to have difficulty reaching him or anyone else in the city, and she had to settle for brief exchanges with him in July and August, while he was in Hong Kong appealing to Father to return to Shanghai. By the end of the summer she could no longer communicate directly with Second Son because he had left Hong Kong and gone back to Shanghai. Of the family members who were close to her, the only one she could contact any longer was Father.

With Father by Letter

Before seeing off Eighth Son, Youngest Daughter had decided that she wanted to remain at the Garland School in 1949–50, and in July and August 1949 she sought Father's approval for her decision, writing to him in Hong Kong. Beyond what she had already received, she did not need his help in preparing for her coming year in school, she wrote. In planning it, she was well aware of the requirements she had to fulfill to complete Garland's two-year course of study within the coming year. As for financing, she already had in hand ample funds to cover the costs of her tuition, board and room, and incidental expenses. Although she had no request to make of Father, she wanted his approval for her plans and his reaffirmation of the closeness of their relationship.

Youngest Daughter was well aware that Eighth Son and others in the family had given Father a low evaluation of Garland, and she countered their views by mounting a vigorous defense of it. On August 1, she wrote to Father (in Chinese, inserting the English words italicized here): "The *Garland School* is not a *finishing school* as you have all imagined. They have never taught me social etiquette or things like that." Her courses had been substantive, not superficial. "I have really learned a lot since coming to *Garland*," she claimed. In the coming year, "I plan to major in *Child Study* and the *Garland School* is famous for this subject."[58]

She was also sensitive to Eighth Son's criticism of the Garland School for being expensive. She freely admitted to Father that it charged high tuition, but she proudly reported to him that the cost would be reduced in the coming year because she was to receive a scholarship. This kind of scholarship was the first ever awarded by Garland, she told Father. "The *Garland School* has never awarded scholarships before. But because of my good academic record and China's extraordinary domestic circumstances, the school is willing to help me with part of the cost of tuition." She realized that Father might assume that Garland was coming to her aid merely because of her status as a refugee from the Communist Revolution in China rather than because of her achievements, so she added: "I've learned that many Chinese students have applied for scholarships, but most have been turned down." The honor of being selected for a scholarship greatly boosted her morale. "I am really happy about this," she wrote to Father, "and I imagine that you will be happy for me too."[59]

Youngest Daughter helped pay her way not only by winning a scholarship but also by taking a job. During the summer of 1949 she served as a governess for the five children of an American physician and his wife, Dr. and Mrs. Simmons, at a summer resort in Duxbury, near Boston. She earned US$80 per month and was proud of herself for devoting her summer to work rather than play. "Most of my friends thought that I worked too hard," she told Father, "but I feel that the experience was valuable and the hard work was worth it." The experience was somewhat comparable to the internships her brothers had held during their summers abroad. After living and working with the Simmons family for two months, she wrote to Father on August 21, "I have really had a great experience, and I have come to understand quite a bit about American family life."[60]

She considered what she learned on the job to be relevant to her major field, child study, because she had become a kind of participant-observer within the Simmons family. "They don't treat me as a maid but rather as a member of the family, so I am quite comfortable here," she reported to Father, characterizing her relations with the Simmons family in the same favorable terms she had used in writing about her relations with the Mullin family a year earlier.[61]

She pleaded with Father to approve her decision to stay at Garland for all of these reasons—her respect for Garland's high standards, especially in her major field; her success at winning a scholarship; and her resourcefulness at landing a summer job and earning an income. She assured him that she would remain in the United States only for this one year before coming home and rejoining her family. "Maybe I can use what I learn after returning to my own country," she proposed hopefully.[62]

In the future, as in the past, she would value family happiness above all else, she promised Father. "How can there be any happiness in this world better than family happiness?" she asked rhetorically. Her plan was to benefit once again from this family happiness in Shanghai as soon as she finished her degree at Garland in the spring of 1950. Reflecting on the past and projecting into the future, she assured Father: "During the past year I have not forgotten any of our family happiness, not even a single moment of it. I can only hope that the political situation will soon become stable and that my studies will soon be completed so that we can all enjoy that happiness again. When I return this time, I hope that I'll be loved more than ever by all of our family members, big and small, and especially by my dear father."[63]

Characteristically distinguishing among the "big and small" within the Liu family, Youngest Daughter elevated Father above the rest and begged for his attention. "My dear Father, may I ask you for one thing?" she wrote in closing. "I wouldn't expect a letter from you every week," she claimed, while noting that her cousin at Garland did receive one from her father in Hong Kong every week, "but can I expect one from you each month? Thank you. I know that you still love your little daughter. I will study hard this year. I hope you will take care of yourself. Don't get too tired. Goodbye. Your precious little daughter."[64]

When Father received these letters from Youngest Daughter, he was in the midst of his own decision making about whether to return from Hong Kong to Shanghai, but he took time to give his blessing to her plans. Reading her reports of her past year's academic achievements "gives me immense pleasure," he told her. "I think your time in the States has not been spent in vain as can be seen from what you write."[65] In light of her successes in her first year, he endorsed her decision to proceed with her second year. "Your decision to continue your studies at Garland School is wise and practical," he told her. "So keep on with your good work. I am very proud to hear that the Garland School has granted you a scholarship so that you find partial self-support."[66]

In approving his daughter's plan, Father absolved her of any responsibility for coming to Hong Kong to take care of him. "Please do not worry about your father," he said. "Although I am alone here in Hongkong I am quite able to look after myself. I am still as healthy as ever and keep myself occupied all the time." As the only Liu in Hong

Kong, he volunteered to keep Youngest Daughter informed about the rest of the family in Shanghai. "It is now impossible for you to write to Shanghai from the States," he noted on August 23. "It is also difficult for me to correspond with them. I shall, however, be able to gather news about the family here and there and shall write you about them once in a while. Your mother and the rest of the family are all well. If you want to write to any of them you can send the letter to me and I can find ways and means of contacting them."[67]

Father then let her know, a few weeks later, that Second Son had agreed to be the Shanghai link. In a letter to Youngest Daughter on September 3, he quoted Second Son as saying: " 'If it is at all possible, I shall keep you constantly informed of our well being in Shanghai.' "[68] So Youngest Daughter was kept up to date by her two favorite members of the family, Father and Second Son.

As long as Father was in Hong Kong, he forwarded news to Youngest Daughter, usually in brief and general summaries. "I hear from your mother and others in Shanghai once in a while," he wrote to her on September 26. "Things are relatively quiet. You do not have to worry about them." He gave her his word that he would regularly and unfailingly write to her from Hong Kong. "As long as I am in Hongkong, I promise to answer your letters."[69]

When Father began to consider leaving Hong Kong, he warned Youngest Daughter that he would not be able to communicate as directly or fully with her if he went back to Shanghai. Second Son "has requested me to return home," Father informed her, "and if I do I shall not be able to correspond with you freely." He assured her that he would try to keep up their correspondence, but he could not make her a firm promise that he would be able to do so. "I think," he vaguely suggested to her, "there are always ways and means of keeping in contact."[70] This contact by letter with him and the other Lius in Shanghai became especially important to Youngest Daughter now that she had ceased to have contact in person with any member of her family in the United States.

With Her Husband in Beijing

After Youngest Daughter said farewell to Eighth Son, she had no contact in person with any member of her immediate family in the United

States for the next year and a half, from July 1949 to January 1951. In her last year at the Garland School, 1949–50, she spent a lot of time with a cousin, Rio, who was her classmate and close companion, but she did not consider herself a member of Rio's family.[71] In the fall of 1950, after graduating from Garland's two-year program, she transferred to Michigan State University, entering a four-year program as a junior and majoring in home economics. She chose this school because of her friendship with another Garland classmate, Geraldine Rounds, whose family lived in nearby Detroit and offered Youngest Daughter a home away from home during holidays from Michigan State and even on a permanent basis. But she did not envision a future for herself with the Rounds family either.[72]

Staying with one of these families was not her only option. Because of her past experience with other families, she could have sought shelter in the home of the Mullins, or she could have joined Eighth Son, who had established a residence in Hong Kong and taken a job there. But she considered these short-term measures at best, and by the end of 1950, after the People's Republic had been firmly in place for more than a year, she became eager to return to Shanghai while she had the chance.

In 1949 and 1950, she had not been completely cut off from Father, Second Son, and the other Lius in Shanghai, and she had continued to receive letters and money from them via Hong Kong. But what if she were to lose touch with them? If she postponed her return to Shanghai any longer, would deteriorating relations between the United States and China make it impossible for her to go home? If she were suddenly cut off, even though she still had some savings, how would she survive in the long run without financial support from the Lius in Shanghai? If either Father or Second Son had chosen to stay permanently in Hong Kong, Taipei, or an American city, she might have moved in with one of them, but with them ensconced in Shanghai, she could not imagine a secure future for herself anywhere else, so she decided to join them there.

In early 1951 she booked passage on the S. S. *Wilson* for a trans-Pacific voyage. As she traveled westward overland to San Francisco and prepared to leave the United States, she did not imagine that she would discover a new family option—a prospective husband—while at sea. But once on board, she quite unexpectedly met, through a mutual friend, another passenger, Zhang Qinshi (C. H. Chang), and they were immediately attracted to each other. They found that conversation came easily because they had a lot in common. Both were born in Shanghai in 1929, had Ningbo as a native place, and came from distinguished families. Zhang's paternal grandfather was Zhang Shouyong, a notable scholar and past president of Guanghua University in Shanghai, and his maternal grandfather was Weng Wenhao, the former head of the Nationalist government's ministry of economics and National Resources Commission. He had been Father's associate and had arranged for Sixth and Eighth Sons to go to the United States on their government internships in 1945. Zhang's grandfathers were retired, but his father, Zhang Yuelian, was active and prominent, holding a position in the Nationalist government as its representative at the World Bank in Washington, D.C.[73]

Although Zhang Qinshi's family had credentials that seemed to identify him with Chiang Kai-shek's Nationalist government, he was leaving the United States because the U.S. Immigration and Naturalization Service (INS), which operated under the Department of Justice, had accused him of being a Communist and threatened to deport him. While in the United States, he had spent four years earning a BA in civil engineering at Ohio University in Athens, Ohio, class of 1950, and he had begun to earn an MA in the same field at the University of Illinois in the fall of 1950. But when he applied for an extension of his year-by-year visa to complete his graduate degree, his request was denied, so he was forced to withdraw from the University of Illinois on January 4, 1951, and return to China.[74]

In all likelihood, Zhang was not guilty as charged. At the time, he was one of about five hundred Chinese students (out of a total of 4,675 then at universities and colleges in the United States) whose requests for visa extensions were denied because they were said to be "poor security risks." These allegations were based on so little evidence that the American universities where the students were enrolled made public protests on their behalf. As the historian Rose Hum Lee has noted, "by the spring of 1951, their plight had created sufficient sympathy to warrant the intervention of various college and university administrators who believed they were wrongly suspected."[75] But the INS rejected these academic leaders' advocacy for the students on the grounds that the national interests of the United States were at stake. "We certainly ought not to let them stay," an immigration official declared in March 1951, "if we believe they are security risks. They are taking advantage of our educational facilities. We must consider justice for each individual and we also must consider justice for the nation as a whole."[76] To protect the nation, the INS refused to grant extensions on visas for Zhang and other Chinese students and ordered them to depart or face arrest and deportation in the spring of 1951.

The timing of Zhang's expulsion suggests that he was a victim of American anti-Communist hysteria. In early 1950 Senator Joseph Mc-Carthy had suddenly risen to national prominence by launching a campaign against Americans who, he charged, had "lost" China in 1949 by letting it slip away from America's ally, Chiang Kai-shek, and into the hands of Mao Zedong. Although McCarthy's allegations were vague and undocumented, he and his supporters began whipping up anti-Communist sentiment in the United States, especially after October 1950, when Mao's new Communist government sent Chinese forces into the Korean War to fight against Americans and other United Nations troops on the battlefield. With McCarthy's campaign on the rise, the U.S. government forcing Zhang to leave the country without investigating him very carefully was probably part of a broad and indiscriminate hunt for Communist subversives.[77]

Whether or not Zhang had been a member of the Chinese Communist Party before he left the United States, Youngest Daughter regarded him as an ardent progressive and was attracted to him by his politics along with everything else about him. By the end of their trans-Pacific journey, the two young people had become seriously interested in each other. Although they had maintained a sense of propriety and refrained from having a passionate shipboard romance, they had begun to discuss the possibility of marriage. Before they parted at Hong Kong (where she was scheduled to spend a week and he was unable to disembark without a visa), he promised to write her in Shanghai from his destination, Beijing.

On her arrival in Shanghai, Youngest Daughter was given a warm welcome home, but she was preoccupied with Zhang—not least because she received letters from him every single day. Over the following months, as his letters poured in, she discussed him with her family, especially her favorite brother, Second Son. By chance, Second Son had known Zhang's father as a classmate, fraternity brother, and tennis partner when they were undergraduates at St. Johns University in Shanghai, and he held the Zhang family in high regard. He strongly preferred Zhang to Youngest Daughter's previous boyfriend, and as usual, she took his advice to heart. With blessings from him and the rest of the Liu family, she and Zhang announced their engagement in the Shanghai newspapers on October 31, 1951, and she then joined her fiance in Beijing, where they planned to be married.[78]

In late 1951, on her arrival in Beijing, her decision to move there was put to a stern test. Before they were married, she lived in a Women's Association dormitory that was attached to the military hospital where she worked, and she was shocked by the primitive nature of her accommodations. Particularly appalling were the latrine-like toilets, which struck an unsettling contrast with the flush toilets and other amenities she had left behind in the Liu family home at Shanghai and college dormitories in the United States. Uncomfortable from the start, she soon found that her life went from bad to worse because she became a target of the Five Anti campaign, which began in January 1952. In support of this campaign, her dormitory mates labeled her "the capitalist's daughter" and tormented her by stuffing her pillow full of soiled sanitary napkins and human excrement. Day after day she absorbed this punishment, and night after night she cried herself to sleep.[79]

Living in separate dormitories, Youngest Daughter and Zhang seldom saw each other until they were finally married in the spring of 1952. At their wedding, they kept the celebration extremely simple. With the Five Anti campaign still under way, they had no desire to be accused of extravagance, so they served nothing more than cheap candy and peanuts. They had in attendance only a few friends and no family members—not even her parents from Shanghai or his from the United States. In the absence of their families, the newlyweds started their married life entirely on their own.[80]

Aligning with Allies and against Enemies

Youngest Daughter's marriage out of the Liu family separated her physically and geographically from her relatives, but it by no means provided her with her first opportunities to take the initiative in family life. Even though she was born with the potential disadvantages of her female gender and low rank in the birth order, she showed from an early age that she was far from powerless as she grew up in the Liu family. Unlike her brothers, she did not seek independence for herself by confronting, defying, or arguing with Father. Instead, she persuaded him to give her an education and approve her other proposals by taking advantage of his indulgence toward her and maintaining an alliance with him and her other allies against her enemies in the family.

On the one hand, Youngest Daughter was effective at fending off unwanted attempts to impose authority on her. In wartime Shanghai with Father away, she successfully evaded Mother's attempts to discipline her. In fact, she mounted such staunch resistance that Mother finally surrendered to her, leaving her upbringing in her early teens to Second Son and his wife. Later, when she was in the United States in her late teens and received unwelcome advice from her guardian, Eighth Son, she flatly rejected it and left him feeling angry and defeated. Ultimately he, like Mother before him, capitulated to her and transferred his responsibilities as her guardian to Second Son.

On the other hand, even while tenaciously standing her ground against Mother and Eighth Son, Youngest Daughter painstakingly built up an alliance with Father and Second Son. Before and after the war, she endeared herself to Father, and she persuaded him to grant her most important requests, notably to go to the United States for college during the Chinese civil war and to continue her studies there after the founding of the People's Republic. In Shanghai during the war, she became like a daughter to Second Son and his wife (who were childless), and while in the United States she convinced him to serve as her guardian by letter from China, even though Eighth Son was supposed to hold this position in person.

In a period of war and revolution, Youngest Daughter's success at talking her family into supporting her travel and education demonstrated her extraordinary resourcefulness at forming family alliances and turning them to her advantage. But for all her aggressiveness at fighting for what she wanted, she never questioned her parents' most fundamental rule that required every child who went abroad for an education to return to China and live there permanently. In early 1951, as soon as she began to fear that China and the United States might be cut off from each other, she readily booked passage home. In obeying this rule, she followed the example that had been set by almost all of her older brothers and sisters. Her only sibling who considered disobeying this rule was Eighth Son.

15

———✥———

A Son Who Refused to Return to China

IN THE late 1940s, Eighth Son was available to meet Youngest Daughter and serve as her guardian in the United States because he had been given a second chance to complete his education there. He set out to redeem himself after ending up at McLean Hospital on his first trip. After holding an internship in the United States for one year, from June 1945 to June 1946, he went on to complete his senior year at MIT in 1946–47 and graduate on June 13, 1947.

Up to then, Eighth Son had never questioned Father's long-standing rule that all the Liu children should return home to work in the family business as needed, and at the time, he renewed his promise to obey this rule. But he had already acted contrary to Father's instructions in reapplying to MIT before returning home and being readmitted there before he received his parents' permission to complete his degree. Similarly, he applied to Harvard Business School for the fall of 1947 even though his parents had told him to come home at that time, and he did not inform them of his intentions to remain in the United States until Harvard Business School had already granted him admission. Only after he had his letter of acceptance in hand did he appeal to his parents to support his decision to extend his stay for two more years so that he could earn an MBA before returning home.

Postponing a Return to China

On June 2, 1947, Eighth Son telegraphed Father: "Intend to enter Harvard Business School. October admission obtained. Letter follows!"[1] In the letter that followed, he pointed out how difficult it was to gain admission to Harvard Business School and urged Father to approve and finance his plans to attend. "I secured the admission unexpectedly early on May 28 from Harvard Business School, to which many have failed to gain admission," he proudly reported. "They, I hear, prefer men with a background of technical training and men who have some practical experience." He was delighted that his record had met their standards, and at his interview, he recalled, "I may have appeared to be a forward-looking young man that day." Rather than take all of the credit for overcoming the competition, he gave some to Father, acknowledging: "I have the advantage of being your son, with your worldwide prestige."[2]

To win Father's support, Eighth Son argued that he should be allowed to enter Harvard Business School for both his own sake and the sake of his future in China. "It is very selfish of me," he admitted, "to ask for further education." But he believed that this strong personal interest in his studies was a good thing because it would motivate him to achieve academic success. He had lacked motivation in his earlier years at MIT, and since then he had developed it as he had come to realize what kind of career he wanted to pursue. "I have now great interest in engineering administration," he wrote to Father. "I must have inherited this interest from you."[3]

Eighth Son's reference to his earlier years at MIT might well have reminded Father of Eighth Son's bad psychiatric experience, but he was confident that he was now far better emotionally prepared to pursue his education than he had been earlier. "I assure you," he wrote to Father, "that I find myself much more capable of taking care of myself than I could while I was here for the first time over in this country, 1937. The great enjoyment I now have is really that I have finally a chance to test myself against what I wanted, and get the satisfaction of it."[4] Healthy and energetic, Eighth Son felt primed to accomplish this time what he had failed to do the first time that he had come to the United States.

Besides giving him self-satisfaction, his MBA would also help him serve China, he maintained. "I am making this appeal," he told Father, "because I think it is better for me to be outspoken what I think is best for me, and because I honestly believe by studying administration on top of my technical training, I shall be better equipped to serve my own people." He would be wiser to prepare himself for future service rather than attempt to serve China at the present moment, he pointed out, because of the conditions in China. "Under the present chaos in China," he wrote to Father in June 1947, he could not imagine what he, "even with a world of good intention, can do without falling into either frustration or corruption."[5]

Eighth Son was convinced that he would be better off not returning to China because his friends who were stuck in China had assured him that they and other young Chinese would not hesitate to attend Harvard Business School if they had the chance. "I have discussed with several of my intimate friends [the decision to attend Harvard Business School]," he reported to Father. "They all advise me not to lose this golden opportunity, saying that hundreds of people are waiting to get into Harvard Business School but are unable to obtain admission, and thousands of people are trying to come to this country to study but cannot come out."[6] Already admitted to Harvard and already in the United States on an appropriate visa, Eighth Son took pride in being the envy of students in China.

For all these reasons, he implored Father to let him accept Harvard's offer of admission. "I beg that you trust my sincerity in acquiring further education in Business Administration," he wrote to Father. "Only with your kind permission," he acknowledged, would he be able to carry out this plan.[7]

In reply, Father granted Eighth Son permission to matriculate at Harvard Business School but expressed his preference that his son should come home. On June 25, 1947, as soon as Eighth Son's request for permission to enter Harvard arrived in Shanghai, Father cabled him in Boston:

FINANCE STUDY ABSOLUTELY NO QUESTION
ADVISE RETURN ONLY BECAUSE OF JOB AWAITING AND FOR
YOUR PERSONAL BENEFIT THEREFORE SUGGEST RETURN AFTER
INVESTIGATION ON SPECIFIC PROBLEMS[8]

While Father left no doubt in this telegram that he would finance Eighth Son's education at Harvard Business School, he made clear that he preferred to have him conduct an investigation of "specific problems" in the U.S. wool industry (which he had described in an earlier letter) and come home rather than remain in the United States any

longer. But Eighth Son unhesitatingly set aside Father's other suggestions and promptly cabled back: "DEEPEST GRATITUDE ATTENDING
HARVARD OCTOBER 8."[9]

Even after Eighth Son enrolled at Harvard Business School, Father
regularly reminded him that he had mixed feelings about letting him
stay abroad. "You have studied abroad and done well at it, which gives
me great satisfaction," Father wrote to him from Shanghai on December 3, 1947, near the end of Eighth Son's first semester in business
school. "There are, however, many things that need to be taken care of
here, and I sincerely hope that you can return home as soon as possible
so that you can put your knowledge into practice and offer me a helping
hand."[10]

In early February 1948, as Eighth Son began the second semester
of his first year at Harvard, he wrote home for permission to complete
the second and final year of his MBA in 1948–49. He was eager to continue at Harvard, but he acknowledged that he had been abroad for a
very long time. "It has been six full years since I said goodbye to Mother
in Shanghai," he wrote to his parents on March 2, and he had spent the
last three of those six years in the United States.

> Living in a foreign land, I can't help but long for my homeland, and I
> always think about both of my parents now being past the age of sixty.
> This puts me in a sentimental mood. It is your hard work that has made
> it possible for me to continue my studies here while many of our coun-
> trymen are suffering from starvation. If I have children, I doubt very
> much that they will receive the same education. The recent situation in
> China is so chaotic that it is not possible to predict what's going to hap-
> pen. If I return to China now, what I can do is probably very limited. If
> I want to do well in the future, I must prepare better now.[11]

Even though he missed his aging parents and had already received an
extraordinary education abroad, he pleaded with them to support him
at Harvard for one more year.

While valuing his opportunity to study at Harvard, Eighth Son did
not naively claim that his MBA would immediately qualify him to become a top manager of industrial enterprises in China or would prepare
him to put Harvard's principles of management directly into practice in
Chinese plants. On the contrary, he was well aware that his courses at
Harvard on production, marketing, administration, public relations,
finance, accounting, and statistics were designed for MBAs seeking em-

ployment in the United States, not China. "What I learn about industrial administration at Harvard may not be applicable to our country," he acknowledged to his parents. But he was confident that he could avoid the dangers of American parochialism because "Father has instructed me to rid myself of my shortcomings, hold on to my strong points, and work with humility, and if I can do so, I will not run the risk of being Americanized."[12] After leaving the United States, he planned to rid himself of any trace of Americanization that he had picked up at Harvard Business School by working his way up the employment ladder and acquiring experience on the job in China.

Eighth Son emphasized his willingness to return home and work his way up as part of his plea to Father to pay the tuition for his final year at Harvard Business School. Concerned that Father might withdraw support under the chaotic circumstances of the civil war, Eighth Son wrote: "Father, you seem not to have taken a firm stand about whether I should stop halfway through my studies here. Why don't you set down clear instructions which unequivocally allow me to finish this semester. Then I myself will make the decision regarding the last year, and we will avoid problems resulting from indecisiveness. I hope that Father and all my brothers understand my position. I also hope you will all give me lots of encouragement."[13]

Contrary to Eighth Son's hopes, Father did not take a firm stand in favor of him staying at Harvard. In fact, Father questioned the wisdom of his doing so. "You mentioned in your letter," Father wrote to Eighth Son on February 23, 1948, "that you wish to stay on another year in the U.S. so that you can complete your study at Harvard. It's not a bad idea, but you must also realize that there's no end to learning and that even if one devotes one's entire life to it, one will find that something still remains to be done." Father preferred to have Eighth Son bring his studies to an end and return home as soon as possible. At age sixty, Father wrote, "I am getting old, and I often find it physically difficult to deal with all the demands made on me. Your older brothers have been very helpful, but I still feel we can use more help. I hope you can return as soon as you can to help out."[14] Yet, despite his desire for Eighth Son's speedy return to Shanghai, Father gave permission to let Eighth Son complete his studies at Harvard in 1948–49.

Eighth Son was relieved to receive Father's permission to continue at Harvard, and he accepted it even though it did not come with Father's unequivocal endorsement of the idea. In thanking his parents for giving permission, he acknowledged their eagerness to have him return home, and he promised them that after graduating with his MBA in the spring of 1949, he would immediately return to China and devote himself to serving the Chinese people through the Liu family business. "I only hope," he wrote to Father and Mother on April 4, 1948, "that after returning to China I can be involved in things which will truly benefit the masses of common people so that my life will not be a total waste in the end. For this reason, I have decided to return to China right after my graduation."[15]

To remove lingering doubts about his preference for life in China, he compared it favorably with life in America. "In the quality of life, Shanghai is much better than the United States. After all, we are Chinese, and Father is a person with an outstanding reputation." Not merely Shanghai but all of China was better, Eighth Son maintained. "China's culture is far superior to that of America. In China, if you have sons and grandsons, the older you get, the more blessings you can enjoy. In America, many couples over the age of seventy still have to work hard because their children are scattered around and are not living with them. Even very rich people get lonely in old age."[16] Equating "China's culture" with high-quality family life, Eighth Son committed himself to return home to his family regardless of what government was in power.

In the winter of 1949, on the eve of his final semester at Harvard, he remained unwavering in his commitment to return to China after graduation. Despite the failure of the Nationalist government's gold yuan reform in the fall of 1948 and the Communists' victories in north China in January 1949, Eighth Son wrote from Harvard to his parents in Shanghai: "Even if the situation changes further in China, I still plan to return. It will be far too late if I don't start working right away." At the same time, he began to imagine the possibility that China would be under Communist rule, and he expressed concern about this eventuality (writing in Chinese; inserted English words italicized here):

> I read from the American newspapers that the Communist Party does not intend to give in. China's future will depend on a single roll of the dice. I hope that each party will not be too rigid and will first consider the people's welfare. History has shown that dictatorships always end up in failure. Only the *democratic* endures. Playing a deceptive trick can

only work once. Otherwise, *policy-makers* will use *totalitarian* methods to massacre the common people and *steer the country into destruction*. It only takes a handful of *power or money mongers* to massacre the great majority of the innocent, good people. We must be extremely careful about the future.[17]

These words seem to have come from U.S. newspapers that drew on Cold War rhetoric to identify the Chinese Communist Party with Soviet-style dictatorship and totalitarianism as opposed to American-style democracy and the common people.

While quoting anti-Communist U.S. newspapers, Eighth Son left no doubt that he identified with the Chinese people, not Westerners, and he pledged his allegiance along explicitly racial lines. "We must wake up fast," he urged, calling for an immediate end to the civil war. "Up to now white people have always taken care of white people first. If we Chinese do not unite, we will surely be wiped out." His experience convinced him that racial differences were insurmountable and that he should not stay in the United States because of the racial prejudice he faced there. "After all," he wrote to his parents in January 1949, "we are members of the yellow race, and we have our own high moral standards. Although friends of mine at school have treated me well, it would only be a fantasy to expect equal treatment if I stay on permanently."[18]

In April 1949, as the People's Liberation Army crossed the Yangzi River and prepared to take Shanghai, Eighth Son once again affirmed his intention to go home. He wrote to Eldest Brother in Shanghai: "Father has repeatedly urged me to begin to establish a career and has said that as a Chinese I can only make a limited contribution while abroad so I should return to China immediately after graduation. I fully agree with him."[19]

Even if China underwent a revolution, Eighth Son fully expected that his training at Harvard Business School would assure him a prominent place in his home country. After thanking Eldest Brother for supporting his plans for education at Harvard, he acknowledged that "some others, lacking any real information, have concluded that I will not be able to obtain practical knowledge at HBS. That is unfair. I don't wish to advertise or anything, but when opportunity presents itself, I will help to make clear that even if our society undergoes drastic changes, business administrative techniques will be indispensable. I often read in newspapers that in the Communist controlled areas, technicians, especially those with administrative expertise, are in short supply. China is such a huge country, it can make use of all kinds of people."[20]

Whether in Communist-controlled areas or any other parts of China, he and his family would always be needed and welcomed, he told his brother, as long as they were not carried away by the passionate causes that blind others to harsh realities. "What we should all do is control our emotions and think constructively. . . . We should not be too idealistic. We should be clear about our goals and approach them with a cool head."[21] Yet, even as he claimed that his education and attitude were still suitable for a career in China, he began to question whether he should go back.

Reconsidering a Return to China

In May 1949, with the People's Liberation Army on the verge of taking Shanghai, Eighth Son for the first time expressed his doubts to his parents about whether to come home. He questioned the viability of China's political and economic future under Communist leadership, and he pleaded with his parents for information and advice.

> The policies of the Chinese communists have not appeared to be open and liberal. If the war goes on, the country's economy will collapse, and I am worried about whether or not I can find a job when I come home. But it is not right for a Chinese to stay abroad for too long a period of time. Therefore, I find myself in a predicament of not knowing what to do next. Here information about China is not always reliable so it is very difficult for me to make a decision. You must also be feeling badly about the situation. Still, I'd be very grateful if you could take time to give me your instructions so that I can follow them as guides for my own future.[22]

His parents' guidance, he seemed to say, would ultimately determine his decision about whether to return home.

If he delayed his return to China, he had the option of finding work in the United States. Only a few weeks before his commencement ceremonies were to be held at Harvard Business School, he suggested to his parents: "After I graduate, I can also try in every way to look for employment to support myself here. Then I can wait until the situation becomes stabilized to return to China. That's of course a possibility."[23]

Another possibility was for him to go to Taiwan. "Taiwan is one of China's industrialized areas," he observed to his parents, making no mention of the retreat of Chiang Kai-shek's government to Taiwan, which was under way. "Do you want me to go there?" While seeking his parents' advice, he also gave his own answer to this question. "My thinking," he told them, "is that during such an unstable time, the best thing to do is to go to Taiwan or Hong Kong for a little while, so as to avoid being robbed either by the Chinese communist troops or by the demobilized armies."[24]

In late April and early May 1949, while reading U.S. newspaper reports on the Communist takeover of Shanghai and weighing his options, Eighth Son heard nothing from Father and only discouraging news about poor job prospects in Shanghai from his brothers. He was eager to receive up-to-date instructions from Father, and when none came, he remained willing to follow earlier ones. As he replied to Eldest Brother on May 4, 1949,

> Father has written me several times from Shanghai, urging me to return home. But the situation is very different from a month ago, and I haven't heard from him for quite some time. Also, both you and Second Brother have written to say that I may not find much to do if I return. All this has made it difficult for me to decide what to do next. I will definitely return if there is a job for me. If not, it would seem better to seek employment here first. Time does go by very quickly, and because of that I am eager to return to China to work. I hope you will ask Father what he thinks.[25]

In late May, he finally heard what Father thought.

Writing on May 11, Father explained that he had recently been out of touch because he had been busy dealing with the tense situation in Shanghai. The People's Liberation Army was on the verge of taking the city. Father wrote to Eighth Son: "The fighting is approaching Shanghai's suburbs, and gunfire can already be heard even in the downtown area. The government has been trying to evacuate the civilian population, but transportation has become tied up. Those who can leave are long gone, and those who can't are sitting and waiting."[26]

The Nationalist government and local organizations in the city were desperately trying to make preparations for an invasion and counted on Father to play a leading role in them. "I am also president of the National Chinese Association of Industries, and there is much business to attend to in this Association. Since many Executive Committee members have left Shanghai, I can find no one to whom to delegate authority, so colleagues in the Association have persuaded me to remain in Shanghai. Also, owing to the current intense situation, authorities in the military and the local government have summoned me every day for consultation. I have either been running around or sitting at meetings. Further, since your mother has no intention of leaving Shanghai, all I can do is wait to see what comes next."[27] Whether Father voluntarily attended to business or involuntarily came under surveillance, he was unquestionably busy.

In the midst of his other work, Father found time to reply to Eighth Son, and he sent pragmatic advice that allowed for contingencies. "With respect to your plans after graduation, I have considered them from a number of angles. It would be all right for you to remain in America to work, but being Chinese, you would ultimately find it more meaningful to work in your own country. When returning, if the situation in Shanghai proves to be too chaotic, you should stay in Hong Kong for a while. When the time comes, I will be writing to let you know what steps to take."[28] In giving this advice, Father implied that he would be in Shanghai when Eighth Son reached Hong Kong and apparently assumed that he would reside permanently in Shanghai with his wife and family. But less than two weeks later Father himself left Shanghai and headed south, first to Guangzhou and then to Hong Kong.

Moving to Hong Kong

In June 1949 Eighth Son graduated from Harvard Business School, and at first he was reluctant to follow Father's advice that he should move to Hong Kong because he felt confident that he would easily land a good job in the United States. But after a few weeks of surveying the U.S. job market, he came up empty-handed, and his confidence waned. "I have now graduated from Harvard Business School," he wrote to Father. "Everyone would be very happy in my position as told by the way they congratulated me but I feel very heavy at heart. I feel more insecure and uncertain after my graduation for not being able to find anything permanent and anyone to work for."[29]

Eighth Son reacted emotionally to his failure to find a job even though he recognized that he was one of many recent graduates victimized by a sudden downturn in the U.S. economy. "It could not be more unopportune to be graduating this summer," he lamented to Father. "American business has definitely lapsed into a recession. One has to know someone to get a decent job."[30] On June 12 he wrote to Father: "Now I realize that I may have made the wrong decision to apply for a job to remain in this country." Besides facing a job shortage, he suffered from guilt for having led a protected life in the United States while the rest of his family endured the hardships of civil war and revolution in China. He wrote to Father: "I cannot enjoy staying in this country, remaining as an escapist."[31]

By the end of June, he was ready to leave for Hong Kong if Father would reconfirm his support for this plan. "Please let me know whether you still advise me to return to Hongkong or not," he wrote. Desperate for work, he bluntly asked: "What kind of assistance can you give me in getting a job either in China or in America?" No longer stalling for time or postponing his trip home, he assured Father that he would come without hesitation. "I am ready to come straight home if there is something useful I can do, on which I can earn a living but not by participating in a civil war. Please let me know also if you want me to find my own way out in this country. The present suspense is really almost unbearable."[32]

Father broke the suspense for Eighth Son by sending him two answers: first a quick one and then a promise of help. The quick one came by telegram and was a direct order: "RETURN VIA HONGKONG." It was followed by a letter in which Father offered to meet face-to-face and work out a plan to his son's satisfaction. "I have given thought to your problem for some time and have been trying to thrash it out. I think you will come straight to Hongkong where I expect to greet you. Then we can talk things out and see what is the best I can do for you."[33] Whatever the final outcome would be, Father left no doubt that the first step should be for Eighth Son to come back to Asia. In closing, he added: "Looking forward to your early return home."[34]

Following these instructions, Eighth Son immediately began booking his passage from the United States to Hong Kong, and he assured Father: "I have made up my mind to return and like to stick to my principle of working and living in China, and of sharing the responsibilities of our people."[35] On July 27, 1949, he departed from the United States with his traveling companion, P. Y. Chao (Zhao), who had been his classmate and fraternity brother at MIT. They ended up taking a four-month journey via Canada, Europe, and the Suez Canal, and along the way, Eighth Son wrote Father anxious letters inquiring about the fate of the family. On November 17, he mailed one from Colombo, Ceylon (Sri Lanka), that expressed his doubts and fears. "I have been wondering all this time about your future plan of action. I have the understanding that all my brothers and sisters are in Shanghai. I have been trying to get hold of newspapers whenever I am in port in order to inform myself since I have been on board M/S 'Bengal' from Genoa. The last news I got from Radio was that plane service between Hongkong and Peiping [Beijing] had been resumed. I suppose those at Shanghai have trouble to come to Hongkong."[36]

Even if Liu family members found a way to emigrate to Hong Kong, Eighth Son was afraid they would not be safe from the Communists there. In mid-November, a month after the People's Liberation Army had occupied Guangzhou and six weeks after the People's Republic had been officially founded, he wrote to Father: "I don't see how we Chinese can maintain ourselves in Hongkong much longer since the Communists took over Canton [Guangzhou] and the surrounding territories."[37]

Despite his apprehension, Eighth Son followed Father's instructions, proceeding to Hong Kong with the intention of living and working there. Before leaving the United States, he had mailed all of his belongings to Father's office in Hong Kong, and in anticipation of his arrival, he expressed his expectations that he would be given a job there. "I hope," he wrote to Father from the M/S *Bengal* at sea in November 1949, "that you can soon put me to work in Hongkong or anywhere near you so that I can be useful to you and learn from your experience."[38] Little did he know when he wrote these words that by the time he reached Hong Kong, Father would already have left there.

Summoned to Shanghai

Before Eighth Son reached Hong Kong, he expected to find Father and possibly the whole Liu family there. Instead, he discovered that Father had departed for Shanghai and had left a message telling him to do the same. In a quandary, Eighth Son moved into the Hong Kong hotel room Father had vacated and began to receive telephone calls from

Shanghai. He heard repeatedly from Second Son, who insisted that he should return to Shanghai and rejoin the family there. But Eighth Son was upset with Father for leaving Hong Kong before his arrival, and he was reluctant to enter China now that it was under Communist rule. Not until he was summoned by Father did he consider returning to Shanghai.

On December 17, 1949, Father wrote to him that Shanghai was the place where all of the Lius should be. "Since liberation [in 1949], everything in our country has returned to normal. The corruption and decadence of the old days have been wiped out entirely. The army's discipline is especially impressive. It is the first we've seen in the republican period [since 1911]. Although life is still hard at the moment, people from all walks of life are working diligently to overcome difficulties. It is generally believed that great hope lies ahead. I share this view. At home, everything is fine."[39]

Besides giving the new government this blanket endorsement, Father specified the exact role Eighth Son should play under its leadership. During the Sino-Japanese War of 1937–1945, Father had appointed Eighth Son to a job in one of his woolen mills in southwest China, and now he proposed that he should pick up where he had left off by taking a position as a wool specialist in northwest China. Setting a tone that combined the personal with the professional, Father wrote to Eighth Son:

> You are going to turn thirty this year, and your mother hopes very much that you will return home to celebrate this birthday. With regard to trends in industry and commerce, the emphasis will be on self-reliance. Foreign imports will include only that equipment necessary for production purposes. Consumer goods will definitely not be allowed to come in. Wool is on the list of prohibited imports. Therefore, I am now joining those involved in Shanghai's woolen industry to find ways to purchase raw materials from various locations in the northwest to meet the needs of each of the mills here. You have acquired special expertise in this area, and after you return to Shanghai, you will definitely not be short of work to do. I very much hope you will soon return to assist me.

Father also instructed Eighth Son to bring with him Fifth and Seventh Sons, who had been sent to Taiwan in the late 1940s and were the only other sons still abroad. These two should immediately move to Hong

Kong and then come with Eighth Son to Shanghai, Father told him, "so that we can all have a joyous family reunion together."[40]

In response, Eighth Son did not take his fifth and seventh brothers to Shanghai, but he did make the trip himself in February 1950 for Chinese New Year. In Shanghai, he had a happy reunion with Mother, who had always favored him and had faithfully corresponded with him but had not seen him for more than seven years—ever since he had left Shanghai in 1942 and gone first to Chongqing, 1942–1945, and then to the United States, 1945–1949.

With his father and brothers, his relations were not so cordial, especially on the question whether he should move permanently to China and live and work under Communism. Father again offered him a position as a wool specialist in northwest China, and Eldest Son tried to interest him in working at a plant that made powdered eggs in central China. Second and Sixth Sons also wanted him to stay in China, but they did not show such high respect for his training. In fact, they questioned whether it had prepared him to take any job. His education at Harvard Business School had been "very reactionary," they told him, so he should begin his life in socialist China by undergoing "reeducation." Only Fourth Son advised him to return to Hong Kong. By doing so, he would be able to satisfy himself and at the same time provide the Lius with a representative outside Shanghai in accordance with the family's time-tested strategy of "not putting all their eggs in one basket." After spending two months in China, Eighth Son seized on Fourth Son's advice and took the train from Shanghai back to Hong Kong.[41]

Once Eighth Son had returned to Hong Kong, Father continued to insist that he as well as Fifth and Seventh Sons should come to live permanently in China and expressed mounting frustration with them for refusing to do so. He was particularly impatient with Eighth Son for arguing that life under Communism would be intolerable because it would deprive him of his freedom. On March 28, 1950, Father wrote to Eighth Son in Hong Kong:

> I read your letter dated the 20th and learned that you are afraid our country lacks freedom of thought, and you think it would be better to stay abroad. This attitude has resulted from egocentrism plus the influence of bogus international propaganda, so you do not know the truth, you vacillate, and you cannot make a decision. You are already thirty

years old, and your viewpoint may be different from that of someone
over sixty like myself, but we can arrive at the same view if we study
the facts carefully.[42]

To bring Eighth Son around to "the same view" on the issue of freedom, Father challenged Eighth Son's assumption that freedom existed
in the United States, Hong Kong, and preliberation Shanghai. "The so-
called freedom [in these places], if examined realistically, is completely
false," Father contended.

   While in the United States, Father claimed, Eighth Son had become
imbued with the wrong ideas about freedom because of his special circumstances in residence there. "You went abroad too early," he recalled
with regret, referring to Eighth Son's first trip to the United States in
1937 at age sixteen. "There wasn't any older person in America to consult, so you had to deal with all matters exclusively on the basis of your
own ideas. Gradually you have come to doubt your father's and your
elder brothers' guidance." As Eighth Son had pulled away from his father and brothers, he had fallen under the sway of American propaganda. "You stayed in America for a long time and were influenced by
American propaganda, so your prejudices have become deeply rooted
and cannot be changed right away." If Eighth Son would critically assess American propaganda and free himself from American prejudices,
then he would be able to see that America lacked freedom, especially
for Chinese and blacks. "In America," Father told his U.S.-educated son,
"both the Chinese and the black people have their residential areas
restricted. They cannot freely choose where to live. When the Chinese
enter U.S. territory, they are subjected to all kinds of abusive treatment
that is heartbreaking."[43]

   By comparison with the United States, Father noted, Hong Kong
"may be a place that has more freedom," but any freedom there for
Chinese was undercut by British colonial rule. Based on his recent
experience, he observed: "In Hong Kong, our fellow countrymen who
have taken up residence may think that they have all kinds of freedom in whoring, gambling, and excessive eating and drinking. But
when it comes to conducting legitimate business—say, in international trade through shipping companies—the chairmen of the boards
of directors and the chief executive officers must all be Englishmen or

of some other foreign nationality." Even vaunted Anglo-Saxon law did not give Chinese freedom in Hong Kong, Father explained, because "the British laws used in the courtroom are designed to protect bad elements in the society for the sake of ensuring the continued prosperity of Hong Kong, so those Chinese who now consider Hong Kong to be a comfortable nest are as pitiful as I was before I traveled abroad and came to realize that I had lost my freedom [in preliberation Shanghai]."[44]

In preliberation Shanghai, Father admitted, he and other Chinese had grown up with the belief that they had freedom, and he had not realized that this belief was an illusion until 1927, when he was nearly forty years old. In old Shanghai, as he now remembered it,

> the speech and movements of high-class Chinese living inside the foreign concessions were all controlled by the foreign police, but they themselves didn't realize it. I myself grew up in the foreign concessions, and at first I, too, was not conscious of the loss of freedom. But when I traveled to Europe and America in 1927, I saw that all the public parks in their countries allowed everyone to enter freely, and yet the public parks in Shanghai's foreign concessions still had a prominently posted public notice that read "Dogs and Chinese Not Admitted." I then suddenly woke up to the fact that Europeans and Americans have not treated the Chinese right.[45]

In both Shanghai and Hong Kong, Father charged, privileged Westerners and corrupt Chinese officials deprived the Chinese people of freedom. "You ought to know," he told Eighth Son,

> that Europeans and Americans occupied Shanghai and Hong Kong and amassed great fortunes under the protection of unequal treaties with all kinds of special privileges. The abnormal prosperity of Hong Kong and Shanghai is also attributable to Chinese officials' corruption and ineptitude and to the people's ignorance, lack of a world view, and obsession with comfort and pleasure. I'm sure you understand fully the indisputable fact that these people have been blind to the widespread poverty and the declining standard of living throughout our country.[46]

Such myopic leaders would never give the Chinese people a chance to experience genuine freedom, Father argued, and he concluded that the leaders of the People's Republic were succeeding in transforming China precisely because they did not have this blind spot.

"It's been over five months since I returned here to Shanghai," Father reminded Eighth Son, writing in March 1950, "and I can see with my own eyes that Shanghai since liberation is much different than before." The revolutionaries, according to his observation, took away freedom only from those who deserved to lose it and not from anyone else. "The Communists conduct themselves with attentiveness and restraint. Everywhere they emphasize practicality, and they always seek to achieve a thorough understanding. There is no corruption and no show of personal favors. People are prohibited from concealing wrongdoing, and they do not dare break the law. Tax evaders and law breakers have lost their freedom, but law-abiding people do not feel any so-called 'lack of freedom.' "[47]

After making his case, Father once again gave assurances that he would find a suitable position for Eighth Son in China's woolen industry—as long as he was willing to embrace the principles and adopt the point of view Father espoused.

> If you agree with all the points I've made above, if you are willing to change your thinking, and if you resolutely decide to return to our country to serve in productive enterprises, I will be sure to shoulder the responsibility of finding you a suitable position either in the private sector or in a joint public-private enterprise in the northwest. You once learned to evaluate wool samples in an American woolen mill, and now you can put your ability to great use. I have high hopes for you.[48]

Father's impassioned arguments and expressions of high hopes for Eighth Son did not persuade him (or Fifth or Seventh Sons) to move back to China. By then, Eighth Son considered himself independent. Less than a decade earlier, while enrolled at MIT, he had lamented that he was incapable of achieving independence as a mature adult, and after being diagnosed as a victim of depression and spending nine miserable months in a psychiatric hospital, he had returned home lacking in self-confidence and willing to leave all decisions about his future in his family's hands. But now, after making his second trip to the United States, completing his degrees at MIT and Harvard, and landing his first major job in Hong Kong, he stood his ground and refused to move back to China even under Father's direct orders. By making this decision, he seemed prepared to separate himself from his family members permanently. But as it turned out, his separation from them proved to be very brief.

Coming Home Involuntarily

In December 1951, after Father's letters to Eighth Son had failed to achieve their intended effect, Sixth Son traveled from Shanghai to Hong Kong and resorted to more drastic measures to bring Eighth Son home. Ostensibly, Sixth Son made the trip to attend the wedding of his wife's sister. He and his wife had no difficulty securing permission to leave China because Sixth Son had been a member of the Chinese Communist Party since the 1930s, and he had demonstrated his unwavering loyalty to the new government of the People's Republic since it was founded in 1949.

On December 29, 1951, after attending the wedding at St. Andrew's Church and the reception in the posh Peninsula Hotel, Sixth and Eighth Sons met to discuss family matters.[49] In age they were close—thirty-six and thirty-one—and between 1945 and 1947, while in their twenties, they had come to know each other particularly well during their internships with businesses in the United States. Since they had not seen each other for more than two years, they brought each other up to date. Eighth Son proudly described his work as a sales engineer with the Swiss-owned Overseas Trading Company, offering proof that his brothers in Shanghai had been wrong when they had warned him that he would never find a job in Hong Kong. For his part, Sixth Son discussed the Liu family's life in China.

At the climax to his report on the family, Sixth Son dramatically revealed his most important news: Mother, age sixty-four, was gravely ill and wanted Eighth Son at her bedside. Both men knew that this news was particularly poignant for Eighth Son because Mother had doted on him during his childhood, and she had faithfully corresponded with him throughout his long sojourns: first in the United States, 1937–1941, then in Chongqing and other inland cities, 1942–1945, and most recently in the United States again, 1945–1949, and Hong Kong, 1950–1951.

Deeply concerned about Mother's health, Eighth Son packed his bags and joined his sixth brother and sister-in-law on their return trip to Shanghai. But they had barely crossed the Hong Kong–China border before Sixth Son confessed that he had lied. In Shenzhen, at the Luohu Railway Station, as the brothers carried their bags from their Hong Kong train to their Shanghai-bound one, Sixth Son assured his brother that their mother was not ill and admitted that he had said so only to lure his brother back to China. On hearing the truth, Eighth Son was stunned and dropped his suitcases, sending them crashing onto the station platform. At that moment and from then on, he was desperately eager to leave China, but he was not able to secure permission to do so for the next twenty-seven years. In 1979, when he finally had the chance to leave, he emigrated from the People's Republic, moving permanently to the United States.[50]

16

Parents' Deaths and Children's Dispersal

IN THE early 1950s, with most of their family living near them in Shanghai, Father and Mother could look back on more than forty years of marriage and take satisfaction in their children's record at carrying out their original plan at least to the extent of following their three cardinal rules: first, to return to Shanghai after being educated abroad; second, to work in the family business when needed; and third, not to marry foreigners.[1] But by then Father and Mother were in their midsixties, and they began to lose their ability to pursue their long-term goals of uniting their family and preserving their business dynasty. With their children they became less influential, not only because they weakened and suffered from ill health but also because they ceased to live together.

The Parents' Separation

In their last years, Father and Mother were not divorced, but they lived wholly separate lives. Their separation occurred after they attempted to live together with He Guiying, the woman who had been Father's mistress since the 1930s. Between the end of the war in 1945 and 1953, Father had lived with Mother in the Liu family home and had kept secret from her the fact that he continued to maintain for He the same separate residence he had bought for her before the war. Father undoubtedly had some trepidation about resuming this pattern because it had not always permitted him to avoid conflicts with Mother during the prewar period. Nonetheless, he resolved to continue his life with both women, one publicly and one secretly, on the premise that Mother would not tolerate the idea of living together with him and his mistress under one roof.

For eight years, 1945–1953, Father led two family lives, one with Mother and the other with He Guiying. This plan did not unravel until he fell ill with heart trouble and failed to see He or deliver her regular stipend, so she came in person to the Liu home looking for him and met Mother for the first time. Mother graciously welcomed her into the house, and they had a pleasant conversation in which He subtly but clearly let it be known that she was Father's mistress. Mother was favorably impressed with He's charming manners and disarming personal style, and she offered to let He take Father to her home and nurse him back to health. Acknowledging Mother's kindness, He declined the offer and proposed that she should instead stay in the Liu home and help Mother with Father. The two women agreed on this arrangement, with He sleeping in Mother's bedroom, not with Father.[2]

During Father's recovery, He remained in the Liu home and continued to spend time with Mother as well as Father. The three of them ate at the same table, took walks in the garden, and appeared together at social occasions. But this cordial triangle did not last. From the time of He's arrival in the family home, the Lius' sons had objected to her presence there, and Fourth Son, who had known He in Chongqing, was particularly skeptical of her motives and critical of her behavior. The other eldest sons joined him in pleading with Father to move He out of the family home, and they refused to attend any social gathering where she was present.

Eventually Mother turned against He. She heard from her sons or saw with her own eyes that He treated Father in ways Mother regarded as outrageous. She sat on Father's lap and peeled oranges for him, feeding them to him one section at a time. She played with Father in the garden, running on her unbound feet as they launched a kite into the air and flew it high in the sky. She joined him in the bath and scrubbed his back. Always at his beck and call, she performed these and other tasks that seemed to Mother to be at best childish and at worst lewd. Out of Mother's earshot, He dared to call herself Father's "resistance-war wife" [a self-characterization that was also used by other women who had lived with married Shanghai men in Chongqing during the war]. Perhaps even more disturbing, Father referred to He as his "wife" (*tata* in Shanghainese, the equivalent of *taitai* in Mandarin)—the same term of endearment he used to refer to Mother.[3]

Ultimately, Mother lost her temper. Confronting He upstairs in the house, she accused her of improper behavior and slapped her so hard in the face that she fell to the floor. Momentarily He considered leaping to her feet and fighting back against Mother, who was thirty years her elder and seemingly frail, but Fourth Son emerged from his room and joined them when he heard the commotion. Standing next to Mother and glowering down on He, he was as incensed with He for her intrusion into the Lius' family as he had been during the war. Looking up at the two of them, He put aside any thoughts of retaliating and promptly moved out of the Liu home and back into the house Father had earlier bought for her.[4]

After the confrontation between Mother and He Guiying, Father and Mother separated. Father moved into He Guiying's house with her and their son, and Mother moved into Second Son's home. Mother's psychological condition, which had been delicate and unstable throughout her life, markedly deteriorated. Meanwhile, the eldest sons in the family, who had been critical of He Guiying's behavior at Chongqing during the war, continued to exclude her and her son from relations with any member of the Liu family other than Father. Father and Mother remained in these separate residences during the last years of their lives.[5]

The Parents' Deaths

Separated from his wife, Father also became separated from his businesses in the years before he died. In October 1953, he heard the Communist Party's call for the "transition to socialism" at the first meeting of China's National Federation of Industry and Commerce. According to Fourth Son, he immediately lent his approval to the idea, and the Liu family's companies were subsequently transformed into "joint public-private enterprises" in early 1956. Asked at the time about his loss of ownership and managerial authority, Father told Fourth Son that he had no regrets. According to Fourth Son, he felt grateful to the Communist Party for the nationalization of his enterprises because it had relieved him of his two greatest fears: bankruptcy in his lifetime and a fight within his family over his property after his death. In his last days, Fourth Son said, Father was comfortable living on a state pension of 5 percent of the value of his enterprises, which were assessed at 20 million yuan in 1956. On his deathbed, he told Fourth Son that all his children in China should divide his pension equally among themselves after his death, and then they should voluntarily return a portion to the state as a token of Father's appreciation for the Communist Party.[6]

It seems unlikely that Father was quite as sanguine and serene in 1956 as he is portrayed above by Fourth Son, especially in light of all that he and his family had recently been through: the upheavals during the revolution, the humiliations during the Five Anti campaign, the losses of ownership of and managerial authority over the family business during the transition to socialism. It seems more likely that after devoting his life to the founding of a business dynasty, he was disappointed to see in his final years that his family firm would not outlive him.

Whatever final pronouncements Father may have made on the fate of his businesses, he did not speak his last words to Mother or their children. On September 30, 1956, he had He Guiying bring Fourth Son to him for a brief conversation, and the next day, October 1, 1956—the day China celebrated the seventh anniversary of the founding of the People's Republic—he died of heart failure at age sixty-eight. On the last day of his life, the only person with him was his mistress.[7]

Father's funeral was conducted on a grand scale. It was held at the Wangguo Funeral Home, Shanghai's biggest mortuary. The entire building was reserved for the occasion, and crowds formed around it, causing the police to block off the surrounding streets. All of China's top leaders in Beijing—including Mao Zedong, Zhou Enlai, and Liu Shaoqi—sent flowers and eulogies. Shanghai's leading officials attended in person, and Ke Qingshi, representing Shanghai's Government Council under Mayor Chen Yi, read the official eulogies aloud.[8]

Prominent people from outside the government were also in attendance, with Father's children and grandchildren leading the way. As Buddhist monks played bamboo flutes and Buddhist nuns chanted, the mourners filed by Father's coffin, which had a glass cover and was open for the viewing of his body. Some members of the Liu family wept, and as they emerged from the funeral home, people in the crowd threw them handkerchiefs for drying their eyes. Father's body was then cremated, and his ashes were kept in a box. Later, the family observed the custom of honoring the deceased by meeting forty-nine days after the death, when they had a meal together at Gongdelin Restaurant, the best vegetarian restaurant in Shanghai.[9]

Mother did not attend Father's funeral, and she was never informed of his death. During the last years before Father died, she was considered by her family to be mentally ill and was confined to a room in Second Son's home. A high bamboo fence was built around the house so that Mother would not fall, jump, or escape, and at her most unstable moments, she was strapped down under restraints. In these quarters, she retained her most trusted servants, and on June 24, 1960, the night before she died, she asked one of her servants whether she was "a nice person." Her servant replied, "Yes, you are." She then had her servant make up two beds, one for herself and one for Father (whom she thought was still alive), and she had her servant sleep in Father's bed while Mother slept in her own. The next morning her servant discovered that she had died peacefully in her sleep.

Mother's funeral was modest compared to Father's. Her children and grandchildren were there, but no officials were in attendance, no crowds came to watch, and no streets were blocked off. Like Father, she had an open casket so that her family members could see her as they filed by and paid their last respects. Her body, like her husband's, was cremated.[10]

Throughout their long marriage, Mother and Father had planned to keep their family united and bequeath a dynasty to their children. While she had dreamed of gathering together her children and grandchildren under one roof, he had trained his sons to take over the family firm. But if, as late as the early 1950s, they held out hope that they might preside over a smooth succession, they lost all such hope in the last years of their lives. Their separation ended their joint management of the family, and even before their deaths, some of their children began to leave China.

The Children Who Left China

By the time Father died in 1956, three sons had already emigrated from China, and eventually the majority of the Liu children ended up abroad. Leaving China permanently, these members of the family took no interest in reuniting the family, reviving the family firm in Shanghai, or reconstituting family connections for business purposes anywhere else.

As early as 1947, when the family was considering Taiwan as a "back way out," Seventh Son was sent to preside over the family's in-

vestments there, and in 1949 Fifth Son joined him in Taipei. Both of
them were surprised by Father's decision to return from Hong Kong to
Shanghai in November 1949, and Fifth Son, who had accompanied Father from Shanghai to Hong Kong in May 1949, was deeply shaken by
it. When news of Father's move reached Taiwan, Fifth and Seventh
Sons were investigated by the Nationalist government, which considered Father's return to the People's Republic to be an act of treason and
branded him "Liu the Bandit." Already upset by Father's decision, Fifth
Son became psychologically disturbed when soldiers from the Nationalist army interrogated him and searched his home, and he never fully
recovered from this ordeal. Fifth and Seventh Sons lived the rest of
their lives in Taiwan, and they managed to hold onto the Lius' property
there, but they did not go into business with other members of the Liu
family, and none of their brothers or sisters ever settled in Taiwan.[11]

If Fifth and Seventh Sons were the first of the Lius to emigrate
from China, Eldest Son was the first to emigrate from the People's Republic. In 1951, before the new government began to place severe restrictions on travel, he left Shanghai abruptly, taking his wife and telling no one. (He had no children.) In Hong Kong he took a job at China
Wool Manufacturing Company, which had been founded by Father in
Shanghai but had come under the ownership of the Lius' former business associate Cheng Nianpeng in Hong Kong. Eldest Son was criticized
by his brothers in Shanghai for working with Cheng, who, in their estimation, had wrongly appropriated the Lius' technology from China
Wool without seeking their permission or giving them proper compensation. Eldest Son soon resigned from this post and emigrated to the
United States. As a young man he had received his education at Baldwin-
Wallace College, Harvard, and the University of Pennsylvania, and now
at age forty he took up residence first in Los Angeles and later in Washington, D.C. Even before he left China, he had begun developing business interests independent of the Liu family, and after reaching the
United States, he never collaborated with his brothers and sisters in
business.[12]

Between Eldest Son's departure from China in 1951 and the late
1970s, very few Chinese were allowed to emigrate from the People's
Republic, but in these years three members of the Liu family arranged
to leave the country. In 1960 Eldest Daughter and her husband, Xue
Diyi, received exit permits and emigrated to Hong Kong, where she lived

with Xue until she died of cancer in 1971 at age fifty-three. In 1976 her husband moved to the United States, where he lived the remainder of his long life, not dying until 2004 at the age of 103. The couple had worked in their own businesses and remained independent of the Liu family firm since Father had disinherited Eldest Daughter in 1936, and after leaving China, they made no attempt to cooperate in business with her brothers and sisters.[13]

In 1962, Third Son emigrated to Hong Kong. He was already divorced from his first wife, Liane, who had lived in the United States since 1949, but she helped arrange for his emigration and the eventual emigration of their three sons. Third Son lived in Hong Kong until his death in 1995. His income there came from the liquidation of Great China Match Company, which he and Father had established in Hong Kong during the Sino-Japanese War. He shared the proceeds from the sale with co-investors in the company, but he did not restore the family firm as a financial unit or economic enterprise, and he did not go into business with any of his brothers or sisters.[14]

Also in 1962, Youngest Daughter, with her husband, Zhang Qinshi, and their four sons, left China to visit Zhang's parents in Hong Kong. They had ample opportunity to remain there because Zhang's father, a leading figure at the World Bank, had lined up a job for Zhang, and Youngest Daughter linked up with Eldest Daughter. But Zhang was still imbued with an idealistic commitment to Communism that he had retained ever since his return from the United States to China in 1951, and he took his family with him from Hong Kong back to Beijing in 1962. With the coming of the Cultural Revolution (1966–1976), he and Youngest Daughter lived to regret this decision. In 1970 the entire family was sent to live and work in a village in central China near Wuhan, where they endured much greater hardships than Youngest Daughter had suffered after moving from Shanghai to Beijing in 1951 and 1952.[15]

After three years in the countryside, 1970–1973, Youngest Daughter and Zhang returned to Beijing and decided to take advantage of his family's offer to help them emigrate. For them the time was right because in 1972 President Richard Nixon had made his trip to China as a first step toward normalization of relations between the United States and China, opening the way for Zhang's father to begin the process of obtaining Chinese passports and U.S. visas for Youngest Daughter's family. In 1976, Youngest Daughter and Zhang emigrated from China permanently, and by 1978 their four sons had all joined them in the United States.[16]

One year later, in 1979, Eighth Son emigrated from China at long last, after yearning to do so for twenty-seven years. Ironically, just as he and Youngest Daughter had lived near each other in the United States in the 1940s, they again took up residence near each other thirty years later. Over time they had both changed. In the 1940s they had been in their twenties, and their trip abroad had been sponsored and financed by their family. He attended MIT and Harvard Business School, she went to Pine Manor, the Garland School, and Michigan State University, and they both aspired to make contributions to the Liu family in China. In the late 1970s, by contrast, they were in their fifties, and they were sponsored by their spouses' families. Like their brothers and sisters who had emigrated, they had no ties to the Liu family business. With no plans for living in China ever again, they both settled in California. Eighth Son died there at ninety-one in 2012, and Youngest Daughter—the last surviving member of the family—still lives there.[17]

The Children Who Stayed in China

The three sons who lived out their lives in China—Second, Fourth, and Sixth Sons—were leaders in their generation of the family and the family firm before 1949, and each became prominent in the People's Republic. But none of them pulled the family back together or revived the family business.

Of all the Liu children, Second Son made the most concerted effort to reunite the family in Shanghai at the time of the Communist Revolution, and his life came to the most tragic end. In 1949, he was the one who traveled from Shanghai to Hong Kong not once but twice to coax Father into coming home, and in the 1950s, he, like Father, became an active political figure under Communist rule in Shanghai. In the 1950s and early 1960s, he held official posts in the All-China Federation of Industry and Commerce and was a delegate from Shanghai to the National People's Congress. In his political life, he became well known for his unofficial connections as well as his official ones. But whatever efforts he made to preserve the Lius as a capitalist family in Shanghai were cut short during the Cultural Revolution. While all the Lius who were still in China suffered during the Cultural Revolution, Second

Son was singled out as a prime target, and he and Fourth Son were shown on television and publicly denounced as capitalists. On December 28, 1967, after being hounded by his attackers, Second Son fell from the top of the Enterprise Building (Qiye lou), an eight-story office building that had been constructed near the Shanghai Bund by Father in 1933 and used by the family ever since. Whether Second Son jumped or was pushed, he plunged to his death.[18]

Fourth Son managed to survive the Cultural Revolution, and he kept a low profile in China until he came into political prominence in the 1980s. After Mao Zedong's death and Deng Xiaoping's triumph over the leaders of the Cultural Revolution in 1976, Deng launched reforms that led to opportunities for Fourth Son to become a model capitalist under Communism. As early as 1980, he was recruited at age sixty-eight to lead a delegation of former Chinese capitalists on a mission to Hong Kong, and in the 1980s and 1990s he rose to a high position in the Chinese People's Consultative Conference and served as a representative at the National People's Congress. But he did not reunite the Liu family or revive the family firm at Shanghai. In fact, he moved to Beijing in 1980 and lived there until his death on March 26, 2003. After he died, even though he had been a capitalist and not a member of the Communist Party, his family received condolences from China's former president Jiang Zemin and other Communist leaders, and his ashes were deposited near Beijing at Babaoshan, a site normally reserved for Communists who are heroes of the revolution.[19]

Sixth Son, a member of the Communist Party since the late 1930s, also made his home in the People's Republic in Beijing, moving there to assume an official post at the Ministry of Industry in 1956. Like Second and Fourth Sons, he was attacked in the late 1960s during the Cultural Revolution. When he and his family were labeled capitalists and persecuted by Red Guards, he did not try to save himself or his family by revealing his membership in the Communist Party. His fellow party members tried to protect him by intimating to Red Guards that he had long served as an underground agent for the revolution, but when these Red Guards followed up and demanded to know whether he belonged to the party, he denied it, honoring his pledge of secrecy even under attack.[20]

Not until 1972 did Sixth Son make his party membership public.[21] Even then, he refused to accept a car, preferential housing, and other privileges as a party member. Later, when he fell ill, he was offered

treatment at the best hospital in Beijing because of his party membership, but he declined the offer, preferring to be admitted to a common
hospital like any ordinary patient. Apparently receiving poor care, he
died in 1988 at the age of seventy-two. He was honored as a hero of
the revolution, and his ashes, like Fourth Son's, were deposited at Babaoshan in Beijing. A dedicated Communist to the very end, Sixth Son
refused to take any of the inheritance Father had left, and he objected
on principle to any proposal for reviving the family firm or participating in any form of capitalist enterprise under socialism.[22]

Middle Daughter, like Fourth and Sixth Sons, stayed in China and
moved away from Shanghai. She lived along China's northern border
at Zhangjiakou until 1962. At that time, Third Son left Shanghai for
Hong Kong, and she moved into his Shanghai apartment. She was the
only member of her generation of Lius to have been a permanent resi-
dent of Shanghai after Fourth Son moved to Beijing in 1980, but her
home did not become a base for reuniting the Liu family or reviving the
Liu family firm. She died in Shanghai in January 2009.[23]

As these brief profiles of the Lius all show, they did not sustain
their family as a cohesive unit and their family firm as a capitalist enterprise in or outside China beyond the death of the patriarch in 1956.
Father and Mother had raised their family and established their business with the hope and expectation that their children would live and
work together and perpetuate a business dynasty. In the 1930s, 1940s,
and early 1950s, they made an impressive start by educating their children at leading academic institutions in the capitalist world and by devising successful survival strategies for keeping their family together
and operating their business even during tumultuous events—the
Sino-Japanese War, the Chinese civil war, and the early years of the
People's Republic. But no matter how well the Liu family had prepared
for the future and adapted when encountering unforeseen dangers, the
second generation of Lius did not preserve the family's unity or sustain
its business inside or outside Mao's China.

The Liu family and its family firm were radically transformed during the history of the People's Republic. Especially after the father's death
and the nationalization of the family's businesses in 1956, the sons and
daughters gave priority to their separate nuclear families over their natal family, pursued careers outside the family firm, and made decisions
without close consultation with brothers, sisters, and other Lius. If we

confine the history of the Liu family to the period after 1956, it points to the inescapable conclusion that the family was fundamentally changed by political pressures brought to bear on it. But if we take a longer view of the history of the family, do we find that it began to change earlier, during the first half of the twentieth century? This question arises as we reflect on the relevance of the Lius' experience to issues in Chinese family history.

—◆—

Conclusion

The Inner History of a Chinese Family

IN RECENT years, historians of China have differed over the issue of whether Chinese families have been fundamentally changed when their members have been physically separated for long periods of time. Recent research has convincingly demonstrated that Chinese commonly experienced long separations from their families during the late imperial period and the first half of the twentieth century; the stereotype of "China as a nation of stay-at-homes" has been largely discredited.[1] Some Chinese may have separated from their families voluntarily (for the purpose of seeking education and jobs), and others may have been forced to separate against their will (by war and revolution). Whatever their motivations, many lived for long periods of time away from home, so these questions arise: What effects did absent members have on their families? Did the families retain their form and cohesion or were they pulled apart and transformed?

Continuity and Change in Chinese Families

Two books have produced sharply contrasting answers to these questions. In a history of an elite family in north China since the fourteenth century, Joseph Esherick has concluded that this family was fundamentally transformed by its members' experiences outside the home during the first half of the twentieth century. In earlier times, a son who completed his education away from home immediately returned to serve his father. But in the 1920s and 1930s, twelve sons in one generation of the family left home for boarding school and college, were exposed to a nationalistic curriculum, and became independent from their family. In 1930, when the eldest of these sons was only twenty-two, their father died, but Esherick considers the death of the patriarch a minor event compared to the sons' newfound independence as a centrifugal force pulling their family apart and causing the sons to lead their lives in separate nuclear families.

During the Sino-Japanese War, with their ties to their family already attenuated, the sons in this family became scattered across China, and they proceeded to make decisions about their careers, marriages, and political commitments on their own. Acting as independent individuals, they created an unbridgeable cultural gap between their lives inside their original family, which they left behind, and their new lives outside it, which they pursued. Thus, even before the founding of the People's Republic, this family was transformed.[2]

Esherick's analysis of an elite Chinese family that fragmented in the early twentieth century is strikingly different from Parks Coble's characterization of elite Chinese families that held together during the same period. Whereas Esherick shows that the sons became independent individuals and served as agents of change in their family, Coble argues that Chinese patriarchs kept families together by retaining authority and dictating policies that their sons readily obeyed.

During the Sino-Japanese War, these sons, like the ones in the family in Esherick's study, ceased to live together in their natal families. But they did not become independent individuals or place nationalism above family, and they were not randomly scattered across China. Instead, the sons in each family continued to defer to their patriarch, dutifully accepting his assignments and following his orders. From his wartime headquarters, the patriarch placed his sons in strategic locations, sending some to parts of China under Japanese occupation and others to parts outside the occupation. After the war, the patriarch followed the same survival strategy when encountering the Communist Revolution of 1949. Once again the patriarch adopted the business strategy of "disperse the family and resources, divide the risk," and once again the patriarch held his family together by retaining unquestioned authority, which kept his children deferential to him whether they lived with him or were separated from him.[3]

Esherick's and Coble's interpretations frame a debate over how Chinese have coped with separations from the family. In the early twentieth century, when members of the younger generation lived separately from their families for extended periods of time, did they achieve independence as individuals, become imbued with nationalism, and cease to participate in the collective life of their families, as Esherick concludes? Or during this period did patriarchs retain their authority, take advantage of their family members' deferential attitudes, and keep their families intact, as Coble argues?

To some extent, the apparent contradiction between these two interpretations may be attributable to the authors' choices of subject. Esherick focuses on a family whose members descended from officials and became best known for their accomplishments in the political arena. By contrast, Coble has researched different kinds of families—ones that made their marks primarily in the business world. But the conflicts between the two authors' conclusions raise questions that are worth asking of any family, including the Lius, and the history of the Lius offers a basis for reconsidering both interpretations.

Independence within the Family

The history of the Liu family contains examples that may be marshaled in support of both Esherick's and Coble's interpretations. In the 1930s, some of the sons in the Liu family followed a pattern very similar to the one Esherick has described. While studying outside the home, they became imbued with nationalism and sought independence as individuals. Second, Third, and Fourth Sons went through these phases during the Shanghai Incident of 1932. As students at Cambridge University in England, their declarations of independence in the family were triggered by Father's proposal that they should acquire British citizenship so that they could give the family business British ownership and prevent the Japanese military from confiscating it. Each of the sons took an independent stance in opposing Father's proposal, and they defended their positions on nationalistic grounds. Expressing their views passionately, they told Father that they did not want to become British citizens because they believed that they should place their patriotism ahead of their family's economic interests.

In the Liu family's history, there are several other examples of sons taking independent stances—some invoking nationalism in support of their positions and some subscribing to other causes. During the Shanghai Incident, Eldest Son, who was studying in the United States, aligned with his three younger brothers in England and attacked Father's proposal more aggressively than they did, citing racial as well as nationalistic reasons for his position. After the Sino-Japanese War broke out in 1937, Sixth Son established a broad ideological basis for his independence by committing himself not only to nationalism but also to Christianity and Communism. Moreover, he acted on his beliefs by moving to Yan'an without informing his parents in advance and by joining the Chinese Communist Party without telling anyone outside the party.

All of these examples seem similar to the ones Esherick has cited as illustrations of sons' nationalism leading to their independence. But other examples in the history of the Liu family show that some Liu sons followed different paths in their quests for independence. During the Sino-Japanese War, the three eldest sons sought independence from Father based on an ideology that was the antithesis of nationalism—a kind of antinationalism. Before the war, they had criticized Father for not being nationalistic enough, but during the war, when they worked with the Japanese occupying forces more closely than he did, they criticized him for being too nationalistic.

Whether nationalistic or not, the sons in the Liu family certainly did seek independence, and several of them achieved it. To this extent, they resembled the sons in the family described by Esherick. If so, then did they, as independent individuals, pull away from their family and lead separate lives especially during the tumultuous Sino-Japanese War and Communist Revolution? On the contrary, like the families described by Coble, the Lius held together.

Empowerment under the Patriarch

While sons and daughters in the Liu family sought and achieved independence as individuals, nearly all of them continued to participate in the family. Following the pattern described by Coble, the patriarch placed the family above the nation, systematically laid plans for his sons in the family business, and gave each of them assignments to carry out. Even when sons and daughters left home for long periods of time, Father as patriarch and Mother as matriarch stayed in touch with them and kept almost all of them continuously involved in the family before and during the Sino-Japanese War and the Communist Revolution.

Before the war, although Mother preferred to keep her children nearby, Father insisted on educating them abroad. On sending off his sons, he emphasized that they should prepare themselves to return home and serve as leaders of the family firm, and he specified what their major subjects should be. Once they were abroad, he was not able to force each one to pursue the exact subject he had proposed, but to a remarkable extent they ended up majoring in fields that trained them for service in the family firm: business administration (Eldest and Eighth Sons), economics (Second, Fourth, and Fifth Sons), law (Third Son), and engineering (Sixth and Eighth Sons). Moreover, as Father had hoped, most of them were admitted to and attended highly prestigious academic institutions: Cambridge University, Harvard University, the University of Pennsylvania, MIT, the Tokyo Institute of Technology.

Once Father had prepared his sons to serve the family and family firm before the war, he deployed them across China during the war. Following the pattern Coble has described, Father left some of his sons (the three eldest) in charge of the family's businesses in Shanghai and Hong Kong—cities ultimately occupied by Japan—and arranged for three others (Fourth, Sixth, and Eighth Sons) to join him and work with him in Chongqing, Chiang Kai-shek's wartime capital outside the Japanese occupation. He found places for all of his sons in the family firm, and none of them declined to work for it. Even Sixth Son, who spent the first part of the war in Mao's Communist base area, and Eighth Son, who had to cut short his education in the United States because of hospitalization for depression, both accepted the positions Father assigned to them in the family firm during the war.

After the war, with the coming of the Communist Revolution, Father initially continued to follow the strategy of coping with instability by deploying members of the family in more than one location, as described by Coble. In the late 1940s as the Communists claimed victories over Chiang Kai-shek's Nationalist forces, Father and several other members of his family traveled from their base in Shanghai to Taiwan, where Chiang had retreated, and they considered moving part or all of the family there. Soon thereafter, Father became disillusioned with

Chiang's government, rejected this alternative, and moved instead to Hong Kong, where he remained for six months in 1949. Not until November 1949, a month after the People's Republic was founded, did Father decide to return to Shanghai, abandon the strategy of deploying family members in more than one location, and bring them all home.

In the last years of his life, Father pursued the strategy of gathering all his family members around him in Shanghai. Since the end of the Sino-Japanese War, he and most of the members of his family had returned to Shanghai and regrouped there. In the early 1950s, Father urged the ones remaining abroad to come home, and by 1952, all except two did so. Youngest Daughter voluntarily returned, and Eighth Son was dragooned by the family into returning. The only children who did not come back were Fifth and Seventh Sons, who remained in Taiwan.

So, paradoxically, the history of the Lius lends support to Coble's interpretation as well as Esherick's. In the Liu family, Father retained patriarchal authority, gave his children assignments, and held his family together throughout the 1930s, 1940s, and early 1950s. Despite his separations from some members of the family because of their educations abroad and their experiences with war and revolution, he consistently found places for nearly all of them as full participants within the extended family.

If Esherick's and Coble's interpretations fundamentally differ, how is it possible that the history of the Liu family lends credence to them both? We think the answer lies in the nature of the Liu family correspondence.

The Lius' Exchanges

The value of Coble's and Esherick's interpretations is that each shows how historical figures took actions in relation to other members of their families, especially when they were physically separated from each other. Coble describes patriarch-entrepreneurs who issued orders to their sons, and Esherick characterizes sons who declared independence from their elders. The limitation of these two historians' research is that they lack records showing how members of families responded to these initiatives. When a patriarch ordered his sons or daughters to attend a university, take a position in the family firm, choose a marriage partner, or adopt a political affiliation, how did they reply? By the same token, when sons or daughters did not follow their parents' orders along these lines, how did the parents react?

If the Lius' correspondence is any indication, then the dynamics of a family's decision making cannot be fully understood on the basis of one side of the exchanges within families. It is not enough to consider a parent's pronouncements on family policies as final or to assume that a son's or daughter's declaration of independence marks the end point of his or her participation in a family's future. Only by going beyond these unilateral assertions and considering bilateral and multilateral exchanges with other family members is it possible to evaluate the dynamics and consequences of a family's decision making. The Liu family correspondence provides a window on these exchanges.

In the Liu family, Father self-consciously rejected the idea that he would dictate orders to his children. In his letters to them he strongly encouraged them to take independent positions and express themselves freely on family issues even when their views differed from his own. In the early 1930s, when his eldest sons were in their late teens and twenties, he began consulting them about decisions in the family and the family firm, and he continued to exchange opinions with them for the rest of his life.

In his style of parenting, Father contrasted sharply with the classic image of the Chinese father as a stern, forbidding, unbending disciplinarian coldly dictating every decision to his wife and children. To some extent, his conception of himself as a father derived from his understanding of Western thought. As noted, in 1934 Father maintained, citing Lord Chesterfield's letters to his son, that he aimed, like Chesterfield, to be his sons' best friend. "As ruler of our house," he assured Fifth Son in encouraging him to seek independence, "I wish to be, to use a political parlance, a democratic leader, instead of being an autocrat or a dictator."[4]

Father's children considered him "modern" by contrast with Mother, whom they characterized as "conservative," and he fits this description to the extent that he showed more awareness of the ideas of Chinese modernizers than Mother did. For example, when Mother insisted on Third Son and Liane demonstrating their filial piety by honoring her list of nine ritual obligations, Father took the position that these filial obligations could be evaluated from either a traditional Chinese or a modern Western point of view. But he by no means abandoned his

Chinese heritage or uncritically embraced a Western identity. In advising the young couple on Mother's list of filial obligations, he did not align himself fully with a Western or a Chinese interpretation, and initially he joined Mother in objecting to Third Son's choice of a bride because she seemed too Westernized. Not until he was persuaded otherwise did he give his blessing to the marriage.

By encouraging all of his children to seek independence and consistently engaging them in arguments about the issues the family faced, Father did not merely accommodate them; he empowered them. Thus empowered, they argued vehemently with their parents and each other, but even when they became physically separated from one another, they conducted these arguments as members of the family, not as outsiders distancing themselves from it or abandoning it.

To be sure, some members of the family threatened to leave the family or the family firm, but in the end they relented and withdrew their threats. In 1933, while studying in the United States, Eldest Son proposed to seek work with a bank outside the family firm as a ploy to persuade Father to let him transfer from Harvard to the University of Pennsylvania. But after he made this transfer and received Father's belated approval for it, he dropped the threat. On his return to China, he became the first son to take a full-time position in the family firm. Subsequently, all of his brothers did the same.

Women also threatened to leave the family. During the war, Mother warned Father that she was prepared to return to her natal family unless he would let her reunite with him during their long wartime separation. But when the war ended and Father returned from his wartime home in Chongqing to her in Shanghai, she dropped her threat. Also during the war, Youngest Daughter felt trapped living with Mother in Shanghai and desperately wanted to escape from her. In this case, at the tender age of thirteen, Youngest Daughter carried out her threat to the extent that she moved out of Mother's residence, but she did not leave the family. Instead she moved in with her older brother, Second Son, and his wife. Of all the children in the family, only one, Eldest Daughter, actually left it, after Father disinherited her in the wake of revelations about her affair with a married man and her resulting pregnancy. But even she reconciled almost immediately with Mother and eventually with Father.

Thus, even while the sons and daughters sought and frequently achieved individual independence, the Lius held together as a family under a patriarch. For all of their passionate arguments, the Lius maintained relations with each other that were, in a word, civil. They overcame or found ways of living with their differences by negotiating with each other. Sometimes the negotiations were bilateral (involving Father and Mother, Father or Mother and one child, or one child and another child), and sometimes they were multilateral (based on alliances of family members). In either case, their power as negotiators was relational, in the sense that they exercised it in exchanges with each other. As patriarch, Father frequently took the lead in initiating discussions and debates, but even under great stress in war and revolution, neither he nor any other member of the family had a monopoly on power in the family, and no one member became permanently alienated from the rest. However independent each one became and however contentious each one's dealings with the others might have been, they stayed in touch and found ways to reconcile with each other.

The Lius' Legacy

The Lius did not survive as a cohesive family after Father's death and the nationalization of their business in 1956, and in light of their long-term separations from then on, one might well wonder what legacy, if any, the family has bequeathed to the twenty-first century. As historians, we have no illusions about our ability to make predictions—let alone predictions based solely on the case of a single family. But a few years ago, thanks to an invitation from members of the Liu family, we witnessed an event that impressed on us the possibility that they and perhaps members of other Chinese families still relate to each other as we have seen the Lius do in this book.

On October 14, 2006, twenty-four members of the Liu family held a ceremony to commemorate the fiftieth anniversary of the death of their ancestor Liu Hongsheng, known in this book as Father. Arriving in Shanghai from various locations in China and the West, they traveled outside the city in chartered buses to a new and very grand cemetery, Fu Shou Yuan, which opened in 1995. Of the family members described in this book, only one, Youngest Daughter, age seventy-seven, was able to attend. At the culmination of the ceremony, she unveiled a massive bronze bust of Father and a smaller cameo of Mother, and in a spontaneous gesture, she reached up and stroked Father's cheeks as tears flowed down her own.

If Father and Mother started the first generation of the Liu family, and if Youngest Daughter represented the second generation, then the others present for this occasion were from the third and fourth generations. After hearing several eulogies in the ceremony at the site of the new monuments, they moved to a dining room in a nearby pavilion and took seats at round tables, where they were served dishes of delicious Shanghai food. In conversations over their meal, they turned inevitably to the topic of the Liu family's history. At first they all praised and paid deference to Father as the patriarch of their family. But before long they brought up controversial points about the roles each of their ancestors had played in their family's history, and then many of them—men and women, young and old—began to argue.

ARCHIVES AND WORKS CITED

NOTES

ACKNOWLEDGMENTS

INDEX

Archives and Works Cited

Archives

Baldwin-Wallace College Archives, Berea, Ohio.
Cambridge University Archives, Cambridge, England.
Chongqing Municipal Archives, Chongqing.
Colorado College Special Collections, Colorado Springs, Colorado.
Harvard University Business School Archives, Cambridge, Massachusetts.
Hong Kong Public Records Office, Hong Kong.
Liu Hongsheng Papers. Center for Research on Chinese Business History, Institute of Economics, Shanghai Academy of Social Sciences, Shanghai.
Michigan State University Archives, East Lansing.
National Archives of the United States, Washington, D.C.
Public Record Office, National Archives, Kew Gardens, England.
Shanghai Municipal Archives, Shanghai.
Simmons College Archives, Boston.
Tokyo Institute of Technology Archives, Tokyo.
University of Illinois Archives, Urbana.
University of Manchester Archives, Manchester.
University of Pennsylvania Archives, Philadelphia.

Works Cited

Beam, Alex. *Gracefully Insane: The Rise and Fall of America's Premier Mental Hospital.* New York: Public Affairs, 2001.
Bernal, Martin. "The Triumph of Anarchism over Marxism, 1906–1907." In *China in Revolution: The First Phase, 1900–1913,* edited by Mary Clabaugh Wright. New Haven: Yale University Press, 1968, 97–142.

Bernhardt, Kathryn. "Women and the Law: Divorce in the Republican
    Period." In *Civil Law in Qing and Republican China,* edited by Bernhardt and
    Philip C. C. Huang. Stanford: Stanford University Press, 1994, 187–214.

Bernstein, Gail. "Kawakami Hajime: A Japanese Marxist in Search of the
    Way." In *Japan in Crisis: Essays on Taisho Democracy,* edited by Bernard S.
    Silberman and H. D. Harootunian. Princeton, N.J.: Princeton University
    Press, 1974, 86–109.

Bickers, Robert A., and Jeffrey N. Wasserstrom. "Shanghai's 'Dogs and
    Chinese Not Admitted' Sign: Legend, History, and Contemporary
    Symbol." *China Quarterly,* no. 142 (June 1995): 444–466.

Boorman, Howard L., and Richard C. Howard, eds. *Biographical Dictionary of
    Republican China.* 5 vols. New York: Columbia University Press, 1968.

Brown, Jeremy, and Paul G. Pickowicz, eds. *Dilemmas of Victory: The Early Years
    of the People's Republic of China.* Cambridge, Mass.: Harvard University
    Press, 2007.

Cardwell, D. S. L. "Introduction." In *Artisan to Graduate,* edited by D. S. L.
    Cardwell. Manchester: Manchester University Press, 1974, 1–10.

Chan Kai Yiu. *Business Expansion and Structural Change in Pre-war China: Liu
    Hongsheng and His Enterprises, 1920–1937.* Hong Kong: Hong Kong Univer-
    sity Press, 2006.

Chan, Wellington K. K. "The Origins and Early Years of the Wing On
    Company Group in Australia, Fiji, Hong Kong, and Shanghai: Organiza-
    tion and Strategy of a New Enterprise." In *Chinese Business Enterprise in
    Asia,* edited by Rajeswary Ampalavanar Brown. London: Routledge,
    1995, 80–95.

———. "Tradition and Change in the Chinese Business Enterprise: The
    Family Firm Past and Present." *Chinese Studies in History* 31.3–4 (Spring–
    Summer 1998): 127–144.

Chang, Iris. *The Chinese in America: A Narrative History.* New York: Viking,
    2003.

Chen Chieh-ju. *Chiang Kai-shek's Secret Past: The Memoir of His Second Wife, Chen
    Chieh-ju,* edited by Lloyd E. Eastman. Boulder, Colo.: Westview Press,
    1993.

Chen Guangfu. *Chen Guangfu riji* [Diary of Chen Guangfu]. Edited by Shang-
    hai dang'an guan [Shanghai City Archives]. Shanghai: Shiji chuban
    jituan and Shanghai shudian chubanshe, 2002.

Cheng Nianqi. "Liu Hongsheng: Zai gou'an yu minzu dayi zhijian jueze" [Liu
    Hongsheng: Choosing between a false peace and a national cause]. In
    Guonan zhong de Zhongguo qiyejia [Chinese entrepreneurs during national
    difficulty], edited by Shen Zuwei and Du Xuncheng. Shanghai: Shanghai
    shehui kexue yuan chubanshe, 1996, 29–44.

Cheng Yu-Kwei. *Foreign Trade and Industrial Development in China.* Washington,
    D.C.: University Press, 1956.

Choi Chi-cheung. "Competition among Brothers: The Kin Tye Lung Company and Its Associate Companies." In *Chinese Business Enterprise in Asia,* edited by Rajeswary Ampalavanar Brown. London: Routledge, 1995, 96–114.

Coble, Parks M., Jr. *Chinese Capitalists in Japan's New Order: The Occupied Lower Yangzi, 1937–1945.* Berkeley: University of California Press, 2003.

———. *Facing Japan: Chinese Politics and Japanese Imperialism, 1931–1937.* Cambridge, Mass.: Council on East Asian Studies, Harvard University, 1991.

———. "The Soong Family and Chinese Capitalists." In *Madame Chiang Kaishek and Her China,* edited by Samuel C. Chu. Norwalk, Conn.: EastBridge, 2005, 69–79.

Cochran, Sherman. "Capitalists Choosing Communist China: The Liu Family of Shanghai, 1948–56." In *Dilemmas of Victory: The Early Years of the People's Republic of China,* edited by Jeremy Brown and Paul G. Pickowicz. Cambridge, Mass.: Harvard University Press, 2007, 359–385.

———. *Chinese Medicine Men: Consumer Culture in China and Southeast Asia.* Cambridge, Mass.: Harvard University Press, 2006.

———. *Encountering Chinese Networks: Western, Japanese, and Chinese Corporations in China, 1880–1937.* Berkeley: University of California Press, 2000.

Dillon, Nara. "New Democracy and the Demise of Private Charity in Shanghai." In *Dilemmas of Victory: The Early Years of the People's Republic of China,* edited by Jeremy Brown and Paul G. Pickowicz. Cambridge, Mass.: Harvard University Press, 2007, 80–102.

Dillon, Nara, and Jean C. Oi, eds. *At the Crossroads of Empires: Middlemen, Social Networks, and State-Building in Republican Shanghai.* Stanford: Stanford University Press, 2008.

Eastman, Lloyd E. *Family, Field, and Ancestors: Constancy and Change in China's Social and Economic History, 1550–1949.* New York: Oxford University Press, 1988.

———. *Seeds of Destruction: Nationalist China in War and Revolution 1937–1949.* Stanford: Stanford University Press, 1984.

Engels, Friedrich. *The Condition of the Working Class in England.* Edited by David McLellan. Oxford: Oxford University Press, 1999.

Epstein, Maram. "Writing Emotions: Ritual Innovation as Emotional Expression." *Nan Nu* 11 (2009): 155–196.

Esherick, Joseph W. *Ancestral Leaves: A Family Journey through Chinese History.* Berkeley: University of California Press, 2011.

Faure, David. "The Control of Equity in Chinese Firms within the Modern Sector from the Late Qing to the Early Republic." In *Chinese Business Enterprise in Asia,* edited by Rajeswary Ampalavanar Brown. London: Routledge, 1995, 60–79.

Feuerwerker, Albert. *China's Early Industrialization: Sheng Hsuan-huai (1844–1916) and Mandarin Enterprise*. Cambridge, Mass.: Harvard University Press, 1958.

Freedman, Maurice. "The Family in China, Past and Present." In *The Study of Chinese Society: Essays by Maurice Freedman*, edited by G. William Skinner. Stanford: Stanford University Press, 1979, 240–254.

———. *Lineage Organization in Southeastern China*. London: Athlone Press, 1958.

Gardner, John. "The *Wu-fan* Campaign in Shanghai: A Study in the Consolidation of Urban Control." In *Chinese Communist Politics in Action*, edited by A. Doak Barnett. Seattle: University of Washington Press, 1969, 477–539.

Glosser, Susan L. *Chinese Visions of Family and State, 1915–1953*. Berkeley: University of California Press, 2003.

Goodman, Bryna. *Native Place, City, and Nation: Regional Networks and Identities in Shanghai, 1853–1937*. Berkeley: University of California Press, 1995.

Graham, Stephen A. *Ordinary Man, Extraordinary Mission: The Life and Work of E. Stanley Jones*. Nashville: Abington Press, 2005.

Gu Wenhu. "Dianxing qiye ziben jituan de xingcheng ji jiyun gaikuang" [An outline of the evolution and cycles of typical capitalist enterprise groups]. In *Bainian cangsang: Zhongguo jindai qiye de guiji, jingyan, jiaoxun* [One hundred years of flux: Norms, experiences, lessons], edited by Huang Yiping and Gu Wenhu. Taiyuan: Shanxi chubanshe, 2000, 130–203.

Han, Yelong. "An Untold Story: American Policy toward Chinese Students in the United States, 1949–1955." *Journal of American-East Asian Relations* 1 (Spring 1993): 77–99.

Harrell, Paula. *Sowing the Seeds of Change: Chinese Students, Japanese Teachers, 1895–1905*. Stanford: Stanford University Press, 1992.

Harrison, Henrietta. *The Man Awakened from Dreams: One Man's Life in a North China Village, 1857–1942*. Stanford: Stanford University Press, 2005.

Hershatter, Gail. *Dangerous Pleasures: Prostitution and Modernity in Twentieth-Century Shanghai*. Berkeley: University of California Press, 1997.

Ho Ping-ti. "Aspects of Social Mobility in China, 1368–1911." *Comparative Studies in Society and History* 1.4 (June 1959): 330–359.

Honig, Emily. *Sisters and Strangers: Women in Shanghai Cotton Mills, 1919–1949*. Stanford: Stanford University Press, 1986.

Hsiung Ping-chen. *A Tender Voyage: Children and Childhood in Late Imperial China*. Stanford: Stanford University Press, 2005.

Hsu, Madeline. *Dreaming of Gold, Dreaming of Home: Transnationalism and Migration between the United States and South China, 1882–1942*. Stanford: Stanford University Press, 2000.

Isaacs, Harold R. *Scratches on Our Minds: American Images of China and India*. Westport, Conn.: Greenwood Press, 1973.

Jones, Susan Mann. "The Ningpo Pang and Financial Power in Shanghai." In *The Chinese City between Two Worlds*, edited by Mark Elvin and G. William Skinner. Stanford: Stanford University Press, 1974, 73–96.

Judd, Ellen. "*Niangjia:* Chinese Women and Their Natal Families." *Journal of Asian Studies* 48.3 (August 1989): 525–544.

Kaysen, Susanna. *Girl, Interrupted.* New York: Turtle Bay Books, 1993.

Ko, Dorothy. *Teachers of the Inner Chambers: Women and Culture in Seventeenth-Century China.* Stanford: Stanford University Press, 1994.

Koo Hui-lan. *No Feast Lasts Forever.* New York: Quadrangle, 1975.

Kuhn, Philip A. *Chinese among Others: Emigration in Modern Times.* Lanham, Md.: Rowman and Littlefield, 2008.

Kwei. "Mrs. O. S. L. Family History" (unpublished report, February 1930), Liu Hongsheng Papers.

Laing, Ellen. *Selling Happiness: Calendar Posters and Visual Culture in Early Twentieth-Century Shanghai.* Honolulu: University of Hawai'i Press, 2004.

Lang, Olga. *Chinese Family and Society.* New Haven: Yale University Press, 1946.

Lee, Leo Ou-fan. *Shanghai Modern: The Flowering of a New Urban Culture in China, 1930–1945.* Cambridge, Mass.: Harvard University Press, 1999.

Lee, Rose Hum. *The Chinese in the United States of America.* Hong Kong: Hong Kong University Press, 1960.

Lin Man-houng. "Overseas Chinese Merchants and Multiple Nationality: A Means for Reducing Commercial Risk (1895–1935)." *Modern Asian Studies* 35.4 (October 2001): 985–1009.

Liu Gongcheng. "Dui diliushibaji 'Kangzhan qijian Liushi qianchuan jingguo' de dingzheng [A correction of "The experience of moving the Liu family enterprises to Sichuan during the war of resistance" in issue number 68]. *Wenshi ziliao xuanji* no. 76 (1981): 198–199.

———. "Kangzhan chuqi xian fu Liu Hongsheng dui zhonggong de taidu" [My father's attitude toward the Chinese Communist Party during the early stages of the War of Resistance]. *Shanghai wenshi ziliao xuanji* (1989): 182–187.

Liu Haiming. *The Transnational History of a Chinese Family: Immigrant Letters, Family Business, and Reverse Migration.* New Brunswick, N.J.: Rutgers University Press, 2005.

Liu Hua-yu. *Mao and Economic Stalinization of China, 1948–1953.* Lanham, Md.: Rowman and Littlefield, 2006.

Liu Nianzhi. "Cong Kangri shengli dao quanguo jiefang de Liu Hongsheng" [Liu Hongsheng: From the victory in the war of resistance to national liberation]. *Wenshi ziliao xuanji,* no. 68 (1980): 185–203.

———. "Kangzhan Qijian liushi qiye qianchuan jingguo" [The transfer of the Lius' enterprises to Sichuan during the war of resistance]. *Wenshi ziliao xuanji,* no. 68 (1980): 170–184.

————. *Shiyejia Liu Hongsheng chuanlu—huiyi wode fuqin* [A biography of the industrialist Liu Hongsheng—reminiscences of my father]. Beijing: Wenshi ziliao chubanshe, 1982.

Lu Fangshang. "Lingyizhong 'wei zuzhi': Kangzhan shiji hunyin yu jiating wenti chutan" [Another "illegitimate organization": Practical problems with marriage and the family during the War of Resistance]. *Jindai Zhongguo funu shi yanjiu* [Research on women in modern Chinese history] 3 (1995): 97–121.

Lu Yan. *Re-understanding Japan: Chinese Perspectives, 1895–1945.* Honolulu: University of Hawai'i Press, 2004.

Lu Zhilian. "Qiye da wang Liu Hongsheng" [King of the Matches Liu Hong-sheng]. *Zhejiang wenshi ziliao* 39 (March 1989): 132–156.

Lufrano, Richard John. *Honorable Merchants: Commerce and Self-Cultivation in Late Imperial China.* Honolulu: University of Hawai'i Press, 1997.

Lutz, Jesse Gregory. *China and the Christian Colleges, 1850–1950.* Ithaca, N.Y.: Cornell University Press, 1971.

Mann, Susan. "The Cult of Domesticity in Republican Shanghai's Middle Class." *Jindai Zhongguo funushi yanjiu* 2 (June 1994): 179–201.

————. "Grooming a Daughter for Marriage." In *Marriage and Inequality in Chinese Society,* edited by Rubie S. Watson and Patricia Buckley Ebrey. Berkeley: University of California Press, 1991, 204–230.

————. *Precious Records: Women in China's Long Eighteenth Century.* Stanford: Stanford University Press, 1997.

————. *The Talented Women of the Zhang Family.* Berkeley: University of California Press, 2007.

Mao Tse-tung [Mao Zedong]. *The Selected Works of Mao Tse-tung.* Beijing: Peking Foreign Languages Press, 1969.

Mao Tun [Mao Dun]. *Midnight* [Zi ye]. Beijing: Peking Foreign Languages Press, 1957.

Men of Shanghai and North China. Shanghai: University Press, 1935.

Morris, Andrew D. *Marrow of the Nation: A History of Sport and Physical Culture in Republican China.* Berkeley: University of California Press, 2004.

Morton, W. E. "The Manchester College of Science and Technology, 1914–1956." In *Artisan to Graduate,* edited by D. S. L. Cardwell. Manchester: Manchester University Press, 1974, 167–207.

Pan, Lynn. *Sons of the Yellow Emperor: A History of the Chinese Diaspora.* Boston: Little, Brown, 1990.

Phillips, Roderick. *Putting Asunder: A History of Divorce in Western Society.* Cambridge: Cambridge University Press, 1988.

Pickowicz, Paul G. "Victory as Defeat: Postwar Visualizations of China's War of Resistance." In *Becoming China: Passages to Modernity and Beyond,* edited by Wen-hsin Yeh. Berkeley: University of California Press, 2000, 365–398.

Rankin, Mary Backus. *Early Chinese Revolutionaries: Radical Intellectuals in Shanghai and Chekiang, 1902–1911.* Cambridge, Mass.: Harvard University Press, 1971.

Reardon-Anderson, James. *The Study of Change: Chemistry in China, 1840–1949.* Cambridge: Cambridge University Press, 1991.

Record of Proceedings of the Thirty-First Session of the International Labour Conference, San Francisco, 1948. Geneva, Switzerland: International Labour Office, 1950.

Record of Proceedings of the Thirty-Third Session of the International Labour Conference, Geneva, 1950. Geneva, Switzerland: International Labour Office, 1951.

Romanus, Charles F., and Riley Sunderland. *Time Runs Out in CBI.* Washington, D.C.: Office of the Chief of Military History, Department of the Army, 1959.

Rowe, William T. *Hankow: Commerce and Society in a Chinese City.* Stanford: Stanford University Press, 1984.

Rush, James R. *Opium to Java: Revenue Farming and Chinese Enterprise in Colonial Indonesia, 1860–1910.* Ithaca, N.Y.: Cornell University Press, 1990.

Saari, Jon L. *Legacies of Childhood: Growing up Chinese in a Time of Crisis, 1890–1920.* Cambridge, Mass.: Council on East Asia Studies, Harvard University, 1990.

Saneto Keishu. *Chugokujin Nihon ryugakushi* [A history of Chinese students in Japan]. Tokyo: Kuroshio shuppan 1970.

Sangren, P. Steven. *Chinese Sociologics: An Anthropological Account of the Role of Alienation in Social Reproduction.* London: Athlone Press, 2000.

Schran, Peter. *Guerrilla Economy: The Development of the Shensi-Kansu-Ninghsia Border Region, 1937–1945.* Albany: State University of New York Press, 1976.

Seagrave, Sterling. *The Soong Dynasty.* Cambridge: Harper and Rowe, 1985.

Seshagiri, Urmila. "Modernity's (Yellow) Perils: Dr. Fu-Manchu and English Race Paranoia." *Cultural Critique* 62 (Winter 2006): 162–194.

Shanghai shehui kexue yuan jingji yanjiu suo [Shanghai Academy of Social Sciences Institute of Economics], comp. *Liu Hongsheng qiye shiliao* [Historical materials on Liu Hongsheng's enterprises]. 3 vols. Shanghai: Shanghai renmin chubanshe, 1981.

Shanghai zhizao chang shang gailan [A commercial survey of industrial factories in Shanghai]. Shanghai: Lianhe shengxin suo, 1947.

Shen Kuiyi. "Wang Yiting in the Social Networks of 1910s–1930s Shanghai." In *At the Crossroads of Empires: Middlemen, Social Networks, and State-Building in Republican Shanghai,* edited by Nara Dillon and Jean C. Oi. Stanford: Stanford University Press, 2008, 45–64.

Shi Qun. "Guangfang jingying gezhong de Liu Hongsheng" [Liu Hongsheng and his knowledge about managing various enterprises]. In *Zhongguo qiyejia liezhuan* [Biographies of Chinese entrepreneurs], vol. 2, edited by Xu Dixin. Beijing: Jingji ribao chubanshe, 1988, 103–122.

Shiba Yoshinobu. "Ningpo and Its Hinterland." In *The City in Late Imperial China,* edited by G. William Skinner. Stanford: Stanford University Press, 1977, 391–439.

Skinner, G. William. "Mobility Strategies in Late Imperial China: A Regional Systems Analysis." In *Regional Analysis,* vol. 1 of *Economic Systems,* edited by Carol A. Smith. New York: Academic Press, 1976, 327–364.

———. " 'Seek a Loyal Subject in a Filial Son': Family Roots of Political Orientation in Chinese Society." In *Family Process and Political Process in Modern Chinese History.* Taipei: Institute of Modern History, Academia Sinica, 1992, 943–993.

Spence, Jonathan D. *The Gate of Heavenly Peace.* New York: Viking, 1981.

———. *The Search for Modern China.* New York: Norton, 1999.

Sulloway, Frank J. *Born to Rebel: Birth Order, Family Dynamics, and Creative Lives.* New York: Pantheon, 1996.

Sutton, S. B. *Crossroads in Psychiatry: A History of the McLean Hospital.* Washington, D.C.: American Psychiatric Press, 1986.

Sze Szeming. "Chinese Students in Great Britain." *Asiatic Review* 28.90 (April 1931): 311–314.

Theiss, Janet M. *Disgraceful Matters: The Politics of Chastity in Eighteenth-Century China.* Berkeley: University of California Press, 2004.

Thorne, Christopher. *The Limits of Foreign Policy: The West, the League and the Far Eastern Crisis of 1931–1933.* London: Hamish Hamilton, 1972.

UNRRA in China, 1945–1947. Washington, D.C.: UNRRA, 1948.

Wakeman, Frederic, Jr. " 'Cleanup': The New Order in Shanghai." In *Dilemmas of Victory: The Early Years of the People's Republic of China,* edited by Jeremy Brown and Paul G. Pickowicz. Cambridge, Mass.: Harvard University Press, 2007, 21–58.

———. *Policing Shanghai, 1927–1937.* Berkeley: University of California Press, 1995.

———. *The Shanghai Badlands: Wartime Terrorism and Urban Crime, 1937–1941.* Cambridge: Cambridge University Press, 1996.

———. *Spymaster: Dai Li and the Chinese Secret Service.* Berkeley: University of California Press, 2003.

Walsh, William Sebastian. *The Inferiority Feeling.* New York: Dutton, 1928.

Wang Shimin, ed. *Shanghai minyong hangkong zhi* [A gazetteer of civil airlines in Shanghai]. Shanghai: Shanghai shehui kexueyuan chubanshe, 2000.

Wang Zheng. *Women in the Chinese Enlightenment.* Berkeley: University of California Press, 1999.

Wasserstrom, Jeffrey. "Cosmopolitan Connections and Transnational Networks." In *At the Crossroads of Empires: Middlemen, Social Networks, and*

State-Building in Republican Shanghai, edited by Nara Dillon and Jean C. Oi. Stanford: Stanford University Press, 2008, 206–223.

Watanabe Takujuro. "Shihonka no jiko kaizo" [Self-reform among capitalists]. In *Chugoku no ho to shakai* [Law and society in China], edited by Nihon horitsuka ho-Chu daihyodan, Kokusai horitsuka renraku kyokai [Representatives of the Japanese legal specialists' delegation to China and the Association of Specialists in International Law]. Tokyo: Shin doku-shosha, 1960, 162–173.

Watson, James L. *Emigration and the Chinese Lineage: The Mans in Hong Kong and London*. Berkeley: University of California Press, 1975.

Wen Chu. "'Zhongguo shiye da wang,' Liu Hongsheng zhuanji" ["King of China's entrepreneurs": A biography of Liu Hongsheng]. *Shanghai Tan* no. 216 (December 2004): 14–20.

Weng Wenhao. "Zhang Qinshi, Liu Mingqiu jiehuan" [The wedding of Zhang Qinshi and Liu Mingqiu]. In *Weng Wenhao shi ji*. Beijing: Tuanjie chuban-she, 1999.

Whyte, Martin King, and William L. Parish. *Urban Life in Contemporary China*. Chicago: University of Chicago Press, 1984.

Williamsen, Marvin. "The Military Dimension, 1937–1941." In *China's Bitter Victory: The War with Japan, 1937–1945*, edited by James C. Hsiung and Steven I. Levine. Armonk, N.Y.: M. E. Sharpe, 1992, 135–156.

Wolf, Margery. *Women and the Family in Rural Taiwan*. Stanford: Stanford University Press, 1972.

Wong Siu-lun. "Business Networks, Cultural Values and the State in Hong Kong and Singapore." In *Chinese Business Enterprise in Asia*, edited by Rajeswary Ampalavanar Brown. London: Routledge, 1995, 136–153.

———. "The Chinese Family Firm: A Model." *British Journal of Sociology* 36. 1 (1985): 58–72.

———. *Emigrant Entrepreneurs: Shanghai Industrialists in Hong Kong*. Hong Kong: Oxford University Press, 1988.

Wright, Tim, ed. *The Chinese Economy in the Early Twentieth Century: Recent Studies*. New York: St. Martin's Press, 1992.

———. "The Spiritual Heritage of Chinese Capitalism." In *Using the Past to Serve the Present*, edited by Jonathan Unger. Armonk, N.Y.: M. E. Sharpe, 1993, 205–238.

Yamada Tatsuo. *Gendai Chugoku jinmei jiten: Gaimusho Ajiakyoku kanshu* [Dictionary of contemporary Chinese elites]. Tokyo: Kazankai, 1972.

Yan Yunxiang. *Private Life under Socialism: Love, Intimacy, and Family Change in a Chinese Village, 1949–1999*. Stanford: Stanford University Press, 2003.

Yang Zhigang. "Jin Weiying yu Liu Gongcheng zai Yan'an di yici huimian" [The first meeting between Jin Weiying and Liu Gongcheng at Yan'an]. *Shanghai Tan* no. 224 (August 2005): 33.

Yeh Wen-hsin. *The Alienated Academy: Culture and Politics in Republican China, 1919–1937.* Cambridge, Mass.: Council on East Asian Studies, Harvard University, 1990.

Yu Xinfang, ed. *Zhang Shouyong xiansheng zhuan* [Collected works of Zhang Shouyong]. Beijing: Beijing tushuguan chubanshe, 2003.

Zelin, Madeleine. *The Merchants of Zigong: Industrial Entrepreneurship in Early Modern China.* New York: Columbia University Press, 2005.

Zhang Qinshi. "Ji zufude jiaohui er san shi" [Recalling a few of my grandfather's teachings]. In *Yue yuan zhuzuo xuanji* [Selected works from the Yue garden], edited by Zhang Zhilian. Beijing: Zhonghua shuju, 2003.

Notes

Introduction

1. Whyte and Parish, *Urban Life in Contemporary China*, 167.

2. Wong, "Chinese Family Firm," 63. For historians' expressions of their debts to Wong, see Wellington K. K. Chan, "Tradition and Change in the Chinese Business Enterprise," 132–133; and Coble, *Chinese Capitalists in Japan's New Order*, 108.

3. Zelin, *Merchants of Zigong*, 114.

4. On cooperative brothers in a Chinese family firm, see Wellington K. K. Chan, "Origins," 85; and on "the primacy of paternalistic authority" in the Chinese family firm, see his "Tradition and Change in the Chinese Business Enterprise," 132. On competing brothers in a Chinese family firm, see Choi, "Competition among Brothers," 108.

5. Faure, "Control of Equity," 75.

6. Coble, *Chinese Capitalists in Japan's New Order*, 111–113 and 213–214.

7. Kai Yiu Chan, *Business Expansion and Structural Change*, 66–67, 74–76, 155–165.

8. As Siu-lun Wong has noted in a brief discussion of the subject, "the role played by women in Chinese business is shadowy and remains poorly understood." See his "Business Networks, Cultural Values and the State in Hong Kong and Singapore," 140–141.

9. Ko has derived her concept of power from theoretical ideas she has quoted from Michel Foucault and Pierre Bourdieu. See her *Teachers of the Inner Chambers*, 10–12.

10. On the seventeenth century, see ibid.; on the eighteenth century, see Mann, *Precious Records*; on the nineteenth century, see Mann, *Talented Women of the Zhang Family*.

11. Wolf, *Women and the Family in Rural Taiwan*, 33, 37–38. For a recent reconsideration of the issues Wolf has raised, see Sangren, *Chinese Sociologics*, 160–161.

12. The man who served as the mother's secretary, Song Guanlin, also tutored her children in English. Interviewees E and F. Song Guanlin to Father, January 8, 1929; Fourth Son to Father, July 4, 1932; Father to Second, Third, and Fourth Sons, August 19, 1933, all originally written in English. Eighth Son to Mother, June 29, 1945, originally written in Chinese.

13. Eastman, *Family, Field, and Ancestors,* 22.

14. For an example of sons becoming independent after the death of their father, see Esherick, *Ancestral Leaves,* chaps. 8–10. The history of this family, named Ye, is strikingly parallel with the history of the Liu family. The twelve Ye sons were born in Tianjin between 1908 and 1924, making them almost exact contemporaries of the nine Liu sons, who were born in Shanghai between 1909 and 1923. As long as the father in the Ye family was alive, he tightly controlled his sons' upbringing, confining them as boys to the family compound and sending them as day students (not boarding students) to middle school, where they had contact with ideas from the outside world "only in small doses" (145). Not until after the father in the Ye family died prematurely did any of his sons achieve independence. He and his sons had little opportunity to argue with each other over the issue of independence because at the time of his death in 1930, his sons were still quite young, ranging in age from six to twenty-two. By contrast, as shown in the following chapters, the Liu father and his sons had ample opportunity to argue over this issue. At the time of the Liu father's death in 1956, his sons were much older, age thirty-three to forty-seven.

15. Hsiung, *Tender Voyage,* 240, 248–249.

16. Saari, *Legacies of Childhood,* chaps. 3 and 4. Quotations from 105.

17. Esherick, *Ancestral Leaves,* 218–219, 231–232, and 311–316.

18. As Susan Mann has recently pointed out, "studies of the Chinese family system seldom address the profound impact of siblings on child socialization, preferring to stress the importance of parental or even grandparental dominance over the young." Mann, *Talented Women of the Zhang Family,* 179.

19. It is no exaggeration to say that both parents and all twelve children are represented in the Liu family correspondence as found in the archives, but some of the children are not well represented. In particular, the lives of the seventh and ninth sons and the middle daughter are poorly documented. With only a few letters by and about them, we have not devoted a chapter to any of these three (as we have done in the cases of the parents and each of the other children), but we discuss them briefly in Chapter 16.

1. Parents Who Dreamed of a Business Dynasty

1. Liu Nianzhi, *Shiyejia,* 14. On October 30, 1938, Ye Suzhen noted in a letter to Liu Hongsheng: "We have shared life together for thirty-one years up to this day." Originally written in English.

2. Father to Sixth Son, May 28, 1934. Originally written in English.

3. Liu Nianzhi, *Shiyejia,* 14; interviewee G. On the persistence of concubinage from late imperial China into the 1930s, see Lang, *Chinese Family and Society,* 50–52 and 254–255. Under Nationalist law at the time, a man was allowed to set up permanent relationships with other women and have children by them with legal rights equal to those of children borne by his principal wife, as long as his principal wife gave her tacit consent. See Freedman, "Family in China," 247–248; Bernhardt, "Women and the Law," 210–214.

4. Father to Sixth Son, May 28, 1934. Originally written in English.

5. Jones, "Ningpo Pang and Financial Power in Shanghai," 73–96; Shiba, "Ningpo and Its Hinterland," 437; Rowe, *Hankow,* 231; Goodman, *Native Place, City, and Nation.* On the use of Ningbo native-place ties in the Ye and Liu families, see Cochran, *Encountering Chinese Networks,* 16–17 and 152–155.

6. Yeh, *Alienated Academy,* chaps. 2–3.

7. Cochran, *Encountering Chinese Networks,* 13–19.

8. Mother to Fourth Son, May 9, 1941. Originally written in English.

9. Ibid.; Kwei, "Mrs. O. S. L. Family History."

10. Mother to Fourth Son, May 9, 1941. Originally written in English. On Ningbo women, see Mann, "Cult of Domesticity," 179–201.

11. Kwei, "Mrs. O. S. L. Family History"; interviewees A, C, and G.

12. Interviewee G. Liu Hongsheng later claimed that Ye Suzhen's younger brother, Ye Chenghe, had squandered his inheritance of 150,000 ounces of silver (approximately US$232,500) within a span of ten years; Shanghai shehui kexue yuan jingji yanjiu suo, *Liu Hongsheng qiye shiliao,* vol. 3, 471 (hereafter LHS QY SL). Liu was probably not exaggerating, because by 1936 Ye Chenghe was reduced to begging for money from him, Ye Suzhen, and their sons. See Ye Chenghe to Liu Hongsheng, May 24, June 26, October 23, and December 4, 1936; Fourth Son to Ye Chenghe, September 11, 1936; Ye Chenghe to Fourth Son, September 25 and October 23, 1936; Ye Chenghe to Eldest Son, September 25 and 28 and October 23, 1936. All originally written in Chinese.

13. Mother to Fourth Son, May 9, 1941. Originally written in English.

14. Ibid. Liu's mother died on April 15, 1931, and was buried in Ningbo (Father to Fourth Son, April 15, 1932). Both originally written in English. Relationships between Ningbo mothers-in-law and daughters-in-law were reputed to be even tenser than those in other Chinese families. See Mann, "Cult of Domesticity," 193.

15. Cochran, *Encountering Chinese Networks,* 152. On Ningbo financiers' domination in Shanghai, see Mann, "Ningpo Pang and Financial Power in Shanghai," 73–96.

16. Liu Nianzhi, *Shiyejia,* 14; Lu Zhilian, "Qiye da wang Liu Hongsheng," 138.

17. Kwei, "Mrs. O. S. L. Family History."

18. Ibid., February 1930. Liu identified Kwei as the doctor who conducted this medical examination in his letter to Second, Third, and Fourth Sons,

March 21, 1930. On opium in Shanghai at the time, see Wakeman, *Policing Shanghai,* 34–39 and 268–275.

19. Kwei, "Mrs. O. S. L. Family History."

20. Ibid.

21. Father to Second, Third, and Fourth Sons, October 15, 1932. Originally written in English.

22. Ibid.

23. Ibid.

24. Gu Wenhu, "Dianxing qiye ziben jituan de xingcheng ji jiyun gaikuang," chap. 4.

25. Father to Eldest Son, May 11, 1933. Originally written in English.

26. Third Son to Father, December 24, 1933. Originally written in English.

27. Liu Nianzhi, *Shiyejia,* 31–32.

28. Father repeatedly reminded their children of these rules. For examples of his earliest reminders, see Matthews (who reported Father's rules) to Ballard, June 10, 1929; Father to Second, Third, and Fourth Sons, August 19, 1932; Father to Fourth Son, September 6, 1933. All originally written in English. Father to Fifth Son, August 19, 1933. Originally written in Chinese.

29. On a scholarly family's adoption of children's names based on Confucian virtues and feminine ideals of beauty in early twentieth-century China, see Esherick, *Ancestral Leaves,* 130.

30. The eldest daughter, Ming Tsu, and the youngest son, Lien, used these romanizations of their Chinese names in English and apparently had no Western names.

31. When writing letters to one another in English, the Liu children commonly used their Western names, but officially they always used their Chinese names in the West as well as China. As Second Son wrote to Father when he and two of his brothers were about to graduate from Cambridge University, "We do not use our English Christian names for official purposes. They are known only to our good friends. They, therefore, will not be written on our diplomas." Second Son to Father, June 3, 1934. Originally written in English. In an e-mail (February 15, 2007), Jacqueline Cox, Department of Manuscripts and Archives at Cambridge University, confirmed that this was the case. Second, Third, and Fourth Sons' Chinese names were given on their diplomas in romanized form (Lieu Nyan Nyi, Lieu Nyan Li, and Lieu Nyan Tse), and their Western names (Julius, Hannibal, and Johnson) did not appear.

32. See Chapters 2, 4, 5, 7, 9, 10, 14; interviewee C; Father to Seventh Son, October 18, 1932. Originally written in English. This strategy of having each member of a family take up a different specialty was by no means unprecedented in Chinese history. On "a policy of family division of labor" among families in late imperial China, see Ho, "Aspects of Social Mobility in China, 1368–1911," 338.

2. Sons Who Tried for Admission to Cambridge

1. Third Son to Father, April 8, 1930; Second Son to Father, July 1, 1930. Both originally written in English.

2. Sze, "Chinese Students in Great Britain," 312.

3. On Father's network in Shanghai, see Cochran, *Encountering Chinese Networks,* 148–156. For essays on other networks in Shanghai and up-to-date bibliographies on this subject, see the essays in Dillon and Oi, *At the Crossroads of Empires.* In this volume Jeffrey Wasserstrom has pointed out that there is a "bifurcation in the literature" on networks in Shanghai's history: some scholars have written about Chinese networks, and others have written about foreign networks, but hardly any have investigated "border crossers" in networks that spanned "the Chinese/foreign divide." The Lius provide an illustration of border crossers who spanned the Chinese/foreign divide for the purpose of seeking admission for Second, Third, and Fourth Sons at Cambridge University. On border crossers, see Wasserstrom, "Cosmopolitan Connections and Transnational Networks," 208–209.

4. Matthews to Ballard, June 10, 1929. Originally written in English. Second, Third, and Fourth Sons to Mother, c. January 6, 1930; Father to Second, Third, and Fourth Sons, [January] 30, 1932. Originally written in Chinese.

5. Ballard to Matthews, July 2, 1929.

6. Father to Alfred Hunter Ballard, "Power of Attorney to Act as Guardian," October 9, 1929.

7. Second Son to Father, June 25, 1930. Originally written in English.

8. Ibid.

9. Ibid.; Third Son to Father, February 1, 1930. Originally written in English.

10. Quoted in Isaacs, *Scratches on Our Minds,* 116. On the Fu Manchu films, see Seshagiri, "Modernity's (Yellow) Perils," 163.

11. Second Son to Father, June 25, 1929. Originally written in English.

12. Third Son to Uncle, December 16, 1929. Originally written in English.

13. Second Son to Father, June 25, 1930. Originally written in English.

14. Matthews to Ballard, June 6, 1929.

15. Father to Third Son, June 6, 1930. Originally written in Chinese.

16. Ballard to Matthews, July 12, 1929.

17. Third Son to Father, April 8, 1932. Originally written in English.

18. Matthews to Ballard, June 6, 1929; Ballard to Matthews, July 12, 1929.

19. Second Son to Father, May 5, 1930. Originally written in English.

20. Fourth Son to Father, April 9, 1930. Originally written in English.

21. Third Son to Father, November 27, 1929. Originally written in English.

22. Fourth Son to Father, September 27, 1930. Originally written in English.

23. Third Son to Father, October 12, 1930. Originally written in English.

24. Fourth Son to Father, September 27, 1930. Originally written in English.

25. On sports at St. John's University, see Yeh, *Alienated Academy,* 72–73; Morris, *Marrow of the Nation,* 19.

26. Third Son to Father, December 13, 1930. Originally written in English.

27. Fourth Son to Father, n.d., c. January 6, 1930. Originally written in Chinese.

28. Fourth Son to Father, late January, 1930. Originally written in Chinese.

29. Ibid.

30. A minister had a lower diplomatic rank than an ambassador. Not until 1933 did the British government allow China to have an ambassador or an embassy in England. Boorman and Howard, *Biographical Dictionary,* vol. 2, 379.

31. Fourth Son to Father, n.d., c. January 6, 1930. Originally written in Chinese.

32. On Shi, see Boorman and Howard, *Biographical Dictionary of Republican China,* vol. 3, 123–126.

33. Second Son to Father, January 6, 1930. Originally written in Chinese.

34. Fourth Son to Father, n.d., c. January 6, 1930. Originally written in Chinese.

35. Second Son to Father, January 6, 1930. Originally written in Chinese.

36. Fourth Son to Father, n.d., c. January 6, 1930. Originally written in Chinese.

37. Ibid.

38. Ibid.

39. Third Son to Father, February 1, 1930. Originally written in English.

40. Fourth Son to Father, late January 1930. Originally written in Chinese.

41. Second Son to Father, n.d., c. late January 1930. Originally written in Chinese.

42. Second Son to Father, c. mid-February 1930. Originally written in English.

43. Third Son to Father, February 27, 1930. Originally written in English.

44. Fourth Son to Father, March 10, 1930 (misdated as March 10, 1929, in the original). Originally written in English.

45. Third Son to Father, April 8, 1930. Originally written in English.

46. Ibid.

47. Second Son to Father, n.d., early April, 1930. Originally written in English.

48. Second Son to Father, n.d., c. early April 1930. Originally written in English.

49. Matthews to Father, March 13, 1930. Originally written in English.

50. Third Son to Father, May 2, 1930. Originally written in English.

51. Second Son to Father, May 5, 1930. Originally written in English.

52. Ibid.

53. Ballard to Arthur Gray, May 5, 1930.

54. Second Son to Father, May 5, 1930. Originally written in English.

55. Ibid.

56. Ibid.

57. Father to Second Son, June 6, 1930. Originally written in Chinese.

58. Father to Third Son, June 6, 1930. Originally written in Chinese.

59. Fourth Son to Father, June 20, 1930. Originally written in English.

60. Third Son to Father, May 25, 1930. Originally written in Chinese.

61. Ibid.

62. Third Son to Father, June 1, 1930. Originally written in Chinese.

63. Ibid.

64. Father to Second, Third, and Fourth Sons, July 8, 1930. Originally written in English.

65. Fourth Son to Father, June 20, 1930. Originally written in English.

66. Third Son to Father, June 21, 1930. Originally written in Chinese.

67. Ibid.

68. Second Son to Father, June 25, 1930. Originally written in English.

69. Third Son to Father, May 2, 1930. Originally written in English.

70. Father to Second, Third, and Fourth Sons, July 8, 1930. Originally written in English.

71. Ibid.

72. Second Son to Uncle, October 16, 1930. Originally written in English.

73. Ibid.

74. Father to Second Son, October 15, 1930. Originally written in English.

75. Father to Second, Third, and Fourth Sons, November 7, 1930. Originally written in English.

76. Ibid.

77. Fourth Son to Father, June 20, 1930. Originally written in English.

78. Second Son to Father, June 25, 1930. Originally written in English.

79. Ibid.

80. Cochran, *Encountering,* 148–150.

81. Second Son to Father and Mother, July 5, 1930.Originally written in Chinese. In reply, Father agreed. "From the photographs that you sent, I can see that the architecture of Cambridge University is absolutely magnificent, and the setting is beautiful." Father to Second, Third, and Fourth Sons, November 7, 1930. Originally written in English.

82. Third Son to Father, October 12, 1930. Originally written in English.

83. Second Son to Father, October 27, 1930. Originally written in English.

84. Fourth Son to Father, October 29, 1930. Originally written in English.

85. Father to Second, Third, and Fourth Sons, July 29, 1932, and August 9, 1932. Originally written in English. The three boys' majors were confirmed by Jacqueline Cox, Department of Manuscripts and Archives, Cambridge University, e-mail, February 15, 2007.

3. Sons Who Did Not Want to Become British Citizens

1. Father served on the Shanghai Municipal Council from 1931 to 1933. Boorman and Howard, *Biographical Dictionary*, vol. 2, 399.

2. On the Shanghai Incident, see Coble, *Facing Japan*, 39–55.

3. Father to Second, Third, and Fourth Sons, February 14, 1932. Originally written in English.

4. Ibid.

5. Ibid.

6. Third Son to Father, February 1, 1932. Originally written in English. For sensational newspaper coverage of the Shanghai Incident in England at the time, see, for example, the full page of photographs in the London *Times*, February 24, 1932.

7. Second Son to Father, February 10, 1932. Originally written in English.

8. Ibid.

9. Third Son to Father, March 4, 1932. Originally written in English.

10. Third Son to Father, February 22, 1932. Originally written in English.

11. Ibid.

12. Ibid.

13. Third Son to Father, March 11, 1932. Originally written in English.

14. Fourth Son to Father, March 13, 1932. Originally written in English.

15. Ibid.

16. Second Son to Father, March 13, 1932. Originally written in English.

17. On dual citizenship, see Man-houng Lin, "Overseas Chinese Merchants and Multiple Nationality," 991–997. On British attitudes toward China and Japan in 1932, see Thorne, *Limits of Foreign Policy*, 141 and 225–226.

18. Third Son to Father, March 11, 1932. Originally written in English.

19. Ibid.

20. Second Son to Father, March 13, 1932. Originally written in English.

21. Eldest Son to Third Son, March 23, 1932 Originally written in Chinese.

22. Ibid.

23. Ibid.

24. Ibid.

25. Third Son to Father, March 31, 1932. Originally written in English.

26. Father received Eldest Son's letter, as forwarded by Third Son, on April 29, 1932. See Father to Second, Third, and Fourth Sons, April 29, 1932. Later Father complained that Shanghai–Cambridge mail delivery became markedly

slower after the Japanese takeover of Manchuria in 1931. Between 1929 and 1931, his letters had taken only sixteen days to go from Shanghai to Cambridge overland on the Trans-Siberian Railway. After the Japanese takeover of 1931, his letters required a full month to go by sea across the Pacific and Atlantic oceans. Father to Second, Third, and Fourth Sons, November 3, 1931. All originally written in English.

27. Father to Third Son, March 22, 1932. Originally written in English.

28. Father to Second Son, April 6, 1932; Father to Third Son, April 6, 1932. Both originally written in English.

29. Father to Second Son, April 6, 1932. Originally written in English.

30. Father to Third Son, April 6, 1932. Originally written in English.

31. Father to Second, Third, and Fourth Sons, June 17, 1932. Originally written in English.

32. Ibid.

33. Father to Eldest Son, April 29, 1932. Originally written in English.

34. Fourth Son to Father, April 30, 1932; Second Son to Father, June 6, 1932. Both originally written in English.

35. Father to Third Son, April 6, 1932. Originally written in English.

4. A Son Who Wanted to Drop Out of Harvard

1. Father to Eldest Son, October 19, 1932. Originally written in English. Youngest Daughter (quoting Mother) to Eldest Son and others, September 15, 1948. Originally written in Chinese.

2. In the words of anthropologist G. William Skinner, "parents could be said in effect to be 'buying' the gratitude, loyalty and filial devotion of [their eldest son] at the cost of [their youngest son's] alienation. . . . [In] serving his own interests, the eldest son can do no wrong; in serving his, however, the youngest son can do little that is right." See Skinner, " 'Seek a Loyal Subject in a Filial Son,' " 957–958.

3. Father to Eldest Son, September 19, 1931. Originally written in Chinese.

4. Eldest Son to Father, April 4, 1932. Originally written in English. E-mail from Louise Kiefer, Archivist and College Historian, Baldwin-Wallace College, May 1, 2007.

5. Father to Eldest Son, June 27, 1932. Originally written in English.

6. Eldest Son to Father, April 4, 1932. Originally written in Chinese.

7. Father to Eldest Son, March 17, 1932. Originally written in English.

8. Father to Eldest Son, April 29, 1932. Originally written in English.

9. Father to Eldest Son, October 19, 1932. Originally written in English.

10. Ibid.

11. Cochran, *Encountering Chinese Networks,* 150–151.

12. Ibid.

13. Ibid.

14. Father to Eldest Son, November 3, 1932. Originally written in English.

15. Ibid.

16. Father to Eldest Son, October 19, 1932. Originally written in English.

17. Ibid.

18. Father to Eldest Son, November 30, 1932. Originally written in English.

19. Father to Eldest Son, October 19, 1932. Originally written in English.

20. Eldest Son to Father, November 14, 1932. Originally written in Chinese.

21. Ibid.

22. Eldest Son to Father and Mother, November 28, 1932. Originally written in Chinese.

23. Father to Eldest Son, January 20, 1933. Originally written in English.

24. Ibid.

25. Eldest Son to Father, January 29, 1933. Originally written in Chinese.

26. Ibid.

27. Ibid.

28. Ibid.

29. Ibid.

30. Ibid.

31. Ibid.

32. Father to Eldest Son, February 27, 1933. Originally written in English.

33. Ibid., quoted in Eldest Son to Father, March 17, 1933. Originally written in Chinese.

34. Father to Eldest Son, February 27, 1933. Originally written in English.

35. Ibid.

36. Ibid.

37. Ibid.

38. Ibid.

39. Eldest Son to Father, March 17, 1933. Originally written in Chinese.

40. Ibid.

41. Ibid.

42. Ibid.

43. Eldest Son to Father, March 30, 1933. Originally written in Chinese.

44. Ibid.

45. Ibid.

46. Ibid.

47. Father to Eldest Son, March 23, 1933. Originally written in English.

48. Ibid.

49. Ibid.

50. Father to Eldest Son, April 10 and 28, 1933. Both originally written in English.

51. Father to Eldest Son, May 16, 1933. Originally written in English.

52. Father to Eldest Son, April 28, 1933. Originally written in Chinese.

53. Father to Eldest Son, June 16, 1933. Originally written in English.

54. Eldest Son to Father, June 21, 1933. Originally written in Chinese.

55. Father to Eldest Son, July 24, 1933. Originally written in English.

56. Eldest Son to Father, October 16, 1933. Originally written in English.

57. Eldest Son to Father, July 11, 1933. Originally written in English.

58. Eldest Son to Father, August 6, 1933. Originally written in Chinese.

59. Eldest Son to Father, August 25, 1933. Originally written in Chinese.

60. Eldest Son to Father, September 16, 1933. Originally written in Chinese. On Chen, see Boorman and Howard, *Biographical Dictionary,* vol. 1, 192–196.

61. Eldest Son to Father, September 16, 1933. Originally written in Chinese.

62. Father to Eldest Son, May 16, 1933. Originally written in English.

63. Father to Eldest Son, September 22, 1933. Originally written in English.

64. Ibid.

65. Eldest Son to Father and Mother, February 28, 1934. Originally written in Chinese.

66. Father to Eldest Son, April 12, 1934. Originally written in English.

67. Eldest Son to Father, January 24, 1935. Originally written in English.

68. Ibid.; Father to Second, Third, and Fourth Sons, April 9, 1935. Originally written in English.

69. McNiven to Eldest Son, July 24, 1936; e-mail from Kaiyi Chen, University Archives, University of Pennsylvania, January 26, 2007.

70. The graduation date of June 19, 1934, was confirmed by Jacqueline Cox, Department of Manuscripts and Archives, Cambridge University, in an e-mail, February 15, 2007, based on Cambridge's central student record cards for Lieu Nyan Nyi (Second Son), Lieu Nyan Li (Third Son), and Lieu Nyan Tse (Fourth Son).

71. Father to Eldest Son, July 6, 1934. Originally written in English.

5. A Son Who Was Sick

1. Fifth Son to Shi, May 28, 1935. Originally written in English.

2. Fifth Son to Father, February 5, 1935. Originally written in Chinese.

3. Second Son to Mother, July 10, 1930. Originally written in Chinese.

4. Father to Eldest Son, January 6, 1931. Originally written in English.

5. Fifth Son to Father, August 9 and September 25, 1931. Both originally written in Chinese. Father to Eldest Son, September 19, 1931. Originally written in English.

6. Eldest Son to Father, October 2, 1931. Originally written in English.

7. Father to Eldest Son, March 17, 1932. Originally written in English.

8. Fifth Son to Father and Mother, December 15, 1934. Originally written in Chinese.

9. Roehm to Father, June 22, 1932.

10. Father to Eldest Son, June 17, 1932. Originally written in English.

11. Father to Eldest Son, August 21, 1932. Originally written in English.

12. Eldest Son to Father, March 19, 1933. Originally written in Chinese.

13. Ibid.

14. Ibid.

15. Father to Eldest Son, July 6, 1933. Originally written in English.

16. Fifth Son to Mother, August 28, 1933. Originally written in Chinese.

17. Fifth Son to Father, September 9, 1933. Originally written in Chinese.

18. Ibid.

19. Ibid.

20. Eldest Son to Father September 16, 1933. Originally written in Chinese.

21. Father to Fifth Son, October 16, 1933. Originally written in English.

22. Ibid.

23. Fifth Son to Father, November 14, 1933. Originally written in Chinese.

24. Fifth Son to Father, October 28, 1933. Originally written in Chinese.

25. Stone to Father, November 17, 1933. Originally written in English.

26. Father to Fifth Son, December 19, 1933. Originally written in English.

27. Father to Stone, December 19, 1933. Originally written in English.

28. Father to Fifth Son, October 30, 1933. Originally written in English.

29. Fifth Son to Father, February 5, 1934. Originally written in English.

30. Father to Eldest Son, October 16, 1933. Originally written in English. Eldest Son to Father, October 16, 1933. Originally written in Chinese.

31. Eldest Son to Father and Mother, February 28, 1934. Originally written in Chinese.

32. Father to Fifth Son, March 10, 1934. Originally written in English.

33. Ibid.

34. Fifth Son to Father, April 10, 1934. Originally written in English.

35. Fifth Son to Father and Mother, December 25, 1933. Originally written in Chinese. Shi's title was "Minister" until it was changed to "Ambassador," when the United States upgraded China's diplomatic status and allowed China to replace its legation with an embassy in Washington, D.C. in June 1935. See Boorman and Howard, *Biographical Dictionary,* vol. 3, 126.

36. Father to Fifth Son, August 1, 1934. Originally written in English.

37. Ibid.

38. Ibid.

39. Ibid.

40. Fifth Son to Father, September 15, 1934. Originally written in English.

41. Ibid.

42. Fifth Son to Mother, September 20, 1934. Originally written in English.
43. Ibid.
44. Father to Fifth Son, November 17, 1934. Originally written in English.
45. Ibid.
46. Fifth Son to Father, December 15, 1934. Originally written in Chinese.
47. Ibid.
48. Fifth Son to Father, September 15, 1934. Originally written in English.
49. Fifth Son to Father and Mother, December 15, 1934. Originally written in Chinese.
50. Ibid.
51. Ibid.
52. Ibid.
53. Fifth Son to Father and Mother, December 25, 1934. Originally written in English. Fifth Son is perhaps alluding to a metaphor used in a Chinese saying attributed to Confucius: "Rotten wood cannot be carved."
54. Fifth Son to Father and Mother, December 26, 1934. Originally written in Chinese.
55. Ibid.
56. Ibid.
57. Third Son to Father, January 31, 1935. Originally written in English.
58. Father to Fifth Son, January 23, 1935. Originally written in English.
59. Ibid.
60. Ibid.
61. Ibid.
62. Ibid.
63. Ibid.
64. Fifth Son to Father, February 5, 1935. Originally written in Chinese.
65. Ibid.
66. Ibid.
67. Ibid.
68. Fifth Son to Father and Mother, March 10, 1935. Originally written in Chinese. Father to Fifth Son, September 11, 1935. Originally written in English.
69. Father and Mother to Sixth Son, April 19, 1938; Mother to Father, October 19, 1938. Both originally written in Chinese. *Colorado College Alumni Directory* (June 1938), Special Collections, Colorado College; e-mail from Jessy Randall, Colorado College Special Collections, February 14, 2007.
70. Father to Second Son, December 12, 1935. Originally written in English.

6. A Son Who Proposed Marriage to a Westernized Woman

1. Matthews to Ballard, June 10, 1929.
2. Father to Second, Third, and Fourth Sons, August 19, 1933. Originally written in English.

3. Fourth Son to Father, June 8, 1933. Originally written in English.

4. Fourth Son to Liu Jisheng, December 15, 1929; Fourth Son to Father, March 19, 1933. Originally written in English.

5. Third Son to Father, September 27, 1932. Originally written in English.

6. Ibid.

7. Ibid.

8. Ibid.

9. Father to Second, Third, and Fourth Sons, May 30, 1933; Third Son to Father, July 1, 1933. Originally written in English.

10. Father to Second Son, May 12, 1933. Originally written in English.

11. Second Son to Father, n.d., c. July 1933. Originally written in English.

12. Fourth Son to Father, September 10, 1933. Originally written in English.

13. Third Son to Father, July 1, 1933. Originally written in English.

14. Ibid.

15. Ibid.

16. Father to Second Son, August 18, 1933. Originally written in English.

17. Father to Third Son, August 8, 1933. Originally written in English.

18. Third Son to Father, February 16, 1935. Originally written in English.

19. Ibid.

20. Lee, *Shanghai Modern,* chap. 2; Laing, *Selling Happiness,* chap. 6; Cochran, *Chinese Medicine Men,* chap. 3.

21. Third Son to Father, February 16, 1935. Originally written in English.

22. Ibid.

23. Rush, *Opium to Java,* 248.

24. Koo, *No Feast Lasts Forever,* 28.

25. Pan, *Sons of the Yellow Emperor,* 151.

26. Ibid.

27. Koo, *No Feast Lasts Forever,* 74.

28. Pan, *Sons of the Yellow Emperor,* 150–152.

29. Ibid.

30. Ibid.

31. Koo, *No Feast Lasts Forever,* 189.

32. Ibid., 189.

33. Ibid., 139–190; *Men of Shanghai and North China,* 470; interviewee P. Liane's mother left unchanged the name of Liane's brother, Robert "Bobby" Kan.

34. Third Son to Father, March 31, 1935. Originally written in English.

35. Ibid.

36. Ibid.

37. Ibid.

38. Ibid.

39. Father to Sons, April 9, 1935. Originally written in English.

40. Third Son to Father, June 3, 1935. Originally written in English.

41. Ibid.

42. Ibid.

43. Quoted in Second Son to Father, May 24, 1935. Originally written in English.

44. Third Son to Father, August 9, 1935. Originally written in English.

45. Ibid.

46. Ibid.

47. Ibid.

48. Ibid.

49. Father to Third Son, telegram dated August 23, 1935. Originally written in English.

50. Father to Sons, n.d., c. August–September 1935. Originally written in English.

51. Ibid.

52. Ibid.

53. Ibid.

54. Father to Sons, September 11, 1935. Originally written in English.

55. Ibid.

56. Ibid.

57. Father to Second and Third Sons, September 11, 1935. Originally written in English.

58. Father to Sons, September 11, 1935. Originally written in English.

59. Father to Third Son, September 26, 1935. Originally written in English.

60. Father to Sons, September 11, 1935. Originally written in English.

61. Father to Third Son, September 26, 1935. Originally written in English.

62. Second Son to Mother, September 22, 1935. Originally written in Chinese.

63. Ibid.

64. Ibid.

65. Ibid.

66. Third Son to Mother, October 24, 1935. Originally written in Chinese.

67. Ibid.

68. Ibid.

69. Third Son to Fourth Son, October 5, 1935. Originally written in English.

70. Ibid.

71. Boorman and Howard, *Biographical Dictionary,* vol. 2, 279.

72. Father to Quo, September 25, 1935. Originally written in English.

73. Third Son to Father, October 27, 1935. Originally written in English.

74. Third Son to Father, telegram, September 30, 1935. Originally written in English.

75. Third Son to Father, October 4, 1935. Originally written in English.

76. Third Son to Father, October 27, 1935. Originally written in English.

77. Ibid.

78. Ibid.

79. Ibid.

80. Ibid.

81. Ibid.

82. Father to Sons, November 7, 1935. Originally written in English.

83. Ibid.

84. Ibid.

85. Father to Third Son, December 23, 1935. Originally written in English.

86. Father to Second Son, December 12, 1935. Originally written in English.

87. Ibid.

88. Father to Third Son, November 23, 1935. Originally written in English.

89. Ibid.

90. Ibid.

91. Father to Second Son, December 12, 1935. Originally written in English.

92. Father to Third Son, December 27, 1935. Originally written in Chinese.

93. In the 1920s, while Chinese intellectuals attacked filial piety, Chinese social scientists conducted surveys that indicated most young Chinese in Shanghai preferred to live with their parents after getting married. See Glosser, *Chinese Visions of Family and State, 1915–1953*, chap. 1, especially 57–64. The staying power of filial piety has also been emphasized by specialists on late imperial China. In Maram Epstein's words, it was "a core emotion at the center of people's lives"—not "just a form of ritual duty" as Chinese critics of it claimed. "Writing Emotions," 155. In the early twentieth century outside big cities like Shanghai, according to Henrietta Harrison, there was actually an increase in "the demands for an emotional expression of filial piety in the villages"; *Man Awakened from Dreams*, 80.

94. Father to Third Son, December 27, 1935. Originally written in Chinese.

95. Ibid.

96. Interviewee P; Father and Mother to Liane Yen, September 16, 1937; Mother to Liane Yen, September 27, 1937; Mother to Third Son and Liane Yen, October 11, 1937; Mother to Liane Yen, November 15, 1937; Father and Mother to Third Son and Liane Yen, December 4 and 9, 1937; Mother to Liane Yen, December 9, 1937; Father and Mother to Third Son and Liane Yen, December 22, 1937; Mother to Liane Yen, December 22, 1937; Father and Mother to Third Son and Liane Yen, January 3, 1938; Mother to Liane Yen, January 3, 1938. All originally written in English.

7. *A Daughter Who Spoiled a Marriage Alliance*

1. Boorman and Howard, *Biographical Dictionary,* vol. 3, 137. On the political prominence of the Song family, see Coble, "Soong Family and Chinese Capitalists," 69–79. Father investigated the possibility of making a marriage for Eldest Daughter with at least one other family besides the Songs. He went so far as to send a photograph of her to Ye Chongzhi, who presided over a family that included twelve sons and was well connected in business and politics in Tianjin, but Ye declined to pursue the matter. See Esherick, *Ancentral Leaves,* 139.

2. Boorman and Howard, *Biographical Dictionary,* vol. 3, 137–140.

3. On the history of "matching doors" in late imperial China, see Mann, *Precious Records,* 12–13.

4. Interviewee G.

5. Second Son to Father, September 16, 1932. Originally written in English.

6. Kwei, "Mrs. O. S. L. Family History;" Eldest Son to Father, February 19, 1932. Originally written in Chinese. Father to Eldest Son, March 17, 1932 and March 19, 1933. The first originally written in English and the second originally written in Chinese.

7. Second Son to Father, September 16, 1932. Originally written in English.

8. Ibid.

9. Ibid.

10. Third Son to Father, October 10, 1932. Originally written in English.

11. Eldest Son to Father, March 19, 1933. Originally written in Chinese.

12. Eldest Son to Father, February 19, 1932. Originally written in Chinese. The book cited by Eldest Son is William Sebastian Walsh, *The Inferiority Feeling* (New York: Dutton, 1928), which was written for a general audience and attempted to popularize the concept of inferiority as originally formulated by the psychologist Alfred Adler.

13. Eldest Son to Father, March 19, 1933. Originally written in Chinese.

14. Fifth Son to Mother, September 20, 1934. Originally written in Chinese.

15. Fifth Son to Mother, September 9, 1934. Originally written in Chinese.

16. Ibid.

17. Fifth Son to Mother, September 20, 1934. Originally written in Chinese.

18. Father to Sixth Son, May 28, 1934. Originally written in Chinese.

19. Father to Sixth Son, August 15, 1935. Originally written in Chinese.

20. Father to Fifth Son, June 22, 1935. Originally written in English. Eldest Daughter was one of many young women to attend schools for physical education in early twentieth-century Shanghai. See Wang, *Women in the Chinese Enlightenment;* and Morris, *Marrow of the Nation.*

21. Father to Second Son, September 18, 1935. Originally written in English.

22. Third Son to Father, October 4, 1935. Originally written in English.

23. Father to Fifth Son, October 30, 1935. Originally written in English.

24. Father to boys, November 7, 1935. Originally written in English.

25. Father to Sixth Son, August 15, 1935. Originally written in Chinese.

26. Fifth Son to Father, December 5, 1935. Originally written in English.

27. Father to Second, Third, and Fourth Sons, November 7, 1935. Originally written in English.

28. Father to Seventh Son, November 7, 1935. Originally written in Chinese.

29. Father to Second, Third, and Fourth Sons, November 7, 1935. Originally written in Chinese.

30. Father to Second Son, December 11, 1935. Originally written in English.

31. Interviewee E.

32. Father to Fifth Son, December 31, 1935. Originally written in English.

33. Father to Second Son, July 28, 1934. Originally written in English.

34. Interviewees E and G.

35. On Sheng and his family, see Feuerwerker, *China's Early Industrialization,* chap. 3.

36. Interviewees E and G.

37. St. John's University and Nanyang (later Communications) University were comparable in many respects. For example, both used English as a prominent medium of instruction in the classroom, and both emphasized the importance of extracurricular activities outside the classroom. See Yeh, *Alienated Academy,* chaps. 2–3, especially 92–95, 196. The precursor to Nanyang University and Communications University had been founded in 1896 by Xue's relative, Sheng Xuanhuai. See Feuerwerker, *China's Early Industrialization,* 69–70.

38. University Calendars, University Archives, John Rylands University Library, University of Manchester, Manchester, England, as reported by James Peters, University Archivist, e-mails, April 19 and 20, 2007.

39. Engels, *Condition of the Working Class.*

40. Cardwell, "Introduction," 8–9; Morton, "Manchester College of Science and Technology, 1914–1956," 185–189. On Chinese students at Manchester University, see Sze, "Chinese Students in Great Britain," 311–314.

41. Interviewee G.

42. Interviewees G and P.

43. Interviewee G.

44. Interviewee E.

45. Interviewees A and J.

46. Interviewee G.

47. Interviewees E and G. Song Zi'an married Jih-iung Woo, the daughter of Y. C. Woo, who ran the San Francisco branch of the Song family's Bank of Canton. See Seagrave, *Soong Dynasty,* 383.

48. Interviewees E, G, and J.

49. Interviewee E.

50. Fourth Son to Third Son and other brothers, October 30, 1943. Originally written in Chinese.

51. K. K. Ting to Eldest, Third, and Fourth Sons, November 15, 1936. Originally written in English.

52. Mother to Third Son's wife, September 14, 1937. Originally written in English.

53. Mother to Shi Meiyu, December 30, 1937. Originally written in Chinese.

54. Mother to Third Son's wife, October 11, 1937. Originally written in English.

55. Mother to Third Son's wife, December 5, 1937. Originally written in English.

56. Mother to Sixth Son, February 14, 1938. Originally written in Chinese.

57. Father and Mother to Sixth Son, March 7 and May 2, 1938. Both originally written in Chinese. Mother to Father, July 23, 1938. Originally written in English.

58. Mother to Father, August 5, 1938. Originally written in English.

59. Mother to Fourth Son, May 9, 1941. Originally written in English.

60. Youngest Daughter to Eldest Son, September 15, 1948. Originally written in Chinese. Interviewee P.

8. Sons Who Became Leaders in Wartime

1. The only children not in Shanghai were Sixth Son, who was in Chongqing, Seventh Son, who was in Japan, and Eighth Son, who was in the United States. Mother to Seventh Son, July 19, 1938. Originally written in Chinese.

2. Coble, *Chinese Capitalists,* 184–187.

3. Fourth Son, who was present at the meetings with Ueda, recorded his recollections in Liu Nianzhi, "Kangzhan," 171–173, and *Shiyejia,* 83–85. On the waves of pro-Japanese and pro-Nationalist assassinations in Shanghai at this time, see Wakeman, *Shanghai Badlands.* Perhaps the case that paralleled Father's most closely at the time was that of Wang Yiting, a Chinese businessman who fled to Hong Kong when the Japanese occupying forces tried to recruit him to serve as mayor of Shanghai. See Shen, "Wang Yiting in the Social Networks of 1910s–1930s Shanghai," 63–64.

4. Father to Eldest Son and others, July 6, 1938. Originally written in English.

5. Father to Fourth Son, September 24, 1938. Originally written in English.

6. Eldest Son's memo, n.d., c. 1937; Liu Nianzhi, *Shiyejia,* 37–41. Kai Yiu Chan has argued that the Liu Hong Ji (a.k.a. Lieu Ong Kee) accounts office was Father's "core business institution" for channeling financial resources into his various enterprises. See Chan, *Business Expansion and Structural Change in Prewar China.* Quotation from 155.

7. Chen Baozhi, an interview recorded in July 1964, in Shanghai shehui kexue yuan jingji yanjiu suo, *Liu Hongsheng qiye shiliao* (hereafter *LHS QY SL*), vol. 3, 315–316. For examples of Father refereeing sparring matches before the war between his sons on the one hand and his senior managers on the other, see Father to Fourth Son, September 6, 1933, Fourth Son to Father, October 9, 1933, Father to Fourth Son, November 15, 1933, Father to Second, Third, and Fourth Sons, March 7, 1935, Second Son to Father, August 6, 1935, and Eldest Son's memo, n.d., c. 1937. All originally written in English.

8. Father to his sons in Shanghai, April 23, 1939. Originally written in English.

9. Father to Sons, June 25, 1939. Originally written in English.

10. Ibid.

11. Ibid.

12. Third Son to Brothers, June 23, 1939. Originally written in English.

13. Ibid.

14. Second Son to Father, August 5, 1940. Originally written in English.

15. Ibid.

16. Ibid.

17. Second Son to Father, November 6, 1940, in *LHS QY SL,* vol. 3, 77. Translated from a Chinese translation of the original English.

18. Second Son to Father, January 31, 1941, in *LHS QY SL,* vol. 3, 77. Translated from a Chinese translation of the original English.

19. Second Son to Father, December 28, 1940, in *LHS QY SL,* vol. 3, 77. Translated from a Chinese translation of the original English.

20. Coble, *Chinese Capitalists,* 192–193.

21. Third Son to his brothers in Shanghai, July 22, 1941. Originally written in Chinese.

22. Ibid.

23. Ibid.

24. Ibid.

25. Third Son to Eldest and Second Sons, June 22, 1942, *LHS QY SL,* vol. 3, 19.

26. Third Son to Father, June 22, 1942, *LHS QY SL,* vol. 3, 19. Originally written in Chinese.

27. Ibid.

28. Ibid.

29. Ibid.

30. Third Son to Eldest Son and Second Son, June 22, 1942, *LHS QY SL*, vol. 3, 19. Originally written in Chinese.

31. Coble, *Chinese Capitalists,* 191–192.

32. Third Son to Liu Jisheng, November 23, 1942, in *LHS QY SL*, vol. 3, 147–148. Translated from a Chinese translation of the original English.

33. Third Son to Liu Jisheng, December 18, 1942, in *LHS QY SL*, vol. 3, 148–149. Originally written in Chinese.

34. Liu Nianzhi, *Shiyejia,* 89–91.

35. Coble, *Chinese Capitalists,* 184–187.

36. Liu Nianzhi, *Shiyejia,* 88–89.

37. Ibid., 89–90.

38. Ibid., 91–92.

39. Ibid., 92.

40. Ibid., 91–94.

41. Coble, *Chinese Capitalists,* 188.

42. Fourth Son to Third Son and brothers, October 30, 1943. Originally written in Chinese.

43. Quoted by Eighth Son in his reply to Father, March 14, 1942. Originally written in Chinese.

44. Mother to Father, May 6, 1942. Originally written in English.

45. Mother to Fourth Son, July 17, 1943. Originally written in English.

9. A Son Who Joined the Communists

1. The second youngest was Eighth Son, who went to the United States in 1937 at age sixteen, and the third youngest was Fourth Son, who set out for England in 1929 at age seventeen. See Chapters 2 and 10.

2. On the Manchurian Incident and the Chinese protests against it, see Chapter 3, and Coble, *Facing Japan,* 1–38. On the number of Chinese students in Japan, see Saneto, *Chugokujin Nihon ryugakushi,* 146.

3. Father to Eldest Son, n.d., c. November 1931. Originally written in English.

4. Sixth Son to Father, September 23, 1931. Originally written in Chinese.

5. Eldest Son to Father, November 19, 1931. Originally written in Chinese.

6. Second Son to Father, February 10, 1932. Originally written in English.

7. Father to Eldest Son, July 29, 1932. Originally written in English.

8. On Mitsui, see Cochran, *Encountering Chinese Networks,* chap. 4.

9. Onoda to Father, August 17, 1931. Originally written in Japanese.

10. Father to Second, Third, and Fourth Sons, July 29, 1932; Father to Eldest Son, July 29, 1932. Both originally written in English.

11. Sixth Son to Mother, January 14, 1938. Originally written in Chinese.

12. Father to Eldest Son, n.d., c. 1932. Originally written in English.

13. Father to Eldest Son, July 29, 1932. Originally written in English.

14. On Eldest Son and coal, see Chapter 4.

15. Liu Gongcheng, "Kangzhan chuqi xian fu Liu Hongsheng dui zhonggong de taidu," 182; Eighth Son to his brothers, July 15, 1939. Originally written in Chinese.

16. Fourth Son to Father, August 31, 1933. Originally written in English.

17. Father to Sixth Son, May 28, 1934. Originally written in Chinese.

18. Eldest Son to Father, March 18, 1933. Originally written in Chinese.

19. Second Son to Father, September 22, 1935. Originally written in Chinese.

20. Father to Second, Third, and Fourth Sons, August 19, 1933. Originally written in English.

21. Liu Gongcheng, "Kangzhan chuqi xian fu Liu Hongsheng dui zhonggong de taidu," 182.

22. Coble, *Chinese Capitalists*, 11.

23. Liu Gongcheng, "Kangzhan chuqi xian fu Liu Hongsheng dui zhonggong de taidu," 182.

24. Ibid.; Sixth Son to Father, Mother, Mr. Song, Brothers, and Sisters, April 22–26, 1938. Originally written in Chinese.

25. Sixth Son to Father and Mother, October 22, 1937. Originally written in Chinese.

26. Father to Sixth Son, November 4, 1937. Originally written in Chinese.

27. Father to Third Son, September 16, 1937. Originally written in Chinese.

28. Sixth Son to Father and Mother, September 9, 1937. Originally written in Chinese.

29. Sixth Son to Father, Mother, and brothers, September 21, 1937. Originally written in Chinese.

30. Sixth Son to Father and Mother, September 25, 1937. Originally written in Chinese.

31. Sixth Son to Father, Mother, Mr. Song, Brothers, and Sisters, November 29–December 2, 1937. Originally written in Chinese.

32. Father and Mother to Sixth Son, November 4, 1937. Originally written in English.

33. Father to Sixth Son, November 27, 1937. Originally written in Chinese.

34. Coble, *Chinese Capitalists*, 183.

35. Father to Sixth Son, November 27, 1937. Originally written in Chinese.

36. Sixth Son to Father, Mother, Mr. Song, Brothers, and Sisters, November 29–December 2, 1937. Originally written in Chinese.

37. Ibid.

38. Father and Mother to Sixth Son, January 3, 1938. Originally written in Chinese.

39. Ibid.

40. Sixth Son to Father, Mother, brothers, and sisters, November 19, 1937. Originally written in Chinese.

41. Ibid.

42. Ibid.

43. *Time,* December 12, 1938, 47, quoted by Graham, *Ordinary Man, Extraordinary Mission,* 212.

44. Quoted by Graham, *Ordinary Man, Extraordinary Mission,* 256.

45. Graham, *Ordinary Man, Extraordinary Mission,* 252–263.

46. Sixth Son to Father, Mother, Mr. Song, brothers, and sisters, April 22–28, 1938. Originally written in

47. Sixth Son to Father, Mother, brothers, and sisters, November 19, 1937. Originally written in Chinese.

48. Boorman and Howard, *Biographical Dictionary,* vol. 2, 103.

49. Sixth Son to Father, Mother, brothers, and sisters, November 19, 1937. Originally written in Chinese.

50. Ibid.

51. Ibid.

52. Ibid.

53. Sixth Son to Father, Mother, Mr. Song, brothers, and sisters, November 29–December 2, 1937. Originally written in Chinese.

54. Father and Mother to Sixth Son, December 6, 1937. Originally written in Chinese.

55. Ibid.

56. Ibid.

57. Father and Mother to Sixth Son, January 3, 1938. Originally written in Chinese.

58. Chan, *Business Expansion and Structural Change in Pre-war China,* 82, 213 n. 47.

59. Sixth Son to Father, Mother, Mr. Song, brothers, and sisters, November 29–December 2, 1937. Originally written in Chinese.

60. Ibid.

61. Ibid.

62. Ibid.

63. Father and Mother to Sixth Son, December 15, 1937. Originally written in Chinese.

64. Ibid.

65. Father and Mother to Sixth Son, January 3, 1938. Originally written in Chinese.

66. Father and Mother to Sixth Son, March 7, 1938. Originally written in Chinese.

67. Sixth Son to Father, Mother, Mr. Song, brothers, and sisters, April 22–26, 1938. Originally written in Chinese.

68. Ibid.

69. Ibid.

70. Ibid.

71. Ibid.

72. Ibid.

73. Ibid.

74. Ibid.

75. Ibid.

76. Ibid.

77. Sixth Son to Father, Mother, brothers, and sisters, November 19, 1937. Originally written in Chinese.

78. Ibid.

79. Williamsen, "Military Dimension, 1937–1941," 136.

80. Liu Gongcheng, "Kangzhan chuqi xian fu Liu Hongsheng dui zhonggong de taidu," 183.

81. Ibid. Zhang had known Zhou Enlai since Zhou's days as a student in Zhang's Nankai Middle School, class of 1917.

82. Yang Zhigang, "Jin Weiying yu Liu Gongcheng zai Yan'an di yici huimian," 33. For examples of contemporaries of Sixth Son changing their names when joining the Chinese Communist Party in the 1930s, see Esherick, *Ancestral Leaves*, 130.

83. Liu Gongcheng, "Kangzhan chuqi xian fu Liu Hongsheng dui zhonggong de taidu," 183.

84. Sixth Son to Shen Shuyu and Wang Jingci, July 17, 1938. Originally written in Chinese. Yang Zhigang, "Jin Weiying yu Liu Gongcheng zai Yan'an di yici huimian," 33.

85. Sixth Son to Shen Shuyu and Wang Jingci, July 17, 1938. Originally written in Chinese. These two were Sixth Son's coworkers at the Sichuan Cement Company in Chongqing, where he mailed them the postcard. They, in turn, forwarded it to his family in Shanghai.

86. Sixth Son to Father, February 26, 1937. Originally written in Chinese.

87. Yang Zhigang, "Jin Weiying yu Liu Gongcheng zai Yan'an di yici huimian," 33. On Kawakami, see Bernstein, "Kawakami Hajime," 86–109. On Chinese students' interest in Japanese radicalism, see Bernal, "Triumph of Anarchism over Marxism, 1906–1907," 97–142; Rankin, *Early Chinese Revolutionaries;* Harrell, *Sowing the Seeds of Change;* Lu, *Re-understanding Japan.*

88. Sixth Son to Father, February 26, 1937. Originally written in Chinese.

89. Ibid.

90. Schran, *Guerrilla Economy,* 99.

91. Sixth Son to Shen Shuyu and Wang Jingci (who forwarded the card to Sixth Son's family), July 17, 1938. Originally written in Chinese.

92. Sixth Son to Father and Mother, May 6, 1939. Originally written in Chinese.

93. Ibid.

94. Ibid.

95. Father and Mother to Sixth Son, May 11, 1938. Originally written in Chinese.

96. Liu Gongcheng, "Kangzhan chuqi xian fu Liu Hongsheng dui zhong-gong de taidu," 182.

97. Mother to Father, July 11, 1938. Originally written in English.

98. Ibid.

99. Mother to Father, August 2, 14, 25, 30, September 9, October 16, 19, 27, 1938. Originally written in English.

100. Mother to Father, August 14, 1938. Originally written in English.

101. Mother to Father, August 25, 1938. Originally written in English.

102. The host at the dinner was Huang Jiangchuan (K. T. Oei), a relative of Third Son's wife. Father to Fourth Son, July 2, 1938. Originally written in Chinese.

103. Boorman and Howard, *Biographical Dictionary,* vol. 1, 438–439.

104. Father to Fourth Son, July 2, 1938. Originally written in Chinese.

105. Ibid.

106. Father to Mother, September 24, 1938, in Shanghai shehui kexue yuan jingji yanjiu suo, *Liu Hongsheng qiye shiliao,* vol. 3, 138–139. Originally written in Chinese.

107. Liu Gongcheng, "Dui diliushibaji 'Kangzhan qijian liushi qianchuan jingguo' de dingzheng," 198–199. Sixth Son recorded this recollection in reply to the publication of Fourth Son's article in which he claimed that Sixth Son had gone from Yan'an to Chongqing because Father had "summoned" him there. Sixth Son maintained that after reaching Yan'an in July 1938, he had not left there for the duration of the year and that in the summer of 1939 he had left Yan'an for Chongqing on his own initiative—not in response to any summons from Father. For the article to which Sixth Son reacted, see Liu Nianzhi, "Kangzhan Qijian liushi qiye qianchuan jingguo," 176. For Fourth Son's subsequent revision of his interpretation, see Liu Nianzhi, *Shiyejia,* 88.

108. Liu Gongcheng, "Dui diliushibaji 'Kangzhan qijian liushi qianchuan jingguo' de dingzheng," 198–199.

109. Sixth Son to Father and Mother, May 6, 1939. Originally written in Chinese.

110. Quoted by Reardon-Anderson, *Study of Change,* 343–344.

111. Liu Gongcheng, "Kangzhan chuqi xian fu Liu Hongsheng dui zhong-gong de taidu," 186.

112. Liu Nianzhi, *Shiyejia,* 88.

113. Mother to Eighth Son, October 20, 1939. Originally written in Chinese.

114. Father to his sons in Shanghai, January 30, 1940. Originally written in Chinese. Liu Nianzhi, *Shiyejia,* 98–99.

115. Ibid., 98.

116. Skinner, "Seek a Loyal Subject in a Filial Son," 974–975; see also Sulloway, *Born to Rebel*. For an example of an early twentieth-century Chinese family in which younger sons seem to have been "born to rebel" more than older ones, see Esherick, *Ancestral Leaves*, 157–158.

10. A Son Who Battled Depression

1. Eighth Son to Fourth Son, n.d., c. January 1939.
2. Eighth Son to Father and Mother, January 7, 1939.
3. Eighth Son to Father and Mother, January 9, 1939.
4. Ibid.
5. Ibid.
6. On the number of Chinese students at MIT, see Eighth Son to his brothers, April 23, 1939.
7. Mother to Eighth Son, January 9, 1939.
8. Eighth Son to Mother, May 14, 1941.
9. Mother to Eighth Son, January 20, 1939.
10. Mother to Eighth Son, January 9, 1939.
11. Mother to Eighth Son, February, 12, 1939.
12. Mother to Eighth Son, June 8, 1939.
13. Mother to Eighth Son, August 1, 1939.
14. Mother to Eighth Son, November 6, 1939.
15. Ibid.
16. Eighth Son to Fifth Son, n.d., c. fall 1939.
17. Eighth Son to Eldest Son, March 19, 1939.
18. Eldest Son to Eighth Son, March 18, 1939.
19. Ibid.
20. Eighth Son to Fourth Son, n.d., c. spring 1939.
21. Ibid.
22. Eighth Son to Eldest Son, June 4, 1939.
23. Eighth Son to his brothers and sisters, April 1, 1939.
24. Eighth Son to Fourth Son, n.d., c. 1939.
26. Eighth Son to Fifth Son, n.d., c. fall 1939.
27. Ibid.
28. Eighth Son to Fifth Son, n.d., fall 1939.
29. Eighth Son to Fifth Son, c. fall 1939.
30. Ibid.
31. Ibid.
32. Ibid.
33. Ibid.
34. Eighth Son to Fifth Son, fall 1939.
35. Eighth Son to Eldest Son, n.d., c. spring 1940.
36. Ibid.

37. Ibid.

38. Eighth Son to Eldest Son, June 4, 1939.

39. Eighth Son to Fourth Son, August 21, 1940.

40. Ibid.

41. Ibid.

42. Ibid.

43. Eighth Son to his brothers, April 1, 12, 23, 1939.

44. Eighth Son to Fourth Son, August 21, 1940.

45. Ibid.

46. Eighth Son to Mother, January 21, 1921[1941].

47. Eighth Son to Mother, May 14, 1941.

48. Raeder to Frick, n.d., c. February 1941.

49. We are grateful to Howard Feinstein, who is both a psychiatrist and a historian, for explaining the meanings of these terms. For examples of "changing psychiatric concepts" for diagnostic purposes in the history of McLean, see Sutton, *Crossroads in Psychiatry,* 150–152, 212, 224–227, 270–271.

50. Tong to Hsiao, November 14, 1940.

51. Frick to Hunt Engineering Company, November 15, 1940.

52. Ku to Woo, December 7, 1940.

53. Report from McLean, December 12, 1940.

54. Ibid. In late November 1940, visitors were still being discouraged from seeing or even forbidden to see Eighth Son. W. David Woo to Eldest Son, January 16, 1941.

55. Tong to Hsiao, November 14, 1940.

56. Eighth Son to Mother, May 14, 1941.

57. Eighth Son to Eldest Son, January 21, 1921 [1941].

58. Liu Jisheng to Eldest Son, January 18, 1941.

59. Ibid.

60. For favorable assessments of McLean by Eighth Son's visitors, see Tong to Hsiao, November 14, 1940; Frick to Hunt Engineering Company, November 15, 1940; and Frick to Wei, n.d., c. February 1941, in which Eighth Son's psychiatrist, Dr. Oscar Raeder, is characterized as "one of the outstanding brain specialists in the United States." For a history of McLean, see Sutton, *Crossroads in Psychiatry.* On experiences of patients at McLean, see Kaysen, *Girl, Interrupted;* and Beam, *Gracefully Insane.*

61. Eighth Son to Mother, May 14, 1941.

62. Ibid.

63. Ibid.

64. Father to sons in Shanghai, April 7, 1941.

65. On Eighth Son's behalf, Frick claimed reimbursement from MIT for his tuition, transferred the funds to McLean for his hospital costs, stored his car, held his passport, secured his personal effects, and ultimately made arrangements for his trip home. Frick reported on these transactions to the

members of the Liu family through Hunt Engineering Corporation's branches in Shanghai and Hong Kong. Frick to Hunt Engineering Corporation, November 15, 1940; Eldest Son to Hunt, December 20, 1940; Eldest Son to Frick, December 20, 1940; Frick to Wei, n.d., c. February, 1941; Father to Eldest Son, May 13, 1941; Wei to Father, June 13, 1941.

66. Father to Eldest Son, May 13, 1941.

67. Eighth Son to brothers and sisters, July 26, 1941.

68. Ibid.

69. Father to Frick, April 7, 1941.

11. Mother's Struggle to Save Her Marriage

1. On Chinese "resistance war wives" appearing in public with their "husbands" during the Sino-Japanese War of 1937–1945, even though the husbands had not been divorced from their prewar wives, see Lu Fangshang, "Lingyizhong 'wei zuzhi,'" 97–121. On the dramatic rises in the divorce rate throughout the Western world during and immediately following World War I and World War II, see Phillips, *Putting Asunder,* chap. 13.

2. Quoted in Lang, *Chinese Family and Society,* 50.

3. Freedman, "Family in China," 247–248.

4. In not taking a concubine, Father followed a pattern that seems to have been prevalent among elite men in Shanghai and other cities of the lower Yangzi region at the time. According to a survey of them in 1920, no less than 82 percent declared that they would not take concubines. Of the small minority who conceded they would take concubines, most said they would do so only if their wives failed to produce children—a rationale that certainly did not apply in Father's case. See Glosser, *Chinese Visions of Family and State, 1915–1953,* 74–75.

5. Interviewees N and O.

6. Interviewee G. On the hierarchy of prostitution in Shanghai at the time, see Hershatter, *Dangerous Pleasures,* chap. 2.

7. Interviewee D.

8. Interviewee G.

9. Father to Sixth Son, May 28, 1934. Originally written in English.

10. Ibid.

11. Ibid.

12. Ibid.

13. Ibid.

14. Interviewee G.

15. Interviewee D.

16. Pan, *Sons of the Yellow Emperor,* 201. Pan was referring to Koo Hui-lan (nee Oei) (who was the sister of Third Son's wife's mother—see Chapter 6) and her husband, Gu Weizhun (Wellington Koo), a diplomat who served as the

Nationalist government's ambassador to France, Great Britain, and the United States. On this couple, see Koo, *No Feast Lasts Forever*. On Chinese capitalists with mistresses, see Mao Dun's classic novel *Midnight*, which was originally published in 1933. Other examples of leaders with mistresses include the political leader Chiang Kai-shek and the literary figures Xu Zhimo and Guo Moruo. On Chiang, see Chen Chieh-ju, *Chiang Kai-shek's Secret Past*; on Xu, see Spence, *Gate of Heavenly Peace*, 193; and on Guo, see Lu, *Re-understanding Japan*, 94–96.

17. For the duration of the war, Mother and other members of her family kept their residences in the French Concession even while they moved from one house to another. In the late 1930s, she moved to Rue Chapsal, and in early 1941 she settled into a house on Jubilee Court. Mother to Eldest Daughter, December 3, 1940, and February 19, 1941; Mother to Eighth Son, April 5, 1941. All originally written in English.

18. Father to Fourth Son, sons, daughters, son-in-law, and daughters-in-law, July 1, 1938. Originally written in English.

19. Father to Fourth Son, July 9, 1938. To be sure that Fourth Son followed these instructions, Father repeated them to him in a letter on July 25, 1938. Originally written in English.

20. Mother to Father, August 14, 1938. Originally written in English.

21. Ibid.

22. Mother to Father, September 14, 1938. Originally written in English.

23. Mother to Father, August 14, 1938. Originally written in English.

24. Mother to Father, September 14, 1938. Originally written in English.

25. Mother to Father, September 16, 1938. Originally written in English.

26. Ibid.

27. Ibid.

28. Father to Mother, September 24, 1938. Originally written in Chinese.

29. Ibid.

30. Mother to Liu Jisheng, October 30, 1939. Originally written in English.

31. Sixth Son to brothers and sisters, January 24, 1940. Originally written in Chinese.

32. Mother to Liu Jisheng, n.d., ca. summer 1940. Originally written in English.

33. Father to Eldest Son and Second Son, n.d., c. 1940. Originally written in Chinese.

34. Father to Eldest Son, March 15, 1941. Originally written in English.

35. Mother to Fourth Son, April 5, 1941. Originally written in English.

36. Ibid.

37. Ibid.

38. Mother to Fourth Son, May 9, 1941. Originally written in English.

39. Ibid.

40. Ibid.

41. Ibid.

42. Ibid.

43. Ibid.

44. Ibid.

45. Ibid.

46. Ibid.

47. Mother to Father, June 19, 1941. Originally written in English.

48. Ibid.

49. Third Son to Eldest, Second, Fifth, and Seventh Sons, July 31, 1941; Mother to Phoebe Tsoh (Fourth Son's wife), September 3, 1941. Both originally written in Chinese.

50. Mother to Phoebe Tsoh, September 3, 1941; Mother to Fourth Son, September 4, 1941. Mother wrote to Fourth Son in Chongqing, and she anticipated that his wife would soon join him there, but in fact his wife did not arrive there until several months later in May 1942. Mother to Fourth Son's wife, June 29, 1942. All originally written in English.

51. Father to Eldest Son and siblings, October 14, 1941. Originally written in English.

52. Ibid.

53. Ibid.

54. Ibid.

55. Sixth Son to Brothers and Sisters, January 24, 1940. Originally written in Chinese.

56. Eighth Son to brothers, May 23, 1942. Originally written in Chinese.

57. [Illegible signature probably of Lily Lieu, Fourth Son's cousin, who was living in Kunming at the time] to Fourth Son, January 16, 1943. Originally written in Chinese. Chongqing Municipal Archives, 0230/0102, juan 29, 189; Liu Nianzhi, "Cong kang Ri shengli dao quanguo jiefang de Liu Hongsheng," 195; interviewee D; Shi Qun, "Guangfang jingying gezhong de Liu Hongsheng," 116.

58. Fourth Son to Third Son and brothers, October 30, 1943. Originally written in Chinese.

59. Fourth Son to Second Son, October 29, 1943. Originally written in Chinese.

60. Fourth Son to Third Son and brothers, October 30, 1943. Originally written in Chinese.

61. Ibid.

62. Fourth Son to Second Son, October 29, 1943. Originally written in Chinese.

63. Eldest Sons (judging by context—signatures missing) to Fourth Son, July 17, 1943. Originally written in Chinese.

64. Ibid.

65. Ibid.

66. Ibid.

67. Ibid.

68. Fourth Son to Third Son and brothers, October 30, 1943. Originally written in Chinese.

69. Ibid.

70. Fourth Son to Second Son, October 29, 1943. Originally written in Chinese.

71. Fourth Son to Third Son and brothers, October 30, 1943. Originally written in Chinese.

72. Ibid.

73. Chinese women supposedly married into their husband's families permanently, but if Mother had left her husband's household and returned to her natal family for help and refuge, she would not have been the first Chinese woman to do so. On this practice in Chinese history, see Judd, *"Niangjia,"* 525–544; Mann, "Grooming a Daughter for Marriage"; and Theiss, *Disgraceful Matters,* 91–92.

12. The Family's Postwar Disunion and Reunion

1. Father to Liu Jisheng, August 15, 1945. Originally written in Chinese.

2. Interviewee G.

3. Liu Nianzhi, *Shiyejia,* 89–91.

4. Ibid., 94–95; Father to Liu Jisheng, August 15, 1945. Originally written in Chinese.

5. Boorman and Howard, *Biographical Dictionary,* vol. 1, 254.

6. Liu Nianzhi, *Shiyejia,* 99.

7. Ibid.

8. Father to Eldest Son, Second Son, and Third Son, August 15, 1945, in Shanghai shehui kexue yuan jingji yanjiu suo, *Liu Hongsheng qiye shiliao* (hereafter *LHS QY SL*), vol. 3, 240. Originally written in Chinese.

9. Father to Liu Jisheng, August 15, 1945, in *LHS QY SL,* vol. 3, 239–240. Originally written in Chinese.

10. Liu Nianzhi, *Shiyejia,* 103.

11. Liu Nianzhi, "Cong Kangri shengli dao quanguo jiefang de Liu Hongsheng," 190.

12. Ibid.

13. Liu Nianzhi, *Shiyejia,* 103; Liu Nianzhi, "Cong Kangri shengli dao quanguo jiefang de Liu Hongsheng," 190. There was no question of Second Son aligning himself with both Xuan Tiewu and Dai Li because Dai considered Xuan to be (in Dai's words) an "absolutely irreconcilable" enemy. See Wakeman, *Spymaster,* 354.

14. Coble, *Chinese Capitalists,* 193; Cheng Nianqi, "Liu Hongsheng: Zai gou'an yu minzu dayi zhijian jueze," 43–44.

15. Interviewees A and F.

16. Liu Nianzhi, *Shiyejia,* 99–101; Liu Nianzhi, "Cong Kangri shengli dao quanguo jiefang de Liu Hongsheng," 186–187.

17. Liu Nianzhi, *Shiyejia,* 101.

18. Ibid.

19. Ibid., 101–102; Liu Nianzhi, "Cong Kangri shengli dao quanguo jiefang de Liu Hongsheng," 188; National Archives of the United States, 84/350/53/8, Margaret K. Gardner to the files, June 11, 1946.

20. Romanus and Sunderland, *Time Runs Out in CBI,* 257–258.

21. Liu Nianzhi, *Shiyejia,* 103; Liu Nianzhi, "Cong Kangri shengli dao quanguo jiefang de Liu Hongsheng," 190.

22. Cheng, *Foreign Trade and Industrial Development in China,* 174.

23. Liu Nianzhi, "Cong Kangri shengli dao quanguo jiefang de Liu Hong-sheng," 192.

24. Ibid., 190.

25. Liu Nianzhi, *Shiyejia,* 106.

26. Cheng, *Foreign Trade and Industrial Development in China,* 174.

27. *UNRRA in China, 1945–1947,* 39.

28. Sixth Son to Father, October 28, 1945. Originally written in Chinese. Eighth Son to Father, June 4, 1947. Originally written in English. Liu Nianzhi, *Shiyejia,* 88–89 and 98–99.

29. On Weng, see Boorman and Howard, *Biographical Dictionary,* vol. 3, 411–412.

30. Interviewee A.

31. Liu Nianzhi, "Kangzhan Qijian liushi qiye qianchuan jingguo," 183.

32. Father to Sixth Son, December 3, 1945. Originally written in Chinese.

33. Sixth Son to Father, May 27, 1946. Originally written in English.

34. Sixth Son to Father, June 18, 1946. Originally written in English.

35. Father to Eighth Son, March 19, 1945. Originally written in Chinese.

36. Eighth Son to Father, March 27, 1945. Originally written in Chinese.

37. Eighth Son to his brothers, June 29, 1946. Originally written in Chinese.

38. Eighth Son to Eldest Son, August 14, 1946. Originally written in English.

39. Mother to Sixth and Eighth Sons, February 15, 1947. Originally written in English.

40. Ward to Eighth Son, May 28, 1947; Eighth Son to Wang, June 1, 1947; Eighth Son to Liu, September 12, 1947; Eighth Son to Father, September 16, 1947. All originally written in English.

41. Mother to Sixth Son, March 22 and 24, April 5, July 30, 1942; Mother to Eldest Daughter, September 8, 1942; Mother to Fourth Son, January 30, 1943; Fourth Son to his brothers in Shanghai, July 10, 1943. All originally written in Chinese. Mother to Fourth Son, May 9, 1941. Originally written in English.

42. Interviewee E. Eldest Daughter arranged for Father to take a portion of their savings, 1 million Chinese dollars (*fabi*, the unit of the Nationalist government's currency), for her to Shanghai when he returned there in early October 1945, so that it could be invested right away, two months before she and her family were able to leave Chongqing for Shanghai. Father delivered it to Eldest Son, who made the investment for Eldest Daughter. Eldest Daughter to Mother, September 22, 1945; Eldest Son to Eldest Daughter, November 6, 1945. Both originally written in Chinese

43. Wang Shimin, *Shanghai minyong hangkong zhi*, 146–147.

44. On Tao Guiji and Baohua, see *Shanghai zhizao chang shang gailan*, 966 and 982.

45. Interviewee E. On Xu's holdings see Cochran, *Chinese Medicine Men*, 90.

46. Wang Shimin, *Shanghai minyong hangkong zhi*, 147.

47. Interviewee E. Wang Shimin, *Shanghai minyong hangkong zhi*, 148.

48. Wang Shimin, *Shanghai minyong hangkong zhi*, 148.

49. Interviewees E and G.

50. While in Chongqing, Eldest Daughter had made efforts to reconcile with Father, but there is no evidence that he had reciprocated. Between the end of the war and their return to Shanghai, for example, Eldest Daughter offered her parents a valuable gift—a wood fungus from Yunnan. She proposed to give it to Father in Chongqing so that he could carry it back to Shanghai, but rather than approach him directly about it, she made this proposal by writing to Mother in Shanghai. See Eldest Daughter to Mother, September 22, 1945. Originally written in Chinese.

51. Interviewees E and G.

52. Ten of Father's eleven sons lived in Shanghai if sons by his mistresses are included.

53. Mother to Eighth Son, February 15, 1947. Originally written in English.

54. For other examples, see Coble, *Chinese Capitalists*, pt. 3.

13. Father's Decision to Live in the People's Republic

1. Father to Eighth Son, February 23, 1948. Originally written in Chinese.

2. The Lius who moved to Taiwan at this time included Eldest Son and his wife (who had no children); Third, Fourth, Fifth, and Seventh Sons and their wives and children; Eldest Daughter's husband, Xue Diyi, and their children; and Middle Daughter and her husband and children. Even Sixth Son, a member of the Chinese Communist Party since the late 1930s, went to Taiwan in 1948 with his wife on their honeymoon. Although he showed no signs of settling there permanently, his wife accompanied her parents there and helped them to establish their residence in Taipei in 1949 before she returned to China via Hong Kong and rejoined her husband in Shanghai. Seventh Son to Father, September 1, November 12, and December 11, 1947; Eighth Son to

Father and Mother, February 9, 1948; Father to Eighth Son, February 23, 1948, Yan Xiangqing (Eldest Son's wife) to Eldest Son (probably July) 13, 20, and 24, 1948; and Eldest Son to Chen Yuanzhang, (probably August) 18, 1948; Xu Jingshu (Sixth Son's wife) to Father and Mother, November 26, 1948. All originally written in Chinese. Eighth Son to his brothers, June 19, 1948; Eighth Son to Eldest Son, August 16, 1948. Both originally written in English. Liu Nianzhi, *Shiyejia*, 110.

3. Quotations in this paragraph are from Eastman, *Seeds of Destruction*, 182–183.

4. Liu Nianzhi, *Shiyejia*, 108–109.

5. Quoted by Eastman, *Seeds of Destruction*, 192.

6. Ibid., 196–197.

7. Sixth Son's wife to Father and Mother, November 26, 1948. Seventh Son had become fluent in Japanese during his student days in Tokyo, 1932–1938, and he took a special interest in Japan's trade with Taiwan, which had been a Japanese colony for fifty years, 1895–1945. Seventh Son to his elder brothers, September 1947; Seventh Son to Father, June 15, 1949. All originally written in Chinese.

8. Liu Nianzhi, *Shiyejia*, 110–111.

9. Ibid., 112–113.

10. Ibid., 111.

11. Ibid., 112–113.

12. Ibid., 114–115.

13. Zhang Dehua to Father, April 28, 1949. Originally written in Chinese.

14. Liu Nianzhi, *Shiyejia*, 111–112.

15. Even though Father chose not to emigrate to Taiwan, representatives of the Nationalist government continued to cite him as a key example of a Chinese capitalist victimized by the Communist Revolution. In 1950 in a speech to the International Labour Conference in Geneva, Switzerland, for example, the Nationalist delegate Xu Xueyou (Hsu Hsueh-yu) claimed that "with the coming of the Communist usurpers, [Father's] textile mills, cement works and match factories were all expropriated." According to Xu, after fleeing to Hong Kong in May 1949, Father "could not but brood over his new loss of property, a gigantic industrial network he had built up over a span of some forty years with his commendable ingenuity and foresight." *Record of Proceedings of the Thirty-third Session of the International Labour Conference, Geneva, 1950*, 143–144.

16. For detailed descriptions of several other Chinese capitalists and analyses of their decisions whether to stay in China or leave or return to it in 1949, see the papers presented at the conference "The Capitalist Dilemma in China's Communist Revolution," held at Cornell University, Ithaca, New York, October 9–11, 2009.

17. Liu Nianzhi, *Shiyejia*, 116.

18. Second Son to Father, June 4, 1949. Originally written in Chinese.

19. Ibid.

20. Ibid.

21. Ibid.

22. Liu Nianzhi, *Shiyejia,* 115–116.

23. Father to Eighth Son, July 14, 1949; Mother to Father, August 6, 1949; Father to Youngest Daughter, August 23, 1949. All originally written in Chinese.

24. Mother to Father, August 6, 1949. Originally written in Chinese.

25. Sixth Son to Father, June 9, 1949. Originally written in Chinese.

26. He Guiying to Father, June 30, 1940. Originally written in Chinese.

27. Interviewee F.

28. Liu Nianzhi, *Shiyejia,* 115–116. In this passage, Father did not identify Zhou's emissaries by name. They might have been Pan Zongyao and Zhang Huinong, two emissaries Zhou Enlai sent to Hong Kong to persuade the banker Chen Guangfu and other leading financiers and capitalists to return to China in 1950. See Chen Guangfu, *Chen Guangfu riji,* 249–251. We are grateful to Dr. Pui Tak Lee for this reference.

29. Father to Hu Yigeng, July 14, 19, 25, and 27, 1949, in Shanghai shehui kexue yuan jingji yanjiu suo), *Liu Hongsheng qiye shiliao,* vol. 3, 368–372; and Fifth Son and Seventh Son to Father, August 25, 1949, in vol. 3, 454. All originally written in Chinese. Eighth Son to Eldest Son, August 16, 1948. Originally written in English.

30. Liu Nianzhi, *Shiyejia,* 116.

31. Ibid., 115–116.

32. *Wenhui bao* (Shanghai), November 5, 1949.

33. On December 25, 1947, at the height of the Chinese Civil War, Mao Zedong introduced this distinction between "national capitalists" and "comprador bureaucratic capitalists." He envisioned "genuine national capitalists" as the ones who would contribute to the "new democratic national economy" of China after his Communist forces ousted Chiang Kai-shek's Nationalist government and took power. Less than two years later, in 1949, when Mao claimed victory and established a new government, the Chinese Communist Party began to use Mao's terminology to separate capitalists into two groups: national capitalists, who were regarded as patriotic and were encouraged to stay as citizens of the People's Republic; and comprador bureaucratic capitalists, who were not eligible for citizenship because they were said to be in league with foreign imperialists and corrupt officials. Since then, scholars in China have continued to make this distinction and have argued with each other about whether Chinese capitalists at all points in modern history deserve to be praised as nationalists or condemned as compradors and bureaucrats. For Mao's original formulation, see Mao Tse-tung (Mao Zedong), *Selected Works,* vol. 4, 167–169. For examples of historical writing in China and a helpful

historiographical analysis of it, see Wright, *Chinese Economy in the Early Twentieth Century,* and Wright, "Spiritual Heritage of Chinese Capitalism," 205–238.

34. Liu Nianzhi, *Shiyejia,* 116–117.

35. Wakeman, "'Cleanup,'" 21–58.

36. *Wenhui bao* (Shanghai), December 18, 1949.

37. *Wenhui bao* (Shanghai), December 17, 1949.

38. *Wenhui bao* (Shanghai), February 8, 1950.

39. *Wenhui bao* (Shanghai), December 17, 1949, and February 8, 1950.

40. Liu Nianzhi, *Shiyejia,* 118–123.

41. For other examples, see Wong, *Emigrant Entrepreneurs,* 31–32.

42. Liu Nianzhi, *Shiyejia,* 120.

43. For examples of other capitalists contributing to the Korean War effort, see Dillon, "New Democracy and the Demise of Private Charity in Shanghai," 89–90.

44. *Wenhui bao* (Shanghai), January 16, 1951.

45. Liu Nianzhi, *Shiyejia,* 120–121. For a fuller analysis of nationalism and transnationalism as explanations for Chinese capitalists' decisions to stay in China or leave during the late 1940s and early 1950s, see Cochran, "Capitalists Choosing Communist China," 359–385.

46. Gardner, "*Wu-fan* Campaign in Shanghai," 477–539. On the range of suffering among capitalists during the Five Anti campaign, see Dillon, "New Democracy and the Demise of Private Charity in Shanghai."

47. *Wenhui bao* (Shanghai), September 5 and December 2, 1950. Quotations are from the latter.

48. Liu Nianzhi, *Shiyejia,* 120.

49. Watanabe, "Shihonka no jiko kaizo," 165.

50. Ibid., 164.

51. Ibid., 164–166. On Mao Zedong's efforts to court Chinese business leaders in the fall of 1953, see Li, *Mao and Economic Stalinization of China, 1848–1953,* 139.

14. A Daughter Who Forged Family Alliances

1. Father to Eldest Son, October 2, 1931. Originally written in English.

2. Father to Sixth and Seventh Sons, November 30, 1932. Originally written in Chinese.

3. Father to Fifth Son, June 22, 1935. Originally written in English.

4. Youngest Daughter to Eldest Son and others, September 15, 1948. Originally written in Chinese.

5. Ibid.

6. Ibid.

7. Mother to Fourth Son, May 9, 1941. Originally written in English.

8. Ibid.

9. Mother to Father, March 23, 1942. Originally written in English.

10. Mother to Fourth Son, May 9, 1941. Originally written in English.

11. Mother to Father, March 23, 1942. Originally written in English.

12. Mother to Father, February 18, 1943. Originally written in English.

13. Mother to Father, March 23, 1942. Originally written in English.

14. Mother to Eighth Son, April 5, 1941; Mother to Father, March 23, 1942. Both originally written in English.

15. Youngest Daughter to Father, n.d., c. 1945. Originally written in Chinese.

16. Sixth Son's telegram to Father, January 7, 1947; Father's telegram to Sixth Son, January 8, 1947. Both originally written in English.

17. On Aurora College, see Lutz, *China and the Christian Colleges, 1850–1950,* 533.

18. At this meeting, Father gave a speech, which was published in *Record of Proceedings of the Thirty-first Session of the International Labour Conference, San Francisco, 1948,* 157–159.

19. Father to Mullin, September 21, 1948. Originally written in English. Father came to know Mullin through T. G. Ling, who had worked as a research scientist for Father and had known Mullin as a fellow chemist.

20. Youngest Daughter to brothers et al., September 15, 1948. Originally written in Chinese.

21. Ibid.

22. Youngest Daughter to Father, August 21, 1949. Originally written in Chinese.

23. Youngest Daughter to brothers et al., September 15, 1948. Originally written in Chinese.

24. Ibid.

25. Ibid.

26. Ibid.

27. Ibid.

28. Eighth Son to Father and Mother, September 9, 1948. Originally written in English.

29. Youngest Daughter to Father and Mother, December 29, 1948. Originally written in Chinese.

30. Ibid.

31. Ibid.

32. Eighth Son to Brothers, July 15, 1948. Originally written in English.

33. Ibid.

34. Up to that time, they had barely caught a glimpse of each other because she had lived her whole life in Shanghai, and he had resided in the United States, 1937–1941, wartime Chongqing, 1942–1945, and the United States again, 1945–1948.

35. Youngest Daughter to Brothers et al., September 15, 1948. Originally written in Chinese.

36. Eighth Son to Father and Mother, September 9, 1948. Originally written in English.

37. Youngest Daughter to brothers et al., September 15, 1948. Originally written in Chinese.

38. Youngest Daughter to Father and Mother, November 20, 1948. Originally written in Chinese.

39. Ibid.

40. Eighth Son to Father and Mother, November 18, 1948. Originally written in Chinese.

41. Ibid.

42. Ibid.

43. Youngest Daughter to Father and Mother, November 20, 1948. Originally written in Chinese.

44. Eighth Son to Father and Mother, November 18, 1948. Originally written in Chinese.

45. Youngest Daughter to Eldest Son, n.d., c. Spring 1949; Eighth Son to Eldest Son, April 12, 1949. Both originally written in Chinese.

46. Eighth Son to Father and Mother, November 18, 1948. Originally written in Chinese.

47. Youngest Daughter to Father and Mother, November 20 and December 29, 1948. Both originally written in Chinese. In letters to his family in Shanghai, Eighth Son also referred repeatedly to Youngest Daughter's correspondence with Second Son. See Eighth Son to Father and Mother, January 5, 1949, and Eighth Son to Eldest Son, April 12 and 21, 1949. All originally written in Chinese.

48. Eighth Son to Eldest Son, April 21, 1949. Originally written in Chinese.

49. Youngest Daughter to Second Son, n.d., c. spring break, 1949. Originally written in Chinese.

50. Ibid.; Eighth Son to Eldest Son, May 4, 1949. Originally written in Chinese.

51. Eighth Son to Father and Mother, May 3, 1949; Eighth Son to Father, June 12, 1949. Both originally written in Chinese. Eighth Son had offered to leave "most or all" of his half to the US$4,500 for Youngest Daughter on his departure from the United States. But he apparently changed his mind because he took US$2,000 with him on his trip to Hong Kong. Eighth Son to Father, August 12, 1949. Originally written in English.

52. Eighth Son to Eldest Son, May 4, 1949. Originally written in English.

53. Eighth Son to Father, c. June 1949. Originally written in English.

54. Eighth Son to Father, June 12, 1949. Originally written in English.

55. Eighth Son to Father, July 30, 1949. Originally written in English.

56. Youngest Daughter to Father, July 28, 1949. Originally written in Chinese.

57. Eighth Son to Father, July 30, 1949. Originally written in English.

58. Youngest Daughter to Father, August 1, 1949. Originally written in Chinese.

59. Ibid.

60. Youngest Daughter to Father, August 21, 1949. Originally written in Chinese.

61. Youngest Daughter to Father, July 28, 1949. Originally written in Chinese.

62. Ibid.

63. Ibid.

64. Youngest Daughter to Father, August 1, 1949. Originally written in Chinese.

65. Father to Youngest Daughter, September 3, 1949. Originally written in Chinese.

66. Father to Youngest Daughter, August 23, 1949. Originally written in Chinese.

67. Ibid.

68. Father to Youngest Daughter, September 3, 1949. Originally written in Chinese.

69. Father to Youngest Daughter, September 26, 1949. Originally written in Chinese.

70. Father to Youngest Daughter, September 3, 1949. Originally written in Chinese.

71. Youngest Daughter to Father, July 28 and August 21, 1949. Both originally written in Chinese.

72. Interviewee J; e-mail from Donna Webber, Simmons College Archives, February 12, 2007; e-mail from Fred Honhart, University Archives and Historical Collections, Michigan State University, East Lansing, April 30, 2007.

73. Interviewees A, J, and K. On Zhang Shouyong, see Yu Xinfang, *Zhang Shouyong xiansheng zhuan.* Zhang Qinshi recalled that during his boyhood he was taught by his grandfather, Zhang Shouyong. See Zhang Qinshi, "Ji zufude jiaohai er san shi."

74. Interviewee J; e-mail from William J. Maher, University Archives, University of Illinois, Urbana-Champaign, February 16, 2007.

75. Rose Hum Lee, *Chinese in the United States of America,* 307.

76. Quoted by ibid., 308.

77. On Chinese as targets of McCarthy's campaigns in the 1950s, see Iris Chang, *Chinese in America,* chap. 14. For more detailed research on this subject,

including a reference to the arrests of eleven Chinese students at Zhang's institution, the University of Illinois, Champaign-Urbana, in early 1951, see Han, "Untold Story," 77–99, especially 85.

78. Interviewees A, G, and J. The wedding announcement appeared in *Shen bao*, October 31, 1951.

79. Interviewee J.

80. Interviewee J. Zhang's grandfather, Weng Wenhao, wrote a poem in honor of this wedding. See Weng, "Zhang Qinshi, Liu Mingqiu jiehuan."

15. A Son Who Refused to Return to China

1. Quoted in Eighth Son to Father, June 4, 1947. Originally written in English.

2. Eighth Son to Father, June 4, 1947. Originally written in English.

3. Ibid.

4. Eighth Son to Father, October 27, 1947. Originally written in English.

5. Eighth Son to Father, June 4, 1947. Originally written in English.

6. Ibid.

7. Ibid.

8. Father to Eighth Son, telegram, June 25, 1947. Originally written in English.

9. Eighth Son to Father, telegram, July 9, 1947. Originally written in English.

10. Father to Eighth Son, December 3, 1947. Originally written in Chinese.

11. Eighth Son to Father and Mother, March 2, 1948. Originally written in Chinese.

12. Ibid.

13. Ibid.

14. Father to Eighth Son, February 23, 1948. Originally written in Chinese.

15. Eighth Son to Father and Mother, April 4, 1948. Originally written in Chinese.

16. Ibid.

17. Eighth Son to Father and Mother, January 24, 1949. Originally written in Chinese.

18. Eighth Son to Father and Mother, January 5 and 24, 1949. Both originally written in Chinese.

19. Eighth Brother to Eldest Brother, April 12, 1949. Originally written in Chinese.

20. Ibid.

21. Ibid.

22. Eighth Son to Father and Mother, May 3, 1949. Originally written in Chinese.

23. Eighth Son to Father and Mother, May 3, 1949. Originally written in English.

24. Eighth Son to Father and Mother, May 3, 1949. Originally written in Chinese.

25. Eighth Brother to Eldest Brother, May 4, 1949. Originally written in Chinese.

26. Father to Eighth Son, May 11, 1949, in Shanghai shehui kexue yuan jingji yanjiu suo, *Liu Hongsheng qiye shiliao* (hereafter *LHS QY SL*), vol. 3, 451–452. Originally written in Chinese.

27. Ibid.

28. Ibid.

29. Eighth Son to Father, c. June 1949. Originally written in English.

30. Ibid.

31. Eighth Son to Father, June 12, 1949. Originally written in English.

32. Eighth Son to Father, c. late June 1949. Originally written in English.

33. Father to Eighth Son, July 14, 1949. Originally written in Chinese.

34. Ibid.

35. Eighth Son to Father, July 1949. Originally written in English.

36. Eighth Son to Father, November 17, 1949. Originally written in English.

37. Ibid.

38. Eighth Son to Father, November 5, 1949. Originally written in English.

39. Father to Eighth Son, December 17, 1949, in *LHS QY SL*, vol. 3, 456–457. Originally written in Chinese.

40. Ibid.

41. Interviewee A.

42. Father to Eighth Son, March 28, 1950, in *LHS QY SL*, vol. 3, 457–458. Originally written in Chinese.

43. Ibid.

44. Ibid.

45. Ibid. On the controversial sign that is mentioned in this quotation, see Bickers and Wasserstrom, "Shanghai's 'Dogs and Chinese Not Admitted' Sign," 444–66.

46. Father to Eighth Son, March 28, 1950, in *LHS QY SL*, vol. 3, 457–458. Originally written in Chinese.

47. Ibid.

48. Ibid.

49. Hong Kong Public Records Office, HKRS 272-1-74 Marriage Notice Book, October 19, 1951–February 26, 1952. We are indebted to Pui Tak Lee for this reference.

50. Interviewee A. Father was not unique in his concerted efforts to bring Eighth Son home in 1949 and the early 1950s. For another example of a sexagenarian father summoning his son from Hong Kong back to Shanghai to

manage family enterprises in 1949 and the early 1950s, see Wong, *Emigrant Entrepreneurs*, 34.

16. Parents' Deaths and Children's Dispersal

1. The only son who did not study abroad or hold an executive position in the Liu family firm was Ninth Son. Born in 1923, he apparently sustained a head injury as a small child and suffered from physical and mental disabilities throughout his life. He died in 1949 at the age of twenty-six. For brief comments on his boyhood and death, see Mother to Eighth Son, January 20, 1939. Originally written in English. Eighth Son to Father and Mother, January 24, 1949. Originally written in Chinese.

2. Interviewee J.

3. Interviewee G. Immediately after the war, the term "resistance-war wife" as a description of a second wife that a man took in unoccupied China while he remained married to his prewar wife in occupied China was popularized in the film *A Spring River Flows East (Yi jiang chun shui xiang dong liu)*, 1947. See Lu Fangshang, "Lingyizhong," 97–98; and Pickowicz, "Victory as Defeat," 380–384.

4. He Guiying to Father, n.d, 1949. Originally written in Chinese. Interviewees G and J.

5. Interviewees E, F, and G.

6. Liu Nianzhi, *Shiyejia*, 123–126.

7. Interviewee A; Liu Nianzhi, *Shiyejia*, 123–126.

8. Interviewees E and G.

9. Interviewee G.

10. Interviewees E and G.

11. Interviewee A.

12. Eldest Son to Wolf, November 12, 1949; interviewees A, E, and J.

13. Interviewees E, F, and G.

14. Liane Yen to Father and Mother, June 28, 1949. Originally written in English. Interviewees E, G, H, and L.

15. Interviewees E, H, J, and L.

16. Interviewees J and K.

17. Interviewees A and J.

18. Yamada, *Gendai Chugoku jinmei jiten*, 1068; *Shanghai jiefang ribao*, February 17, 1979; interviewees E, G, and N.

19. Interviewees A, E, and M; *Wenhui bao* (Shanghai), November 20, 1980; *Zhongguo renda xinwen*, March 31, 2003.

20. Interviewees E, G, H, and L.

21. Liu Nianzhi, *Shiyejia*, 98.

22. Interviewees H and L.

23. Interviewees C and G.

Conclusion

1. Kuhn, *Chinese among Others*, 15. On Chinese men's constant travels away from home in a scholarly elite family, see Mann, *Talented Women of the Zhang Family*, 128, 198, 203. On merchants' travels and relocations for purposes of long-distance trading, see Skinner, "Mobility"; Rowe, *Hankow*; and Lufrano, *Honorable Merchants*. On peasants as internal migrants to Chinese cities, see Honig, *Sisters and Strangers*. On overseas connections, see Watson, *Emigration and the Chinese Lineage*; Skinner, "Chinese Peasants and the Closed Community"; Hsu, *Dreaming of Gold Mountain*; and Liu, *Transnational History*.

2. Esherick, *Ancestral Leaves*, 218–219, 231–232, and 311–316.

3. Coble, *Chinese Capitalists in Japan's New Order*, 111–113 and 213–214.

4. Father to Fifth Son, August 5, 1934. Originally written in English. Father's approach to parenting may also have drawn inspiration from a softer and warmer approach to fatherhood in Chinese history that dates back to an era before China had extensive contact with the West. According to Ping-chen Hsiung, "by the end of the sixteenth and beginning of the seventeenth centuries . . . the old, haughty air of a 'Confucian patriarch' was on the wane. An ethical and aesthetical appreciation for a softer, warmer, socially more domestic and more sociable father, husband, and man had gained a fresh respectability in the sophisticated circles of Chinese society." Hsiung, *Tender Voyage*, 115.

Acknowledgments

The members of the Liu family ventured into a wide variety of arenas—business, politics, society, foreign affairs. As we have followed them through history, we have had the benefit of advice from historians and social scientists from a wide range of specialties. We are grateful to all of our numerous friends and colleagues who have answered our questions and given us guidance. We wish to thank most of all Maria Cristina Garcia, who has commented passionately and helpfully on multiple drafts of this book in manuscript. We are also indebted to others who have read it and made suggestions for improving it: Joseph Esherick, Michael Hunt, Daniel Kaiser, Michael Kammen, Jon Saari, an anonymous reader for Harvard University Press, and especially Thomas Lyons, who not only provided valuable comments on the manuscript but also made the maps. We have tried to rise to their challenges, and we take full blame wherever we have fallen short.

We have received generous help from members of the Liu family. Since 2000, we have interviewed several of them, and we are grateful to them for sharing their memories with us. All of them who have spoken with us and sent us emails, letters, and photographs have agreed to allow us to include their comments and materials in this book. Some of them have preferred not to be cited by name, so we have decided to cite all of them anonymously, representing each one in the footnotes by a random letter of the alphabet. We want them to know how deeply we appreciate their vital contributions and warm encouragement.

The only members of the Liu family whom we wish to thank by name are Liu Hongsheng (O. S. Lieu) and his fourth son, Liu Nianzhi (Johnson Lieu), both deceased. We are especially indebted to them because they preserved our single most important documentary source: the Liu family correspondence. Throughout his career, Liu Hongsheng had his staff keep copies of all the incoming and outgoing letters—not only the ones to and from him but also the ones exchanged by all the members of his family. This correspondence was filed in his accounts office, Liu Hong Ji (Lieu Ong Kee), which he first established in the 1910s and then moved in 1930 to his newly built eight-story Enterprise Building in Shanghai. Subsequently, up to the early 1950s, his staff at this accounts office continued to file original copies of his family's incoming letters and carbon copies of their outgoing letters on a regular basis. If he had not maintained this policy of retaining original and carbon copies of family letters along with business correspondence in his files, it seems likely that these letters would have become at best scattered and at worst lost.

In 1958, two years after Liu Hongsheng's death, his son Liu Nianzhi was approached by Huang Yifeng, Vice President of the newly founded Shanghai Academy of Social Sciences (SASS), who appealed to him to give the Liu family's papers to SASS for the use of scholars. Liu Nianzhi decided to donate the whole vast collection—including the originals and copies of the family's letters and the family firm's business correspondence and other records—none of which had ever been published.

Since then, several scholars have worked intensively on this unique set of papers and have produced important studies based on it. The most monumental publication is a documentary history, *Liu Hongsheng qiye shiliao* (Historical materials on Liu Hongsheng's enterprises) (1981), which was compiled and published in three volumes by a team of scholars at SASS under the leadership of Ma Bohuang. In addition, other scholars have come from all parts of China and abroad to consult the unpublished Liu Papers at SASS. Although we are the first to make extensive use of the Liu family letters, many scholars have relied on Liu Hongsheng's business records as the basis for writing books and articles.

We are very fortunate to have met Liu Nianzhi in 2000, three years before his death, and although we were not able to converse very well with him because of his ill health, we thanked him for donating this remarkable collection of unpublished materials. In expressing our gratitude at that time and again here, we convey thanks from ourselves and all other scholars who have benefited from this collection in the past and will do so in the future.

At SASS, we had the good fortune to work on the Liu correspondence under the guidance of learned scholar-archivists, first Huang Hanmin and, since his retirement, Lu Xinglong. While we have been researching this book, they have been the successive directors of the Center for Research on Chinese Business History, where the Liu Papers are housed at SASS. They and their staff members, especially Shen Qiusheng, have been extremely helpful. In Shanghai, we have also benefited from our discussions of the history of the Liu family with other scholars, including Ding Richu, Du Xuncheng, Ma Bohuang, Qian Shaoming, Shen Zuwei, Wang Xi, Xu Xuejun, Zhang Zhongli, and Zhang Zhongmin.

Outside China, several archivists promptly replied to our requests for information about the records the Lius compiled when they were students at colleges and universities. Liren Zheng and Elaine Engst of Cornell University showed us how to contact their fellow librarians and archivists in England, the United States, and Japan. Among the archivists who came to our aid are Jacqueline Cox, Fiona Colbert, and Susan Sneddon at Cambridge University, Richard Densmore and Louise Kiefer at Baldwin-Wallace College, Kaiyi Chen at the University of Pennsylvania, Jessy Randall at Colorado College, James Peters at Manchester University, Donna Webber at Simmons College, Frederick Honhart at Michigan State University, George Burn at Ohio University, and William Maher at the University of Illinois.

While working on this book, we have had strong support from colleagues, students, and staff members at our home institutions. At Grinnell College, Karen Groves has spent years preparing a database containing the Lius' letters, and Ilana Meltzer has constructed a useful index to them. At Cornell University, sources have been checked and editorial work done by several students: Kelly Foss, Xiaojia Hou, Amy Kardos, Peter Lavelle, Soon Keong Ong, and Kun Qian. In his days as a graduate student (long before he assumed his current position as curator of Cornell's Wason Collection on East Asia), Liren Zheng made the greatest contribution of all. These and numerous other Cornell students have contributed insights based on their readings of draft chapters that were circulated in seminars, especially one on Chinese family history.

We also are grateful to our "homes away from home": Nanjing University, especially for help from Hu Zhengning; and the National Humanities Center, in Research Triangle Park, North Carolina, where the staff provided unfailing support and fellow scholars gave valuable advice.

For improving the manuscript even after we thought it was in final form, we thank our editors at Harvard University Press, Kathleen McDermott, Andrew Kinney, Barbara Goodhouse, and Martha Ramsey.

In writing this book about a family, we have come to realize more than ever that our lives are inextricably entwined with our own families. We are grateful to our family members for everything they have done for us, and we thank, above all, our wives, Maria Cristina Garcia and Ming Yang, to whom this book is dedicated.

Index

Accounts office (Liu Hong Ji; Lieu Ong Kee), 3, 88, 130, 167–168, 300, 396n6

Agriculture, 91, 93

Apprenticeships: of Second, Third, and Fourth Sons, 46–47; of Eldest Son, 71–74, 77–78, 85–86; of Sixth and Eighth Sons, 88, 267–269, 270, 320, 325, 342; of Eldest Daughter, 153–155; of Youngest Daughter, 316

Autonomy. *See* Independence

Baldwin-Wallace College, 92, 94, 349; Eldest Son at, 58, 67, 68; Fifth Son at, 95–99, 105

Ballard, Arthur H., 24, 27–30, 31, 36, 37–38, 43, 46–47, 116

Ballard, Mrs. J. G., 25–26, 31

Bao Shuzhen, 238, 240, 241, 257

Battle of Shanghai, 189–190

Beijing, 9, 124, 125, 288

Beipei, 202

Bethel Hospital, 159

Birth order: Eldest Son in, 67, 88–89, 126–127, 385n2; rebellious sons in, 216, 402n116; Youngest Daughter in, 298–299, 323

Burma Road, 181

Cambridge (England), 23–64

Cambridge (Massachusetts), 67–83, 217–227, 309

Cambridge University, 1, 67, 68, 88, 92, 156, 181, 293; Father's strategy for admission to, 23–24, 37, 46–47; Ballard's strategy for admission to, 36–38, 46–47; sons' strategy for admission to, 37

Central China Match Company (Japanese), 176

Chen Guangfu (K. P. Chen), 85–86

Chen Yi, 290, 347

Cheng Nianpeng, 284, 349

Chiang Ching-kuo, 280–281

Chiang Kai-shek, 1, 189, 264; in wartime Chongqing, 9, 175, 176, 180, 211–212, 260; in prewar China, 49, 147, 148, 206–210; in Chinese civil war, 275, 283, 284, 321

Childbearing: by Mother, 18–19; by Eldest Daughter, 158–161; by Bao Shuzhen, 238; by He Guiying, 253

China Coal Briquette Company, 17

China Match Company, 17

China Merchants Steam Navigation Company, 14, 75, 77, 289

China National Relief and Rehabilitation Administration, 264–267, 289

China Trading Corporation, 288

China United Engineering Company, 272–273

China Wool Manufacturing Company, Limited, 17, 179, 266, 284, 291, 349

China Woolen Company, 181

Chinese Communist Party, 215; in Yan'an, 203; Sixth Son in, 206–210, 213–215, 268, 342; Father's attitude toward, 282–283, 290–293, 295, 352–353

Mitsui Company, 174–175, 186–187
Modernity, 19, 102, 127, 144–145, 365
Mother (Ye Suzhen): in family alliances, 5, 245; as devoted wife, 13, 18–19, 241–244; in her natal family, 15–16; as opponent of Third Son's marriage to Liane Yen, 131–145; as campaigner to bring Sixth Son back from Yan'an, 210–211; as advisor to Eighth Son on his depression, 219–221; as opponent of Father's mistresses, 237–241; as threat to splitting Liu family, 248–257, 362; in postwar Liu family reunion, 259–260; in final confrontation with Father's mistress, 344–346; death of, 348; cameo of, in her honor, 364
Mother-in-law, 4, 17, 254
Mullin, C. E., 304, 305–308; and his family, 306–308

Naming: of Liu children in Chinese and English, 20–22; by Ye parents (Tianjin), of their children, 21, 380n29; by Sixth Son, of himself, 206, 400n82; for official purposes, 380n31
Nanchang, 158
Nankai University, 195
Nanyang University, 155
Natal families: of Father, 6, 14–15; of Mother, 15–16, 17–18, 249–250, 254, 362, 378n18, 407n73; of Liane Yen, 122–125; of Xue Diyi, 155–156; of Wu Yuying, 198–200
National capitalists, 287–288, 289–290, 292–293, 297, 411n33
National Match Monopoly, 260
National Monopoly Bureau, 260
National Science Research Institute, 213, 214
Nationalism, 175; of Liu sons, 51, 52–63, 356, 357–358; of Chinese, 51, 52, 411–412n33; of Father, 52, 62, 289–290, 292–293, 297; of Sixth Son, 185, 190–191, 198–199, 203, 211
Nationalist Army, 205, 275, 283
Nationalist government, 9, 49, 290; in Sino-Japanese War, 175, 176, 180, 207, 242, 260, 297; in Chinese civil war, 275, 289, 320
Nationalization, of the Lius' enterprises, 346–347

Native-place ties, 228, 273, 279, 308, 320; of Father, 14, 23, 267–268; of Mother, 15
Naturalization, proposal by Father for his sons to become British citizens, 50–63, 170–171
Networks: of Father, 14, 17, 24, 26–27, 36, 37, 73, 260–267; of Liu sons at Cambridge University, 32–39, 46–48; of Mother, 245–257; of Dai Li, 262–263, 407n13; of Fourth Son, 263–267; of Youngest Daughter, 298–324; in Sino-foreign border crossing, 381n3. *See also* Native-place ties
Newspapers, 8, 119, 157, 208; in the People's Republic, 289, 290, 293; in the Cold War, 330–332
Nineteenth Route Army, 50, 52
Ningbo, 14–15, 228, 261, 267, 279, 308, 320
Ninth Son (Liu Nianlian), 378n19, 418n1
Northwest Woolen Manufacturing Company, 181

Olmstead, George, 265–266
Onoda Satoshi, 186–187
Opium, 18–19, 239
Oxford University, 32, 33–34, 35, 38, 68

Pacific War, 259
Pan, Lynn, 122, 124, 240
Parish, William, 1
Patriarch, 20–21, 62; sternness of, 1–4, 5; friendliness of, 101–102, 419n4; family's deference to, 356, 358–359; empowerment under, 358–363
Peking Union Medical College, 91
People's Liberation Army, 9, 282, 283, 288, 313, 314, 331–333
Philadelphia, 229; Eldest and Fifth Sons in, 99, 100, 101, 103, 104, 106
Pine Manor Junior College, 307–312, 351

Qingli Iron Works, 272–273

Racism: of English toward Chinese, 24–30, 48, 58; of Liu sons toward Cantonese, 26; of Americans toward Chinese, 58, 331, 358
Raeder, Oscar, 230, 403n60
Rangoon (Burma), 180